The History of American Funeral Directing

The Histor

PUBLISHED BY BULFIN PRINTERS, INC. MILWAUKEE, WISCONSIN 19

f American

Funeral

Directing

Robert W. Habenstein

William M. Lamers

iv

Acknowledgements

Permission to use quoted material has kindly been granted by the publishers and agents noted below:

Blades, East and Blades, London, *Annals of the Barber-Surgeons of London*, c. 1890, by Sidney Young.

B. T. Batsford, London, *London Tradesmen's Cards of the XVIII Century*, c. 1925, by Ambrose Heal; and *The Signboards of Old London Shops*, c. 1947, by Ambrose Heal.

Cambridge University Press, Cambridge, England, *A History of Epidemics in Great Britain*, c. 1891, by Charles Creighton; *The Road to Hel: A Study of the Conception of the Dead in Old Norse Literature*, c. 1943, by Hilda Ellis.

Catholic University of America Press, Washington, D. C., *Death and Burial in Christian Antiquity*, c. 1941, by Alfred C. Rush; *Ecclesiastical Sepulture in the New Code of Canon Law*, c. 1923, by John A. O'Reilly.

Columbia University Press, New York, *Medieval Handbooks of Penance*, c. 1938, by John T. McNeil and Helena M. Gamer.

Crane and Breed Casket Company, *The Evolution of the Modern Casket*.

Curtis Publishing Co., Philadelphia, *Saturday Evening Post*, "Their Last Words Had a Punch," by Charles L. Wallis, April 17, 1954.

Frederick A. Stokes Co., New York, *Funeral Customs, Their Origin and Development*, c. 1926, by Bertram S. Puckle.

George Allen & Unwin, London, *Heart Burial*, c. 1933, by Charles A. Bradford.

H. S. Eckels and Company, Philadelphia, "The Funeral Director in Grandpa's Time," *Clinical Topics*, May, 1938, by Frederick A. Frantz.

Harvard University Press, Cambridge, Mass., "Cremation and Burial in the Roman Empire" in *Harvard Theological Review*, XXV, October, 1932, by Arthur D. Nock.

Houghton Mifflin Company, Boston and New York, *Economic and Social History of New England 1620-1789*, 2 vols., c. 1890, by William B. Weeden.

Indiana University Press, Bloomington, Indiana, *Main Street on the Middle Border*, c. 1954, by Lewis Atherton.

Alfred A. Knopf Incorporated, New York, *A History of Medicine*, c. 1947, by Arturo Castiglioni.

The Macmillan Company, London, *Life and Labor of the People of London*, 9 vols., c. 1895, Charles Booth, editor.

The Macmillan Company, New York, *Spiritism and the Cult of the Dead in Antiquity*, c. 1921, by Lewis B. Paton; by special permission of Katharine H. Paton.

▼

Macy-Masius, New York, *Samuel Sewall's Diary*, c. 1927, Mark Van Doren, editor.

Massachusetts Historical Society, Boston, Mass., *Proceedings*, Vol. 17.

Methuen & Co. Ltd., *The Life and Times of Sir Edwin Chadwick*, c. 1952, by Samuel E. Finer.

New-York Historical Society, New York, *The Arts and Crafts in New York*, c. 1938.

Oxford University Press, New York and Oxford, *Stories on Stone*, c. 1954, by Charles L. Wallis; *Burial Reform and Funeral Costs*, c. 1938, by Arnold Wilson and H. Levy.

New York University Press, New York, *The Colonial Craftsman*, c. 1950, by Carl Bridenbaugh.

Random House, New York, *The Persian Wars*, c. 1942, by Herodotus, George Rawlinson, translator.

F. C. Riddle & Bro. Casket Company, St. Louis, *Funeral Customs Through the Ages*, published in 1929.

The Ronald Press Company, now Alfred A. Knopf Incorporated, New York, *Cities in the Wilderness*, c. 1938, by Carl Bridenbaugh.

Charles Scribner's Sons, *Social Life in the Reign of Queen Anne*, c. 1925, by John Ashton; *Dawn of Conscience*, c. 1946, by James H. Breasted; *Customs and Fashions in Old New England*, c. 1894, by Alice M. Earle; "Death and Disposal of the Dead," in *Encyclopaedia of Religion and Ethics*, c. 1912, John Hastings, editor.

University of Chicago Press, Chicago, *The Merchant Class of Medieval London*, c. 1948, by Sylvia Thrupp.

Yale University Press, New Haven, *Colonial Folkways*, Vol. VIII of The Chronicle of America Series, c. 1918, by Charles M. Andrews; *After Life In Roman Paganism*, c. 1923, by Franz Cumont.

William Wood & Co., New York, now Williams & Wilkins Co., Baltimore, *Outlines of Greek and Roman Medicine*, c. 1914, by James S. Elliott.

Preface

This book represents an attempt to tell in broad outline the story of American Funeral Directing. Although its major emphasis is upon matters of the past century it looks backward across the long record of Western Civilization in an effort to give selective historical depth and meaning to funeral beliefs and practices as found in America today.

This study is only incidentally a personal record. Few names have been mentioned, and these usually as a matter of rightful identification of man with idea or event. Rather the major emphasis has been upon beliefs, customs, practices, institutions, and social processes as they have appeared in the course of the development of funeral directing as a unique occupation in its own right. No effort has been made to present a comprehensive, encyclopedic account of everything that has been said, done, or happened in Western Civilization as it might possibly pertain to death and burial. At any period exceptions to and deviations from customs and arrangements set out in this book may be pointed out, either by the historian, the ethnographer, or the funeral director whose memory is long or in whose family the accounts of funeral customs of yesteryear have been chronicled. The focus has been, as far as the historical materials have permitted, upon the dominant profile of an emergent occupation, and the social, economic, and cultural conditions of its growth and change. While it might well be a profitable venture to note, classify and record the welter of minor deviations in custom and practice as they may be found to exist within the broad framework of American funerary belief, such an effort has not been attempted in the present work.

There is no task connected with the writing of a book more pleasant than that of acknowledging generous and competent assistance, cheerfully given. The debt to authors and publishers is summarized in the preceding section. Mr. Harry J. Gilligan, long a leader in associational activities of funeral directors because of his close scrutiny of the manuscript and his extensive factual and textual criticism, was particularly helpful. Mr. H. Fremont Alderson and Mr. Jerry Spears, both outstandingly knowledgeable in matters pertaining to funeral directing, read the manuscript thoroughly and gave the authors the benefit of their criticism and suggestions. Mr. Howard C. Raether, Executive Secretary of the National Funeral Directors Association and his staff stood ready at all times to help. Jane (Mrs. Robert W.) Habenstein and Miss Anna Louise Nestmann worked indefatigably at the task of editing the manuscript, and Mr. William M. Lamers, Jr. was responsible for a portion of the research on early embalming and the funeral practices of the Middle Ages. Good use was made of the library of the National Foundation of Funeral Service, Evanston, Illinois. Generous provision of factual and illustrative materials was made by officers of many of the major manufacturing concerns, trade publications, and funeral directors' associations. Names of these will be found in the citations, references, and acknowledgments at various points throughout the book.

The authors feel that they should make explicit that although without the suggestions, criticisms, and guidance of the above-mentioned and many others the work could never have been completed, responsibility for the writing of this book in its final form has been solely theirs.

Robert W. Habenstein
William M. Lamers

Milwaukee, Wisconsin
August 1, 1955

Contents

List of Plates

xiii

List of Figures in Text

Part One:
Early Mortuary
Behavior

~Pagan Roots of Modern Funeral Practice

Americans today are of a common mind with regard to many matters. They take it for granted that every man has a right to "life, liberty, and the pursuit of happiness." They believe without questioning that equality before the law is a part of their natural birthright, that people should be permitted to select their places of residence, their mates, their occupations, and freely make the most of their own critical life decisions. They hold that every child has the right to a common school education, to be provided, if the parents so desire, at public expense. Although less often popularly expressed, but nonetheless firmly taken for granted is the assumption that every person, no matter what the circumstance, has the right to a decent burial.

This bundle of common beliefs—what people take for granted, the opinions which become the firm premises

3

upon which they base their final group thinking and their individual judgments without questioning the broad underlying assumptions—these constitute the core of any social institution. An example may serve to clarify the point. Assume that we are confronted with the dead body of a man. What disposition shall we make of it? Shall we lay it in a boat that is set adrift? Shall we take the heart from it and bury it in one place and the rest of the body in another? Shall we expose it to wild animals? Burn it on a pyre? Push it into a pit naked to rot with other bodies? Boil it until the flesh falls off the bones, and throw the flesh away and treasure the bones? Such questions provoke others which may not even be consciously articulated, such as: "What do men generally think this body is?" And, "What do they think is a proper way of dealing with it?"

By complicated individual and group processes there are built up laws, customs, traditions, fashions. Once people have begun to think and act in a certain way it is hard to make them change their minds.

As a result of a long slow development, with its roots deep in the history of Western civilization, it is the common American mind today that the dead merit professional funeral services from a lay occupational group. These services include embalming, the preparation of the body for final viewing, a waiting period between death and disposition, the use for everyone of a casket that is attractive and protects the remains, a dignified and ceremonious service with consideration for the feelings of the bereaved, and an expression of the individual and group beliefs. Finally, convention demands burial in the ground or other disposition in a dignified place and manner that reaffirms those beliefs, insofar as not contrary to public health, expresses the esteem of the bereaved, and satisfies them that they are acting in accord with their means and that esteem.

All this is to be in the nature of a lay, professional service, rendered by an occupational group set apart to serve these functions, and supplementary to the service that may be offered by the clergy as an independent occupational group. In a word, the "decent funeral" is a universally accepted part of American thought and life, and the funeral director "belongs." It is taken for granted that his services are to be used in the burial of the dead.

What lies behind these contemporary American beliefs and practices? In dealing with their dead why do Americans today strive to provide a certain type and standard of burial, and call upon an occupational group to take the leading role in the laying away of the dead?

Obviously some part of the so-called "reverential roots" of American mortuary belief descends from humanitarianism—the doctrine that man's obligations are limited to and dependent alone on man and human relations—which developed as an outgrowth of the later, Pagan Renaissance, as distinguished from the earlier Renaissance, which was Christian. But to stop here would clearly commit the error of over simplification of historical origins. Humanitarianism alone neither explains nor accounts for the basic social interpretations of life and death in which the funeral customs of our day are anchored. To discover these, and to find out why people act as they do toward their dead, we must look to early Christian behavior; and beyond this, to the funeral behaviors of certain earlier civilizations. The long backward glance will show not merely customs that are related in the direct line, but interesting resemblances, unrelated but born out of a common need. Thus if two peoples, separated by thousands of years and half the globe, both use a litter to carry a body to the grave it is likely that the same necessity in each case was the independent mother of invention, and that the practice of the latter group in spite of its similarity, may be entirely unrelated to the practice of the earlier. With these and other common sense reservations before us we propose to examine the most pertinent and common of ancient and medieval funeral practices in an effort to develop backgrounds for an improved understanding of present day American methods of caring for the dead.

In spite of some variants in the formula, repeated so frequently that it has become an historical truism, the larger part of Western culture today is a composite of Greek aesthetics and philosophy, Roman law and administrative genius, and ancient Teutonic vigor, superimposed upon the dominant Judaeo-Christian tradition. Nevertheless, the largest determinant in modern American funerary practice stems from the Christian tradition.[1] In turn the rudiments of the Christian funeral outlook are in the main derived from Hebrew religious and ethical concepts. These, again, were undoubtedly influenced by the death beliefs and mortuary practices of the early Egyptians and other ancient civilizations. Before these, in the uncounted ages of prehistory, were practices whose nature we can only guess, guided in part by the practices of later primitive peoples of whom we have some knowledge.

To the new doctrines of Christ the early Christian church added interpretations having significance for funeral beliefs and practices still with us today. To a much lesser extent contributions were made by the mystical and philosophical beliefs of the Greeks and Romans. Some pagan customs prevalent during the period of the early Christian church undoubtedly were absorbed in the Christian burial complex. To understand better this original Christian complex and the contemporary American funeral beliefs and practices that stem from it we will look backwards along a few of the roads that lead to it.

FUNERAL CUSTOMS OF THE ANCIENT EGYPTIANS

Of all the great civilizations of ancient times springing up in the general area surrounding the Mediterranean basin —that is, Southern Europe, Western Asia, Northern Africa —including, among others, the Babylonian, Assyrian, Chaldean and Persian, that of Ancient Egypt has had perhaps more influence than any other upon civilizations intermediate to our own, and through these upon the modern Western World. For that reason, and without denying that other ancient civilizations may have contributed indirectly to modern funeral practices, Egyptian civilization is singled out for consideration.

For five thousand years in the Nile delta and southward along its flood plain, there flourished a culture in which the fine and practical arts, the abstract and applied sciences, reached an early advanced development. Here, too, in the ordering of human affairs there appeared, perhaps for the first recorded time, a morality of group life based on internal conscience rather than on external authority supported by force.[2] Although it is hazardous to attempt to settle such matters with finality at a distance as much as six or seven thousand years, we are fortunate in that of all ancient civilizations, the material culture of the Egyptians is best preserved. Its magnificent cities, now in ruins, its monuments, tombs, pyramids and the wealth of objects made by human hands—all these testify to the splendor of a remarkable era. Archaeologists, who dig into the laden sands and reconstruct from the remains the life of the people who made a civilization, have by no means exhausted the cultural treasures of the Nile country. Newer discoveries, plus an intensified interest in the social life of the ancient Egyptians[3] have led to a sharper appreciation of the high social, political, economic and religious achievements attained during five thousand years of Egypt's historical development.

Death Beliefs: One of the most persistent themes to pattern the thought and culture of the ancient Egyptians was that of death and the life beyond. The theologies of both sun-worship and the cult of Osiris—god of the underworld and judge of the dead—were profoundly affected by the idea of death. In a dry, warm climate, where the elements dealt benignly with the bodies of the dead and natural mummification was often the result, the earliest settlers of the Nile valley were stimulated to ponder the prospects of continued life in and beyond the grave. One of the universal responses to death has been to attribute some life to the body lying in the grave, while believing at the same time that an element or aspect of the dead person resides elsewhere apart from the grave.

The Egyptians attributed a divine origin to the soul; they held that throughout life it was engaged in a struggle with good and evil; and that after life its final state was determined by judgment, according to its behavior on earth. Those who were justified before Osiris, passed into perpetual happiness; those who were condemned, into perpetual misery. The justified took the name of Osiris, the judge, under which name they indeed already had appeared for judgment.

It has been found in the tombs that everyone who could afford a sculptured record was described as justified; every mummy was already an Osiris. It is probable that the performance of ceremonies and the whole process of embalming, together with charms attached to the mummy, and prayers said by those who visited the tomb, were held necessary to secure future happiness. The practice of embalming attained major importance from the belief that the deceased would resume his normal, everyday activities in the after-life, and thus in the earlier periods it was not unusual to sacrifice servants and make presentations of food and money to aid the soul on its journey to the sun.

The Egyptians believed that the sun was the center, the focus of the universe, from which all things emerged and to which they returned. The death beliefs of the Egyptians pivoted around the idea that the complex elements that joined to make a person could be reassembled in the body of the dead. These elements included The Ba (Soul), The Yakhu (Shining one), The Name, The Shadow, The Heart (as the seat of the intellect and emotions) and the Ka.[4] The last is most significant, as it remained by the dead and demanded attention from the living. In earlier times this attention took the form of food offerings, but later it was reduced to the saying of prayers. Central to the Egyptian concept of life after death was the belief in the resuscitation of the body. Although at death the various elements of the dead person were thought to depart, it was believed that they could be reconstituted or brought together again as was the case in the miracle of Osiris, through a series of ritualistic actions. The body, itself, was therefore to be preserved in natural form so that the restoration of *the person* in its complex parts, the bringing together of the elements which at death had been separated, might take place. Thomas Greenhill, Surgeon, author of *The Art of Embalming*, published in 1705, ascribed human fastidiousness to the soul, saying that it left the body only when the body was "corrupt and putrified, as abhorring so loathsome an habitation; whereas on the contrary, it never forsook it when it was preserved incorrupt and entire. . . . By its being dressed in fine linen (the body) might court and incline its best companion, the soul, to cohabit with it."[5]

To this end the art of embalming was employed, and, as is commonly known, reached an amazing state of perfection. James H. Breasted, who has made extensive studies in the history of ancient Egypt notes, however, that "it is . . . not correct to attribute to the Egyptians a belief in the *immortality* of the soul . . . or to speak of his ideas of immortality."[6] It would be more accurate instead to say that the soul, in a sense, had to be "mortalized" by being brought back to the body. When soul and name and shadow and heart and body were joined, the "person" was restored.

Among the oldest of Egyptian funeral ceremonies are those associated with offering the dead such fare as various kinds of cakes, oils, beer and wine. To provide for this offering, a regular portion of a man's estate was set aside. While the food generally was permitted to decay, or was consumed by attendants on the theory that it nourished the shade spiritually even though eaten by the living, a tube down which food could be passed was sometimes extended from the exterior of the grave to the mouth of the corpse.[7]

Yet, despite the elaborate ritual and the practical provisions taken toward the dead to secure reconstitution of the person, continued attention to the grave and spirits of the dead by surviving relatives was thought to be necessary. The need for protecting the body, the coffin, and funeral treasures gave impetus to the building of tombs. In consequence, tomb chaplains or priests, to whom the necessary ritualistic actions on behalf of the dead were delegated, came into Egyptian funerary customs. The most enduring monuments in the world, the great pyramids, were both memorials and tombs for the rulers of Egypt. (See Plate 1.) Thus for nearly four thousand years, Egyptian society at every level, from the Pharaohs down to the least slave, was given over in great part to the task of preparing and caring for the dead. Appreciation of this fact has led Breasted to remark:

In no other land, ancient or modern, has there ever been such attention to the equipment of the dead for their eternal sojourn in the hereafter. The beliefs which finally led the Egyptian to the devotion of so much of his wealth and time, his skill and energy to the erection of the "eternal house" are the oldest conceptions of a real life hereafter of which we know.[8]

After the burial, offerings were made at stated times throughout the year by the family, and the chief inscription on the tomb begged the passer-by to say a prayer for the good of the inhabitant thereof. The making of prescribed offerings at the tomb must have been most inconvenient; and possibly because of this, burial grounds became peopled by a tribe of mercenary professional embalmers and lesser priests, who made their living not only by their profession, but by fraud and even theft. Yet all in all we must admire the generosity with which the Egyptians lavished their riches upon this mode of affection, to be repaid not only by a natural satisfaction, but also by the wholesome recognition that there are unselfish and unproductive uses of wealth.

The Threat of Plague as a Burial Motive: Combined with the religious motive, the concern of the ancient Egyptians for the proper disposal of the dead had some kind of sanitary purpose. Like the ancient Chinese they sometimes used dry burials to keep the products of putrefaction from seeping into the soil and thus generating plague. In dry burial, bodies were shrouded in coarse cloth and were laid upon beds of charcoal under six or eight feet of sand on the edge of the great plain at Memphis, and above the reach of the flooding Nile. The dry air and nitrous soil provided for their slow and inoffensive decomposition, and they were as well preserved from putrid decay as if they had been embalmed. For the great masses of Egypt this disposal practice and not cavity embalming was also an economic necessity, and tends to reinforce the theory that the national practice of elaborately ritualized embalming and entombment originated in the utilitarian purpose of sanitation as much or more than in ends that were primarily religious and ceremonial. Dry burial was in effect a cheaper form of embalming available to the Egyptian masses. Herodotus observed that the people of Egypt felt themselves continually menaced by some great epidemic scourge, and took precautions accordingly.[9]

Against this backdrop of beliefs concerning death and the afterlife, specific Egyptian death customs come to have meaning and logic, even though over the course of nearly five thousand years, and through successive historical epochs, they grew and changed, responding to fashion and, possibly, even to outside influence. Some, such as the dismemberment of the body, passed out of existence completely. Yet in spite of superficial changes, the basic beliefs remained unchanged. There was life after death, no matter what form it might take. This life demanded not only the preservation of the body in its natural appearance, but ritualistic actions to restore to the body the elements that with it formed the person and continued attention to the dead for their protection and comfort in the hereafter.

Embalming: As practiced during the peak of artistic performance in the New Kingdom period (1738-1102 B.C.) embalming presents one of the most universally interesting aspects of Egyptian care for the dead.[10] Later classical writers, Herodotus and Diodorus in particular, have described the process fairly accurately, noting that three grades of embalming were in vogue, these varying by the amount of time, attention, and the quality of materials used in the operation.

For the well-to-do and those of high rank the most elaborate and expensive process was used. In it the brain and the
viscera were removed, embalmed or preserved separately, and
placed in a series of four canopic jars, or burial vases. (See
Plate 1.) In the New Kingdom period these jars had
four heads, representing four Children of Horus, the hawk-
headed god of day. Mestha, the man-headed, protected the
stomach and large intestines; Hapi, the dog-headed, guarded
the small intestines; Tuamutef, the jackal-headed, watched
over the lungs and heart, and Qebhsennuf, the hawk-headed,
protected the liver and gall bladder.[11] The cavities in the
head and body were washed clean and filled with spices and
resins. The body was then immersed in a soda solution for
forty days, following which time it was wrapped in fine
linen. A second method, less costly, called for the injection
of cedar oil into body cavities without evisceration. The
body was laid in natrum or natron—a fixed alkali—for the
prescribed period, after which the cedar oil, which had dissolved the soft organs, was released; and the body, its flesh
dissolved by the natron, was reduced to preserved skin and
bones. The third mode, practiced for the poorer classes,
consisted in purging the intestines and soaking the body in
a soda solution for seventy days. The use of bitumen, or
pitch, was a later development, and resulted in the hard,
black mummy which tended to last almost indefinitely. It is
this type that in the Western mind constitutes the popular
image of an Egyptian mummy. Bodies embalmed with expensive unguents, spices, oils and resins quickly lost their
preserved condition when unwrapped, and were not likely
to remain long on public display.

The most celebrated description of Egyptian embalming
was written by Herodotus (484 to 424 B.C.) a Greek and the

"Father of History." He writes, in *The Persian Wars,* that in Egypt,

. . . There are certain persons appointed by law to the exercise of the profession of embalming. When a dead body is brought to them, they exhibit to the friends of the deceased, different models highly finished in wood. The most perfect of these they say resembles one whom I do not think it religious to name in such a matter; the second is of less price, and inferior in point of execution; another is still more mean; they then require after which model the deceased shall be represented; when the price is determined, the relations retire and the embalmers thus proceed. In the most perfect specimens of their art, they draw the brain through the nostrils, partly with a piece of crooked iron, and partly by the infusion of drugs; they then with an Ethiopian stone make an incision in the side, through which they extract the intestines; these they cleanse thoroughly, washing them with palm wine and afterwards covering them with pounded aromatics; they then fill the body with powder of pure myrrh, cassia, and all other perfumes except frankincense. Having sewn up the body, it is covered with nitre for the space of seventy days, which time they may not exceed; as at the end of this period it is washed, closely wrapped in bandages of cotton, dipped in a gum which the Egyptians use as a glue; it is then returned to the relations, who enclose the body in a case of wood, made to resemble a human figure, and place it against the wall in the repository of their dead. The above is the most costly mode of embalming. They who wish to be less expensive adopt the following method: they neither draw out the intestines nor make any incision in the dead body, but inject an unguent made from the cedar; after taking proper means to secure the injected oil within the body, it is covered with nitre for the time specified above; on the last day they withdraw the liquor before introduced; which brings with it all the bowels and intestines; the nitre eats away flesh, and the skin and bones only remain: the body is returned in this state, and no further care taken concerning it. There is a third mode of embalming appropriate to the poor. A particular kind of ablution is made to pass through the body, which is afterwards left in nitre for the above seventy days, and then returned. The wives of men of rank, and such females as have been distinguished by their beauty or importance, are not immediately on their decease delivered to the embalmers: they are usually kept for three or four days, which is done to prevent any indignity being offered to their persons. An instance of this once occurred.[12]

Coffins: The desire to keep bodies from touching the earth was characteristic not only of the Egyptians but of most early African peoples. Mats and skins, reed, wooden and earthenware baskets, had been employed to this end during the earlier periods of Egyptian history. As concern with perfection in preservation developed, so did the art of producing more elaborate coffins. From the XIth dynasty (about 2,500 B.C.) down to the days of the Empires, coffins play an important role in Egyptian burial. In the earlier historical periods they were rectangular, and tended to be massive, along the lines of a sarcophagus. Hieroglyphic inscriptions which covered the exterior were devoted to prayers, genealogies, and religious and magical texts, intended not only to help the restoration of the body and thereby the reconstitution of the person, but to aid and give power to the dead in the afterlife. (See Plate 2.) Between the XIIth and XVIIIth dynasties the shape of the coffin was changed, probably as a result of the growth of the cult of Osiris, and the anthropoid (or man-resembling) coffin came into use.[13] Here the face of the dead was reproduced, first by wood carving, later by cartonnage—a mixture of linen and stucco —painted in lifelike resemblance. (See Plate 3.) Usually this outer casing was given the appearance of a laborer bearing the implements of husbandry, with only the face and hands exposed, the rest of the body being painted with subjects relating to the future state, and bearing the principal inscription, giving the name and titles of "the Osiris justified." The final development of this form is seen in the portrait coffin, developed under the Romans about the second century A.D., in which, instead of a modelled head, the face was painted on a wooden panel held in place by bandaging.[14] (See Plate 3.) The realism and representational quality of this portraiture far surpasses the Earlier Egyptian art with its unresolved problem of perspective and proportion. Budge describes these painted coffins in some detail:

The finest and most beautiful painted coffins found in Egypt date from the XVIII dynasty, and the nobles and priests of Amen-Ra were provided with most luxurious funerary equipment. It was no uncommon thing for a great noble to be buried in three coffins, the outermost serving as a sarcophagus. The coffins are well shaped and well made, and both inside and outside are covered with Vignettes and long texts from the Theban Book of the Dead, and from the Book of Gates, the Book "Ammi Tuat" and scenes from the work describing the passage of the dead Sun-god Afu-Ra through the hours of the night. Numerous small scenes, in which the deceased is seen adoring Osiris and his company of gods of the dead, and various forms of the Sun-god, are painted on every available space. Vignettes and texts were painted in bright colours upon the layer of plaster with which the coffin was overlaid, and the whole coffin, both inside and out was given a thick coat of yellowish varnish. The passage of thirty-four centuries has diminished the brightness of the colours . . . but when such a coffin left the hands of the scribe and artist the effect of this medley of hard, uncompromising colours and disconnected subjects must have been somewhat crude and startling.[15]

Some of the most opulent of these coffins had rich inlays of lapis-lazuli, variously colored opaque glass, mother of pearl, and semi-precious stones. That of Tut-ankh-Amon was made of gold and jewels. (See Plate 3.) Although stone and granite coffins were occasionally used by the nobility, such materials were generally reserved for the massive sarcophagi, which in turn were also engraved with appropriate scenes and texts.

a) Aerial View of Pyramids at Gizeh

b) Canopic Jars, Containers of Vital Organs

PLATE 1

a) Canopic Chest, Tut-ankh-Amon

b) Egyptian Outer Coffin, Inscribed with Magical Texts

PLATE 2

Undertaking Specialists and the Ritual of Embalming: In a society where so much time, energy and materials were expended on the disposal and care of the dead it was necessary to develop an elaborate division of labor with the usual accompanying specialization of tasks and offices. While primarily it was the duty of the family and relatives to take the necessary measures to insure the appropriate immediate and continued care of the dead, as wealth and rank permitted these duties could be delegated to specialists; and as Egyptians succeeded in meeting the economic and social problems of life on this earth, they tended more and more . to let these specialists handle the complexities of securing an agreeable afterlife for the dead. It followed, then, that as a family's wealth and prestige grew, so did the luxury and costs of its funerals, as well as the number of specialists that were engaged in them.

For an Egyptian of rank, most arrangements and operations necessary to appropriate burial were *undertaken* by various classes of occupational specialists. The setting of death and burial was overwhelmingly sacred, combining magical and religious elements; and the actions toward the dead took place at all stages within a thorough-going ritualistic context. Upon the death of the head of the house, women of the household "rush frantically through the streets, beating their breasts, and from time to time clutching at their hair, which is sprinkled with the thick dust of the streets, and uttering wailing cries of grief."[16] The *Kher-heb*, or priest who superintended embalming and funeral arrangements was called, and, with his assistants, arrived as quickly as possible. The body was then removed to the embalming chambers while the priest discussed the method of preserving it. Arrangements also got under way for final entombment, to take place some two or three months hence.

Meanwhile the tomb was properly inscribed, or plastered with texts and scenes of the departed's life, tomb furniture was built, and among other things, a group of professional mourners was immediately organized to sing funeral dirges throughout the city.

In the embalming chamber the *Kher-heb* was in complete charge; and under him the surgeon and his assistants proceeded with the embalming operations. Since embalming basically had a ritualistic and symbolic aspect, representing the dismemberment and restoration of Osiris, each step in the operation was taken in conjunction with prayers and protective formulas. One assistant, the scribe, indicated the path of the incision. Another, using a sacred stone knife, made the incision, and might be subject to ritualistic stoning for any violation of the sacred body. Other assistants completed the evisceration, the washing, and the application of spices, unguents and gums. Next the viscera were preserved and placed in Canopic Jars, while the body was soaked in a tank of natron solution. Following this, the intricate task of bandaging began, once the body had been properly filled with spices and preservatives. Bandaging was invariably accompanied by a vast body of ritual actions; and the mummy cloth was inscribed with passages from various texts and formulas to give power to the dead in the afterlife. In the process, hundreds of yards of bandages were used by the specialists, and weeks were consumed in completing the task. Meanwhile, scarabs, amulets, and useful artifacts and ornaments were put inside the body, within the bandages, or in the coffin or tomb. (See Plate 4.)

In the entire history of the preparation of the human body for burial it is unlikely that so many specific functions have ever been assigned to so many separate functionaries as among the ancient Egyptians. Thomas Greenhill,[17] a surgeon, writing at the very end of the 17th century, with the works of Herodotus, Diodorus, and other ancient authors before him, finds that Egyptian embalming required five distinct specialists, each performing a separate office: "A *Designer* or *Painter*, a *Dissector* or *Anatomist*, a *Pollinctor* or *Apothecary*, an *Embalmer* or *Surgeon*, and a *Physician* or *Priest*." The last functionary was a "great philosopher" and "instructed others in these ceremonies."[18] Describing the specific functions, Greenhill points out:

The *Surgeon*, Who was the chief *Embalmer*, generally directed and took care to see the several Operations perform'd in due order, and sometimes did them himself; for tho' the *Curatores Corporis*, that were his Assistants and Servants, commonly Dissected, Embowell'd, Wash'd, Anointed and *Embalm'd* the Bodies of the meaner sort of People, yet when any Prince or Nobleman was to be *Embalm'd*, after the richest and most curious manner, he perform'd the chief part of the Work himself, and this he was the more capable of as being both an exquisite *Anatomist*, and well vers'd in the Nature of all *Balsamic* Medicines, whether *Galenical* or *Chymical*, and tho' he might be something inferior to the *Physician*, yet in conjunction with him, was he both the better able to consider the Nature of the deceas'd Person's Distemper, or Cause of his Death, and accordingly to proceed in his *Embalming*; and lastly, he was very dextrous and knowing in the *Art* of *Bandage*, whereby it appears his chief Business was to *Embalm* and Roul up the Body . . . so was there (also) a greater occasion for a skilful Apothecary, to take care of and see to the compounding the *Aromatic Powders*, *Oils*, *Balsams*, *Ointments*, *Cerecloths*, *Tinctures*, *Spirits*, and the like analogous Things, and their Application, according to the Directions of the *Doctor*; and as the *Surgeon* had under him a *Dissector*, &c. who embowell'd and wash'd the Body, and did the like inferior Businesses, so had the *Apothecary* Servants under him to make up the Medicines, administer Clysters and Injections, and to Anoint the Body, thence call'd *Pollinctors*. Thus was the chief Concern of the *Embalming* a Body manag'd by the Advice and Assistnce of the *Physician*, *Surgeon* and *Apothecary*, as indeed it ought also to be perform'd at this Day, and not to have ignorant *Undertakers* direct and act all things at their pleasure.[19]

The funeral procession was also under the organizing genius of the *Kher-heb* who, with his assistants arranged for the transportation of the mummified corpse in its inscribed and ornamented coffin, as well as for all the funeral paraphernalia. The mummy was placed on a sledge drawn by oxen or men; and the procession with its burdened, wailing servants, professional mourners simulating anguished grief, religious functionaries, and relatives set out for the place of entombment. When it reached the river or came to a sacred lake which had to be crossed, the mummy was removed to a sacred boat, which bore the principal mourners and was towed by another boat, and was in turn followed by still others bearing lesser mourners, offerings, and all other goods and equipment necessary for the burial. When the family tomb was reached, in the case of the wealthier, interment was directed by the tomb priests and their assistants. Under their directions the sarcophagus was placed in a sepulchre, usually at the bottom of a pit, but decorated as lavishly as the family could afford. Offerings were then made for the welfare of the deceased in a chapel in the upper part of the tomb. One tomb sufficed for each family, and sometimes for several generations of the same family. In the case of the less wealthy, many were buried in the sepulchral chambers of a single pit, above which was reared no structure or grotto. According to Diodorus, every one was judged by a legal tribunal before the right of burial was permitted, and of this there may be a survival in the practice of the modern Egyptians which prescribes that a witness must answer for the character of the deceased before his burial. When the mummy had been laid away, masons closed the grave for eternity.

Influence of Egyptian Death Customs: It is not proper to conceive of the Egyptians as devoting all their talents and energies to the disposal and care of their dead. Having brought their civilization to a relatively high peak of economic and social development, luxurious treatment of the dead became a potentiality which, it must be admitted, was most fully realized. After the rise of the cult of Osiris, belief in a prosperous afterlife, under special conditions, spread over most Egyptian society. As noted, the basic reason underlying the practice of mummification was the belief that it was necessary to preserve the body in the most perfect form in order that it might be rejoined by the complex entities which make up the total personality or person. Although this belief did not make its way into Christian theology, such was the depth and scope of Egyptian culture that Christians in Egypt were embalmed and mummified as a matter of custom. The Egyptians of the Osiris cult believed that while entry into the world beyond depended in lesser part upon magical and mystical procedures, basically it was contingent upon the candidates having lived a life free from evil. The selective process was symbolically represented by the Egyptians in the popular scene of the "Balance," where the heart of the dead man was weighed by the god of death, Anubis, against a feather. (See Plate 4.) Should the balance be unfavorable the heart was devoured by the monster Ament, and the dead man's desire for the glorious other-world of Osiris remained unattained. The implications of this belief were felt in Hebrew and early Christian religion and represented one of the earliest introductions of a sense of inner values, or conscience, which served to control ancient man in his relations to his fellow man.

The Egyptian custom of embalming the dead was rooted in a system of religious beliefs whose content by and large has not been incorporated into modern Western civilization. Nevertheless, from earliest times until now, Egyptian embalming has continued to rouse lively interest and admiration, and from Ancient Egypt to the present, neither the idea

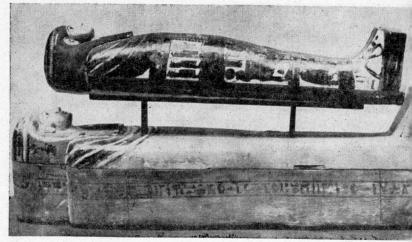

a) Modelled Outer-Coffin and Coffin, Showing Use of Cartonnage

b) Gold Mask, Tut-ankh-Amon

c) Coffin Portrait

PLATE 3

Preparation of Egyptian Mummy, a Painting

b) Examples of Mummy Bandaging

c) The Dawn of Conscience: Weighing of the Heart by Anubis

PLATE 4

nor the practice of embalming has ever been lost, nor for that matter, was there ever an eclipse of knowledge as to the general procedure which the Egyptians used.[20]

In considering Egyptian embalming practices, we should remember again that the embalmers belonged to the priestly class, and that embalming was a religious ritual as well as a physical operation. This double function of embalming was not carried along into later Western funeral practices, even though certain other aspects of burial continue to have both a physical and religious significance.

FUNERAL CUSTOMS OF THE ANCIENT GREEKS

During the two thousand years between the Golden Age of Mycenae (1600 B.C.) and the closing of the University of Athens (529 A.D.), (which latter fact marked the final extinction of Grecian culture on the homeland), on an almost uninhabitable Mediterranean peninsula, there arose a magnificent Greek civilization much of whose cultural heritage has long since been incorporated into the bases of Western thought and action. Though not as rich, perhaps, in historical depth as Egypt, the pinnacle of Greek cultural achievement reached in the 5th century B.C. stands above the comparable development of any other ancient civilization. Art, philosophy, political activity found ample room for the highest development in this classical or "golden" age. Our review of the death beliefs and mortuary customs of the ancient Greeks will seek focus in this period.

Death Beliefs: To the Greeks death was always conceived as one of the harsher lots of mankind. The writings of the classical period used stern and severe epithets for death, although ancient Greek literature is not without consolations for it.[21] Although the belief in a future existence persists in vague form throughout all Greek literature, earlier beliefs conceived of the dead as living a bodily existence under the earth. Later, in Homeric times, (circa 700 B.C.) this belief gave way to the concept of a shadowy afterlife peopled by disembodied souls—a belief not uncommon to Semitic peoples generally.

To A. Rohde, a close student of Greek mortuary customs, this belief in a disembodied existence accounts for the introduction of cremation.[22] But this theory does not explain the fact that cremation first appeared on the Greek peninsula itself three centuries earlier, during the Bronze Age, when the Greek states were loosely organized into the Achaean empire under the leadership of Mycenae. The practice of burning the dead had been brought down into the peninsula from the north by less civilized Greeks who had had contact with neighboring barbarians, and who with their iron weapons conquered their weaker cousins. Although infrequently practiced at first, its acceptance increased in the Proto-geometric period, and it took the place of earth burial shortly before the beginning of the historical period, around 700 B.C.[23]

At its highest point of development the Greek conception of the afterlife involved the separation of the soul from the body, and its ascent, or journey into an eternal and immortal afterlife. Rush writes:

The worship of Dionysius, [the god of wine] originating in Thrace, must have sown the first seed of the belief in an immortal life of the soul. The rites of this cult were intended to produce a wild excitement in which the limitations of ordinary sense life seem to be abolished. In such an ecstacy or *alienatio mentis* the soul was supposed to have left the body and winged its way to union with the god.[24]

Despite the popularity of this cult with its oriental overtones, it is fair to say that the general response of the Greeks to the thought of death was one of resignation, and not of anticipation of the glorious afterlife. The trans-

lation of the individual to the Elysian fields, or the union of
the soul with the cult god, were beyond the expectations
of the many, and only under special circumstances the lot
of the few. At the pessimistic end of the spectrum of Greek
death beliefs, hopelessness and despair prevailed, as revealed
in the revulsion for death expressed by the classic writers.
The revolting character of death in this concept is seen from
the fact that Euripides refers to him as "the sable-vestured
King of Corpses, Death."[25] But, whatever the belief as to
the mode of afterlife—and *some* form of such was always
conceived—the general and overriding concept was material-
istic in the sense that the soul was not forever freed of a
bodily counterpart. Death was real; it was bad, evil and
possibly terrifying. Consequently the funeral ritual and the
attention given to the grave and the memory of the departed
played an important role in the mode by which the living
related themselves to the dead.

Burial Practices: Reverence for the dead permeates the
burial customs of the Greeks through all the ages.[26] Not
only was it customary to give the dead a fitting burial, but in
classical times the law of Athens required the burial, or at
least the covering with earth, of the corpses of strangers. Neglect of the dead was condemned and even urged as a dis-
qualification for office. Greek literature has many examples
to show how important burial was to the Greeks. In the play
Antigone by Sophocles, for instance, when the tyrannical
king, Creon, forbids the burial of the rebel Polynices, Antigone, the sister of the dead man, demands the privilege of
giving at least symbolical burial to the corpse so that its
shade might cease to wander disconsolate upon the earth and
enter into the Elysian fields. When permission is refused, the
girl scatters dust upon her brother's body and so brings death
upon herself by violating the royal decree. In the *Iliad* by

Homer, when Hector, the hero of the Trojans, is vanquished by Achilles, the champion of the Greeks, he drops to his knees, not to ask that his life shall be spared, but to beg that his enemy will take the gold he knows his father, Priam, King of Troy, will offer for his body so that it may be given burial.

Lest the dead remain unburied, the Athenians cremated them on immense pyres erected on the battlefields where they had fallen; and gathering the bones, returned them to Athens to be entombed splendidly and with due honor and ceremony. There is a legend of the mourning parents who stood before the Council of Athens and successfully demanded the execution of the victorious general who had returned in such hot haste to the city to claim his triumphal honors that he had left his dead, the son of the petitioners among them, unburied on the field of glory.[27]

Although the earlier Greeks may have included human sacrifice in their burial rites, this practice was later reduced to a symbolic offering, and as Graves has pointed out, "almost everything connected with the interment of the dead seems essentially modern."[28] As soon as death occurred the eyes and mouth of the deceased were closed by relatives or friends. Greek funerary urns often depict the scene; usually it is the female performing the act, or, possibly the children. (See Plate 5.) Since passage into the netherworld required crossing the river Styx, a coin (obol) valued at about three pence was placed in the dead man's mouth for Charon, the ferryman. Without such fare the unlucky shade was doomed to wander a hundred years along the shores.

Preparation of the body for burial was generally made by family members. The washing of the body with warm water was performed by women chosen from the next-of-kin. The act had more than a symbolic value, since it was thought that those only apparently dead might be revived in the process.

Laying out and dressing the corpse was a sacred duty, entrusted in like manner to female relatives. While the body was anointed with oils, perfumes and spices, in keeping with the belief of the shadowy afterlife of the disembodied soul, no serious attempt at embalming was made. From the earliest times in Greek history, it was customary not to bury the dead naked, but with clothing.[29] Plutarch refers to the fact that the tendency to be extravagant in clothing the dead caused Solon to decree that only three burial robes could be used. These were the covering for the funeral bed, the garment in which the corpse was enveloped, and the outer covering.[30] This early instance of sumptuary law is not, historically, an isolated case. Later periods in Western civilization, including the early American Colonial period, reveal sumptuary decrees and legislation dealing with excessive funerary display.

Flowers, woven into wreaths, were furnished for the dead by relatives and friends of the deceased. Included with the corpse was a honey cake for the dog Cerberus, the three-headed guardian of the lower region. While mourning was indicated by dark, or subdued colors, the dead were robed in white.

Within a day after death the body, washed, anointed, dressed, and ready for burial was laid out in state. Friends and relatives then viewed the corpse, a practice which in part served to guarantee that death had actually occurred (see Plate 5) and that the corpse might not have suffered violence. Meanwhile, ritualistic wailing by female mourners began. After one day of lying in state, unless the social prestige of the dead was such as to require extension of time up to seven days, a funeral procession was formed to accompany the body to the tomb. Usually at an hour before dawn, the procession set out. It consisted of the corpse on a bier carried by relatives or friends, or, possibly hired "corpse bearers,"[31] female mourners, fraternity members, either immediately preceding, or just behind the corpse, and hired dirge singers. (See Plate 6.) Curiously enough, any *man* might join in the dismal march to the grave, but every *woman* was denied the melancholy privilege, unless she had passed her sixtieth year, or was connected with the deceased by blood and was over sixteen years of age.[32]

As noted earlier, cremation of the dead began in Greece about 1,000 B.C. as a burial form adopted from the immigrant Greek-speaking people from the North. At first rarely used, its acceptance increased through subsequent historic periods, until during Homeric and Classical times it was the predominating mode of disposition. While at no time was earth burial entirely superseded, the belief in the power of the flame to set the soul free acted as a strong impetus to the practice of cremation. It might be noted, however, that the ashes of the dead, were still conceived to have personal, or spirit characteristics.[33] Although a choice of inhumation or cremation was available at all late Greek periods, the obsequies at the burial universally indicated a conception of a disembodied soul, or shade, in rather sharp distinction to the Egyptian belief in the reanimation of the dead by restoration to the body of the complex elements which together with it formed the person.

Coffins and Tombs: Wood, stone and baked clay coffins were in use at various periods of early Greek history. Those of baked clay, representing the earlier eras, tended to be rudely fashioned, although some were decorated with painted floral designs. Chests of cypress wood were used in the later periods, yet stone was perhaps the most popular material, although its weight precluded its being carried in the funeral procession. The body was borne on the bier, and if not cremated, was deposited, enclosed in the coffin, in the tomb.

Graves has classified these tombs into four major groups: (a) *stelae*, or shafts, (b) *kiones*, or columns, (c) *trapezae*, or square cut tombs, and (d) the *naidia* or temple-like structures.[34] The *stelae*, which were actually upright slabs of stone, and other tombs, were often covered with figures carved in *bas relief*, finished off with painting. (See Plate 6.) Scenes were apt to be lifelike, showing the deceased on the deathbed, or at work in his home. In a relief, found at Athens, some kind of a repast or feast is shown. A bearded man reclines upon a couch and holds a plate or saucer in his hand; his wife is seated at his feet, and a naked cup-bearer is near at hand. A friend stands at the head of the couch and the dog lies under it.[35] Inside the tomb, and sometimes inside the coffin, there were placed practical and artistic ornaments, jewels, vessels, wreaths, painted vases, articles of toilet, war, and play. As in the case of the Egyptians, preparations were often made by the individual before his demise for the continued care of the tomb. Family tombs were also used.

The final steps were the funeral feast which broke the fast that the bereaved had been keeping, and the offering of sacrifices at the sepulchre on specified days. Although in early times these sacrifices took the form of blood-propitiations to the appropriate gods, the Greeks later substituted offerings of food, wine, and various libational mixtures. Thus, the Greeks of antiquity kept alive their relationship to the dead and to the dreary afterlife which they believed was the common lot of man.

Herodotus tells us that the primitive Greeks sometimes slaughtered slaves and horses to provide servants and beasts for the dead in the material hereafter. This practice of so equipping the dead with all the goods and services needed in a happy life beyond, is to be found in the funerary cultures of many peoples. Suttee—self inflicted or group inflicted cre-

a) Attic Black-Figured Plaque

b) Lekythos of Amasis, Used in
Greek Funerals

c) Mourning Scene,
Greek Lekythos

PLATE 5

a) Funeral Procession, Painted on Grecian Pottery

c) Stelé of Aristion

b) Farewell Scenes, Greek Lekythoi

d) Restored Grecian Funeral Lot

PLATE 6

mation of a Hindu widow—though now illegal, on very rare
occasions is still practiced in India. As facts grow difficult,
symbols tend to replace them. Thus, when the Egyptians
discontinued the custom of sacrificing slaves to be buried in
the tomb with their masters they substituted small clay
figures.[36] In considering objects buried with the dead we
should always bear in mind the fact that while some of
these are designed to serve the dead, others are placed
there primarily as symbols. The many clay scarab beetles
to be found in Egyptian tombs, for example, have no utilitarian purpose in the afterlife, but symbolize resurrection.
To the Egyptian who watched the scarab beetle lay its eggs
in dung which it rolled into balls, and who saw the next
generation of scarab beetles emerge from corruption, the
meaning was clear: new life springs from decay. The Egyptians likewise saw in wheat a respected funerary symbol:
life lies dormant ready to grow from the germ. When wheat
appears on Christian tombs, to this resurrection symbolism
a sacramental meaning is added. Grapes and wheat represent wine and bread, the appearances under which Christ
offers Himself and is received by the faithful on Christian
altars.[37]

FUNERAL CUSTOMS OF THE ANCIENT ROMANS

In the 1,200 years from 753 B.C. when Romulus became
the first king of Rome, to 476 A.D., when the barbarian
Odoacer deposed Romulus Augustus, the last of the Roman
emperors of the West, Roman civilization emerged, flourished, underwent major political, social, economic and religious changes, and finally disintegrated rapidly under the
onslaught of the barbarians from without and moral decay
from within. Left behind was a residue of political, economic, and social institutions to serve as models for the
Western world in the administration of human affairs. Al-

though the Romans borrowed and adapted much of their culture in the areas of the practical and expressive arts from the Greeks, their contributions to the science and árt of administration are substantially their own. Many details of Roman funeral and undertaking operations foreshadowed corresponding operations today. Of particular importance was the emerging role of the secular as distinguished from the religious undertaker, and the assignment to him of specific tasks. Roman burial practices thus mark a major step in defining the status, character, and occupational role of the modern funeral director.

Roman View of Death and the Importance of Burial: Belief in the afterlife among the Romans varied in the course of changing times. In earlier centuries an animistic view— animism is the doctrine which holds that the soul is the vital principle—held that the soul of man, although separated at death from the body, hovered around the place of burial for its continued peace and happiness, and required constant attention from the descendants in the form of offerings of food and drink. Should the offerings be discontinued, the Romans thought that the soul would cease to be happy, and might even become a spirit of evil to bring harm upon those who had neglected the proper rites.[38] Starting about 300 B.C., contact with the civilization of Greece brought to the Romans new religious and philosophical beliefs concerning death and the afterlife. The mystery cults of Greece and the Oriental East emphasized the spiritual aspects of the afterlife, and included the hope of joining with the cult god in a pleasant, wondrous, or ecstatic existence in eternity. Opposed to this joyful lot was another world of torment, gloom and continued unhappiness. A more philosophic conception, proposed by the Epicureans, was that the body and the soul, composed of atoms, simply disintegrated at death.

Thus the afterlife of man was no different than the before-life. However, what was originally a philosophy of moderation became vulgarized into a scheme of life which was characterized by St. Paul as meaning "Let us eat and drink for tomorrow we shall die."[39] Maecenas, writing during the Augustan age (43 B.C.-14 A.D.) revealed in poetry not only some of the dreaded maladies of the period but the grimness with which the Romans held on to the life of the here and now:

> Though racked with gout in hand and foot,
> Though cancer deep should strike its root,
> Though palsy shake my feeble thighs,
> Though hideous lump on shoulder rise,
> From flaccid gum teeth drop away;
> Yet all is well if life but stay.[40]

The emergence of Christianity as the dominant religion of the Roman Empire, a phenomenon well under way by the year 300 A.D., made general for the first time a theological orientation to death. Death had a meaning given it in terms of an organized set of beliefs about man and his Maker, and death customs for the most part were patterned by the Christians after the mode of sepulture of Christ.

In light of these different orientations to death and the disposal of the dead, it is difficult to make generalizations. Generally, some sort of afterlife was envisioned by all Romans at all times. Even Epicurus left instructions in his will that offerings should be made in perpetuity to his dead relatives and for celebrations of his birthday. Moreover, no matter what form of afterlife was conceived, the relation of the living to the dead was held to be continuous and of vital importance, to the quick and the dead alike.

Roman Burial Customs: At various times both cremation and earth burial were practiced by the Romans. Cremation was the normal practice during the period of the Republic and the first century after Christ, but under the Roman Empire fire burial was replaced by inhumation. The causes for this change have been attributed to the spread of oriental mystery cults with their abhorrence of fire, and to the rise of Christianity with its emphasis upon the hallowed nature of the body, and to the operation of fashion.[41]

For reasons of sanitation, burial within the walls of the city of Rome was prohibited, and so it followed that the great roads outside were lined with elaborate and costly tombs erected by the well-to-do. (See Plate 7.) Although most of these were for families, individuals were honored occasionally by monuments or public memorials which, strictly speaking, were not tombs. For the poor of Rome, of course, there was no such magnificence. Corpses of slaves and aliens were laid in the *commune sepulchrum*, the common burial pit, outside the walls.[42]

Great tombs, or *columbaria*, filled with niches for the urns holding ashes of the cremated dead were often erected by speculators who rented urn space to those who were unable to afford appropriate resting places of their own. In imitation of these structures others were erected on the same plan by burial societies formed by persons of the artisan class, and others still by benevolent men, as baths, and libraries were erected and maintained for the public good.[43] (See Plate 7.) Although burial of the *misera plebs* eventually became a function of the state, burial societies were possibly the first agencies to assure appropriate burial for the poorer classes of workers. At Lanuvium between 100 and 200 A.D. the regulations of one such association indicate that social and festive affairs were likewise included in its official functions.[44]

There was little alienation of the dead—that is, avoiding the facts of death or hurriedly putting the dead out of sight—

in Roman funeral behavior. A person died in the presence of the immediate family. Under ordinary circumstances, the body was washed with warm water, anointed, laid out in a white toga, and decorated with whatever insignia of rank the dead had achieved in life. The body was then put upon a funeral couch, feet to the door, to lie in state for a period of three days to a week depending upon the prestige of the person in life. Flowers were strewn about the funeral couch, incense was burned, and outside the door, cypress or pine boughs were set as a warning of the possible pollution by death.

In the case of the well-to-do, the care and laying out of the body was delegated to professional undertakers who also took charge of the arrangements for the funeral procession and burial. Among the Romans the corpse needed preservation not for eternity, as with the Egyptians, but only long enough to lie in state without putrefaction. Added attention signified that the dead had been a person of importance, and therefore required a longer period of lying-in-state. In the scattered references to Roman burial, the role of the physician is not altogether clear. For example, while Pliny remarks that it was customary among the Egyptians to preserve bodies by the physician's art, it does not appear that among Greeks and Romans the physician served as embalmer. Although Roman embalming seems to have consisted for the most part of a superficial anointing of the corpse with spices and perfumes, cavity embalming was sometimes practiced, particularly for rich or important people. Such as it was, embalming was delegated to the *pollinctores*, who were either slaves or employees of the *libitinarius*, the Roman equivalent of the head undertaker. The latter was so called because he exercised his business at the temple or grove of *Libitina*, the goddess of corpses and funerals. Deaths were also registered at this temple.[45] In addition to the *pollinctores* another sub-category of under-taker was the *designator*, who acted as master of ceremonies and director of the funeral procession.[46] The *praeco* or crier was a special functionary who summoned the partici-pants to a public funeral. Interestingly enough, the social status of these tradesmen and functionaries who were not slaves was not high, as indicated by the fact that they were debarred from participation in political life. Should they resign their office, however, they could be elected to the highest magistracies.[47]

Early Funeral Directing: The *libitanarius*, apparently, is the direct ancestor not only of the undertaker but of the modern funeral director as well. In addition to providing anointing or embalming, he supplied hired mourners, mourn-ing costumes and other accessories for funeral pomp, and arranged services designed to ease the grief of the bereaved. One of his more important functions was to arrange with his assistant *designator* the details of the funeral procession, which among the Romans had far more importance than it has now. At mid-twentieth century one funeral procession is much like another, and attracts little attention. The Roman procession on the other hand, gave persons of wealth and importance an opportunity to display their social and eco-nomic position by costly public parade. Johnston describes such a procession:

The funeral procession of the ordinary citizen was simple enough. Notice was given to neighbors and friends. Surrounded by them and by the family, carried on the shoulders of the sons or other near relatives, with perhaps a band of musicians in the lead, the body was borne to the tomb. The procession of one of the mighty, on the other hand, was marshaled with all possible display and ostentation. It occurred as soon after death as the necessary preparations could be made, as there was no fixed in-tervening time. Notice was given by a public crier in the ancient words of style: "This citizen has been surrendered to death. For those who find it convenient, it is now time to attend the funeral. He is being brought from his house." (Author's trans.) Questions of order and precedence were settled by an undertaker (*designator*). At the head of the procession went a band of musicians, followed, at least occasionally, by persons singing dirges in praise of the dead, and by bands of buffoons and jesters, who made merry with the bystanders and imitated even the dead man himself. Then came the imposing part of the display. The wax masks of the *alae* and assumed by actors in the dress appropriate to the time and station of the worthies they represented. It must have seemed as if the ancient dead had returned to earth to guide their descendant to his place among them. Servius tells us that six hundred *imagines* were displayed at the funeral of the young Marcellus, the nephew of Augustus. Then followed the memorials of the great deeds of the deceased, if he had been a general, as in a triumphal procession, and then the dead man himself, carried with face uncovered on a lofty couch. Then came the family, including freedmen (especially those made free by the testament of their master) and slaves, and next the friends, all in mourning garb, and all freely giving expression to the emotion that we try to suppress on such occasions. Torchbearers attended the train, even by day, as a remembrance of the older custom of burial by night.[48]

In selecting the buffoon to portray the dead man an effort was made to obtain the services of an actor who resembled him. This travesty was intended to show that the departed members of the family had come back to escort the newest recruit to the ranks into the underworld. The waxen masks were carefully preserved as heirlooms, to be used only at funerals.[49]

While ordinary funerals were nighttime affairs, persons of higher status were buried by day. Torchbearers attended the day processions, however, as a remembrance of the custom of nocturnal burial. A funeral oration in the Forum was included in the funeral of those with sufficient prestige to be

honored publicly. The body was then moved outside the city
to the tomb where cremation or earth burial took place. At
this point the ceremony included the consecration of the
burial site, the purification of those assembled, and the casting of earth upon the remains. Subsequently, a mourning
period was observed, offerings were made to the gods, and
the memory of the dead was kept alive through later memorial
festivals. Fear that the dead might be jealous of apparent
neglect by the living, who bore grief stoically, led both Greeks
and Romans to introduce professional mourners into their
funeral processions. Hired women shrieked and beat their
breasts with abandon. As the ceremony drew to a close,
the frenzy of their simulated sorrow mounted, and was cli-
maxed with a triple ceremonial farewell, the *conclamatio
mortis*, or calling out of the dead, as tearing their hair, rending their garments and scratching their faces until they drew
blood, they thrice encircled the coffin, shrieking out the name
of the deceased.[50] (See Plate 7.)

By the time of Constantine, the first Christian Emperor
(314 A.D.-379 A.D.) municipal authority had been extended
to include the public disposal of any Roman who needed
but could not afford a proper burial. Companies of functionaries were established to prepare the religious procession, to carry the bier and to dig the grave. Sumptuary
laws prohibiting excessive spending were enacted at the
time, and overcharge for funeral paraphernalia was declared
illegal. "Every person who needed it," writes Puckle, "was
to have a coffin without payment, whilst even the poorest
were to be followed to the grave by a cross bearer, eight
monks, and three acolytes."[51] From this period through
the Middle Ages the management of funerary behavior becomes more and more the province of the Church, and for
the next fifteen hundred years the secular undertaker re-

a) Funeral Procession, Relief from Amiternum

b) Roman Burial Urn

c) Tomb of Cecillia Metella, Appian Way

Columbarium, Vigna Codini

e) Funeral Urn, Depicting the *Conclamatio*

PLATE 7

mains an occupational casualty to the revolution of Western culture.

Influence of Roman Burial Practices: Roman influence upon contemporary funeral beliefs has been on the whole slight. The *conclamatio mortis*, for example, was not taken up by the Christian Church as a formal rite, and must not be confused with occasional spontaneous outbursts of grief in Christian burials. Some direct impact is to be found in the influence that the splendor, pomp and ceremony in which the Romans expressed their social hierarchy in their funerals, had upon the uniform simplicity of the early Christian funerals. Nock points out the operation of *fashion* in Roman funeral behavior, and ascribes the decline of cremation to the desire of Romans to indicate their social position and wealth more advantageously through earth burial:

By fashion we mean the habits of the rich, which gradually permeated the classes below them. Burial seems to have made its appeal to them because it presented itself in the form of the use of the sarcophagus. This was expensive and gratified the instinct for ostentation. The richest could build mausolea. Many whose resources would not suffice for that, could afford sarcophagi, which might well appear a more solid and adequate way of paying the last honors to the dead . . . the sarcophagus reestablished the popularity of burial, and then burial then came in its own right to be the dominant custom of the poor.[52]

Roman influence upon modern funeral practices is to be regarded in the last instance not so much for the *content* of those death beliefs which might have been transmitted to the Western world, but for the *occupational models* useful to mass societies exhibiting an urban way of life. Most important from the point of view of this study is the secular functionary, the Roman undertaker, who as arranger, manager and director of funeral affairs, as well as supplier of mortuary paraphernalia, sets a pattern of occupational behavior meaningful to the funeral director of mid-twentieth century. Additionally, the administrative measures of the Romans have stood as a source of suggestion to modern societies in which a body of mortuary law has been felt necessary to insure adequate public protection in the matter of the disposal of the dead.

CITATIONS AND REFERENCES FOR CHAPTER I

1. For detailed treatment of this subject see Alfred C. Rush, *Death and Burial in Christian Antiquity* (Washington, D. C.: The Catholic University of America Press, 1941); Bertram S. Puckle, *Funeral Customs, Their Origin and Development* (New York: Frederick A. Stokes Co., 1926); Lewis B. Paton, *Spiritism and the Cult of the Dead in Antiquity* (New York: The Macmillan Co., 1921); and Edwin Mitchell, "Death and Disposal of the Dead," John Hastings (ed.), *Encyclopaedia of Religion and Ethics* (New York: Charles Scribner's Sons, 1912).

2. The emergence of a morality of conscience in Early Egypt, has been described by the eminent Egyptologists, James H. Breasted in *The Dawn of Conscience* (New York: Charles Scribner's Sons, 1946), and W. M. F. Petrie, *Religion and Conscience in Ancient Egypt* (London: Methuen and Co., Ltd., 1898).

3. See for example, Margaret A. Murray, *The Splendour That Was Egypt: A General Survey of Egyptian Culture and Civilisation* (New York: Philosophical Library, 1949).

4. After Murray, *Ibid.*, p. 189.

5. Thomas Greenhill, *The Art of Embalming* (London: Printed for the Author, 1705), p. 106.

6. Breasted, *op. cit.*, p. 49.

7. Puckle, *op. cit.*, p. 101.

8. Breasted, *A History of the Ancient Egyptians* (New York: Charles Scribner's Sons, 1903), p. 65.

9. Charles Creighton, *A History of Epidemics in Britain*

(Cambridge: at the University Press, 1891), Vol. I, p. 160.

10. The definitive work of mummification is undoubtedly Sir E. A. Wallis Budge's *The Mummy: a Handbook of Egyptian Funerary Archaeology* (2nd ed.; Cambridge: At the University Press, 1925). For a technical discussion of the process in light of recent investigations into the chemicals used, see Simon Mendelsohn's "The Mortuary Craft of Ancient Egypt," *Ciba Symposia*, Vol. 6, No. 2, May 1944, pp. 1795-1804.

11. For the hieroglyphic representation of these gods see *A Guide to the Egyptian Collections in the British Museum* (London: Harrison and Sons, 1909).

12. Herodotus, *The Persian Wars*, translated by George Rawlinson (The Modern Library ed.; New York: Random House, 1942), Book 2, Ch. 85-90, pp. 155-158.

13. Budge, *op. cit.*, p. 428.

14. Murray, *op. cit.*, p. 189.

15. Budge, *op. cit.*, pp. 428-429.

16. *Ibid.*, p. 340. The description of these burial proceedings follows Budge, pp. 336-351.

17. Greenhill, *op. cit.*, pp. 177-179.

18. *Ibid.*, p. 177. Italics in the original.

19. *Ibid.*, pp. 283-285. Italics in the original.

20. For a description of embalming techniques of the Egyptians together with an extensive bibliography see Edward Johnson's *A History of the Art and Science of Embalming* (New York: Casket and Sunnyside, 1944).

21. Sister Mary Evaristus, *The Consolations of Death in Ancient Greek Literature* (Washington: National Capital Press, n.d.).

22. A. Rohde, *Psyche, The Cult of Souls and Belief in Immortality Among the Greeks*, pp. 19-24, quoted in Rush, *op. cit.*, p. 3.

23. See Martin P. Nilsson, *The Minoan-Mycenaean Religion and Its Survival in Greek Religion*, second revised edition (Lund Norway: C. W. K. Gleerup, 1950), p. 617, *passim*, for indications that the primitive belief of continued life in the grave—basic to the cult of the dead—does not immediately give way as the practice of cremation increases. See also Martin P. Nilsson, *A History of Greek Religion* (Oxford: At the Clarendon Press, 1925), p. 99 ff. Although quite generally the early Semitic and Mediterranean peoples held the belief in an underground community of departed spirits, unlike the Greeks many of them resisted cremation. It is not safe to conclude, therefore, that the cremation of the dead is a logical and necessary product in ceremony and ritual of a certain single set of death beliefs, when these same beliefs are seen to lead to other funeral practices. The persistence of earlier beliefs and customs into newer practices is seen in the bottomless vases found by archaeologists in tombs of the Homeric period containing cremated remains. Offerings poured into such containers ran into the tomb—an indication that side by side with the Greek belief of the shadowy afterlife the belief in the bodily afterlife still lingered. See also, Nilsson, *Greek Popular Religion* (New York, Columbia University Press, 1940), p. 22 ff.

24. Rush, *op. cit.*, pp. 3-4.

25. *Ibid*, p. 5. The use of the term "sable"—that is, "black"—crops up in the late Reformation period with reference to the earliest undertakers. Steele, in the comedy, "Grief a la Mode" uses the expression to indicate an occupational classification.

26. For a scholarly study devoted solely to Greek death customs see Frank P. Graves, *The Burial Customs of the Ancient Greeks* (Brooklyn: Roche and Hawkins, 1891). More recent data from the findings of classical archaeolo-

gists should be added, however, to bring the picture up to date. Recommended particularly are the works of Martin P. Nilsson: *op. cit.*

27. Puckle, *op. cit.*, pp. 237-238.

28. Graves, *op. cit.*, p. 20.

29. Rush, *op. cit.*, p. 125.

30. *Ibid.*, p. 126.

31. Graves, relying upon a passage in Pollux accepts the fact of professional "buriers," whose sole business was pall-bearing. *Op. cit.*, p. 40.

32. *Ibid.*, p. 42.

33. Nilsson, *Greek Popular Religion, op. cit.*

34. Graves, *op. cit.*, p. 53.

35. *Ibid.*, p. 57.

36. Puckle, *op. cit.*, p. 58.

37. *Ibid.*, p. 53 *seq.*

38. Harold W. Johnston, *The Private Life of the Romans*, Revised ed. (Chicago: Scott, Foresmen & Co., 1932), p. 41. This portion of the chapter is indebted to this work. See especially Chap. XIV, pp. 375-394.

39. Isaiah 22:13; I Cor. 15:22.

40. Quoted by James S. Elliott, *Outlines of Greek and Roman Medicine* (New York: Wm. Wood & Co., 1914), p. 66.

41. Arthur D. Nock, "Cremation and Burial in the Roman Empire," *The Harvard Theological Review*, XXV (October, 1932), pp. 321-360.

42. See *Burial Reform and Funeral Costs*, by Arnold Wilson and H. Levy (London: Oxford University Press, 1938), p. 6.

43. Johnston, *op. cit.*, p. 378.

44. See Ludwig Friedlander, *Roman Life and Manners Under the Early Empire*, translated by J. H. Freese (3 vols., 7th ed.; London: George Routledge & Sons, 1913), Vol. I, pp. 151-154.

45. William Smith, *et al*, *A Dictionary of Greek and Roman Antiquities* (2 vols., 3rd ed.; London: John Murray, 1890), pp. 890-893, *passim*.

46. Ethel H. Brewster, *Roman Craftsmen and Tradesmen of the Early Empire* (Menasha, Wisconsin: George Banta, 1917), pp. 44-52.

47. *Ibid.*, pp. 49-50.

48. Johnston, *op. cit.*, pp. 390-391. For a more extended discussion of the role of crier (*praeco*) see Ethel H. Brewster, *op. cit.*, pp. 44-52. The most comprehensive treatise in English bearing on the social life of the Romans is Ludwig Friedlander's *Roman Life and Manners Under the Early Empire*, *op. cit.* See especially "Luxury in Funerals," II, pp. 210-218 for evidence that Roman extravagance in funerals far outstripped the display of modern times.

49. Puckle, *op. cit.*, p. 66.

50. *Ibid.*, p. 68.

51. *Ibid.*, p. 33.

52. Nock, *op. cit.*, pp. 321, *passim*.

Early Christian, Hebrew, and Scandinavian Burial

The resemblance of many pagan funeral customs to our own is so striking as to suggest that the funeral practices of Western civilization today are largely drawn from earlier, non-Christian sources. While certainly there is some connection between them, it is worth remembering that some of these resemblances are accidental, and that the basic system of concepts underlying present Western funeral practice is centrally rooted in Judaeo-Christian mortuary beliefs. To shift the figure, although within this Judaeo-Christian framework, specific rituals and practices have resulted from the rise of sects and denominations; and even within these, some modifications have taken place as a result of local and national customs, fashions, even whims perhaps, the basic ideological under-pinning of Christian orientation to the dead and the provisions for their disposition remain essentially and substantially unchanged today.

51

FUNERAL PRACTICES IN EARLY HEBREW CULTURE

Death Beliefs: Like other Semitic peoples, the early Hebrews regarded man as composed of two elements, *basar*, or flesh—the same word used for the flesh of slaughtered animals—and *nefesh*, or breath.[1] The breath was a spirit-like substance that dwelt in life within the flesh, or more particularly, within the blood. At death, the flesh returned to dust, while the breath or spirit persisted. The Hebrews believed that the dead not only retained in large measure their former powers of thought and feeling, but added to these certain supernatural powers such as the ability to take possession of stones or images, or even of the bodies of men. In addition, the ghosts of the dead looked, acted, dressed like the bodies they had left, although they were as shadows, or weakened images, so that Isaiah could say of them that they "grope as those who have no eyes and stumble at noon as in the twilight."[2] Like other Semites, the Hebrews believed that the soul kept a close connection with the dead body, so that when the corpse was hurt the soul suffered. In like fashion the early Hebrews generally held that the soul led a shadowy after-life in a netherworld called *Sheol*. This belief seems to have been arrived at later, for earlier specific cults of the dead had tended to emphasize the return of the spirits of the dead to the grave, or to the place of residence in life. By the end of the Babylonian captivity (597 to 547 B.C.), however, monotheism (a belief in one God) as distinguished from polytheism (a belief in many gods) had developed as a set of organized beliefs, centering around the figure of Yaweh, to the exclusion of primitive forms of worship. In early Hebrew death beliefs, the soul was not seen as a completely discarnate element, since the close blood-flesh-spirit relation of man to Yaweh made a clear-cut separation of the body and soul difficult for the Hebrews to conceive. Also, earlier con-

ceptions of resurrection proposed that in a manner similar
to Egyptian belief, the breath or spirit was to be put back
into the body. By about 150 B.C. in consequence of two
hundred years of Persian and well over a century of Greek
domination, Hebrew death beliefs were basically these: upon
death, the souls of the righteous, bereft of fleshly adornment,
passed directly into a blessed existence; while the souls of the
wicked were sent into a state of punishment; but both would
be raised from the netherworld at the day of the last judgment to receive their final rewards and punishments.

Burial Customs: Immediately after death the eyes and
mouth of the dead were closed, the body was washed,
anointed with sweet smelling spices, and dressed in its best
attire; in very early days at least, it was bound up in the
position of an unborn child.[3] Although at the time of Christ
the body was wrapped in linen, after it was washed and
anointed with spices, such shrouding seems to have been a
later development, because it is not mentioned in the Old
Testament. The Jewish belief that in the underworld the
dead could be recognized by their garments suggests that
they had been buried in their customary daily apparel. In
keeping with a practice which the Jewish historian Flavius
Josephus (37-100 A.D.) describes as ancient, Jewish officials
and kings were buried with spices, ornaments, and gold and
silver.

Burial commonly took place on the evening of the day of
death. This seeming haste was founded on hygienic necessity. In the warm climate of Palestine putrefaction was
quick to begin, and spread rapidly. The early Hebrews
buried their dead without coffins. These first came into limited use after the Babylonian Captivity (597 to 547 B.C.).
The body was borne to the place of interment on a bier.
When the grave was reached, the poor were laid on the

ground or in a shallow trench, and over them a mound of earth was shovelled. The rich were interred in natural caves or in artificial sepulchres hewn out of rock.

Mourning Customs: When death occurred, the nearest of kin "rent their garments." While originally it seems to have been the practice of the mourner to remain naked until the burial rites were completed, as civilization advanced and social awareness increased, the ceremonial rending became a stripping down to a loin cloth of goat's or camel's hair, and later a removal only of the upper garment. Sandals were discarded, and for a long time bare feet remained a symbol of death. Although the Hebrews removed their clothes they did not uncover their heads but kept them draped or, in lieu of a drape, covered them with their hands. Although later forbidden, cuttings in the flesh once were practiced as a sign of grief. Earlier Hebrews cut off a generous tuft of hair between the eyes or shaved off the beard to parade their sorrow. Their descendants reduced the practice to a symbolical plucking of a few tufts. Similarly, the custom of throwing oneself in the dust was later symbolically represented by sitting in the dust or placing dust upon the head. Fasting for the dead, which began at the moment of death, ordinarily terminated at evening on the day of death.

Lamentation for the dead was a regular and important rite among the Hebrews. Hired mourners swelled the wailing of the family. Although the professionals had a considerable reportory of laments, all addressed to the dead, for special persons they prepared special dirges. Practices that seemed to contain vestiges of earlier ancestor worship, or appeared closely allied to it, were little by little stamped out by the later Hebrews.[4]

Place of Burial: The Jewish belief that family ties were not necessarily severed by death was important in determining their place of burial, inasmuch as family members who were buried together remained together in Sheol.[5] For this reason the earliest tombs were placed upon the family lands or near its dwellings, and burial therein was restricted to family members.[6] To be buried apart from one's kin was a catastrophe regarded as a manifestation of the judgment of Jehovah. The early Hebrews sought to lie with their fathers, and placed offerings in and before family tombs. These were generally easy of access. For example, Abraham's stood at the edge of his field; that of Joseph of Arimathea was in his garden; those of the Kings of Judah were in Jerusalem in the royal gardens. Samuel and Joab were given burial in their own houses. Not all sepulture, however, was so convenient. Aaron, Eleazar, and Joshua were buried in mountains; and Rachel, on the highway from Jerusalem to Bethlehem.[7]

Although for their family use the Kings of Judah erected tombs in Jerusalem, even in early times for reasons of sanitation tombs were generally placed beyond the walls of the city. Gradually the belief crystallized that they were filled with uncleanness and therefore would defile. By the time of Christ they were whitened with lime so that their ceremonial impurity might be recognized at a distance, and shunned. Speaking to the Pharisees Christ says, "Woe unto you, because you are as sepulchres that appear not, and men that walk over and are not aware.[8] Unlike their neighbors the Egyptians and the Phoenicians, who erected tombs of lavish and monumental splendor, the Hebrews preferred simple tombs, natural or artificial chambers, unadorned, and even without inscription, so that it is difficult to date them. At the root of this severity lies not only the general lack of interest of the ancient Jews in the plastic arts but their stern opposition to ancestor worship. An adorned tomb of this period is generally indication of Greek or other foreign influence.

Hebrew graves divide themselves into four varieties: the grave as described below, the sunken grave with a stone cover, the bench-grave, and the trench-grave. The oldest and commonest form is the single chamber containing recess graves, oblong excavations, one and a half feet square and six feet long, hewn lengthwise into the chamber wall. Tombs might be a single chamber with a single grave; a single chamber with several or more graves, or several connected mortuary chambers. The above-ground tomb in Palestine is of later construction and of foreign origin and use.[9]

Among early Hebrews, ancestral burial places were sacred and used for worship, the making of vows, and for sanctuary. Sacrifice to the dead was a practice that continued for a long time. Among offerings made were treasures, incense, spices, food. A double portion of inheritance was given to the first born because the duty of bringing sacrifice and of making libation to the dead was his by law and custom. The anxiety of the ancient Hebrew lest he should not have a son originated in part in a fear that without a male heir no one after his death might provide for him the gifts without which his soul could not enjoy rest.

Interment the General Practice: During all historical periods the ancient Hebrews interred their dead. While embalming was rarely practiced, both Jacob and Joseph were embalmed,[10] according to a custom that was foreign rather than strictly forbidden. No such tolerance was accorded cremation. When cremation took place it was frowned upon as an indignity to the corpse; and, by venerable custom and the priest-code both, it was regarded as a means of intensifying the disgrace of the death penalty.[11] At the root of this dislike was the age-old belief that even after death there was a bond between the soul and body, and that the spirits of the unburied, the cremated among them, on earth wandered disconsolate, and in Sheol—the underworld, the abode of the dead,—found no rest, but in pitiable conditions were driven into nooks and corners. The grave localized the soul in the body so that it there rested secure from harm. To remain unburied was therefore not only a disgrace but a misfortune.[12] For these reasons it was a sacred duty for all to bury an unburied body. Criminals who had been stoned to death were considered buried beneath the mound of stones that had slain them.[13]

Men dreaded the thought that they might remain unburied; worse was the possibility that one's corpse might be devoured by wild animals. Interment was denied as a punitive act only to foreign enemies. To violate a grave and to destroy its contents were considered great outrages. For strangers, criminals, and the extremely poor a public place of burial was provided. When Urias was brought out of Egypt and slain by King Joachim, "he cast his dead body into the graves of the common people."[14] The chief priests took the pieces of silver used to bribe Judas, "and after they had consulted together, they bought with them the potter's field, to be a burying place of strangers."[15]

FUNERAL BELIEFS AND CUSTOMS OF THE EARLY CHRISTIANS

Early Christian beliefs regarding death and the disposal of the dead were built upon the general mortuary ideology of the Hebrews as vivified and expanded by the teachings of Christ.

Death Beliefs: To Hebrew conceptions of the "flesh and blood" relationship of man to God, of an afterworld from which the body is to be resurrected, and of the eventual divine judgment in which each man must give an account-

ing for his life on earth and be punished or rewarded in the
life hereafter, Christ and the Church He founded, made
significant additions. To the Hebrew doctrine of the father-
hood of God, Christ added the great commandment of love,
and the concept of the sonship of man, and therefore the
brotherhood of man. To external conformity to the law He
added internal conformity to its spirit. More significantly, He
preached *the infinite and equal value of every human soul.* The
soul was both spiritual and immortal, and not destined in the
afterlife to be a discarnate spirit. There could be no annihila-
tion of the soul in death; no soul could be totally destroyed.
The teaching of Christ went beyond that of the Hellenistic
Jews of Alexander and the Book of Wisdom. In Paton's
words:

> Wisdom and all the Hellenists maintain that the future life is
> purely incorporeal, that there is no resurrection of any sort,
> but that the body is evil and a clog to the soul from which it is
> delivered by death. This is not the conception of Jesus . . .
> He says "I am the resurrection and the life." This must indi-
> cate . . . that the soul is provided at death with a new body
> adapted to the new environment upon which it is entering.[16]

The Resurrection of the Body and Cremation: In the
resurrection, the glorified body is patently to be, "a superior
body, like unto those worn by the angels of God."[17] The
resurrection concept of the Christians, therefore, certainly
offered more than the promise of pagan immortality—which
signified only continued life of some aspect of the person.
Because Christians held that it was the power of God that
transformed the body on the day of judgment, many felt
that the dead must necessarily be buried in the earth. Cumont
remarks:

> If the Christians of the first centuries no longer feared that
> they would go to join the shades who wandered on the bank of

the Styx, they were still pursued by the superstitious dread that they would have no part in the resurrection of the flesh if their bodies did not rest in the grave.[18]

Yet in St. Paul's memorable passage, ending:

. . . For this corruptible must put on incorruption and this mortal must put on immortality . . . then it shall come to pass the saying that it is written, death is swallowed up in victory. O grave where is thy victory. O death where is thy sting.[19]

there is more than the suggestion that the disposition of the body after death by any one mode of sepulture was a matter of indifference. The resurrection was the *miracle* of God: bodies burned, buried, or lost at sea shared equally in the miraculous transformation, although the Church held it revolting that the human body, "once the temple of the Holy Spirit, once sanctified and refreshed spiritually by the Sacraments" should be burned, except in "well-defined, isolated instances when because of disease or epidemic, cremation is absolutely necessary to prevent the disease."[20] The principle involved here is that of the common good. Cremation, too, has been frowned upon because of its pagan associations, and because in later suspicion of foul play, it rendered an official examination of the body difficult.[21]

Customarily, then, Christians buried their dead, although the practice of cremation was currently prevalent in Greek and Roman culture. There does not seem to have been a rigidly compelling doctrine prohibiting cremation, and Christians *were* occasionally cremated. But there was the example of the Master. "Those who imitated Christ during their lives," Rush observes, "also wished to imitate Him in death and be buried after the manner of His burial."[22] Although cremation was prohibited finally in Christendom during the reign of Constantine The Great, (306-337 A.D.) Christianity as a whole has never taken a final single stand in the matter, and today some of the more "secularized" religious groups, such as the Unitarians, actually favor the practice.[23]

Christian Equality in Death: The doctrine that in death all men are equal, and that the eternal rewards which they gain are not to be assigned according to earthly rank, is a central Christian death belief. While the Egyptian Cult of Osiris and the Grecian belief in the Elysian fields may have contributed to the Christian concept of the afterlife, these theories were basically aristocratic. Not all members of society could hope to share equally in the next-world comforts they offered. Rush comments that the Egyptians, "Seeing the differences among people in this life argued that there must be differences in the afterlife. They imagined there must be a special afterlife of happiness for chosen souls and especially the king."[24] For the Greeks, the shadow-life afterworld, with the separation of soul from body, was a belief more likely born of resignation than of hope; it was the inevitable end to life's journey. The miracle that elevated one's afterlife to the Elysian Plain was beyond the expectation of all but a chosen few. "As an heroic myth it was more likely to capture the fancy of the poet than the allegiance of the average Greek."[25]

These aristocratic concepts of the afterlife are in strong contrast with Christian belief. Christ Himself held out to all men an equal hope of the Kingdom of Heaven, with the joy therein to be in no way allotted according to earthly title or position, but only as each—king or beggar alike—became as a little child.[26]

Death as "Sleep.": The tone and direction of Christian funeral practices were set by the Christian belief in the resurrection. To non-Christians and the very early Hebrews, death was an uninviting reality in which the promise of an agreeable or intolerable afterlife was at best given only to a select few. The changed outlook produced by Christianity is to be clearly seen in the new metaphor in which death is represented as sleep. The "Cemetery" by its etymology designates a sleeping place, where those rest for a while in Christ until they rise with Him in the general resurrection. The concept and terminology of death as sleep have carried through almost two thousand years into modern funerary usage. Death is not only sleep, it is a summons by Christ or by His angels who bear the souls of the elect to heaven. Under another metaphor, death to the early Christian became a kind of birth into eternity, and a triumphal transition; and therefore not an event calling for hopeless and unconfined grief.[27]

Burial Customs: Primitive Christian burial customs, like those of the early Hebrews, were simple, unpretentious, and organized within the context of community living by a group of people to whom the Commandment, "Little children love one another," represented a way of life in which the Supreme law was, "Thou shalt love the Lord thy God with thy whole heart, thy whole soul, and thy whole mind; and thou shalt love thy neighbor as thyself." To bury the dead was one of the seven great enumerated corporal works of mercy enjoined upon all Christians. Early canon law laid down simple requirements for the burial of the dead, asking only that the body should be decently laid out, with lights beside it; that it should be asperged with holy water and incensed at stated times; that a cross should be placed upon the breast, or, in lieu of a cross, the hands should be folded; and that it should be buried in consecrated ground. No regulation required that the dead must be buried in a coffin. A decree of the Council of Auxerre forbade the priest to bestow the ceremonial kiss upon the dead, and prohibited the practice of clothing the corpse in rich raiment.[28]

The Christian doctrine of the equal and inestimable worth of every soul found funerary outlet in the provision that even the poor should receive befitting burial. According to Aristides, "when one of the poorer members of Christianity passes out of this world each one of the Christians, according to his ability, gives heed to him, and carefully sees to his burial."[29] The early Christian community provided its own burial services as a corporal work of mercy without hired pallbearers or other assistants, even in times of plague, when deaths were heavy and the funerary duties onerous. Rush comments on this fact:

During the time of plague and public calamity the bearing of the dead to burial was the work of private friends and charitable Christians. This is exemplified in the conduct of Christians during the plague which swept over the Roman Empire in the third century. Eusebius, describing the conduct of the Christians during this trying time, says: "Thus they would take up the bodies of the saints in their open hands to their bosoms, and close their eyes and mouth, and carry them on their shoulders and lay them out."[30]

The Role of the Family in Early Christian Funerals: Early pagan peoples generally closed the eyes and mouth of the dead as one of the first acts after death; significantly, this intimate duty was not delegated to outsiders but performed by husband or wife, or children or other close relatives of the deceased. Wives and mothers are mentioned in Greek and Roman writings as carrying out the task and among early Christians the family administered to the dying and took charge of the care of the dead.[31] Summing up early Christian funeral practice Mitchell notes:

When death ensued, the eyes were closed, the body washed, the limbs swathed, the whole body wrapped in a linen sheet with myrrh and aloes, and laid upon a couch in an upper room. (Acts 9:37 F.; Mark 15:46; John 11:44) These acts were performed by the elder women—kindred and friends of the family. Relatives and intimates were admitted to view the face of the deceased, and an interval of eight or more hours was required before burial.[32]

Among the Hebrews, certain women of the community were assigned the task of assisting in the laying out of the body. This task was considered a contaminating influence, a legal defilement, and, consequently not to be undertaken by priests, or members of the priestly class.[33] However, this taboo did not extend into Christian funeral practice; quite the contrary, the Christian "Kiss of Peace" marked a major break with Jewish tradition. Christians touched the dead; and since the body was considered sacred and holy it was possible for the laity and even the clergy to handle it without fear of legal defilement or need for ritualistic purification. Even beyond such permissive touching of the corpse Christians "developed a formal liturgical rite in their burial service which involved contact with the dead, namely imparting the Kiss of Peace."[34] The practice survives among the laity to this day in the final kiss sometimes given to the corpse immediately after death, sometimes before the closing of the casket. Among the clergy it has been long since discontinued.

Rush notes other funeral rites in the primitive church:

Certain rites were performed before death which were intimately linked with each other, namely, the stretching out of the feet of the dying, the administration of the *Viaticum*, the catching of the last breath and the imparting of the final kiss. The first two were helps intended to aid the dying person. The stretching out of the feet was a help in the natural order; while the *Viaticum* was a help mainly in the supernatural order.[35]

The naive, disregarding the spiritual nature of the soul, somehow fancied that it would leave the body from the feet, progressing to the mouth. They therefore stretched out the feet to facilitate its egress and, incidentally, the laying out of the body upon death. The Viaticum was the Communion or Eucharist administered to the dying, as a means of giving them strength on the journey into eternity. The word originally signified an allowance of money for transportation and supplies made to Romans sent on duty into the provinces.

Other Christian Funeral Customs: Although on the whole the early Christians anointed the corpse, especially in Rome and in the Holy Land, they showed a tendency to take over the burial practices in vogue in the countries in which Christianity was becoming established. Thus in Egypt, without in any way accepting the basic Egyptian religious beliefs, they embalmed their dead. In other localities they sometimes practiced cremation.

Interestingly enough, the conventional pagan mourning colors of red, black and purple were rejected by early Christians. Basing their reasoning on the belief that the soul went forth into immortality clothed in white, they favored the use of white mourning garments—although the *practice* of mourning was originally discouraged. The return to the conventional dark colors represents one instance where customary usage was not successfully displaced in light of a new death belief. With regard to the clothing of the dead by the early Christians, Rush writes:

The manner in which the Christians clothed their dead can be traced back to similar practices in Jewish and other ancient burial rites. At times, linen garments were employed; at other times the corpse was clothed with the best kind of garments worn during life.[36]

Washing the Corpse: The mortuary customs of the early Greeks and Romans stressed the importance of having the family lay out the body. In both cultures female relatives washed the corpse. While the ablution of the dead was a

purification rite among the Jews, among the Greeks and
Romans the washing of the body with warm water was a
test measure to guarantee that life was extinct. The Christians borrowed from the Jews certain funerary customs
associated with Christ, among them the washing of the
corpse. Puckle believes that this custom originated in the
"dim ages," and was part of the preparation to make
the dead appear to best advantage in the afterlife. Among
the Jews this task was assigned to the eldest son, and signified that the dead, being cleansed of sin, might enter into
heaven. The Christians took over the rite with the interpretation unchanged. The body of Christ had been washed immediately after the descent from the cross. The practice, St. John
Chrysostom (died 407 A.D.) observed, was "hallowed in the
person of our Lord."[37] Even during the visitation of the
plague during the third century the Christians continued to
wash the corpse although they risked contamination by doing
so.[38]

The Hebrews, unlike the Egyptians, did not embalm the
corpse, but anointed it with oils and spices. The purpose
behind anointing in a preservative manner, or perfuming, or
on occasion, burying the body in lime, was to prevent speedy
contamination and to counteract the odor of decay. Again,
in reverential imitation of Christ's burial, the practice was
followed among early Christians of perfuming the dead body
in commemoration of the spices with which Jesus was
wrapped. The pagans did not approve this custom, thinking
it foolish for the living to waste expensive ointments on the
dead, which they thought they might better employ in anointing themselves.[39]

The Wake in Early Christian Funeral Practices: Among
early Christians, as noted earlier, relatives and intimates
were admitted to view the face of the deceased and an interval

of eight or more hours was required before burial.[40] Ancient peoples, including some Asiatic and pre-literate groups, had long observed the custom of keeping the corpse laid out after death, and of keeping a "watch" or "wake" over it.[41] Puckle gives a functional interpretation to this practice, holding that this delay between death and burial, varying in length according to custom and climatic conditions, served a psychological need in gradually conditioning friends and relatives to the changed conditions brought about by death; and a physical need in providing an opportunity for continued close observation of the corpse, in the hope that it might return to consciousness.[42]

The old Jewish custom of "watching" or "waking" the dead was rooted in a genuine concern by relatives and friends that no person should be buried alive. To insure against such terrible contingency the sepulchre was left unsealed for three days so that the corpse might frequently be scrutinized for signs of life. This practice was taken over by the early Christians who used the occasion to gather and say prayers for the repose of the deceased, under the scriptural injunction that it is a "holy and wholesome thought to pray for the dead that they may be loosed from their sins." Those Christians who believe in the purgatorial doctrine still observe the custom of praying for the dead.[43] Gebhart adds a second purpose to the wake, to give comfort to the bereaved family.[44] During the night psalms were occasionally sung, as they were sung on the vigils preceding the feasts of the martyrs.

The Christian wake manifests contributions and adaptations from several burial cultures. Instead of the wailings of the mourners, who might have been hired for the purpose by the Hebrews, or the shouts of the Roman *conclamatio*, outbursts of grief among the Christians were held in check.

The grimness of death, for the latter, had lost its edge; the dead were "asleep in Jesus." While the Hebrew wake took the form of a vigil at the grave or in the sepulchre, the Greek custom was to wait three days before burying the dead. The Romans borrowed this practice from the Greeks, and the Christians from the Romans, so that the Christian wake became transferred from the grave to the home or the church. The element of time, however remained flexible, varying with the prestige of the dead, and the amount of money available for the preservation of the corpse.

If early Christian burial took place in the forenoon, the Requiem Mass was said and Holy Communion distributed; if it took place in the afternoon, the ceremony was limited to the singing of psalms and the saying of prayers, accompanied by the special service of the dead. This service consisted of hymns of thanksgiving for the deceased, and prayers by the living that they too might enter upon eternal life. The bishop pronounced thanks that the dead brother had persevered in his faith and in his Christian warfare, even to death; while the deacon read portions of scripture giving promise of resurrection. A hymn was sung on the same theme.[45]

The Funeral Procession: The early Christian funeral procession reflected in some degree the customs of the localities in which Christians lived. The funeral procession and the wake had been important parts of the burial complex of most peoples. While for the Egyptians, Greeks, and Romans these occasions varied with the social status of the deceased, the display lavished upon them is legendary and has intrigued alike ancient and modern writers, painters and sculptors.[46] It should be noted that the impulse to display emotion at funerals, whether originating in uncontrolled feelings or in sentiment collectively evoked by the social demand of the situation, was subjected to social controls which sometimes crystallized into law. Greeks, Romans, Hebrews and Christians, Rush notes, at some time or other developed formal restraints to funeral behavior.[47] In the earlier periods, the emphasis in Christian funeral processions was upon the maintenance of a subdued and reverent attitude, tinctured by a latent sense of triumph and exhilaration, since death was a victory, marking the beginning of a better life. Instrumental music, actors, buffoons, *praecos* and the like were excluded from the Christian funeral procession. Noisy exhibitions of grief were shunned. Young men, not for pay, but as a corporal work of mercy, carried the bier to the place of interment outside the city or village— "A natural cave, or a tomb hewn in a rock hillside or in a subterranean chamber, or in a simple grave," as local conditions determined.[48] We read in The *Acts of the Apostles* that when Anais died, "the young men rising up, removed him and carried him out and buried him."[49]

The early Christian funeral procession was limited to the corpse, its bearers, and the family and friends of the dead. As it passed solemnly and quietly to the grave, psalms and hymns were sung. If possible, the funeral took place in the daytime, to emphasize the belief that the dead person was entering into eternal light and life and not into gloom. Torches were carried at the head of the procession, not to light the way, since such function was not needed, but as befits the progress of a victorious combatant. Lights carried before the dead symbolized both the glory into which it was hoped he had come, and the triumph of his new state. Many instances are recorded of the use of the daytime torches in early Christian funeral processions. Lamps were employed as substitutes. When the body of St. John Chrysostom was removed from Comana to Constantinople, so many persons bearing lamps came out in ships to meet the corpse that the "sea was covered with lamps." When the abbeys of York were demolished, lamps were found whose light could not be extinguished by wind and water.[50]

Although the funeral sermon as we know it today does not seem to have been part of the funerary practice of the early Christians, the funeral oration honoring those of merit was taken over from non-Christian practice; and after the persecution era, was customarily included in the burial services for leaders or saints. Alms in the form of food and money were distributed to the poor at the grave, and public prayers were offered for the dead, in keeping with purgatorial doctrine. It should be noted in passing, that even in the primitive church, the third, seventh or ninth, thirtieth or fortieth days and the anniversary of death, were designated as special memorial days for remembering the dead with Requiem Masses.[51] Finally, Christian interment traditionally included farewell prayers expressing the belief that, instead of being the end of life, death was in reality only the beginning of a true existence. The rites sometimes ended with the anointing with oil and the "Kiss of Peace." Flowers were occasionally strewn on the grave.

Early Christian Cemeteries: O'Reilly points out the interest of the Christian church from earliest times in the provision of suitable places of interment:

For the burial of her dead, the church has always prescribed the setting apart and designation of places suitable for the tombs and graves. Regarding the bodies of the faithful departed as the habitations of the rational soul, like to the image of God—and the temple of the Holy Ghost—the law of the church demands that the place set aside for their interment should obtain a special religious significance. The ground, venerated by the relics of saints and martyrs, was always considered as sacred and was deputed so by suitable religious rites when such were possible. These designated locations were such as the customs and times preferred.[52]

While the earliest scattered converts to Christianity among the Jews were content to have their bodies interred without distinction among their Jewish brethren,[53] as soon as Christian colonies developed among non-Christians, a demand arose for special places of burial, which could be the scene of a distinct ritual, as befitted a fundamental difference in viewpoint concerning the dead body. It was not possible for the small, struggling, persecuted early Christian Church to possess and maintain cemeteries such as we know today. The earliest Christian burials from apostolic times to the persecution of Domitian were in family vaults erected outside the walls, along the roads leading from great cities.

"Let there be no burial or cremation in the city"—so reads one of the original laws of the Twelve Tables. This sanitary rule was observed by the early Christians in Rome for several centuries, and only disregarded when persecution forced their successors to assemble for worship in cemeteries. Pagan Romans buried their dead along the highways and beyond their cities, and following both law and custom, the bodies of early martyrs were so interred. St. Peter was buried beyond the Tiber on the Via Triumphalis; and St. Paul, three miles beyond the City, on the Via Ostiensis. Other saints were known to have been given burial outside the City walls. Only about the year 258 were the bodies of Saints Peter and Paul transferred into the catacombs, lest they should be profaned during the persecution of the Church. Thus, for three centuries the early Christians in Rome and in many places in the Empire were buried along public roads outside the walls of towns and cities or in catacombs. Of these latter there were some forty in Rome itself.[54] The tombs along the Appian Way constitute a notable instance of such extra-mural burial on privately owned lots. Out of this tomb burial, and in response to an ever increasing need for more room, the catacombs developed. (See Plate 8.) Originally these were galleries, chambers, and passages, openly hewn out of soft rock, with public entrances; their enormous later extension was due to crypt enlargement for burial purposes. Leclercq[55] observes that the catacombs originated in the tombs of the wealthy Christians who had them constructed in their gardens or villas and in place of reserving them to their household, permitted their use to their fellow Christians. This origin is clear from the inscriptions on the tombs in the more ancient Roman cemeteries.

At the time they were commenced, the Roman government approved the construction of these excavated cemeteries, and protected them against vandalism. Their secondary and accidental uses in sheltering and providing places of assembly for Christians driven by merciless persecution into such underground hideaways for the secret performance of their religious rites, and the resultant search and spoliation of the vast shelters, came later, and culminated in 253 A.D. in the decree of the Emperor Valerian which forbade Christians "either to hold assemblies or to enter those places, which they called their cemeteries." Among other cities there were catacombs at Naples, Palermo, and Syracuse. Catacomb burial among the Christians is known to have been practiced in Greece, Persia, Egypt, and in Syria and other places in Asia Minor. The catacombs at Paris are a series of charnel houses in which, by governmental decree, the contents of other cemeteries thought to be pestilential were dumped.[56]

When the great persecutions came to an end at the close of the fourth century, the church emerged from its long exile underground. A sign of its new freedom was the vogue for

open air cemeteries. Archaeological research indicates that
these were established in Rome and North Africa before
the reign of Constantine the Great. Although early Roman
law had decreed that burial must be beyond the city walls,
in the emergent Christian practice of open air burial, cemeteries in most early instances were located mostly within
the walls and in the vicinity of churches so that by the time
of Pope John III (560-575) most burials in Rome were intramural.[57]

Early Christian Burial Practices Grow More Complex:
Concurrent with the growth and acceptance of Christianity
in the early centuries after Christ was the pressure of pagan
burial practices and the use of funeral ritual and display to
indicate the importance, wealth or position of the dead in a
more complex, urban form of society. The burial customs
of the early Christians had been attuned to a community way
of life; Christendom in the Empire period spread across
many lands and included vast numbers of peoples. Consequently, the opportunity for infiltration of local customs was
enhanced in the very process of its spread, and ritual and ceremony were perforce elaborated into the type of display, or
spectacle that could appeal to and socially define situations
for the masses of people who were currently sharing in a
new way of life.[58]

About the fourth century the church established great
religious feast days to commemorate publicly and solemnly
the death of anniversaries of the martyrs. Rush continues:

At this time Christian life tended to center more and more
about the Church. Not only were the death and the anniversaries of the martyrs celebrated in the Church, but the death of
the faithful was linked in the Church service. Thus originated
the practice of bringing the deceased to the Church, and there
holding a wake over him. This became the usual practice
throughout Christendom.[59]

a) Divine Service, Catacombs of St. Calixtus, 50 A.D.

b) Vault in Catacombs of Rome

PLATE 8

a) Mourning Scene, Gallo-Roman Bas-relief

b) German Funeral Sacrifice, a Painting

PLATE 9

O'Reilly notes that the formula of the funeral service of the Roman Ritual, "is composed in three separate sections, the *'levatio corporis,'* or services in the house of death, and conveying the body to the church—the funeral services in the church—and the rites attendant upon the burial in the cemetery."[60] From the standpoint of religion, he observes, the obligations of providing and obtaining the prescribed funeral rite is "not only suitable and becoming, but really urgent." The recognition of this obligation "has always been foremost in the history of the Church." The obligation included the Requiem or Mass for the dead. "However, no explicit law has been codified prior to the New Code, relative to this detail. Now a special canon states that, 'unless there is weighty reason to the contrary, the bodies of the faithful, prior to the funeral, must be transferred from the place where they repose, to the church, where the funeral services—the complete order of ceremonies and functions, which are completed in the approved liturgical books—shall be held.' "[61]

Early Christian Funeral Functionaries: Unlike the Roman funeral, which was conducted by paid secular functionaries and public officials, early Christian funeral functions were carried out by the brethren of the dead under the direction of the clergy. These early simple practices later gave way in the funerals of saints, martyrs, and persons of civil and religious importance, to rites as costly and elaborate as those which had marked the burial of Greeks and Romans of comparable position.[62]

Prior to the assumption by the state of the duty of burying the poor, the poor themselves tried to assure themselves of a decent interment by forming burial clubs. Some of these combined social with funeral functions and at fixed times during the year met for large scale drinking parties. But during the time of Constantine as indicated earlier the state assumed the responsibility of seeing that all who needed it received decent burial. Laws were made to prevent overcharge. Under the supervision of the Church every person who required it was to have a free coffin. Even the poorest was to be borne to the grave in a procession which included a cross bearer, eight monks, and three acolytes. Under the general supervision of overseers, called *decani*, burial parties worked in groups, some preparing for the religious procession, some carrying the body, others lifting the body and digging the grave.[63] Stone indicates that, among the early Christians, friends carried the corpse to burial on their shoulders, and the highest clergy did not find such service beneath their dignity, although by rule, deacons were to carry deacons, and priests, priests. A dead bishop was commonly borne into several churches before being taken to the grave, the body usually resting on a bed of ivy, laurel, or other evergreen.[64] Burial of the poor was not left to indiscriminate care among the early Christians. Two classes of minor functionaries were assigned to visit the sick and bury the dead. The first were called *parabolani*, because they risked their lives in caring for the sick in contagious diseases; the second were designated *laborantes, lectarie, fossarii, sandapilarii,* and *decanii*. As the names indicate, these had the responsibility of digging graves, carrying coffins, placing the remains in the ground, and performing other related services. The Church prescribed rigid rules for these operations and kept careful watch that they should be well performed.[65] While it has been suggested that these functionaries were the forerunners of the modern undertaker, it is more likely that under different titles and management they were the *libertinarii* and their assistants the *pollinctores* and *designatores* of pagan Rome.

After the fourth century the Church itself built an elaborate set of religious and social controls over one of the most significant areas of human experience. In the process, the funeral service moved from the simple and reverential gestures of family and friends to a set of experiences and actions which were organized as part of the wider operation of an urban-type society. In a summary of Christian funerary beliefs and practices it should be said that while on the surface they may seem to have been derived from the corresponding beliefs and practices of adjacent cultures, their basic pattern originated in Hebrew beliefs and customs, as adapted to the changing needs of the Christian viewpoint. Rites and ceremonies tend to follow accepted patterns of belief, as customs and usages tend to be drawn from or to give form to folkways already extant. By the year 400 the basic orientation toward death and the dead in the Western world was set. From this period through the next thousand years death in Western culture will imply a "Christian" funeral, stylized and integrally a part of the panoply of religious behavior organized and controlled by the Roman Catholic Church. The Reformation will divide this traditional behavior into two main streams without changing basically the underlying death beliefs or modifying many of the practices.

Funeral Beliefs and Customs of the Ancient Germans and Scandinavians

Cremation of the dead as a mode of burial held the attention of the Greeks and Romans for over a millenium; yet fire burial was practiced by early Scandinavians independent of the influence of classical civilization for over two thousand years. Since this custom has persisted in Western society, though with widely varying degrees of acceptance, it is quite

likely that the death beliefs and practices of ancient Northern Europe contributed an ideological thread to the tangled
skein of modern mortuary behavior.

Cremation began in Scandinavia during the Middle Bronze
Age, according to Hilda Ellis, having diffused slowly but
with "startling thoroughness" from Indo-European areas
northward through Germany.[66] It persisted through the
Iron Age, and was the predominant mode of disposal of the
dead until the tenth century A.D. Evidently the practice of
burning the dead went on in the North until Christianity
was so firmly established that grave burial once more became the universal custom.[67]

Cremation as a Protection from the Dead: Although
many minor burial customs or "folkways" continue to be
practiced without foundation in basic belief concerning life
and death, the introduction and acceptance of cremation in
Northern Europe had its roots in the acceptance of new
ideas about the afterlife. In this new belief, we can detect
two important themes: one is to burn the body as a method
of keeping spirits of the dead from harming the living; the
other, by the same method, "to free the spirit of the dead
from the clogging prison of the body."[68] Ancient Norse
mythology contains many tales about the harmful spirits
of the dead, who, improperly buried, return to plague the
living. Ellis relates the gruesome story of the foster-brothers
Aran and Asmundr as illustrative of these. The two agree
that whichever of them shall survive the other will spend
three nights with the corpse in the burial room. Aran drops
dead one day and Asmundr is left to fulfill the compact.
Aran is in the mound, with his weapons, his hound and
hawk, and his bridled and saddled horse, and Asmundr on
a stool takes up the vigil beside him. On the first night the
dead man slew the hawk and hound, and devoured them.

On the second night he arose again, slew the horse and began to devour it so that the blood ran from his jaws, meanwhile inviting Asmundr to partake of the feast. On the third
night Aran rises again and attempts to eat Asmundr. But
the foster-brother resists, draws his sword, overcomes the
corpse, and escapes with no more damage than the loss of
his ears.[69]

Cremation to Free the Spirit of the Dead: In the second
theme, cremation to free the spirit of the dead from the
clogging prison of the body, we can discern several contribut-
ing concepts. One of these is the belief that in the afterlife
the dead may enter into the realm of the gods. Ellis notes
that the practice of cremation, or suttee, and certain kinds
of sacrifice, is connected with this belief. Entrance into the
Teutonic Valhall, or Valhalla, where the gods dwell, like
entrance into the Greek Elysian Plain, is not a democratic
right but an aristocratic privilege. Another concept is the
belief that life or spirit continues to exist in the grave
mound itself. From this belief sprang cults of the dead, with
their fertility beliefs, ideas of rebirth and inspiration by a
deity, as well as the conception of the "everlasting battle," in
which animated spiritual bodies engaged in fierce combat,
devoured each other, and returned afresh each night to
renew eternally the battle. To the latter belief are added the
sub themes of supernatural guardian women, the Valkyries,
who give aid to certain heroes during life, and after death
bear them away to their abodes; and the use of the grave
mound and its spiritual residents for magic, inspiration,
wisdom. Like almost all people of Northern Europe and
Asia, the Scandinavians believed in the "journey to the land
of the dead." Among the Scandinavians this belief was reflected in the practice, reserved for those of highest station,
of ship burial. In the ship-burials of the Viking Age in Norway

. . . the dead man rests on a bed within the ship, surrounded by all the necessities of life and many choice possessions, with various animals sacrificed to accompany him, and the dead slave girl laid in the tent beside him.[70]

The ship was then set afire and drifted out to sea, a burning holocaust, carrying its precious cargo into the glorious after-life. Yet other ship burials took place on land; and it is from the burial mounds of ships, some intact and some half burned, found in most North European sea-bordering countries, that archaeologists and students of Scandinavian antiquity have found the richest materials for their reconstruction of the funeral customs and beliefs of these earlier peoples.

From the viewpoint of modern death beliefs, however, most significantly important has been the pre-Christian Scandinavian concept of the disembodied soul, which through ritualistic ceremonies performed by the living is liberated from the body so that it may enter into a spiritual afterlife. Even where this belief is found, however, the two worlds of the here and the hereafter were never completely separated, the nature and strength of the nexus varying with time and place.[71]

Another significant residue of belief incorporated into Western culture from the death customs of the ancient Scandinavian and German cultures was the notion of fire as a proper, perhaps enobling agent in the transforming of a bodily ridden soul into an incarnate spiritual entity. In the words of the historian Karl Blind:

The twirling flame which rose from the pyre towards Heaven did not fill them with the idea of final destruction, but rather with that of enobling purification. They were easily brought to see in it a cleansing of what they conceived to be man's eternal being from mere earthly dross. They looked upon flame as true conductor of the dead, as the emancipator of the soul. The applica-

a) Early Christian Sarcophagus

b) Tomb of Innocent VIII

PLATE 10

tion of the fire to the corpse appeared to them to be a means even of appeasing and purifying the soul: A view we often find among the Greeks and Romans.[72]

Additionally, and perhaps equally as important, was the belief of the pre-Christian peoples of Northern Europe in the soul itself, as potentially an incarnate entity which could be emancipated from the body through the agency of fire. Nevertheless, the worlds of the living and dead were not categorically separated; rather the evidence of archaeology and literature reveals a substantial and reciprocal relationship. Supernatural powers, for good or for evil, were potentially available to persons who could explain the mysteries of the other world. In the last analysis the "cosmology of death" of these peoples turned the world of the dead back upon the world of the living, i.e., one's relations with the dead had more consequence for the living, than one's relations with the living had for the dead.

For centuries commerce and war kept contacts alive between the Teutonic and Mediterranean cultures. The great mingling came with the fall of Rome and the Western Empire before the barbarian hordes. The beliefs and practices of the Germans and Scandinavians were brought into England chiefly through the Danish invasions. The Danes who first appeared on the eastern and southern coasts of England in 787 A.D. made repeated invasions after 832, first wintered on the island in 851 and became firmly established there in 866. In 1016 Canute the Dane became sole monarch of England, and Danish or Norse rulers continued to reign until 1066. In that year William the Conqueror defeated and slew Harold the Saxon at the battle of Hastings, and ushered in the Norman conquest. Strangely enough, though the Danes conquered the Romanized Celts, the burial customs of the defeated people prevailed. As Prenté-Orton points out:

The influence of the British population and of continental neighbors is best seen in the burial customs of the invaders. The Angles and the Saxons brought with them the custom of cremation, though the Jutes of Kent practiced the inhumation of the Roman Empire. In the heathen cemeteries of the North, however, there was a steady growth of inhumation instead of cremation, which lingered longest in East Anglia and Northumbria, where on the whole a Romanized population had been small.[73]

Some Common Elements in the Mortuary Beliefs of Early Peoples: As we take a view across the primary mortuary beliefs of the early peoples and cultures thus far considered, we are able to draw at least one solid conclusion: death does not end all relationship between the dead and the living but merely signalizes the transition from one set of relationships to another. Nock, perhaps better than any other, indicates the two broad orientations which define the continued relations of dead and living:

Through the history of man's conduct in face of the mystery of death run two strands. On the one hand, there is the possibility that the departed one or some part or aspect or transformation of him may pass to a new place of spiritual existence, may enjoy new happiness or face new dangers; the happiness and the dangers are of course thought of in terms of earthly experience, but as subsisting under quite different conditions. This earthly expectation I have spoken of as a "possibility" because, except where a dogmatic religion is fully dominant, the expectation is normally tentative and hesitant; the individual does not and cannot hold it

> As he believes in fire that it will burn
> Or rain that it will drench him.

On the other hand, there is the fact that the dead man's remains, whether buried or burned or exposed are actually localized in a particular spot. Hence that spot retains its importance, even when it is dogmatically held that the essential element in the man whom we loved is elsewhere. Originally the belief in the practical necessity of the rites is strong. The dead man is thought of as an animated corpse, with natural need and natural vindictiveness. And he remains so, even in enlightened communities, in the eyes of many of the less educated. When this has faded, the grave remains the spot at which we took our leave of the dead man and at which his memory can appropriately be honored. This desire for honor remains strong, even after any idea of benefiting the dead man by tendance has disappeared. Epicurus denied the afterlife, but in his will he provided offerings in perpetuity to his father, mother, and brothers, for celebrations of his birthday and the anniversaries of others of his intimates. Hence funerary ritual is associated in the main with the tomb and not with the afterlife, as theoretically conceived, with things done and not with things held, and the variations of practice are normally conditioned by conveniences, safety, and economy or ostentation.[74]

CITATIONS AND REFERENCES FOR CHAPTER II

1. For a comprehensive treatment of the death beliefs and customs of the Hebrews, see Lewis B. Paton, *Spiritism and the Cult of the Dead in Antiquity*, *op. cit.* Sepulture is well described in *The New Schaff-Herzog Encyclopedia of Religious Knowledge*, edited by Samuel Macaulay Jackson, D.D., L.L.D. with the assistance of Charles Colebrook Sherman and George William Gilmore (New York: Funk and Wagnalls Company, 1908) Vol. II pp. 307-309.

2. Isaiah, 59:10.

3. Paton, *op. cit.*, p. 250.

4. *Ibid.*

5. II Samuel 21:14.

6. Mitchell, *op. cit.*, p. 498.

7. Elizabeth Stone, *God's Acre* (London: John W. Parker & Son, 1858), pp. 10-11.

8. Luke, 11:44.

9. Samuel M. Jackson, *The New Schaff-Herzog Encyclopedia of Religious Knowledge*, *op. cit.*, pp. 307-309.

10. Genesis 50:2, 26.

11. I Samuel 31:12; Amos 6:10; Joshua 7:25; Leviticus 20:14.

12. I Kings 14:11, Isaiah, 23:12.

13. Joshua 7:26.

14. Jeremiah, 26:23. See also Isaiah, 4:9.

15. Matthew, 27:7.

16. Paton, *op. cit.*, pp. 295-296.

17. *Ibid.*

18. Franz Cumont, *After Life in Roman Paganism* (New Haven: Yale University Press, 1922), pp. 68-69. Quoting Leblant.

19. I Cor. 15:54, 55.

20. William W. Buechel, "Christian Burial—What it Means," *The Ave Maria*, Vol. 80, No. 19, November 6, 1954, pp. 8-9.

21. Nock, *op. cit.*, pp. 321-360.

22. Rush, *op. cit.*, pp. 247.

23. See Robert W. Habenstein, "The American Funeral Director" (University of Chicago: unpublished doctoral dissertation, Department of Sociology, 1954), p. 22 *seq.*

24. Rush, *op. cit.*, p. 2.

25. Habenstein, *op. cit.* p. 4.

26. For a more detailed account of the genesis of the basic religious beliefs which underpin contemporary orientation to death and burial, see Robert W. Habenstein, "A Sociological Study of the Cremation Movement in America." (Unpublished M.A. Thesis, Department of Sociology, University of Chicago), 1949, pp. 6-21.

27. Rush, *op. cit.*, p. 15, pp. 27-43.

28. Puckle, *op. cit.*, pp. 32 *seq.*

29. Quoted in Rush, *op. cit.*, p. 203.

30. Rush, *op. cit.*, p. 206.

31. Graves, *op. cit.*, p. 23ff.

32. Mitchell, *op. cit.*, p. 456.

33. Numbers, 19:11-14.

34. Rush, *op. cit.*, pp. 101-105.

35. *Ibid.*, p. 91 ff.

36. *Ibid.*, p. 128.

37. St. John Chrysostom, *Eighty-Fourth Homily on St. John,* quoted in Puckle, *op. cit.*, p. 33 *seq.* Puckle stresses the simplicity of funerals during the Age of Faith.

38. Rush, *op. cit.*, pp. 112-117: also Graves, *op. cit.*, pp. 22-25. In this they were more courageous or perhaps more indiscreet than their Fourteenth century successors, lay and clerical, who, during the great plague, abandoned the dead. See Cardinal Francis Gasquet's work, *The Black Death* (London: George Bell and Sons, 1908), especially pp. 46-48.

39. Puckle, *op. cit.*, p. 36.

40. Mitchell, *op. cit.*, p. 456.

41. For an amply documented study of the mortuary practices of selected groups of pre-literates see Effie Bendann, *Death Customs* (New York: Alfred Knopf, 1930).

42. Puckle, *op. cit.*, p. 61.

43. *Ibid.*, p. 62.

44. John C. Gebhart, *Funeral Costs* (New York: G. P. Putnam's Sons, 1928), p. 12.

45. Stone, *op. cit.*, pp. 550-561.

46. The Metropolitan Museum of New York contains numerous excellent examples of these ancient funeral processions as found in friezes and paintings and on pottery.

47. Rush, *op. cit.*, p. 160.

48. Mitchell, *op. cit.*, p. 456; Matthew, 9:23; Luke, 8:2; I Corinthians, 15:54.

49. Acts, 5:6.

50. Stone, *op. cit.*, pp. 550-556.

51. Jackson, *The New Schaff-Herzog Encyclopedia of Religious Knowledge*, Vol. II, *op. cit.*, p. 308 *seq.*

52. John A. O'Reilly, *Ecclesiastical Sepulture in the New Code of Canon Law* (Washington, D. C.: The Catholic University Press, 1923), p. 5.

53. Acts 5:6; 8:2; 9:37.

54. Stone, *op. cit.*, pp. 62-63.

55. Leclercq, *Manual d'Archeologie Chretienne*, quoted in O'Reilly, *op. cit.*, p. 5 seq.

56. O'Reilly, *op. cit.*, p. 11 seq.; J. Spence Northcote and W. R. Brownlow, *Roma Sotterranes, or Some of the Roman Catacombs* (London: Longmans, Green, Reader, Dyer, 1869), p. 54.

57. O'Reilly, *op. cit.*, p. 6 seq.

58. Mitchell, *op. cit.*, p. 457, makes an excellent summary of this reinfiltration of non-Christian burial practices and the corresponding reaction of the Church.

59. Rush, *op. cit.*, p. 160.

60. O'Reilly, p. 49 seq.

61. *Ibid.*, pp. 47, 48.

62. Cf. Puckle, *op. cit.*, Chapter VI, pp. 99-129; Rush, *op. cit.*, pp. 193-235; Mitchell, *op. cit.*, pp. 467-478; and Friedlander, *op. cit.*

63. Puckle, *op. cit.*, p. 33.

64. Stone, *op. cit.*, pp. 56-57.

65. Wilson and Levy, *op. cit.*, p. 8.

66. Hilda Ellis, *The Road to Hel: A Study of the Conception of the Dead in Old Norse Literature* (Cambridge University Press, 1943), pp. 8ff.

67. *Ibid.*, p. 12.

68. *Ibid.*, p. 13.

69. *Ibid.*, pp. 55-56.

70. *Ibid.*, p. 47, An actual eye witness of a Russian ship burial of the tenth century is reported by an Arabian observer, Ahmed Ibn Foszian. See Carleton S. Coon, *A Reader*

in *General Anthropology* (New York: Henry Holt & Co., 1948), pp. 414-416.

71. *Ibid.*, pp. 198-201.

72. Karl Blind, *Fire Burial Among our Germanic Forefathers: A Record of the Poetry and the History of Teutonic Cremation* (London: Longmans, 1875), p. 13.

73. C. W. Prenté-Orton, *The Shorter Cambridge Medieval History* (London: Cambridge University Press, 1952), p. 173.

74. Nock, *op. cit.*, pp. 332-333.

Death and Burial through the Middle Ages and Renaissance

The defeat of the Emperor Romulus Augustulus, last of the western imperial Roman line, by the barbarian Odoacer in 476, was the final one of a series of blows that marked the end of Roman power in the West, although the Eastern Empire with Constantinople as its capital did not fall until 1453, almost a thousand years later. In the first half of the 5th century the Huns under Attila overran the greater part of Rome's empire, and were followed by the Vandals who swept down upon Italy and sacked Rome in 455. Without the stabilizing influence of Rome, western Europe was so transformed from what it had been under the *Pax Romana* that a new era in history was entered upon. In the ensuing chaos, civil society was broken up and new institutions were forcibly superimposed upon the ruins of older civilizations and Roman customs were preserved only in a few towns in southern Europe, in a few isolated localities sheltered by nature from the tidal wanderings of the barbarians, and in the Eastern empire. The great migrations had many causes. The richness of Rome tempted the greedy, the weakness of the degenerated empire created a vacuum, the pressures of Asiatic hordes behind them pushed the nearer barbarians across the Rhine and Danube boundaries. In England, as the Roman garrison withdrew, the wild tribes of the west and north descended upon their Romanized relations. Until the migrations subsided, the arts of peace had lean soil in which to thrive. But if the barbarians conquered the Empire, the Church conquered the barbarians, gave the new nations a pervasive common culture and a common second language, and provided within its walls and through its monks and scholars little islands of peace which served as a matrix for keeping alive the great tradition of Rome. This unsettled period has been frequently referred to as the "Dark Ages." While a case can be made in support of the title, care must be taken to apply it with reasonable limitations. Even at the worst of the long period of turmoil, as Castiglioni points out, the light did not entirely fail:

The Christian idea . . . exercised a determining influence on the development of medicine: it gives a different valuation of human life, a fraternal concept of equality and charity which imposed on all the faithful the most severe sacrifices in order to lessen the suffering of others. The example of the early Christians who during the epidemics of the early centuries were tireless in caring for the sick at the peril of their own lives is an admirable proof of the value and the justifying force of those humanitarian ideas which . . . brought about the creation of a series of institutions designed to care for the aged and the sick.[1]

While quiet did not come of a sudden, simultaneously, all over the troubled Mediterranean area, by the 13th century the descendants of migrant barbarians had built great cathedrals and would build even greater; had created literature in the new tongues, and would write more; had speculated deeply, and summarized their thinking into theological and philosophical treatises which are studied today.

CHRISTIAN INFLUENCE UPON FUNERAL BEHAVIOR
DURING THE EARLY MIDDLE AGES

Funerals: With the emergence of the Christian Church from persecution and the catacombs into daylight the simplicity that had characterized her primitive burial practices gave way to an imposing dignity that better expressed her own importance and that of certain of her members. The dead were brought to church where a Requiem Mass was said or sung. By the late fifth century the *Statuta Antiqua* assigned to penitents in Southern Gaul the duty of bringing the unattended dead to church for burial.[2] In *The Penitentials of Theodore of Tarsus*, the Archbishop of Canterbury, 668 to 690 A.D. gives ten regulations for the burial of clerics, the first two of which provide:

According to the Roman Church the custom is to carry dead monks or religious men to the church, to anoint their breasts with the chrisom, there to celebrate masses for them and then with chanting to carry them to their graves. When they have been placed in the tomb a prayer is offered for them; then they are covered with earth or stone.

On the first, the third, the ninth and also on the thirtieth day a mass is celebrated for them; and, if they wished it, is observed a year later.[3]

Despite the invectives against it by the early Fathers of the Church, ostentation gained way, and the primitive custom of burying the dead in new white garments of linen to signify or prefigure the putting on of the "new clothing of incorruption," yielded by degrees to the practice of burying persons in the costumes by which during life they had indicated their positions, so that they continued "splendid in ashes, pompous in the grave." Kings were arrayed in royal finery, and emperors in imperial robes. Knights were shrouded in military garments; the dead bishop wore his episcopal garb and priests their priestly vestments. Monks wore the habits of their several orders. In 595 A.D. the last rites of the Empress Theodolinda, friend of Pope Gregory the Great, lasted for over a week. After death, her body was brought to the Cathedral of Monza, the interior of which was hung with costly black drapes. There it was placed under a splendid catafalque,—a catafalque being a canopy as well as a platform—and lay in state, surrounded with lighted candles and tapers, so that patrons from all corners of Lombardy might pay their respects. Meanwhile, in hundreds of churches votive Masses—Masses made in fulfillment of vows or promises—were offered for the repose of the soul of the Empress, and bells were tolled. Finally, after the Requiem Mass, the body was interred under the high altar and surmounted with a magnificent shrine. The custom of building shrines, chapels, and chanceries in churches was a pious practice by which the donors strove to remind those who survived and succeeded them of their demise, with a view to securing their prayers.[4]

Anglo-Saxon times in England began when invading Low German tribes conquered the country in the 5th century. When an Anglo-Saxon of importance died, the body was placed on a bier or in a hearse, and on it was laid the book of the Gospels as a symbol of faith, and the Cross, as a symbol of hope. For the journey to the grave, a pall of silk or linen was thrown over the corpse and the symbols. In the procession, priests bearing lighted candles and chanting psalms, marched before and on either side of the dead and the bearers, while behind the bereaved there followd friends who had been summoned, and strangers who deemed it their duty as a corporal work of mercy to join the party. (See Plate 11.) If the procession reached the church in the evening, the night was spent in prayers. When morning came, Mass was sung for the dead, the soul shot or mortuary fee was paid from his estate, the body was solemnly laid in the grave, and liberal alms were given to the poor.[5]

After the Norman Conquest in 1066 the funeral of the rich Englishman from King down to Squire grew in pomp and length, sometimes lasting a full week. It began with tolling of the bells at the moment of death. It continued through the embalming of the body or its anointing with fragrant herbs and spices. When the body had been wrapped in a winding sheet of fine linen—frequently included as a wedding present—it was carried from the death chamber into the great hall of the manor or palace, there to lie in state in the midst of black hangings and under the gleam of many waxen torches. The cost of this illuminating of the face of the dead during long watches was great. Wax was expensive, and as many as 400 large candles were burned at one burial. At the end of three days' vigil the corpse was sealed in a leaden coffin, and brought to the church where a Solemn Requiem Mass was sung, and the deceased's clothes were distributed to the poor. Finally, after the body had been laid to rest, the principals at the funeral, including the officiating clergy, returned to the hall to eat of the "funeral baked meats."[6]

Church and Cemetery Burial in the Middle Ages: When Constantine's Edict of Toleration was passed 313 A.D., by a strange set of circumstances burial within the walls or limits of a city rather than outside of them was given tremendous impetus. Christians had long worshipped at altars in tombs and cemeteries. Now it was safe to transfer these altars and their relics to churches in towns and cities. Long accustomed to the association between place of burial and place of worship, Christians desired to be buried near their churches. When at his own request Constantine was buried in the vestibule of the church of the Holy Apostles, which he had built, he set a precedent not only for his successors, but for church dignitaries and benefactors, and finally for many other people. He also greatly influenced the custom of burial within the walls, and the development of churchyard burial to receive the overflow from the church building itself. Although the spread of the custom of sepulture in church was at first neither general nor rapid, within the first half century after Constantine's death it gained such wide and intense acceptance that it was common practice in Constantinople and other Roman cities. And this in spite of the fact that Roman emperors, whether pagan or Christian, had long manifested concern for community health in the making of burial laws. All feared contagion from the pollution of earth, water and air by the decomposition of corpses. But sentiment winked at sanitation.[7]

The Emperor Theodosius in 381 A.D., renewing the edicts of his predecessors, forbade interment in cities, and decreed that to prevent infections, coffins, urns, and sarcophagi within the walls of Rome should be removed to a distance. The law that no cemetery was allowed in or near the city of Rome was soon extended to other cities of the Roman empire, and was subsequently embodied in the legal code of Justinian (534 A.D.) the Lawgiver, and the greatest of the Emperors of the Eastern empire. Ecclesiastical prohibitions united with the civil law in condemning the practice of mixing the dwellings of the living and the dead. Gregory the Great, who was Pope from 590 to 604, restored the disregarded ban on intramural burial. Oddly enough, Christian religious belief became part of the obstacle to the abolition of the practice. It was not difficult to persuade pagan Romans who regarded a corpse with disgust, to bury it at a distance and outside the walls. But Christians did not look upon their dead with loathing; and as a result, in spite of emperors and popes, at length "tyrannical custom overcame the law," so that that which had been the "prerogative of emperors had at last become the common right of all."[8]

At the end of the 5th Century and during the whole of the 6th, burials within cities were very common, and continued so in spite of the fact that synods and councils of the Church tried to enforce the ancient codes. Charlemagne (742-814) himself attempted to stamp out the practice by first prohibiting the burial of the laity within churches; then extending the prohibition to all persons; and finally ordering the destruction of tombs, and forbidding that in the future they should rise above the ground. But to no avail. So tenaciously did people cling to the outlawed practice that at the end of the 9th century, in codifying and publishing church canons, the Pope himself accepted the established fact, and in one canon erased the old prohibition against church burial, giving as his reasons the fact that it distressed relatives to see their dead carried far from them, and that transportation involved heavy expense to the poor. Such occasional permission notwithstanding, intramural burial proved so great a nuisance and menace that from the 10th to the 18th century, councils and synods in various parts of the Catholic world made vigorous efforts to abate or prohibit the practice. As Wickes points out, no matter how modes of interment were affected by superstition or religion, the belief was universally accepted from the beginning of history to the 9th century that it was injurious to the living to expose them to the corruption of the dead, and that in crowded communities, the dead became a source of disease and pestilence. It was paradoxical, he notes, that intramural burial should have been permitted just when "nature's laws began to be better understood."[9]

Reference has already been made to the practice of using the church building itself for sepulture. From the 6th century on, as a result of the efforts to prevent earth burials within the walls of towns and cities, burial within church buildings themselves became more and more common, until the churches, too, found themselves involved in a most serious problem.[10]

Whether graves were placed under altars, in walls, or under floors, the amount of place available for sepulture within the church was severely limited. In recognition of this fact, in England, a 10th century canon entitled *De Non Sepeliendo in Ecclesiis*—"About not Being Buried in Churches"—calls burial in churches a "privilege" to be granted in the future to priests and to such persons as merited such special recognition by the eminence of their lives. When the Archbishop of Canterbury rebuilt his Cathedral in 1075 he provided vaults in the chancel and even beneath the altar. These were reserved for important personages; while the great majority of people continued to be buried in the churchyard.

Burial within the church itself had its nuisance aspects. The conditions mentioned by Ramazzini, who wrote much later, must have been better, if anything, than in earlier days when preparation of the body was more primitive. "There are so many tombs in the church, and they are so often opened that this abominable smell is too often unmistakable. However much they fumigate the sacred edifices with incense, myrrh, and other aromatic odors, it is obviously very injurious to those present." Ramazzini quotes

Lilio Giraldi of Ferrara (1479-1552) as very properly censuring the custom of interring the dead indiscriminately in churches, as being contrary to the practice which in remote times and in the earliest days of Christianity limited burial within the church itself to martyrs.[11] Although religious orders once restricted church burial to their own members, they came to accept the corpses of persons of rank, and of benefactors, until abuses of such hospitality of sepulture caused the church-going public to become incensed and the clergy to grow indignant. In 1581 Cardinal Bourbon, Archbishop of Rouen, decreed in council that "not even the rich should be buried in churches."

There was some logic in the effort people made to be buried in church precincts. Berner believes that in pagan days, the burial place was considered, if not sacred, at least religious through the *illatio mortui*. The early Christian Church at first upheld this view, but later rejected it by ecclesiastical decree, maintaining; that "among Catholics the place itself is not made holy simply by the burial of the human body." Instead of the body consecrating the soil in which it lay; the body was made sacred by being buried in soil that had been consecrated. Because it was believed that evil spirits were powerless in consecrated ground the term "God's acre" was applied to churchyards. The fear of vampires and ghouls, which in some places was strong during the Middle Ages, made churchyard or at least intramural burial a much sought after privilege. Christian tradition supported this practice. The concern of the Church for the remains and souls of the dead produced regulations concerning burial; and the concept of a consecrated place brought with it a decisive break with the past and communal rather than individual or local places of interment became the rule.

The same Church that consecrated the soil of the grave-yard took measures lest it be profaned. In England from the time of King Egbert (A.D. 740) Christian burial was denied those who "lay violent hands upon themselves," although this severe deprivation was not extended to those whose suicide came in a fit of madness of frenzy. Those found guilty as *felo de se* ("felled by themselves") were sometimes buried at a cross roads with a stake driven through the body: sometimes in unconsecrated ground, in a ditch or on the heath, sometimes in the churchyard by night.[12]

It was common practice throughout Europe until the time of the Black Plague, which swept over the continent in the 14th century, for each church or town to maintain a small churchyard burial ground sufficient for the needs of its pa-rishioners. When, during a brief period of the second half of the 14th century, the Black Death carried off an estimated two-thirds to three-quarters of the population of England, the churchyards proved wholly inadequate. In London, for example, the 120 small churchyard plots had to be supple-mented by three "extramural" cemeteries—two in Smithfield and one at Aldgate. These soon passed into the hands of friars and eventually became monastery grounds.[13]

But extramural burial was the exception, not the rule. Al-though churches were erected near existing centers of popu-lation and became foci for more concentration in normal times, with the natural spacings of births and deaths the ground could be used over and over again for returning the dead to the earth. Thus the church of St. John the Baptist, Widford, Hertfordshire, with less than half an acre available for a graveyard, interred no less than 5000 persons in the beautiful small plot that looks down upon the wide ford of the Ash. But this was uncoffined burial, with no effort made to preserve the remains of the dead. Only in relatively recent times, as coffined burial became the universal practice, have the old churchyards proved too small.[14]

The statement must not be taken, however, to mean that the ability to provide minimum space for disintegration was wholly acceptable then, or a standard to be imitated now. In 1552 Archbishop Latimer denounced the state of St. Paul's churchyard in London as productive of "much sickness and disease," and made reference to its all too familiar odors. That these should have arisen is not surprising. For some years prior to 1582, as many as twenty-three of the parishes of London which had given up their own burial grounds were using St. Paul's churchyard for their dead. In 1582 this number was reduced to thirteen, when ten of the parishes joined in seeking their burial needs in a new cemetery laid out near Bishopsgate. Even with this relief, it is difficult to see how thirteen parishes could find burial facilities in St. Paul's churchyard, which by 1584 was so crowded, with former burials made so shallow, "that scarcely any grave could be made without corpses being laid open."[15]

Disposal and Contagion: "Rightly or wrongly," Creighton comments, "taught by experience or misled by fancy, the medieval world firmly believed that the formal and elaborate disposal of the dead had a sanitary aspect as well as a pious."[16] An illustration in point is the use of the interdict, a spiritual weapon employed on rare occasions by the Pope to enforce discipline on rebellious rulers or peoples. This punishment took the form of a prohibition restraining the faithful from ecclesiastical functions. Stone remarks, "The most fearful part of an interdict has always been felt to be not allowing the rites of sepulture, and the burying of the dead in unconsecrated ground.[17] Writing of the last years of the reign of Richard I (1157-1199) and John II (1167-1216), the Chronicler Ralph of Coggeshall in Essex bewails the decree of Pope Innocent III in interdicting all Chris-

tian rites save only baptism by the Clergy of France: "Oh
how horrible . . . to refuse the Christian rite of burial to
the bodies of the dead, so that they infected the air by their
foetor and struck horror into the souls of the living by their
ghastly looks."[18] The same interdict was extended to England in 1208 during the reign of King John. The belief that
the dead infected the air was current in England for several
centuries before the Black Death. Creighton calls this belief
an "instinct" as wide as human nature; and observes that
among early writers there is a clear perception of the relation between the disposal of the dead, and sanitation and
contagion, with concern growing acute particularly after a
battle, massacre, or natural catastrophe. When the Welsh
raided as far as Shrewsbury in 1234, strewing the country
with naked corpses for the birds and animals to feed upon,
"the faetor of so much corruption infected the air on all sides
so that even the dead slew the living."[19] To prevent contagion, as early as 1348 the Venetian Doge Dandolo appointed a commission entrusted with such precautions as
the "special removal of corpses, the depth of graves, prohibition of exposing the dead on the streets, a guard against
visiting ships, and so on."[20] The theory of the origin of
plague virus from the corruption of the dead was commonly
held in the 16th century and for a long time thereafter. Ambrose Pare (1510-1590), the father of French surgery held it.
Discussing the causes of plague, Dr. Gilbert Skene wrote in
the 16th century about "dead carrions unburied. . . . which
by similitude of nature, is most indecent, as every brute
is most infectant and pestilential to their own kind."[21]

Creighton well summarizes the whole matter of the disposal of the dead and the spread of contagion during the
Middle Ages:

But even if these truths had been generally apprehended,
religious prescription and usage would have been too strong to

allow any radical measures being adopted. The grand provocative of plague was no obvious nuisance above ground, but the loading of the soil generation after generation, with an immense quantity of cadaveric matters, which were diffused in the pores of the ground under the feet of the living, to rise in emanations, more deadly in one season than in another, according as the level of the ground-water and the heat of the earth determined the degree of oxidation, or the formation of the more dangerous half-way products of decomposition . . . the skirts of the city were used also to deposit the soil (sewage) upon. Thus it happened that the ground outside the walls, which came in time to be the densely populated liberties and out-parishes, and the chief seat of all later plagues, had for generations before received the refuse of the city, and a large proportion of the bodies of the dead.[22]

The Purgatorial Doctrine and the Formation of Leagues of Prayer and Other Pious Practice: The Catholic doctrine of purgatory, that is the belief in a state of purgation in which "those whose souls are not perfectly cleansed undergo a process of cleansing" before they can enter heaven, was in part responsible during the Middle Ages for the formation of numerous confraternities, guilds, brotherhoods, or leagues of prayer devoted to burying the dead and praying for the souls of the faithful departed. These lay organizations are not to be confused with the religious orders living in communities and bound together by vows. In medieval England, such lay burial organizations were common. Typical of all of them were the regulations of the Guild of Abbotsbury which, among other matters, provided that "If anyone belonging to this association chance to die, each member shall pay a penny for the good of the soul, before the body be laid in the grave." The Steward of the Guild made the necessary funeral arrangements, which included a Requiem Mass, burial with solemnity, the payment of the soul-shot or mortuary fee, and a liberal distribution of alms. Davey found the inscriptions on the earliest English tombs "pathetic": "Of your charity pray for me." When a member of the Guild of All Souls in London died, the survivors were wont to give the poor a loaf of bread for the repose of his soul. The custom survived into the 19th century.[23] In an age that lacked newspapers and printed death notices, the announcement of demise was made by the human voice. Originally this function was bound up with the purgatorial doctrine. The crier—later named the "Death Crier," and in some parts of England "The Death Watch," and still later dressed in black with a death's-head and cross bones painted on the front and back of his gown or tabard, and, with a bell in hand—after the death of a person of distinction or a member of the League of Prayer, went the rounds crying, "Of a charity, good people, pray for the soul of our dear brother or sister"—naming the dead—"who departed this life at such and such an hour"—stating the time. (See Plate 12.) At this clamor and the ringing of the bell the town or city folk on the crier's itinerary threw open their sash and doors, and murmured an *Ave* or a *Pater Noster*. In London, when royalty died, the death watch was no ordinary public servant paid as an official by the civic corporation, but a nobleman, attended by a procession consisting of a cross bearer and the entire Guild of the Holy Souls, each bearing a lighted candle.

Prior to the Reformation, as the funeral procession bore the corpse to the grave, passers-by and bystanders, uncovered and stood in reverence until it had moved beyond them. When they met a procession, the pious even turned about and joined it, walking with the mourners part of the way to the grave. Vestiges of the old processional dress still survived into the 19th century in the scarf and hood of black silk occasionally worn by ladies, and in the "weepers," bands of black for a dead man and white for a dead woman, worn on the arms of gentlemen in mourning.[24]

The burial guilds survived the Reformation. Wilson and Levy, making special pleading for funeral reform in England, write of these guilds:

> Burial in the early and later Middle Ages was largely defrayed and—apart from the functions of the church—administered and assisted by gilds and corporations in order that the attendant expenses should not bear heavily upon the estate of the dead or the purses of their living relations.[25]

Puckle enumerates some of the equipment paraphernalia provided by the guild:

> The guild supplied a hearse . . . also a pall, bier, candles, etc. These articles were collectively owned, and held always at the disposal of those of the fraternity who might have need of them; they might, moreover, be borrowed by members for the use of friends, in which case a toll was taken of a certain quantity of wax, which would be made up into candles as required.[26]

Many of the same items were also made available through the church.

The Wake During the Middle Ages: During the Middle Ages the vigil for the dead, originating out of the Hebrew practice as an act of precaution against premature burial, was continued as an act of piety. One of the canons enacted under King Edgar in England in the 10th century reads: "Let him (the parish priest) shrive him, give him Housel, and Extreme Unction, and, after death, carefully order, and not allow any absurdity with the corpse, but with the fear of God bury it wisely."[27] (To "shrive" is to give absolution; "Housel" is an old word for the Eucharist.)

In the Irish canons a woman was given a penance of fifty days on bread and water for wailing after the death of a layman or laywoman.[28]

The learned monk Regino, who became an abbot in Lorraine in France in 892, compiled in 906 his work, *"Of Synodical Cases and Ecclesiastical Discipline."* In this book among other matters, he warned that:

Diabolical Songs be not sung at night hours over the bodies of the dead. Laymen who keep watch at funerals shall do so with fear and trembling, and with reverence. Let no one there presume to sing diabolical songs nor make jests and perform dances which pagans have invited by the devil's teaching. For who does not know that it is diabolical, and not only alien from the Christian religion, but even contrary to human nature, that there should be singing, rejoicing, drunkenness, and that the mouth be loosed with laughter, and that all piety and feeling of charity be set aside. . . . But if any one wishes to sing, let him sing the *Kyrie Eleison.* But if he does otherwise, let him be quite silent. If, however, he will not be silent, he shall be forthwith denounced by all, or adjured that he no longer has God's permission to stay there, but is to withdraw and go to his own house. On the morrow, moreover, he shall be so punished that others may fear.[29]

That the custom of behaving riotously at wakes became widespread is evident from the *Corrector* of Burchard of Worms, written a hundred years later, between 1008 and 1012. Burchard asks: "Hast thou observed funeral wakes. . . . when the bodies of Christians are guarded by a ritual of pagans; and hast thou sung diabolical songs there and performed dances which the pagans have invited by the teaching of the devil; and hast thou drunk there and relaxed thy countenance with laughter . . . as if rejoicing over a brother's death."[30]

By the 14th century disorder at wakes had progressed beyond rioting and drunkenness with the addition of the new custom of "rousing the ghost." While some have sought to explain this irreverent custom as originating in an effort to bring back through necromancy or black magic the spirit of the departed, it would seem less strained to account for it as a grim kind of horseplay. Aristotle has defined humor as incongruity intellectually perceived. Not all onlookers at a funeral bear an equal burden of grief. To persons lightly concerned, the heavy solemnity and deep dolor is a startling backdrop for the ludicrous. The dead were "raised" during the 14th century by playing practical jokes on superstitious relatives to frighten them, and by taking liberties with the corpse. The extent to which this grisly roughhouse was practiced is apparent from the fact that the Council of York (1367) condemned "those guilty games and follies, and all those perverse customs which transformed a house of tears and prayers into a house of laughing and excess." In the same vein the Guild of Palmers—returned pilgrims from the Holy Land who wore two palms crosswise in token of their pilgrimage—permitted its members to join in waking the dead only if they abstained from "raising apparitions and from indecent games." In the south of Ireland the vigil keepers entertained themselves with a sham battle, while their Scotch brethren fought mock duels that frequently ended in real fights and bloodshed. Everywhere the families of the dead plied the wakers with intoxicants and food, of which latter pancakes were a favorite item.[31]

Funeral Feasts: In addition to serving as an occasion for praying for the dead, the wake filled several secondary functions, among which was the opportunity it gave those who had been present at the death of clearing themselves of any suspicion of foul play; and those who had not been present at seeing that no foul play had taken place; and all who might inherit, the chance to witness whether an equitable distribution of property was being made. As a further function, the wake served as a feast to welcome the principal heir to his new estate. Etymology reveals the story:

the old word for the funeral feast was "averil" or "arvel," meaning "heir ale" or "succession ale." A common practice in medieval England that persisted even as late as the Stuart Kings—James I the first of the line ascended the throne in 1603—was to place a cup of wine in the coffin next to the corpse. By drinking of it the mourners felt that they had established some kind of communion with the dead.[32]

Funerals of State During the Middle Ages; The Use of the Effigy: The funeral of a great personage often lasted a week, from the time the tolling of the bell announced the death, through the washing and embalming of the body, the exposition in state, the Requiem Mass, burial, and the banquet of the "funeral baked meats." Waxen death masks were often made of the nobility as soon as possible after their expiration. It was not uncommon for a waxen presentment to be exhibited in church upon the catafalque, in place of the real body—a practice originating no doubt in hygienic and aesthetic necessity, especially in hot weather, since the funeral may have lasted many days. The custom persisted in England until the reign of William and Mary (1650-1702), and in France until the middle of the 17th century. It is last mentioned in connection with the death of Anne of Austria (1666): "The Queen-mother died today. She was immediately embalmed, and by noon her waxen effigy was on view at the Louvre. Thousands are pressing in to see it."[33]

The funeral of Henry V (1387-1422), King of England and victor of Agincourt, illustrates not only the elaborate and prolonged funeral rites given to monarchs and great dignitaries, but shows the physical need which these produced for some method of keeping the corpse from becoming offensive. It also displays a quaint refinement of the process of bone burial described in detail below. After the

King's death in France, his body was boiled to obtain a perfect skeleton for transportation to England. Before leaving France, the bones were taken to the church of Notre Dame, where a fitting funeral service was conducted over them. Above them, in the coffin was placed an effigy of boiled leather, robed in purple and shaped to represent the king "as well as might be desired." In its hand the figure carried the royal sceptre, and on its brow it wore the kingly diadem. After the services, the coffin containing the effigy and bones was placed in a splendid chariot or hearse, draped with a covering of red velvet sprinkled with gold leaf. Accompanied by the King of Scotland as chief mourner, and all the princes, lords, and knights of his house, the funeral procession moved from town to town until it reached the port of Calais. From Calais it was taken by boat to London where it was finally laid to rest in Westminster Abbey. Henry's widow caused a silver plated effigy of her husband, with a solid silver-gilt head, to be placed on the tomb. This effigy was destroyed during the Reformation.[34]

Sepulchral Monuments: The beginnings of Christian sepulchral monuments in England are to be found in stone coffins whose lids formed a continuous portion of the pavement of churches. At an early date it became customary to mark these with a carved symbol, such as a cross, to express piety, or some emblem to tell the occupation or position of the deceased. This simple incising was succeeded by the practice of carving an effigy of the dead person in the stone, or even a representation showing the coffin opened, with the dead displayed wholly or partially within. Little by little the tops of the tombs were raised above the level of the pavement, until they could no longer be walked upon. Next the custom grew of surmounting them with a festoon or canopy. As these grew in size and magnificence, they en-

cumbered the church, and were placed at the east end, parallel with the chancel, that part of the church reserved for the
clergy, or were erected in chapels especially constructed to
shelter them, and opening from the side aisles. The beauty,
magnificence, and cost of some of these monuments was
great. Some were enriched with semi-precious and precious
stones, and adorned with life-like figures of solid brass. The
finest on record is that of Henry III (1207-1272), who
had provided for the body of Edward the Confessor (1004-
1066) a coffin of solid gold and precious stones, the workmanship of which was so fine that it surpassed the material
in cost. The first tomb effigies were made of wood, plated
over with bronze or copper, plain or gilt. Later brass was
used, and some monumental effigies were made of silver.
One of the earliest of the latter was placed on the tomb of
Catherine, the daughter of Henry III. She died in 1251.
These monumental effigies, however rich and elaborate, con-
sistently display a humble attitude in the presence of death,
in spite of some identification showing status and occupation. Crusaders, and even those who had been prevented
from fulfilling their vows to visit the Holy Land, were represented with crossed legs; prelates, with the right hand raised,
as if in benediction; bishops carried a crozier in their left
hands, abbots, in the right; priests held a chalice; warriors
bore arms; kings were crowned—and so on through a long
list of ranks, titles, functions. Other symbols represented the
virtues of the deceased; thus stone lions at the feet of the
effigy told of the dead man's courage, industry, vigilance.
Emblems represented achievement, dragons pierced by the
staves of the abbots of Peterborough gave a clue to their
triumph and the church's over the devil. These representa-
tions were more in keeping with the Christian tradition than
the skull and cross bones of later medieval monumentary
art.[35]

a) Funeral of Archduke of Brussels, 1622

ℏIC PORTATVR: CORPVS
EADWARDI: REGIS: AD: ECCLESIAM: STI
PETRI APÚ

b) Funeral Procession of St. Edward the Confessor, from an
11th Century Tapestry

PLATE 11

a) Anglo-Saxon Widow,
9th Century

b) Death Criers, French Costumes, 17th Century

c) Funeral of an Abbess, 10th Century

PLATE 12

The Plagues: Beginning in the 6th century A.D., during the reign of the Emperor Justinian, as a part of the great cycle of pestilence which periodically had been sweeping over the world since the dawn of history, the bubonic plague entered Europe. In 542 it carried off in one day 10,000 people in Constantinople. Again and again plague swept over England, the cycle of epidemics of the 14th century, known as the Black Death, being most severe. Plague, although showing some signs of a decline, recurred in the 15th, 16th and 17th centuries. The years 1664 and 1665 were dismally remembered as marking the Great Plague of London. In 1665 out of a population estimated at 460,000, bills of mortality for the city showed 68,596 deaths.[36]

The successive waves of plague did much to change the economic and social structure of Europe. In England, for example, the earlier visitations wiped out a high percentage of serfs, forced freedom from the land upon those who were left, and did much to end the system of semi-slavery. Because funeral customs and practices depend in part upon what people are able to earn and to provide for the dead, a social revolution of this kind is significant for the present consideration. Apart from this, the plagues produced burial crises that fascinate us by their sheer magnitude. One visitation must have been much like any other.

Shakespeare's contemporary, the poet-playwright Thomas Dekker, described London and its "sinfully polluted suburbs" during the plague of 1603. While walking the streets at night he hears from every house the loud groans and ravings of the sick, the death struggles of the dying, the shrieks of the bereaved, the cries of alarm, servants crying out for masters, wives for husbands, parents for children, children for their mothers. Here a distraught man runs to look for a sexton, there a group sweats as it carries a coffin.

Persons push bodies from their houses into the street by stealth lest the officers of the law seal up their houses with the mark of death. In the plague of 1547 an order was issued prohibiting burial between six in the evening and six in the morning. In 1665, when the time was reversed, the twelve hours of darkness proved too short to bury the dead. In his imaginary *Journal of the Plague Year* the eminent novelist Daniel Defoe (1661-1731) tells of the Aldgate plague pit at midnight, with seven or eight lanterns set on the heaps of earth round the edge, and of the constant journeying to and fro of the dead-carts. Defoe probably got his story from eye witnesses. Certainly this was a case in which truth could be given no heightening by the art of fiction.[37] Fact must have transcended fancy. (See Plate 14.)

The Plagues Overload the Cemeteries: Turner of Boulogne, preaching at St. Paul's Cross, London, on August 8th, 1563, when 5000 a week were dying in London alone of the plague, besought the Lord Mayor to bury the dead in a field beyond the city, and to halt the tolling of the funeral bell, "for that the tolling of the bell did the party departing no good, neither afore their death nor after."[38] The story was repeated of the Pilgrim on the road to Bagdad who was overtaken by a spectral traveler. "Who are you, and to where do you hurry?" the pilgrim asked. "I am Plague," the figure shouted across his shoulder, "and I go to Bagdad to slay a thousand people." On his flight from the city the Pilgrim overtook the grisly traveler. "You told me that you would slay a thousand in Bagdad," he chided, "and yet I found ten thousand slain." "I spoke accurately," answered Plague, "I slew but a thousand. The other nine thousand died from fright."[39]

So great were the numbers dying that Christian burial rites could not be provided. After consecrated ground was quickly filled, great trenches were dug, and into them bodies were placed, layer upon layer, with a sprinkling of earth between layers, until they were filled. On the site of the present Charter House in London it is estimated that more than 50,000 burials were made. Great difficulty was experienced in finding persons who would risk contagion by burying the dead; and, as the sexton's bell tolled the passing, people shut themselves within their houses, lest they be infected by the corpses being carted or borne to the charnal pit.[40] Yet, as Puckle points out, although new cemeteries were hastily constructed as old churchyards were filled, "In all this stress of circumstances . . . no thought was given to the cremation of bodies; surely proof enough that the practice was repugnant to the people, who even in such circumstances as these refused to adopt the pagan practice as being against the usage of the Christian Church."[41]

Various laws were passed in an effort to reduce contagion. The Act of 1547, forbidding burial between six in the evening and six in the morning, doubtless was based upon the belief that during the daytime people were less susceptible to the foul vapors of contagion than they were at night—a belief that popularly persisted far into the 19th century. The curfew also had the effect of forcing plague deaths into the public eye, and of making prowling at night in a cemetery conspicuous, thus rendering it more difficult for ghouls to ply their trade.[42]

Coffined Burial Becomes the Custom: Although the use of coffins appears in many cultures and even antedates written history, the modern American practice of universal coffined burial is a development of recent centuries. The word itself is derived from the Greek *Kofinos*, meaning a basket, coffer or chest. In the Old Testament there is only one record of coffined burial. When Joseph the Hebrew patriarch and son of Jacob died, he was embalmed and "put in a coffin in Egypt."[43]

Herodotus tells how when Cambyses (died 522 B.C.), King of the Medes and Persians, set forth to conquer Egypt, he sent spies ahead. These reported back how they had seen Ethiopian bodies coffined in hollow pillars of transparent crystal. This was probably glass, the manufacture of which was known to the Egyptians as early as 2000 B.C.[44]

Baked clay or earthenware coffins were most common among the Greeks, although they used other substances. The Roman coffin, called *arca* or *loculus*, was generally made of stone. The Romans used coffins of many kinds, among them bricks covered with tiles; stone coffins with urns, *paterae* and lachrymatories in them—a *patera* is a "saucer-like dish of earthenware or metal used for drinking or libations," and a lachrymatory is a "small vessel" found in ancient tombs, and once believed to have contained the tears of mourners; and coffins of lead and glass; but they preferred a particular kind of stone which was quarried in Assos, in Troas, the territory of ancient Troy, lying in northwest Asia Minor south of the Dardanelles. They believed that this stone possessed the power of consuming the body except for the teeth, in a few weeks. Strangely enough, from this supposed power came the Greek word "sarcophagus," or "body-eating," which was applied first to the stone itself and then to the principal object made from it, the sarcophagus. Many early stone coffins have been discovered among Roman antiquities in England. The Celts left simple coffins made of unhewn flat stones set on edge to form the sides, with a crowning flat stone for the lid. These were succeeded by the stone coffin, cut from a solid block, tapering from the upper end in rough resemblance to the body outline, with a hewn recess and a special widening to receive the body extending into another recess for the head, and a hole in the bottom to permit drainage of the fluids of decomposition. Such coffins first appeared among the Anglo-Saxons about 695, and were common for higher class burials for the period through the reign of Henry VIII (died 1547). These solid block coffins, when buried outside, frequently were in excavations so shallow that their tops were clear of the ground, while in churches their lids formed a portion of the pavement. Lead coffins were sometimes used during the Middle Ages.[45]

The earliest known wooden coffin was that of Arthur, a half-mythical king of England who reigned in the 5th or 6th century. In large English *tumuli* or burial mounds, coffins made out of hollow logs have been occasionally unearthed, holding skeletons and charred bones. Other coffins made of elm logs with the bark clinging to them, and with fittings of small rivetted brass strips have been discovered.[46]

A custom of briefer duration, lasting for about a century from the time of the Norman Conquest (1066), was that of wrapping the corpse for burial in the strongest leather or in a bull's hide. Henry I of England (died 1135), his son Prince Henry, King John (died 1216) and James III of Scotland were among notables shrouded in a bull's hide.[47]

All these practices, however, represent exceptions to the general rule that the dead were laid uncoffined in their graves. During the Norman dynasty, (1066-1154) and for a long while afterwards, many persons of distinction preferred to be buried in the plain earth. Such was the general custom during the reigns of Edward II (1284-1327) and Edward III (1312-1377). Knights were sometimes laid to rest uncoffined but clad in full armor. In excavating for repairs to the choir of the Cathedral of Gloucester, workmen discovered the remains of three abbots who had been buried uncoffined in shallow graves, but wearing gloves and garments. Even during the reign of Queen Elizabeth I (1533-1603) it was customary to bury the dead, wrapped only in winding sheets. The practice is further indicated by the implications of a statement to be found in the minutes of the vestry of St. Helen's Church, Bishopgate, March 5th, 1564, "that none should be buried within the church unless the dead corpse be coffined in wood." Presumably even some of those who qualified by wealth and position for church burial still preferred to be carried to their graves on biers and to be removed and placed uncoffined in their sepulchers.[48]

But coffining or shrouding, whether in stone, wood, lead, leather or hide, was reserved for the wealthy and important. The shroud and the shrift of the poor and unimportant were simple and short. In England the humble were usually sewed up in sheets or wrapped in a linen shroud and carried to their graves in the Parish shell, a coarser kind of temporary coffin with a movable lid, used only for conveyance and doing duty for many years. The simple burial service recited, the body of the poor was placed in the earth, covered only with the winding sheet; and the clods were shoveled upon it. Charitable friends paid for masses for the dead, while guilds defrayed all the small expense originating in this simple funeral.[49]

In some places in England, coffined burial was not permitted even to some who could afford it, only certain of the prosperous being allowed a coffin or chest—"to be chested" is the old phrase. In 1580 the City Fathers of Rye in Sussex forbade coffined burial to all but the mayor, the councilmen and their wives, and to such as were licensed by the mayor.[50] By implication the service book of the Anglican Communion, the *Book of Common Prayer*, the burial portions of which date from 1546-1547, indicates the frequency of uncoffined burial in England at the middle of the 15th century. It does not mention a coffin, making reference only to the corpse or body, as when it says "the earth shall be cast upon the body."

In 1563 the General Assembly of Scotland decreed that a bier should be made in every country parish "to carry the *dead corpse* of the poor to the burial place, and that those of the villages or houses next adjacent to the house where the *dead corpse* lieth, or a certain number out of every house, shall convey the *dead corpse* to the burial place and bury it six feet under the earth."[51]

As commerce and industry enriched England, and the standards of living of all classes rose, coffined burials, hitherto only the privilege of the rich, became increasingly the practice of all classes. In 1603 the dramatist Thomas Dekker stated that the coffin makers of London were busily employed and growing rich. Yet Sir Henry Spelman observed that as late as 1650 interments without coffins were common among the humbler classes, decent covering fulfilling the full need for burial. In London, fifteen years later at the worst of the last great visitation of the plague, most burials were in coffins,[52] although registers and churchwardens' accounts bear frequent witness to uncoffined burials through the 16th and 17th centuries.[53]

Social Developments and Funeral Practice

Funeral Ostentation Grows Among the English Middle Classes: As the Middle Ages closed in England, ostentatious public funerals for the rising middle class were the order of the day. Speaking of merchants, Sylvia Thrupp, social historian of Medieval England, says: "The final problem in expenditure that perplexed the merchant arose out of the question as to how he should be buried, the size of the torches and tapers to be placed about his body in the hearse, the number of persons to attend the rites and the funeral baked meats at his house, the number, quality and cost of the mourning clothes to be distributed, the month's mind, and other stipends to be paid, and so on at length."[54]

For any man who cared about his social position it was therefore logical to wish for as splendid a funeral as could be arranged without working hardship to his heirs. On the other hand, the priest would tell him that worldly standards should at this point give way before humility and piety; he should spend his money on alms, not on vain display. Torn between the habits of a lifetime and a fear that his priest might be right, the merchant either compromised or left the problem to his executors.[55]

This tendency toward ostentation intensified in the 15th century, and costs mounted as more wax torches were carried, more shields of arms displayed, more mourning gowns distributed, more lavish entertainments provided. Whether a funeral should be costly or inexpensive, however, was a matter of free choice to a man before his death, and to his heirs after it. As Thrupp puts it: "No commercial organization of the funeral as a whole developed to force expenses up."[56]

A merchant could still provide a funeral for his son for a half a mark during the reign of Edward IV (1461-1483)— a mark was the equivalent of thirteen shillings and four pence—and for less than nine shillings the Grovers Company gave respectable burial to an almsman. Wills afford some indication of funeral costs. Of surviving 14th century wills, that of William Thorneye, an alderman of London, drawn in 1348, provided that 80 pounds, the highest amount so to be set aside, should be spent on his funeral and for the repose of his soul. For 20, 30 and 40 pounds respectively, three other aldermen purchased funerals, Masses, and other memorial works. Some wealthy men firmly set a limit of four pounds, or ten or twenty marks, for expenditures for funerals and for the alms to be distributed to the poor attending them. In 1403 John Doget ordered 25 torches for his hearse, in addition to 20 marks to be spent on other items, and requested that no one wear black except his wife, executors, servants, and debtors. This provision suggests that it may have been customary for all of a dead man's friends to be robed in mourning. There is some evidence to show that while wealthy merchants gave lip homage to a distaste for worldly show as bringing no profit to the soul, they were nonetheless willing to make compromise with it. Thus although Nicholas Wyfold made testamentary provision that he should be buried "without any grete hers, poni ponis, cost or other vaine glorie of the worlde," he set aside the substantial sum of 100 marks to defray costs. "Excess," Thrupp observes, "brought common sense reaction in its train. Not every merchant was gratified to think of his company brethren descending like locusts on the family larder after his memorial services."[57]

Custom, social pressures, and the desire to maintain status or personal and social importance—not to seem, even in death, unworthy of one's occupation—militated against penuriousness or apparent stinginess in the funerals of important people. It would probably be unfair to ascribe all ostentation or lavish expenditure to the vanity of the dead. The surviving family or occupational group, too, had its position to maintain.

The Development of Burial Clubs: To assist people of the working classes, particularly guild members, to defray the heavy expenses of a funeral, and to perpetuate the memory of dead friends, burial clubs were formed. Throughout the Middle Ages great importance was attached to the religious ceremonies attending burial. Guilds provided prayers, Masses, yearly reminders, palls or "mort" cloths. (See

Plate 14.) To defray the cost of these services a small regular contribution called "quarterage" was levied among the living. It became customary for the guild to pay for the services of a chaplain, as well as for candles and other equipment and supplies.[58] Guild members were expected to attend the funerals of departed members, and to pray regularly for the repose of their souls. While the burial clubs were most common among guild members, they were to be found among other groups of the laboring classes as well. The activities they sponsored ultimately gave rise to the setting up of several new full-time occupations. One of these functionaries did nothing but invite people to funerals by rapping on their doors with the key to the house of the departed. Another, the bell ringer, marched through the streets, calling out the names of persons on the first anniversaries of their deaths and requesting prayers for them.[59]

The Shroud in England Changes from Linen to Wool: The shrouding of the corpse presents interesting and significant considerations. Throughout most of the Middle Ages, when the corpse was shrouded at all, the shroud was of linen, often loosened at the feet and hands to permit easy escape on the day of resurrection. Up to the middle of the 16th century the church provided that an infant dying within a month of baptism was to be interred in his chrisom, a primitive baptismal robe, so constructed as to permit the priest to anoint the child on the back and breast, and normally worn by the child for seven days afterwards to protect these places, or until the mother was "Churched," that is, blessed in church after childbirth. For burial, the infant wearing the chrisom was swathed with bandages, or "swaddled."[60]

For some unaccountable reason the priors of Durham

went to their graves in their boots. Such burial in robe of office marked an unconscious return to Roman ways in which magistrates and military men were shrouded in their purple robes of honor or other rich raiment, while persons of rank or wealth were cremated in their official garments.[61]

Creighton could not say when the custom of burial in a sheet or cerecloth was no longer followed in England, although it is certain that it was less and less observed by the poorer classes during the 17th century. As the population increased and funerals became more elaborate, note was taken of the fact that linen of great value was being buried each year in the form of cerecloths (a "cerecloth" is a cloth treated with wax, alum, or gummy matter.) for the dead. Linen was imported, and the expanding paper industry of England wanted all the used linen it could obtain for the production of high grade paper. At the same time the woolen industry wanted customers. And so paper manufacturers joined woolen manufacturers in securing passage of the "Burial in Woolen Act" of 1666. This act provided that woolen cloth should be substituted for linen in the shroud and in the lining of the coffin, but that no penalty should be enacted for burying a plague victim in linen. Because this act was frequently disregarded, amending statutes were added in 1678 and 1670, providing that a relative of the deceased must swear to an affidavit attesting to the use of a woolen shroud. (See Figure 1.) A heavy fine, part of which was given to the informer, was assessed for violation of this law. In spite of these sanctions, many people disobeyed the law, preferring to pay the penalty rather than to abide by it and bury their relatives in wool. Sometimes the law was successfully violated by covering the body with flowers or hay. Not until 1814 were these peculiar acts, passed to aid manufacturers rather than to improve funerals, repealed.[62]

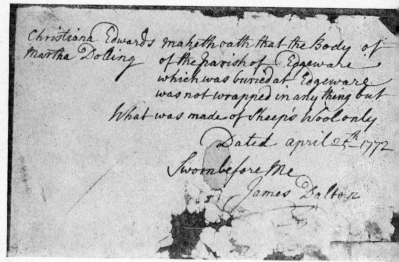

Christiana Edwards maketh oath that the Body of
Martha Dolling   of the parish of Edgeware
                   which was buried at Edgeware
                   was not wrapped in any thing but
What was made of Sheep's Wool only
                   Dated april 25th 1772
                   Sworn before Me
                   James Dalton

Figure 1. Buried in Woolen Affidavit, 18th Century England

The Free Distribution of Mourning Clothes: A curious
medieval custom was that of distributing ceremonial robes
to the mourners. Originally the mourning garment—called
a "weed," although the term is now restricted to the "widow's
weeds," or a "doole," something given away in dolour, a
double etymological pun—was a long black cloak similar to
those now worn by nuns. It was designed as an outer garment, large enough to fit many sizes of people since obviously it could not at short notice be prepared in carefully
personalized and tailored fashion, and to completely cover
ordinary attire. Garments of this type were provided by
close relatives of the dead for other relatives, the clergyman
conducting the services, intimate friends, and poor retainers
—to the last as an act of charity. At the funeral of the Earl
of Oxford over nine hundred black gowns were distributed,
and that done in spite of the fact that the deceased had
been heavily fined during life by Henry VII (1457-1509) for

excessive display of wealth. Such extravagance led to sumptuary regulations in England in the 16th century "restricting
the use of mourning as to quantity and dictating also the
quality of materials, and the exact manner in which the
garments were to be fashioned."[63]

As funerals grew in elaborateness it was to be expected
that establishments would develop devoted exclusively to
the sale of mourning garments and other funeral paraphernalia. Such business in France, called a *Magasin de Deuil*,
was long antedated in Italy by the *Mercerie de lutto*, from
which the Italian could buy or rent in a few hours all that
was needed to conduct a respectable funeral in a country in
which climate made speedy burial necessary.[64]

English Burial Fees During the Waning Middle Ages:
In a large parish like Cripplegate there was an obvious
gradation of dignity of burial according to the importance
of the dead. A few, such as the poet, John Milton (died
1674), were buried within the church in leaden coffins; others,
who paid full burial fees received like interment in the
churchyard; but the majority for whom burial dues were re-
mitted were laid to rest in a sheet, uncoffined in a part of
the graveyard set aside for the poor.[65] The nature of the
burial fees in England can be seen from those set up for
the parish of St. Saviour's Southwark: "In any churchyard
next the church, with a coffin, two shillings, eight pence;
without a coffin, twenty pence; for a child with a coffin, eight
pence; without a coffin, four pence. The College Churchyard, with a coffin, twelve pence; without a coffin, eight
pence."[66]

Mourning Colors: Mourning colors owe their choice
partly to resemblance, real or imaginary, between the facts
of death and burial and certain colors, and partly to the
operation of that whimsical thing called fashion. How much

of fashion there is in funerary color selection can be seen in the fact the ancient Egyptian and Burmese adopted yellow; the Persians and Abyssinians brown; and the Armenians and Syrians, light blue. White symbolizing hope, is the mourning color of the Chinese, as it is, for a different reason, among certain aborigines, who smear their bodies with white clay as a sign of bereavement. The choice of color in this case may originally have been accidental.[67]

Although in modern times black is the generally approved color for mourning, white coffins for children are still customary; and, purple is used to designate death and mourning for royalty and many Christian groups. These conventional uses represent changes from the earlier practices of the Roman Empire, in which white became the mourning color for women, and from the general practice of the Middle Ages throughout Western Europe, when white was the color of mourning worn by all. The vogue of black was given a powerful impetus in 1498 when black was substituted for white by Anne, the widow of Charles VIII of France,[68] even though Mary Queen of Scots as late as 1560 mourned the death of her second husband, Lord Darnley, in white. The French King, Louis XI (1423-1483) forsook purple, the customary mourning color of the French court, for a hunting suit, half red and half white, pleading that he did so "for the sake of simplicity."[69] He did not set a new fashion thereby. Mortuary custom is in part based on an intrinsic seemliness in things in which frivolity has small place.

The Widow During the Middle Ages: Her Lot and Her Raiment: Special conventions governed the conduct and clothes of the widow during the long period when marriage was universally regarded as indissoluble and sacramental, and remarriage was considered with disfavor, except in the case of the very young woman. For the widow of an important man, it was customary to retire to a convent, or to live in strict seclusion in the "dower-house," garbed as a nun, honoring in retrospective contemplation by the practice of the spiritual and corporal works of mercy, the virtues of her late spouse. Puckle sees in this self-immolation and life-long imprisonment the shadow at least of the earlier practice which required the widow actually to be sacrificed and buried with her husband so that he might enjoy her comforts in the afterlife.[70]

Curious customs of dress were also associated with widowhood. One of these was the wearing of the barbe, a long pleated arrangement of fine linen, so called because it resembled a beard—*barba* in Latin. The position of the barbe was determined by rank. Lower orders wore it beneath the chin; those above the rank of baroness, above it. The widow's bonnet, now seldom seen, was derived from the nun's habit, its streamers a survival of the veil, now thrown back and reduced in size, but originally covering the face. The widow's cap represents the ancient custom of cutting off the hair as a sign of mourning or renunciation. While the widow "admitted the principle, she was no longer prepared to part with her hair," Puckle comments. The wearing of white cuffs by the widow as a symbol of mourning also stemmed from the convent. The higher their rank, the more rigidly were women bound by the mourning etiquette of their times and position. Prior to the 15th century a widowed queen kept to her black draped apartment for a year after her husband's death.[71]

Local Customs Add Color: Within the framework of the general cultural beliefs and practices much latitude existed in the Middle Ages, as now, for the development of local customs. The list of these is long. It is a widespread custom among Protestants, for instance, to sprinkle a handful of dirt on the corpse, an act reminiscent of the Roman custom of covering a body found unburied with at least three handfuls of earth while reciting the ceremonious farewell. The custom of sprinkling earth on the coffin was formally instituted for the church of England by a rubric, or rule for conducting the liturgical service, as an assigned part of the duty of the officiating clergy. Later, the gesture could be made by any bystander. The Jews placed a bag of earth in the coffin, and each mourner present helped fill the grave with earth. Among the Irish it was an old custom that the priest should bless and sprinkle a handful of earth upon the corpse before burial. The pious construed this deed as appeasement of the other occupants of the churchyard.[72] Possibly as a disinfectant against the plague, at all English funerals a sprig of rosemary was handed to all who attended the burial rites. The sprig was later thrown into the open grave. This custom was still found in England past the middle of the 19th century.[73] A similar custom, substituting carnations and other flowers pulled from floral pieces, was long observed in America. (See Plate 14.)

It was long customary in various parts of Christendom to bury the clergy with their feet extending toward the east, in the belief that Christ would there appear to summon the world to judgment. Thus the clergy would be first to arise and lead their flocks to the great tribunal. From this practice the east wind in Wales is called the "Wind of the Dead Men's Feet."[74]

A nod should be given to customs that disappeared. Puckle tells of a curious functionary, a sort of male scapegoat called the "sin-eater." It was believed in some places that by eating a loaf of bread and drinking a bowl of beer over a corpse, and by accepting a six-pence, a man was able to take unto himself the sins of the deceased, whose ghost thereafter would no longer wander.[75]

neral Procession, Queen Elizabeth, 1603. No. 1 represents wax effigy of the Queen. Kings at Arms. 3. Noblemen. 4. The Archbishop of Canterbury. 5. The French bassador and train bearer. 6. The great Standard of England. 7. The Master of the rse. 8. The Lady Marchioness of Northampton. 9. Captain of the guard. 10. The at Standard of Ireland. 11. Standard of Wales. 12. Gentlemen of the Chapels Royal. Trumpeters. 14. Standard of the Lion. 15. Standard of the Greyhound. 16. The een's Horse. 17. Poor Women. 18. The Banner of Cornwall, the Aldermen, Recorders, Town Clerks, etc.

PLATE 13

a) "Corpse Bearer," 18th Century
England

b) Coffin Pall, Church of Folleville, Franc
Late Renaissance

c) Funeral Scene in Hogarth's "The Harlot's Progress"; Note Use of Rosemary Sprigs

PLATE 14

Customs that were local, or general customs that have ceased to be followed, should be distinguished from mere individual eccentricities, such as the upside-down burial of Richard Hull. In accordance with a notion once popular that on the day of judgment the world would be turned around, Hull is buried upside down on his horse beneath a stone tower on Leith Hill.[76]

Medieval Preoccupation With the Physical Side of Death: Funeral practices in part depend on the *Zeit-geist*, the spirit of the time, the view men take of death. For whatever reason—could it have been the fact and threat of periodic plague, or the inevitable reaction of men who lived with dangerous zest?—the Middle Ages manifested an intense preoccupation with the physical side of death. Charnal houses were a common sight. The bodies of executed prisoners were suspended from trees so that others might profit from the lesson. Poets sang of death as robbing the body of beauty, power, sensuality. Statues and woodcuts displayed death at its most horrible—as ugliness, putrefaction, filth. The cry, "Memento mori,"—"Remember that thou wilt die," wails through the long period, and is characteristic of it. The great Dutch historian Huizinga points out that the imploration to remember death reached poor and great alike. The poor heard it through the preaching of the mendicant orders, the tolling of the funeral bell, and the cry in the streets, "Bury your dead." The rich heard the message in the sermons of men like Denis the Carthusian who reminded his audience that when a nobleman lay down in bed at night, "he should consider how, in the same manner as he now lies down himself, strange hands will soon lay his body in the grave."[77]

The greatest of the didactic plays of the Middle Ages, called "morality plays," is *Everyman*, which comes out of the early 15th century. The plot concerns Everyman, who as his name indicates, represents the human race. In the play God calls on his servant, Death, to summon Everyman to judgment. But Everyman is "full unready his reckoning to make"; and when Death proves obdurate, pleads with Fellowship, Kindred, Cousin, Goods, Knowledge, Beauty, and other companions to enter the grave with him. They refuse, and so he turns to Good Deeds, unbinds him by being shriven, and enters the grave, while the Doctor tells the audience that at the last all things forsake Everyman save Good Deeds. It is a grim sermon on the boards, a grave play —but quite characteristic of the age that gave it birth.[78]

More terrible than this stately drama was the death dance, which came into vogue during the Middle Ages as a result of popular, morbid preoccupation. To the men and women of these times death was a commonplace fact to be stared at; and because very few bodies were properly preserved man became engrossed with the disposition of the body rather than with the afterlife of the soul. It is easy to understand how the theme of the dance macabre, once conceived, planted itself in the popular imagination and there found fertile soil for growth. This grisly theme was expounded by the woodcuts of Guyat Marchant, the poetry of Jean LeFevre, the murals of the church of La Chaise-Dieu, the frescoes of the cloister of the churchyard of the Innocents at Paris. The theme later led to Holbein's dancing skeleton, and much later to Goethe's *Totendanz*. As men grew obsessed with it, the spiritual side of death seemed less engrossing, less important. The note of promise, the "sleeping in Christ" that characterized the Christian viewpoint, is drowned out in fearsome noises from the grave for those who are caught up in the cult of the gruesome. One is enveloped and pre-occupied with the fear of one's own death; not the fear of living no more, or of being punished for one's sins; but the fear of dying, and decaying with other corpses, naked, with clenched hands and rigid feet, mouth agape and bowels crawling with worms. Here was death graphically and symbolically represented without sentimentality, spoken of without euphemism, lived with starkly and morbidly. Even funeral decoration was influenced. It was not uncommon in the 14th century for painters to picture the dead as rising from their graves to join in the dance macabre in search of new members for their fellowship; and even tombs were decorated with images of decaying corpses.[79] (See Plate 15.)

The Sexton Emerges: With the growth of the practice of churchyard burial, the church of the early Middle Ages naturally extended its authority over the burial processes, and at the same time burials began to lose their domestic or neighborhood character. The desire to be interred near the church and near some saint, martyr or holy person brought revolutionary changes in burial practices. As Wilson and Levy point out:

The rise of the church as an expression of organized Christianity and Christian worship changed the whole aspect of the burial problem. A new epoch opened with public burial in churches and in churchyards, which brought with it profound changes in the popular attitude towards burial and the disposal of the dead. The religious outlook on death began to assume importance: the solicitude of the living for the bodies and spirits or souls of the dead was invested with religious sanctions and brought about, ere long, the first decisive break with the past by prescribing communal instead of local places of sepulture, sanctified by their associations with Christian worship.[80]

During the early Middle Ages there apparently was no secularized person to whom were entrusted any or several or all of the burial tasks as they had been entrusted to *libitinarii* and *pollinctores* among the pagan Romans. The occupation of sexton emerged at this time. The sexton was originally an under officer of the church, to whom were delegated the care of church property, the ringing of bells, and frequently the digging of graves. This absence of mention of other functionaries makes it apparent that until the early Renaissance the tasks of undertaking, earlier assigned to secular officials were undermined, proscribed or absorbed by the officials of the church.

An exception to the foregoing statement is to be found in embalming for mortuary purposes, a practice which at the beginning of the Middle Ages was infrequent, but grew to be much commoner by the close of the Renaissance, and is almost universal now.

We have seen that the Hebrews limited their preservative techniques to the application of oils, perfumes and spices to the surface of the body, seeking to preserve it not for eternity but only until the sepulchre should be closed at the end of the three day vigil. The early Christians, as has been indicated, regarded the body as the temple of the Holy Spirit and generally looked with disfavor upon Egyptian embalming methods as involving mutilation. In spite of this attitude, however, there is well established evidence that some primitive Christians were embalmed, and that some had organs removed for independent burial. Such development is not surprising in view of two facts.

The first is the continued use of Egyptian embalming methods by the pagan Romans. While only a small minority even of the rich and powerful continued to be embalmed, the practice was widespread throughout the Roman Empire during the three centuries after Christ. Thus in 66 A.D., the body of Poppaea, wife of the Emperor Nero, was embalmed in Egyptian fashion before interment in the Mausoleum of Augustus; and in 95 A.D., the body of Annia Priscilla, wife of Flavius Abascantus, freedman secretary of the Emperor Domitian, was mummified and laid in a marble sarcophagus.[81] Quite literally in this case there was a tendency even for Christians when in Rome to do as the Romans did.

The second circumstance tending to break the prejudice of the early Christians against embalming was the close association of their primitive places of meeting and worship with their cemeteries and with the relics of the saints and martyrs. Bradford points out that the "Early Christians primarily disfavoured the mutilation of the body, but subsequently, as a consequence of their churches being built over the tombs of the martyrs and their altars hallowed with their relics, they came to look at things in a new perspective."[82]

Independent Heart Burial: This new perspective grew from the fact that dismembered fragments of the bodies of saints and martyrs began to be preserved and regarded as holy relics. While Bradford dates the formal beginning of the practice of independent heart burial with the enshrinement in 1117 of the heart of D'Arbrissel, Founder of the Order of Fontevrault, he asserts that in essence such separation of parts was ancient, and could be traced to evisceration "which had been in vogue from the later Stone Age and elaborated by the Egyptians with a highly developed ceremonial, of which the embalming of the dead became a leading feature—special prominence being given to the heart."[83]

The heart of St. Ignatius (died 107) has been preserved as a relic. The Emperor Sigismund is reputed to have brought to England the heart of St. George (died 303) when he was made Knight of the Garter in 1416. The crypt of the church of St. Benoit-on-the-Loire exhibits a reliquary said to contain the heart of St. Benoit (died 547). The heart of St. Catherine of Sienna is said to be interred beneath the high altar of the Church of St. Mary Supra Minerva in Rome.

Whether these separations of the heart from the body were made immediately after death or later is not clear; but some seven hundred years after the death of St. Benoit, the body of Peter, Bishop of Poitiers, was entombed at Fontevrault, while his viscera were given burial at St. Cyprian's Church in Poitiers. Two years after this, the remains of D'Arbrissel, to whom reference has just been made, were separated, the heart being buried at Orsan Monastery, while the remainder of the body was buried in the town of Fontevrault itself. Other instances of the ceremonial interment of the heart apart from the body have been recorded. In 1235, for example, the heart of Abbot William of St. Albans was buried apart, near the altar of St. Stephens. Royal prestige was lent to the custom by Jeanne Queen of Navarre who kept the heart of her husband, King Philip, apart from his body until her death, when by her orders it was enshrined in the same urn as her own, in the church of the Jacobins in Paris. In 1480, Rene, King of Sicily directed in his will that the day after his death his heart should be borne to the church of the Friars Minor of Angersto to be buried in the Chapel of St. Bernardine. In 1514 the heart of Anne of Brittany was buried with great pomp at the Carthusian Church at Nantes; in 1621 the heart of Louis of Lorraine, Cardinal de Guise, was buried in pompous ceremony at the cathedral church of Notre Dame of Paris. In medieval visceral embalming it was the practice to remove the viscera, together with the brain, eyes and sometimes the tongue, and to place these in a cask which was often buried later with the embalmed body. Such division of the organs made multiple burial easy; and English King Edward I (1239-1307) took advantage of it to have parts of Queen Eleanore's body deposited in three tombs erected in her honor.[84]

Gannal describes how M. Regner, apothecary to the King of France and to Madame la Dauphine, assisted by his eldest son, prepared Madame's heart for independent burial:

The heart, after having been emptied, washed in spirits of wine and dried, was placed in a glass vessel with its liquor (embalming fluid); and this same organ, having been filled with a balm made of corrella, cloves, myrrh, styrax, and benzoin, was put into a sack of cere-cloth of its own shape, which was again enclosed in a box of lead, cordiform, which was immediately soldered.[85]

Not even a papal decree was able to stamp out this practice of dividing the body for burial, with separate graves for the several portions, and separate funeral rites. Bradford finds that divided burial was "far from rare" in the seventeenth century, and that there were many instances of it in the eighteenth and even in the nineteenth centuries, among which the heart burials of the French statesman, Gambetta, (1838-1882) and the English novelist, Thomas Hardy (1840-1928) were conspicuous. As much as anything, the development of arterial embalming has served to eliminate the practice today so that evisceration and divided burial are now extremely rare.[86]

Independent Bone Burial: Although much importance was attached to being buried in one's native soil, lack of embalming and refrigeration, together with slow transportation, made it virtually impossible to return home the bodies of those who died in foreign countries. Faced with a similar problem, the Macedonians did not embalm the body of Alexander the Great to return it to his native Macedonia, but preserved it in honey for transit. The Spartans used the same material to conserve the corpse of King Agesipoles I during its conveyance to Sparta for burial.[87] The Middle Ages developed another practice to facilitate transportation. The poor and the unimportant who met death at a distance from their homes presumably were disposed of where they fell or died. The noble, the rich, and the important were sometimes brought back in part, their bodies being cut up and boiled to extract the bones. These were placed in a chest and returned home, while the juices and soft portions were buried not without ceremony near the place of death. The crusaders considered human remains sacred, and the bodies of many knights who lost their lives in the East were boiled so that the bones could be packed in a chest for Christian burial at home. This practice was outlawed by Pope Boniface III who pronounced it "an abuse of abominable savagery, practiced by some of the faithful in a horrible and inconsiderate manner." Yet many Englishmen who died in France during the Hundred Years War (1337-1453), including Edward of York and The Earl of Suffolk, both of whom died at Agincourt (1415), were so boiled and buried divided after a dispensation granted by one of the successors of Boniface.[88]

Embalming in the Middle Ages: While actual funeral or other embalming was not common during the Middle Ages, records show that the art as derived ultimately from the practices of the Egyptians was not lost, though actual embalmings were few and far between. As we have seen, the coming of Christianity gradually pushed aside the older pagan burial beliefs and customs and substituted new practices. In this shift, while there is some evidence that a small minority of early Christians in Rome and particularly in Egypt were embalmed, embalming itself, whether because of its intimate associations with the pagan religions, or its costliness, or its attendant mutilation of the body, fell under some ecclesiastical disapproval. In the third century, St. Anthony, the founder of Egyptian monachism denounced the practice as sinful, intimating that the ancient Egyptian rites were out of harmony with Christian doctrine.[89] He probably was protesting, too, against Egyptian death and afterlife beliefs associated with embalming, and attacking the excessive expense of Egyptian funerals. It is not likely that most people of his time regarded embalming as sinful in and by itself, even though it had extremely limited vogue, as only the very wealthy could afford it, or royalty was felt to deserve it.

A few illustrations must suffice. The body of Charlemagne (died 814 A.D.), embalmed and dressed in imperial robes, was placed in sitting position in his tomb at Aachen. The body of Edward I of England (1239-1307), buried in Westminster Abbey in 1307 was found intact in 1770.[90] The preserved remains of Canute (died 1035), were discovered in Winchester Cathedral five hundred years after his death, while in the 16th century the body of William the Conqueror was related to be well preserved at Caen.[91] The corpse of Henry I was embalmed and brought to England in 1135 for burial in the Church of Reading Monastery. The process employed in his case consisted in the removal of the brain, tongue, heart, eyes, etc., by means of incisions, and embalming with various drugs. The viscera were interred in the church of St. Mary de Pré at Emandriville. The salted, eviscerated body was later shipped, wrapped in a tanned bull's hide,[92] according to the custom of the time. In 1281 Cecily Talmache of Hamstead, Suffolk, was embalmed at a charge of six pounds, five shillings and four pence, a total made up of the following itemized costs: for wax and spices, four pounds, four shillings and two pence; for fine linen and silk, one pound, twelve shillings; for the chandler, nine shillings and two pence. Sir John Cullum commented that this sum would purchase 28 quarters of wheat.[93]

Although, as Bradford points out, "Sanitary reasons dictated evisceration and embalming as a corollary to the practice of intramural interment, and was in active operation in the early twelfth century," it must be concluded that embalming could not have been widespread in the medieval period, as descriptions of medieval cemeteries indicate.[94] Moreover, as will be seen, the shortage of persons capable of embalming would have prevented the practice from becoming other than highly infrequent. But even had skilled practitioners been available in large numbers, the cost of their services and of the rare spices, chemicals, unguents and wrappings, all of which were considered necessary, would have put the process far beyond the means of all except the very wealthy. Not even these were commonly embalmed. When, for example, the Princess Mary died in 1481, her unembalmed body was wrapped tightly in a long cerecloth and placed in a leaden coffin. When the coffin was opened in 1810, the body was in an excellent state of preservation due to the very secure wrapping which had excluded the air.[95]

Although embalming was not commonly practiced in England during the Middle Ages, it was reported in *Gentleman's Magazine* in 1789 that there was discovered in the village church in Danbury, Essex a preserved body, sheeted in lead and boxed in an elm coffin. When the lead was opened the body was revealed lying wholly perfect in a "liquor or pickle resembling mushroom catchup." Someone tasted the preservative and found it like "catchup, and of the pickle of Spanish olives."[96]

Great interest in embalming was aroused by the fact that the bodies of certain saints, for example that of St. Rose of Viterbo, were said never to have decayed. Such resistance to decomposition appeared the more remarkable in view of the fact that in certain Paris cemeteries flesh disappeared from the bones in as little as nine days.[97]

Distressing experiences with unembalmed or poorly embalmed corpses could not but help point up the need for better methods of preservation. When Queen Elizabeth I (1533-1608) died, although her wish was respected that she should not be embalmed, Lord Burleigh, the chancellor, gave orders to her surgeon to "open her." Lady Southwell gives an account of the sequel of the dramatic episode: "Now the Queen's body being cered up, was brought by water to White-hall, where being watched every night by several ladies, myself that night watching as one of them, and being all in our places about the corpse, which was fast nailed up in a board coffin, with leaves of lead covered with velvet, her body burst with such a crack that it splitted the wood, lead and cere cloth; whereupon the next day she was fain to be new trimmed up."[98]

The Surgeon and the Anatomist Take Over: While the Middle Ages carried over the Egyptian practice of cavity embalming they did not carry with it the highly skilled Egyptian embalming team, but during this period the task was assigned for funerary purposes to a group already experimenting with it for other ends.

Until the rise and development of the craft guild produced the barber surgeon, medieval embalming was more or less a secondary function of the surgeon and anatomist. Whether they sought this function or not, it was theirs by reason of the fact that their normal occupations gave them an acquaintance with the body—extremely limited, it is true, in many regards. Further, they had access to surgical texts which contained instructions on embalming, such as Pietro d'Argellata's, and they were probably inquisitive enough to welcome the chance to work with a body before it had become deteriorated and obnoxious with decay. Cadavers, moreover, were hard to obtain; and unless they were preserved, the effort to dissect them became a race against putrefaction.

Hence the anatomist and the surgeon had strong motivation for experimenting with embalming. In the early 14th century the practice was established in Italy of acquiring the bodies of executed criminals for the purpose of performing "anatomies." Due to the lack of embalming, it was necessary to eviscerate the corpse, and then hurriedly dissect it before the odor of putrefaction made further work impossible.[99] Quite possibly, too, when the medieval surgeons and anatomists turned their anatomical and embalming skills to the preparation of the corpse of an important person in burial they exacted a substantial fee for their services.

The art of the medieval medical embalmer closely resembled that of his Egyptian prototype. The most obvious and therefore often the first step was to remove those parts of the body most susceptible to rapid decomposition: the intestines, stomach, liver, pancreas, kidneys, and esophagus. On occasions, as an added precaution, the tongue, eyes, and brain were also removed. The opened and eviscerated body cavities were then washed with water, alcohol, and a pleasant smelling substance, such as rose-water. After the cavities were dried they were filled with a variety of spices, chemicals and an absorbent such as cotton. This filling served a three-fold purpose. It aided in the drying-out of the body, gave it a pleasing odor, and helped preserve its natural shape. The body openings themselves were filled with tar or oakum—loose fibers picked from old hemp ropes —to prevent the entry of insects. Finally, the body was securely wrapped in many layers of cloth to reduce contact with the air and to check decay.

It is most likely that Galen of Pergamon (130-200 A.D.), whose autocratic influence dominated medicine for almost thirteen hundred years until the publication of *De Corpora Humani Fabrica* by Vesalius in 1453, left some account of embalming in his works, for his was the voice that carried early medicine from 200 A.D. through the Middle Ages.

The excellent description of Egyptian cavity embalming left by the Greek Herodotus (about 484-424 B.C.) should be compared with Pietro d'Argellata's of the embalming of Pope Alexander V who died at Bonnea in 1410.

In his *Chirurgia*, a treatise on surgery in six books, not published until 1480, Pietro d'Argellata (died 1423), Professor of Anatomy at the University of Padua, gave the earliest complete account of medieval embalming, describing three variants of the basic cavity method. (See Plate 16.) d'Argellata was the pupil of Guy de Chauliac (1300-1368), whose works bear a strong resemblance to the writings of Paul of Aegina, a Byzantine Greek of the 7th century who wrote an *Epitome of Medicine* in seven books, practiced in Alexandria, and may be regarded as the last representative of Greek medicine before the Arabian conquest.[100] Says d'Argellata:

Nevertheless I relate this method to you as it is the same one used to embalm the highest pontiff, Pope Alexander V. His doctor opened up the abdomen to the pubis, making a straight line incision without injuring the viscera, tying up the colon in two places, cutting it between the two ligatures, leaving out the waste. The rest of the intestines were then removed together with all the viscera. He then used a sponge and washed everything clean with alcohol, and proceeded to pour alcohol into the body. He then used a sponge to dry up any moisture that was left. He then filled the whole abdominal cavity with one pound of aloes, caballainies, succatrinol, acaciae, nucis xuperuni, Galluae, and muscatae. Then he covered the abdomen with cotton, powder, and more cotton, repeating this until the whole cavity was filled, after which the domestic appeared and sewed the body up in the same manner in which a furrier would sew up furs. They then put powder into the cavity of the esophagus and larynx, filled it with cotton adding balsam. They put egg white into the rectum. They then made a few more tufts of cotton and put them into the mouth, nostrils, and ears. After all this they covered the entire body with waxed linen to which a little turpentine was added. They also put his thighs and arms close to the body and covered them with linen. When finished they put his ornate Papal cloak on him because he had to lay for eight days without giving offensive odor. This method of embalming the Doctors of that era liked best. In this way the putrefaction of the dead body was prevented. The face of the Pope was washed with thoroughly salted rosewater.[101]

In the same work, d'Argellata is the first to mention the use of low temperatures to retard decomposition, a physiological innovation that remains useful to the present time.

In an early treatise on embalming (1605) written subsequent to the Middle Ages, Peter Forestus, a Dutch physician, describes the embalming experiences of other physicians in some detail:

A renowned doctor from Spirigio embalmed the princess Joan from Burgundy. In 1582 the Countess of Hautekermaken was embalmed by the writer before he knew that the task had been assigned Professor Heurnie of Leyden, Holland. He likewise embalmed Prince Auraici, who died July 10, 1584, in collaboration with a colleague, Dr. Cornelius Busenius.[102]

In the first thousand years of the Christian era there had been considerable retreat in the practice of medicine and surgery, and in the study of anatomy.[103] To explain in part this lack of progress, Park, the medical historian, points out that "dissection was forbidden by the clergy in the Middle Ages on the ground that it was impious to mutilate a form made in the image of God."[104] While agreeing generally with Park's argument, Riesman says in extenuation of this viewpoint of the Middle Ages, that earlier there had been little dissection; that Egyptian physicians had not practiced it; and that while it may have been carried on to some extent in the Alexandrian school, it was not a common practice among the Greeks and was definitely forbidden to the Arabs by the Koran; so that all through the era of Arabian domination in medicine and surgery the science of human anatomy lay dormant. And this in spite of the fact that without dissection, no medical advance could be made beyond Galen, whose own work had not been based on dissection.[105] The first serious anatomist of the Middle Ages was Mondino de'Luzzi (Mundinus) (1270-1326), who served as Professor at the University of Bologna from 1314 to 1324, and who had the advantage of dissection, even though his actual experience was limited to two cadavers, and he did not emancipate himself from the authority of the ancients.[106] The limitations under which anatomists worked can be seen in the decree of the enlightened Hohenstaufen Emperor, Frederick II (1194-1250), making it lawful for each anatomist to dissect the human body at least once in every ten years.[107] By and large, the European anatomists of the early Middle Ages were persecuted and hindered in their studies; and finding it difficult to secure corpses, sought means to preserve those which they had as long as possible.[108]

Perhaps the closest alliance between medicine and religion during the Middle Ages took place in and around cloisters during the period of monastic medicine. Certain monks or churchmen practiced medicine, perhaps out of necessity, as intelligent educated men with access to most of the learning of the day and much collective experience fortified by common sense; and spent a great deal of time translating older medical texts—Greek, Arabic, Latin, etc.— into colloquial Latin.[109] From the close resemblance between the techniques of medieval embalming and the practices of the Egyptians, it is reasonable to assume a direct link between the two. Beyond exceptional cases, however, there is little evidence of any extensive use of visceral embalming during this period. The knowledge more than the practice was preserved.

The Reformation and Christian Funeral Beliefs and Practices: The question of indulgences, or remission of part of the temporal punishment due to sin, was tied up with the doctrine of purgatory, and was a major point at issue in the dispute between Martin Luther (1483-1546) and the Roman Catholic Church. With the rejection of the doctrine of purgatory by the Reformers of the 16th century, and of the Mass and the mediation of the priesthood, the ground work was laid for changes in funeral customs and practices based on these beliefs.

Full change did not come instantly, so ingrained are habits. While the final result in England, for example, was "so radical that little of the ancient ritual remained," Davey observes that it took much longer to penetrate the habits and customs of people than is usually imagined.[110]

The new service of the Church of England, compiled in 1546-1547, consisted of scriptural passages in conformity with a religion that rejected belief in purgatory, and therefore in the validity of prayers for the dead. Little by little older practices disappeared.

Down through the reign of Queen Mary Tudor (died 1558) a period of lying-in-state was common practice even for the poor, as it gave an opportunity for relatives and friends to gather and to pray for the departed soul. The Reformation ended this custom in England, except for those of high rank who lay in state chiefly for purpose of review and ceremony. With the abolition of monastic orders and burial and purgatorial brotherhoods, guilds, and leagues, the funeral street

a) Death Devouring Man and Beast,
Tapestry Design of the
Middle Ages

b) Bones of All Men, an Early Woodcut
by Holbein

c) Angels Praying Over a
Skull, Bas-relief of the
16th Century

d) "Danse of Death," Nohl

PLATE 15

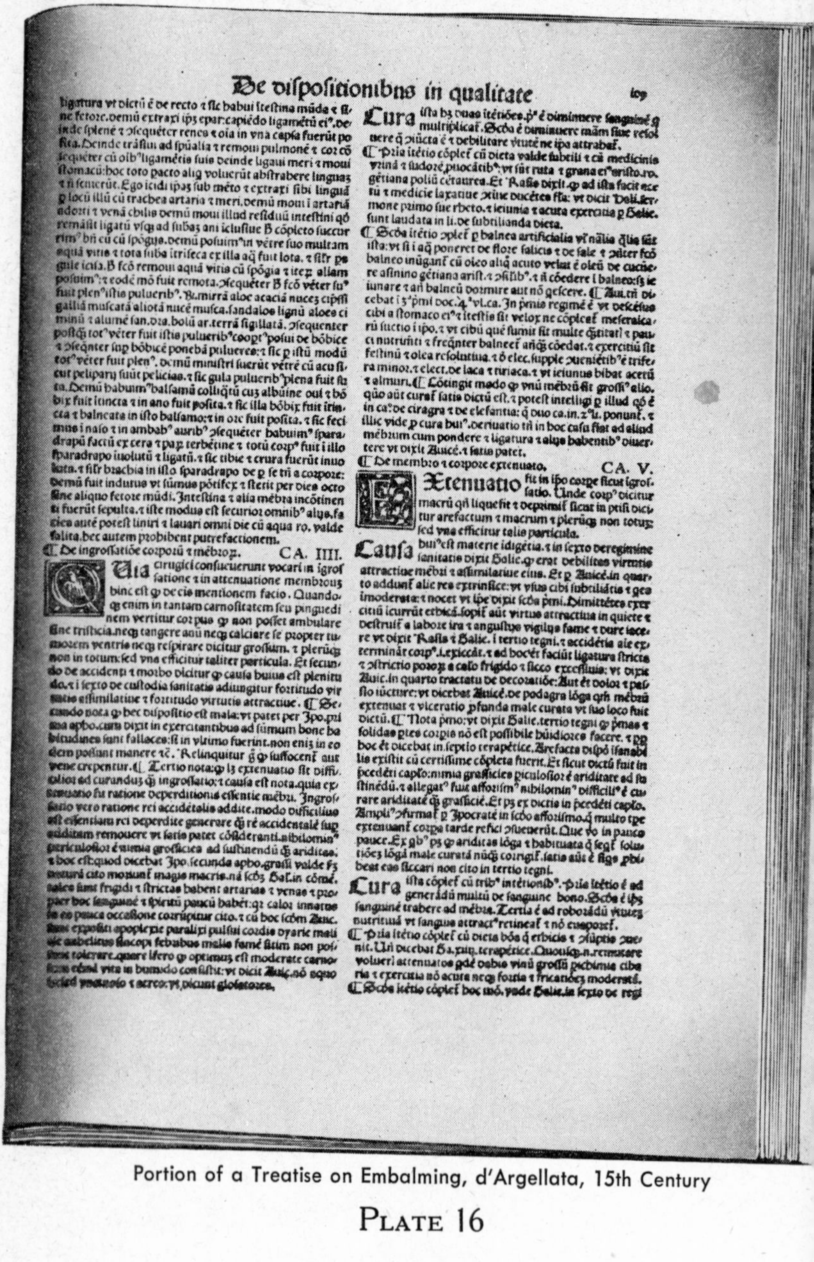

De dispositionibus in qualitate 109

ligatura vt dictū ē de recto ⁊ sic habui intestina mūda ⁊ sine fetore. demū extraxi ip3 epar: capiēdo ligamētū ei⁹. deinde splenē ⁊ ꝯsequēter renes ⁊ oīa in vna capsa fuerūt posita. Deinde trāsiui ad spūalia ⁊ remoui pulmonē ⁊ cor cō sequēter cū oib⁹ ligamētis suis deinde ligaui meri ⁊ moui stomacū: hoc toto pacto aliq volucrūt abstrahere linguā ⁊ nō fecerūt. Ego icidi ipā3 sub mēto ⁊ extraxi sibi linguā p locū illū cū trachea artaria ⁊ meri. demū moui i artariā adorti ⁊ venā chilis demū moui illud residuū intestini qd remāsit ligatū vsq ad subā3 ani iclusiue B cōpleto succurrim⁹ bñ cū cū spōgijs. demū posuim⁹ in vētre suo multam aquā vitis ⁊ tota suba itrifeca ex illa aq̄ fuit lota. ⁊ sic p gnie icisa. B fcō remoui aquā vitis cū spōgia ⁊ iterū aliam posuim⁹: ⁊ eodē mō fuit remota. ꝯsequēter B fcō vēter su⁹ fuit plen⁹ istis puluerib⁹. B. mirrā aloe acaciā nuce3 cipsi galliā muscatā aliotā nucē musca. sandalos lignū aloes ciminū ⁊ alumē san. dra. bolū ar. terrā sigillatā. ꝯsequenter postq̄ tot⁹ vēter fuit istis puluerib⁹ coopt⁹ posui de bōbice ⁊ ꝯseqnter sup bōbicē ponebā puluerē: ⁊ sic p istū modū tot⁹ vēter fuit plen⁹. demū ministri fuerūt vētrē cū acu sicut peliparij suūt pelicias. ⁊ sic gula puluerib⁹ plena fuit suta. Demū habuim⁹ balsamū colliqtū cu3 albūine oui ⁊ bōbix fuit itincta ⁊ in ano fuit posita. ⁊ sic illa bōbix fuit itincta ⁊ balneata in isto balsamo: ⁊ in ore fuit posita. ⁊ sic fecimus i naso ⁊ in ambab⁹ aurib⁹ ꝯsequēter habuim⁹ sparadrapū factū ex cera ⁊ pa. terbētine ⁊ totū corp⁹ fuit i illo sparadrapo iuolutū ⁊ ligatū. ⁊ sic tibie ⁊ crura fuerūt iuoluta. ⁊ sic brachia in isto sparadrapo de p se tñ a corpore: demū fuit indutus vt sūmus pōtifex: ⁊ stetit per dies octo sine aliquo fetore mūdi. Intestina ⁊ alia mēbra incōtinenti fuerūt sepulta. ⁊ iste modus est securior omnib⁹ alijs. fatieu autē potest liniri ⁊ lauari omni die cū aqua ro. valde salita. hec autem prohibent putrefactionem.

De ingrossatiōe corporū ⁊ mēbrorū. CA. IIII.

Uia cirugici consueuerunt vocari in igrossatione ⁊ in attenuatione membrou3 hinc est q de eis mentionem facio. Quandoq enim in tantam carnositatem seu pinguedinem vertitur corpus q non posset ambulare sine tristicia. neq tangere anū neq calciare se propter tumorem ventris neq respirare dicitur grossum. ⁊ plerūq non in totum: sed vna efficitur taliter particula. Et secundo de accidenti ⁊ morbo dicitur q causa huius est plenitudo. ⁊ i sexto de custodia sanitatis adiungitur fortitudo virtutis assimilatiue ⁊ fortitudo virtutis attractiue. Secundo nota q hec dispositio est mala: vt patet per Ipo. qui ma apho. cum dixit in exercitantibus ad sūmum bone habitudines sunt fallaces: si in vltimo fuerint. non eni3 in eodem possunt manere ⁊c. Relinquitur g̃ q suffocent aut vene crepentur. Tertio nota: q l3 extenuatio sit difficilior ad curandu3 q̄ ingrossatio: ⁊ causa est nota. quia extenuatio fit ratione deperditionis essentie mēbri. Ingrossatio vero ratione rei accidētalis addite. modo difficilius est essentiam rei deperdite generare q̄ rē accidentalē superadditam remouere vt satis patet cōsiderāti. nihilominus periculosior ē nimia grossicies ad sustinendū q̄ ariditas. ⁊ hoc est: quod dicebat Ipo. secunda apho. grossi valde ꝯ naturā cito moriunt magis macris. nā fcō3 Gal. in cōmē. talis sunt frigidi ⁊ strictas habent artarias ⁊ venas ⁊ propter hoc sanguinē ⁊ spiritū paucū habēt: q2 calor innatus in eo pauca occasione corrūpitur cito. ⁊ cū hoc fcōm Auic. sunt expositi apoplexie paralisi pulsui cordis dyarie mali vic anhelitus sincopi febribus malis famē sitim non possunt tolerare. quare libero q optimus est moderate carnositas cōsul vita in humido consistit: vt dicit Auic. nō aquo lucido vaporoso ⁊ aereo: vt dicunt glosatores.

Cura ista h3 duas itētiōes. p⁹ ē diminuere sanguinē q multiplicat. Scda ē diminuere mām sue resoluere q̄ ꝯiūcta ē ⁊ debilitare vtutē ne ipā attrahat.

Pria itētio cōplet cū dieta valde subtili ⁊ cū medicinis vrinā ⁊ sudorē puocātib⁹: vt sūt ruta ⁊ grana ei⁹ aristo. ro. gētiana poliū cētaurea. Et Rasis dixit. q ad ista facit acetū ⁊ medicie laxatiue ꝯtue ducētes flā: vt dicit Hali. sermone primo sue rheto. ⁊ ieiunia ⁊ acuta exercitia p Halie. sunt laudata in li. de subtilianda dieta.

Scda itētio ꝯplet p balnea artificialia vt nālia q̄lia sūt ista: vt si i aq̄ poneret de flore salicis ⁊ de sale ⁊ ꝯiter fcō balneo inūgant cū oleo aliq acuto velut ē oleū de cucūere asinino gētiana arist. ⁊ ꝯsilib⁹. ⁊ ā cōedere i balneo: s3 ieiunare ⁊ an̄ balneū dormire aut nō qescere. Aui. tñ dicebat i 3⁰ pmi doc. 4 ⁹ vl. ca. In pmis regimē ē vt deficiat cibi a stomaco ei⁹ ⁊ itestis sit velox ne cōplet meseraica. rū suctio i ipo. ⁊ vt cibū quē sumit sit multe q̄titati ⁊ pauci nutrimēti ⁊ freq̄nter balneet añq̄ cōedat. ⁊ exercitiū sit festinū ⁊ olea resolutiua. ⁊ ō elec. supple ꝯueniētib⁹ ē trifera minor. ⁊ elect. de laca ⁊ tiriaca. ⁊ vt ieiunus bibat acetū ⁊ almuri. Cōtingit modo q vnū mēbrū sit grossi⁹ alio. qūo aūt curet satis dictū est. ⁊ potest intelligi p illud qd ē in ca⁹ de ciragra ⁊ de elefantia: q̄ duo ca. in. 2⁹ li. ponunt. ⁊ illic vide p cura hu⁹. de ituatio tñ in hoc casu fiat ad aliud mēbrum cum pondere ⁊ ligatura ⁊ alijs habentib⁹ diuertere vt dixit Auicē. ⁊ satis patet.

De membro ⁊ corpore extenuato. CA. V.

Extenuatio fit in ipo corpe sicut igrossatio. Unde corp⁹ dicitur macrū qñ lique fit ⁊ deprimit sicut in prisi dicitur arefactum ⁊ macrum ⁊ plerūq non totu3: sed vna efficitur talis particula.

Causa hu⁹ est materie idigētia. ⁊ in sexto deregimine sanitatis dixit Halie. q erat debilitas virtutis attractiue mēbri ⁊ assimilatiue eius. Et p Auicē. in quarto addunt alie res extrinsice: vt vitus cibi subtiliatis ⁊ geo imoderata: ⁊ nocet vt ipe dixit fcda pmi. Dimittētes exercitiū icurrūt erhicā. sopit aūt virtus attractiua in quiete ⁊ destruit a labore ira ⁊ angustie vigilie fame ⁊ dure iacere vt dixit Rasis ⁊ Halie. i tertio tegni. ⁊ accidētia aie extermināt corp⁹. i. exiccāt. ⁊ ad hocēt faciūt ligatura stricta ⁊ ꝯstrictio porou a calo frigido ⁊ sicco excessiuis: vt dixit Auic. in quarto tractatu de decoratiōe: Aut ēt dolor ⁊ passio iūcture: vt dicebat Auicē. de podagra lōga qn̄ mēbrū extenuat ⁊ viceratio pfunda male curata vt suo loco fuit dictū. Nota pmo: vt dixit Halie. tertio tegni q pmas ⁊ solidas ptes corpis nō est possibile huidiores facere. ⁊ p3 hoc ēt dicebat in. septio terapētice. Arefacta dispō isanabilis existit cū certissime cōpleta fuerit. Et sicut dictū fuit in pcedēti caplo: nimia grossicies piculosior ē ariditate ad sustinēdū. ⁊ allegat⁹ fuit affori⁹ nihilomin⁹ difficili⁹ ē curare ariditatē q̄ grassiciē. Et p3 ex dictis in pcedēti caplo. Ampli⁹ firmat p Ipocratē in fcdo afforismo. q multo tpe extenuant corpa tarde refici ꝯsueuerūt. Que vo in pauco pauce. Ex qb⁹ p3 q ariditas lōga ⁊ habituata q̄ seqt solutiōe3 lōgā male curatā nūq̄ corrigit. satis aūt ē sigs phibeat eas siccari non cito in tertio tegni.

Cura ista cōplet cū trib⁹ intētionib⁹. Pria itētio ē ad generādū multū de sanguine bono. Scda ē ip3 sanguinē trahere ad mēbra. Tertia ē ad roborādū vtute3 nutritiuā vt sanguis attract⁹ retineat ⁊ nō euaporet.

Pria itētio cōplet cū dieta bōa q̄ erbicis ⁊ ꝯsūptis ꝯuenit. Un̄ dicebat Ga. xiiij. terapētice. Quousq. n. remutare volueri attenuatos gdē debis vinū grossū pichimie cibaria ⁊ exercitia nō acuta neq fortia ⁊ fricatiōes moderatā.

Scda itētio cōplet hoc mō. vnde Halie. in sexto de regi

Portion of a Treatise on Embalming, d'Argellata, 15th Century

PLATE 16

processions which once had followed the bier lost much solemnity. The solemnity of the requiem mass went with the Reformation, as did vestments, candles, incense, holy water. Growing puritanism found an outlet in the Vestiarian Controversy, in which a group within the English Church sought further to strip away the residuum of Roman Catholic externals of worship. Thus in successive steps pageantry yielded to plainness. With the Counter-Reformation, in Catholic countries on the continent, the ceremonial of the Church moved in an opposite direction, so that, as Davey observes, "nothing can be imagined more theatrically splendid than the church decorations and ceremonies on occasions of funerals of eminence."[111]

The Reformation did not change the fundamental Christian doctrine that the body, no matter what its decay, is not worthless. The reformers kept the belief in the resurrection of the dead. Christians should therefore be fittingly buried, and burial places should be properly maintained. Burial was a concern of the church, to be attended by the congregation, even, if possible, when the poor were buried. The tolling of bells summoned the congregation to a burial, and if all did not come, the minister and school children, or at very least the sexton and the gravedigger, represented it. On the way to the cemetery children and mourners sang Christian burial hymns. At the grave itself prayers were recited, appropriate scriptual passages read, and almsgiving for the poor was encouraged by the passing of alms boxes or collection plates. Custom in some countries provided that after the closing prayer the Creed was pronounced. Burial services in the Reformed Church were very similar to these.[112]

Manifest on every occasion when the congregation gathered was the desire to provide pious instruction and exhortation. A Protestant funeral was no exception. The reading of

Scripture and the singing of hymns, lessons in themselves, were supplemented by a brief discourse on death and resurrection which was given in the home, or in the church or at the grave. For a fee, the minister prepared and delivered a special sermon making particular reference to the life and death of the deceased. Out of this early practice, which joined consideration of the last things—death, judgment, heaven or hell—with the memory of the departed—emerged the Protestant funeral sermon of today. Occasionally, even among the early Protestants, the pious were fond of carrying the cross in the procession and of thrice casting earth upon the body at the grave. Although they were then generally regarded with distrust, these practices have since been widely accepted as additions to the funeral rites. The benediction of the dead was and is even more mooted. Luther and the Augsburg Confession permitted the blessing of the dead, while the Reformed church rejected prayers for the dead unconditionally, the blessing among them.[113]

CITATIONS AND REFERENCES FOR CHAPTER III

1. Arturo Castiglioni, *A History of Medicine* (New York: Alfred A. Knopf, 1947), pp. 245-246.

2. John T. McNeil and Helena M. Gamer, *Medieval Handbooks of Penance* (New York: Columbia University Press, 1938), p. 21.

3. *Ibid.*, p. 202 *seq.*

4. Richard Davey, *A History of Mourning* (London: Jay's, Regent St. W., 1890), pp. 22-23.

5. *Ibid.*, pp. 23-24.

6. *Ibid.*, p. 34.

7. Stephen Wickes, *Sepulture; Its History, Methods and Sanitary Requisites* (Philadelphia: P. Blakiston Son & Co., 1884), p. 44 *seq.*

8. *Ibid.*, p. 46.

9. *Ibid.*, p. 48.

10. J. F. A. Adams, *Cremation and Burial* (1875) A reprint of a review the name of which is not given. The article is to be found in the pamphlet collection of the Cremation Society, Vol. II, p. 267. Quoted in Wilson and Levy, *op. cit.*, p. 12.

11. Bernardini Ramazzini, *De Moribus Artificum*, trans. Wilmer C. Wright (Chicago: University of Chicago Press, 1940), pp. 153-155.

12. Wilson and Levy, *op. cit.*, p. 14.

13. Creighton, *op. cit.*, p. 332.

14. Wilson and Levy, *op. cit.*, p. 13.

15. Creighton, *op. cit.*, p. 334. Quoting *Remembrancia*.

16. *Ibid.*, p. 11.

17. Stone, *op. cit.*, p. 17.

18. Ralph of Coggeshall, Rolls series, No. 66, p. 112. Quoted in Creighton, *op. cit.*, p. 11.

19. Creighton, *op. cit.*, p. 12.

20. Castiglioni, *op. cit.*, p. 361.

21. Quoted in Creighton, *op. cit.*, p. 156.

22. *Ibid.*, p. 336.

23. Davey, *op. cit.*, p. 63.

24. *Ibid.*, p. 54.

25. Wilson and Levy, *op. cit.*, p. 82.

26. Puckle, *op. cit.*, pp. 34-35.

27. Quoted in Stone, *op. cit.*, p. 68.

28. McNeil and Gamer, *op. cit.*, p. 121.

29. *Ibid.*, pp. 318-319.

30. *Ibid.*, p. 333.

31. Puckle, *op. cit.*, p. 64.

32. *Ibid.*, pp. 102-104.

33. Davey, *op. cit.*, p. 34.

34. *Ibid.*, p. 38.

35. Stone, *op. cit.*, pp. 174-176.

36. *Encyclopedia Britannica*, 1890, Vol. XIX, p. 164 *seq.*

37. Creighton, *op. cit.*, p. 649 *seq.*

38. Stow's *Memoranda.* Camden Society, New Series, XXVIII (1880) p. 125. Quoted in Creighton, *op. cit.*, p. 336.

39. After Puckle, *op. cit.*, p. 184.

40. *Ibid.*, p. 185.

41. *Ibid.*, p. 185.

42. See also C. J. Polson, ed., *The Disposal of the Dead* (London: English Universities Press, 1953), pp. 299-300.

43. See Genesis 50:26.

44. Herodotus, *History of the Persian Wars*, Book III. Quoted in Wickes, *op. cit.*, pp. 134-135.

45. Wickes, *op. cit.*, pp. 134-136.

46. *Ibid.*, p. 135.

47. *Ibid.*, p. 136.

48. Davey, *op. cit.*, pp. 137-138.

49. *Ibid.*, pp. 34-39.

50. Puckle, *op. cit.*, p. 42.

51. *Ibid.*, p. 116. Quoted from William Andrews.

52. Creighton, *op. cit.*, Vol. II, pp. 36-37; Davey, *op. cit.*, p. 139.

53. Charles Cox, *The Parish Registers of England* (London: Methuen & Co., 1910), p. 120.

54. Sylvia Thrupp, *The Merchant Class of Medieval London* (Chicago: University of Chicago Press, 1948), p. 152.

55. *Ibid.*

56. *Ibid.*, p. 153.

57. *Ibid.*, p. 154.

58. Sir Ernest Pooley, *The Guilds of the City of London* (London: Collins, 1947), p. 8.

59. Puckle, *op. cit.*, p. 84 *seq.*

60. *Ibid.*, pp. 37, 40-42.

61. Stone, *op. cit.*, p. 55.

62. Polson, *op. cit.*, p. 8; Creighton, *op. cit.*, p. 37; Davey, *op. cit.*, p. 139.

63. Puckle, *op. cit.*, pp. 86-90.

64. Davey, *op. cit.*, p. 95.

65. Baddeley, *Parish of St. Giles, Cripplegate* (London, 1888), quoted in Creighton, *op. cit.*, Vol. I, p. 335.

66. *Old Southwark and Its People* (London 1878), quoted in Creighton, *op. cit.*, Vol. I, p. 335.

67. Polson, *op. cit.*, p. 10; Puckle, *op. cit.*, p. 162.

68. Polson, *op. cit.*, p. 10; Puckle, *op. cit.*, p. 93.

69. Puckle, *op. cit.*, p. 93.

70. *Ibid.*, p. 90.

71. *Ibid.*, pp. 91-94.

72. *Ibid.*, p. 162.

73. Davey, *op. cit.*, p. 55.

74. *Ibid.*, p. 138.

75. Puckle, *op. cit.*, pp. 69-70.

76. *Ibid.*, p. 161.

77. J. Huizinga, *The Waning of the Middle Ages* (London: Edward Arnold Company, 1924), pp. 124-135.

78. J. S. Tatlock and R. G. Martin, *Representative English Plays* (New York: The Century Co., 1924), "Everyman," pp. 31-44.

79. Huizinga, *op. cit.*, pp. 124-135.

80. Wilson and Levy, *op. cit.*, pp. 9-10.

81. Friedlander, *op. cit.*, Vol. II, p. 212.

82. Charles A. Bradford, *Heart Burial* (London: George Allen & Unwin, 1933), p. 5.

83. *Ibid.*

84. *Ibid.*, pp. 5, 6, 14, 56, 58.

85. J. M. Gannal, *History of Embalming (and of Preparations in Anatomy, Pathology, and Natural History)* (Paris,

1838), trans. R. Harlan M.D. (Philadelphia: Judah Dobson, 1840), pp. 113-115.

86. Bradford, *op. cit.*, pp. 5, 6, 14, 19.

87. Friedlander, *op. cit.*, Vol. II, p. 212.

88. Huizinga, *op. cit.*, pp. 128-129, 333.

89. Creighton, *op. cit.*, Vol. I, p. 159.

90. *Encyclopedia Americana* (1932) Vol. X, p. 273.

91. *Encyclopedia Britannica* (1929) Vol. VIII, p. 384.

92. Bradford, *op. cit.*, p. 23; Puckle, *op. cit.*, p. 41.

93. p. 31.

94. Simon Mendelsohn, *Embalming Fluids* (New York: Chemical Publishing Company), pp. 10-12.

95. Bradford, *op. cit.*, p. 25.

96. *Gentleman's Magazine*, 1789, quoted in Polson, *op. cit.*, p. 217.

97. Huizinga, *op. cit.*, p. 133.

98. Davey, *op. cit.*, p. 45.

99. David Riesman, *The Story of Medicine in the Middle Ages* (New York: Paul B. Hoeber, 1935), pp. 3-8 *passim.* Charles Joseph Singer, *A Short History of Medicine* (London: Oxford, 1928).

100. Richard A. Leonardo, *History of Surgery* (New York: Froben, 1943), pp. 118-120.

101. Quoted by Thomas Greenhill in the *Art and Knowledge of Embalming* (London: 1705) from the account of the embalming of Pope Alexander V in the 29th book of Peter Forestus, who in turn drew directly upon Pietro d'Argellata's *Chirurgia.* See also Fielding H. Garrison, *An Introduction to the History of Medicine* (Philadelphia: W. B. Saunders, 1929).

102. Peter Forestus, "On the Art of How to Embalm the Dead Human Body," in *A New Medical Treatise, Embracing the External and Internal Pathological Ulceration of the*

Whole Human Body, edited by Petrum Offenback, M.D. (Frankfort am Main: Printed by Zachariane Palthemium, 1605), translator unknown. In the collection of the National Foundation for Funeral Service Library in Evanston, Illinois.

103. Riesman, *op. cit.*, pp. 3-8 *passim*.

104. Roswell Park, *An Epitome of the History of Medicine* (Philadelphia: F. A. Davis, 1908), p. 3.

105. Riesman, *op. cit.*, p. 173 *seq*.

106. Leonardo, *op. cit.*, p. 114.

107. *Ibid.*, p. 120.

108. Bradford, *op. cit.*, p. 27.

109. Castiglioni, *op. cit.*, pp. 292-294.

110. Davey, *op. cit.*, p. 54.

111. *Ibid.*, pp. 50, 54.

112. Jackson, *op. cit.*, pp. 307-309.

113. *Ibid.*

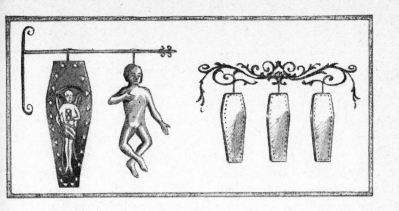

Medical Embalmers and the Rise of English Undertakers

We have seen thus far that while at various times and in various places there have been persons set aside by custom or law or both to carry out the several procedures required for the burial of the dead, there is no unbroken line extending from the modern funeral director back to the ancient Egyptian team of funeral functionaries. Only in embalming can be discovered some kind of continuity. And even in this specialty, while the link between today and ancient Egypt is unbroken, there were almost fifteen hundred years during which funeral embalming was rarely practiced, and then it was carried on only incidentally and secondarily by someone primarily engaged in an occupation other than the burial of the dead.

The present chapter will continue to follow the development of embalming from the late Middle Ages to relatively modern times. Next, it will trace the beginnings and growth of a new, lay occupational group, the English tradesman undertaker. It will show how this new group gradually took to itself a number of functions relating to the burial of the dead, among them funeral embalming. With the development of the English funeral undertaker and his American counterpart we are well on the road that leads to the American funeral director of the twentieth century.

Embalming and the Growth of Medical Science: From the 9th century on, a slow breaking away from Egyptian practices is to be noted in the writings of physicians and surgeons on the subject of embalming. Rhazes (9th and early 10th century), d'Argellata (15th century), Forestus (16th century), and Clauderus (17th century)—all suggest some breaking with the past.[1] For, if by the 15th century decomposition was a morbid preoccupation, it was also something of a challenge, and with the revival of interest in anatomy and surgery, correlative with the rebirth of secular or lay medicine, physicians began to show a professional interest in the preservation of the corpse by other than traditional Egyptian methods. In two cases varying widely as to purpose Huizinga records how in an effort to keep them intact until burial, the features of Pierre of Luxembourg were touched up with paint; and how when an heretical preacher of the sect of the Turlupins died in prison before sentence could be passed, the body was preserved [*sic.*] in quicklime for a fortnight in order that it could be burned in public with a living heretical woman.[2]

The demand for better methods of preservation was seconded by the artists who drew anatomical plates. Most prominent of these was that supreme genius, Leonardo da Vinci

(1452-1519). In the course of his anatomical studies, which he finally summarized in 750 magnificent plates, da Vinci dissected over 50 cadavers, an unusually large number for the time. While so engaged he developed a system of venous injection which years later may have served as an inspiration to Ruysch and Hunter. It is not known whether or not da Vinci ever injected a preservative solution into any of his cadavers. But the mere fact that he anticipated Harvey's injection of the veins by over two hundred years is proof of his anatomical and physiological genius.[3] In any event, whether or not da Vinci's invention was immediately utilized to its full extent for funerary embalming, it was a precursor of modern embalming procedures. Although the early counterpart of the modern undertaker did not appear until the 17th century, it is evident that by the 15th most of the principles of embalming in vogue today were known to medical practitioners. After that time there remained only the discovery of the circulation of the blood in the early 17th century to stimulate the use of arterial embalming. At least two centuries before, cavity injection with compounds of metallic salts had been employed. In 1866, the remains of John of Lancaster, Duke of Bedford (died 1435), consisting of a lock of hair and 50 grams of a blackish substance interspersed with globules of metallic mercury, were transferred from a grave in the Cathedral of Rouen to the Museum of Antiquities of that city. LeRoy in 1918 published the results of an analysis of what he supposed was the mercurial embalming preservative—the "balsamic mercurial unguent"—employed. He was able to identify metallic mercury, phosphates, sulphites, aluminum oxide, ferrous oxide, lime, silicon dioxide, and the oxides of magnesium, sodium, and potassium.[4]

Injection techniques to inflate portions of the body for purposes of tracing the continuity of the blood vessels were practiced by such early anatomists as Jacob Sylvius, Carpi, Eustachius, Stephanus, Malphigi, Gleason, De Graff and Swammerdon. The work of these men was carried on from the middle 15th to the middle 17th century.[5] A 17th century Florentine physician, Girolamo Segato, is known to have turned the human body into stone by injecting the tissues with a solution of silicate of potash. As a second step he immersed the body in a weak acid solution.

From these and other instances it is clear that by the end of the 17th century the medical world understood the possibilities of injection embalming, even though some physicians, surgeons and anatomists kept their precise techniques a secret. The Dutch professor, Fredrick R. Ruysch (1638-1731), while searching for a means of inhibiting putrefaction in anatomical specimens, devised a technique for arterial embalming, but he did not divulge its media and operative details, although it is known that the injection was followed by evisceration. Credit for first taking this step belongs to Gabriel Clauderus, a German physician, who described the process in a work entitled, *Methodus Balsamundi Corpora Humani, Aliaqua Majora Sine Evisceratione.* Meanwhile, in England, William Harvey (1578-1657), physician and anatomist, and greatest of physiologists, injected colored solutions into the arteries to support his theories concerning the circulation of blood, which discovery he announced to his pupils in 1618. Although Harvey's researches are basic to modern embalming techniques, full utilization of them for this purpose was not immediately made.[6]

The 18th century witnessed further great advances in both arterial and cavity embalming. In his lectures, Dr. William Hunter (1718-1783), the great Scotch anatomist, included directions for the use of arterial and cavity embalming for preserving the human body not only for laboratory use but for burial. Because Hunter was the first to report fully and openly the fluid and method to be used, he is generally considered to be the originator of the injection technique of preserving human remains.

Utilizing his brother's methods, John Hunter, younger brother of William, continued to prepare anatomical specimens, and in 1775 embalmed the body of the wife of Martin Van Butchell, the famous London quack, employing both cavity and injection techniques. In this celebrated embalming, Hunter, assisted by Cruickshank the surgeon, employed oil of turpentine and camphorated spirits of wine for arterial injection, and camphor for cavity packing. Van Butchell subsequently kept the body on display, attired in fine garments, in a glass-lidded case in his sitting room. "The dear departed," he called his wife when introducing her to guests. As the news of the exhibit spread, Van Butchell was so besieged by curiosity seekers that he was compelled to announce that "no stranger can see his embalmed wife unless . . . at any day between nine and one, Sunday excepted." When Van Butchell remarried after some years his second wife objected to her predecessor's remains, and they were removed to the Museum of the Royal College of Surgeons in London.[7]

By 1800, physicians, surgeons, and anatomists in many parts of Europe were improving old embalming processes or experimenting with new. Among leaders in the field during the 19th century were Dr. Matthew Baillie; the Neapolitan, Dr. Tranchini; the Frenchman, Dr. Falconry; the Irishman, Dr. Morgan; the Englishmen, Drs. Marshall and Pettigrew, the latter an authority on Egyptian mummies as well as a physician; and the Russian, Dr. Tschniernoff. While the medical profession was improving embalming techniques, a new specialist, the chemist, was providing better fluids with which to work. Of the earlier chemists to be concerned with embalming the best known was the Frenchman, Jean Nicho-

las Gannal, whose *History of Embalming* remains one of the
few classics dealing with the subject.

The Role of the Barber-Surgeons in Embalming: Leonardo tells us in his *History of Surgery* that the barbers
of monasteries were called "Barbers and Reducers." The
latter title referred to the fact that, among other methods
of healing, they reduced the quantity of blood in their patients; that is, they were blood letters. Monks were obliged
to have the crowns of their heads shaved regularly for the
tonsure and in some monasteries were bled five times a year.
From the early 12th to the late 13th century, in seven
councils the Church forbade the clergy to practice medicine
on the grounds that men who had taken religious vows
should have concern for the care of the soul rather than for
that of the body, that the church abhorred the shedding of
blood, and that churchmen should not touch matters
which could not openly be talked about. But the practice
of blood-letting was still the vogue, and since it was forbidden to the monks it was taken up by medieval barbers
who already had some experience in the process.

For the barber, blood-letting led into more general surgery and from this humble beginning ultimately arose the
trade of the barber-surgeons, or "Surgeons of the Short
Robe," as distinguished from the later day surgeons of the
college de St. Come who wore long robes. Lay though they
were, the barber-surgeons thus traced their origins to the
days of monastic medicine. With the rise of guilds in the
late Middle Ages they became a powerful craft, united by
corporate bonds. As such they possessed group organization
and solidarity; restricted admission to their ranks; exercised
strict domain over the right to embalm; took measures to
see that their members were fit to carry out the practice of
surgery, of which embalming was an important subordinate
skill; and addressed the law with the voice of authority.[8]

Although from Egyptian times to the present there had always been embalmers, until the rise of the guild system in Europe and the assumption of authority by the barber-surgeons there existed no single group that exercised strict control over the embalming process and perpetuated the tradition through generations. The success of Ambrose Paré, a barber-surgeon and the father of modern surgery, elevated the prestige of the barber-surgeons to the detriment of the Surgeons of the Long Robe.[9] In 1550 Paré described the embalming practice of his time:

Our countrymen the French embalm the bodies of their Kings and nobles with spices and sweet ointments . . . *but the bodie which is to bee embalmed with spices for very long continuance, must first be embowelled, keeping the heart apart that it may be embalmed and kept as the kinsfolk think fit:* also the brain shall be taken out. Then you shall make deep incisions along the arms, thighs, etc., to let out the blood and give space for putting in the aromatic powders. The whole body should be washed over with aqua vitae and strong vinegar, wherein shall be boiled wormwood, aloes, coloquintidi, common salt, and alum. Then the spices . . . shall be stuffed in and the incisions sewn up, and then let the whole bodie bee anointed with turpentine dissolved with oil of roses and camomile, adding if you think fit, some chymical oils of spices, then let it be strewed over again with the fore-mentioned powder, then wrap in a linen cloth and then in sear-cloths. Lastly let it be put in a coffin of lead and filled up with dry sweet herbs.[10]

A document, dated 1389, found in a bundle of papers dealing with the fraternities and guilds of the city of London, delineates the purposes of the Fraternity of Barbers of that place, and provides some indication of the antiquity of the Guild and of its significant funeral practices:

ITEM. That when any brother of the said Fraternity dies the brethren of the said Fraternity shall go on to the Vigil to the dirge, and on the day (of the funeral) to the Mass, and to the dirge and to the mass of the month's obit, and that each such brother dead have thirty masses from their common box and that each brother who is absent without reasonable excuse at any of the said four times, shall put into their common box in place of his offerings and expenses, as he ought to have done if he had been present, three pence.[11]

On October 20, 1604, the barber-surgeons of London decided to apply for a new charter enumerating twenty-seven clauses which they desired to have included. The sixteenth clause declared:

. . . openinge searinge and imbalmeinge of the dead corpes to be pply belongeinge to the science of Barbery and Surgery, And the same intruded into by Butchers Taylors Smythes Chaundlors and others of mecanicall trades unskillfull in Barbery or Surgery, And unseemely and unchristian lyke defaceinge disfiguringe and dismembringe the dead Corpes, And so that by theire unskillfull searinge and imbalmeinge, the corpes corrupteth and groweth . . . pntlie contagious and ofensive to the place and psons approachinge.[12]

Although the barber-surgeons had been embalming in England for over two hundred years, only at the beginning of the 17th century did they find it necessary to obtain a formal decree that of all men they alone possessed the right "to open, seare and imbalm" the corpse. In addition to the sixteenth, the twenty-fifth clause of the new charter, obtained within three months, read:

No butcher, tailor, waxchandler or other persons (are) to cut, dissect, or embalm any dead body, but the same (is) to be done by members of the Company approved and appointed by the Masters or Governors of the Barber-Surgeons.[13]

On January 7, 1646, the barber-surgeons of London invoked their charter rights against a Mr. Michael Makeland. *The Annals* recount the incident:

Mr. Michaell Makeland appeareing to this Court at the request of our Mr (Master) he was here complayned of to have embalmed severall humane Bodyes within this City against the Ordinance of this Company in that behalf being an Apothecary and not a Surgeon approved according to Law.[14]

Makeland's appearance marks a step forward in the history of funeral undertaking. He is the first person known by name to take positive action to break the prerogative of embalming legally assigned to medical and surgical practitioners.

Again in 1652 the Company of barber-surgeons rose to defend their exclusive chartered right to embalm. The entry of October 26th reads:

26 October, 1612
This daie it is ordered that at the chardge of the howse the pnte . . . Masters wth the Clark shall seeke in the Rowles for the charter of the wax chaundlers and to tak a coppie of that pte of the charter touchinge the libertie gyven unto them for the imbaulmynge of dead bodyes And as they shall finde the same soe to take the advice of my lord cheife Justice about the same at the chardge of the howse.[15]

How they fared in the matter was not recorded.

The Emergence of the Funeral Undertaker: It bears repetition that by the middle of the 17th century the barber-surgeons of London were invoking the law in an effort to defend their exclusive right to embalm. Such action to prevent infringement is indication that by accident or design other occupational groups—butchers, tailors, wax-chandlers among them—were being called upon to give a service that for one reason or another the chartered group was not giving in the manner or, more likely, at a cost the customer desired.

Two conclusions present themselves from the foregoing material. The first is that funeral undertaking as a clear-cut distinct secular occupation had not appeared in Europe

before the 17th century. The second is that embalming
developed as a medical specialty long prior to and independent of undertaking. The appearance of facts and ideas
can sometimes be roughly dated by the appearance of
names for them in the language. The words "embalmer"
and "undertaker" offer an interesting case in point. "Embalm" as an English word is of the 14th century. Its first
written English use on record, according to the Oxford dictionary, was in 1340 in the phrase, "They . . . with oyne-
ments the body embawnyd." Its immediate origin was in the
French word "enbaume," which in turn had been derived
from the Latin "balsamum," "balsam," and farther back
from the Greek "balsomon." To embalm was to preserve with a balsamic resin or aromatic oil. Prior to 1340 it
is likely that any printed reference made to the process in
England would have been in Old French or in Latin. The
use of the word in Middle English in 1340 merely indicates
that funerary embalming in England antedated Chaucer
(1340-1400). Chaucer himself used the phrase, "Let the
corse embalm," in 1385. In 1587 De Mornay speaks of
"Imbalmers . . . of dead bodies," and Bacon in 1626 remarks that, "The Romans . . . were not so good embalmers
as the Egyptians." By 1600 the terms "embalm" and "embalmer" probably had a standardized if not wide usage in
England.[16]

Significantly for the present consideration the word "undertaker," in the sense one who prepares the dead for burial
and takes charge of and manages funerals, has no history
of comparable length in English usage. As early as 1400 the
term "undertaker" can be found. But it describes one who
"undertakes" a task or enterprise, with no reservation as
to the nature of this task. Through the seventeenth century
it also carried the same meaning as "underwriter," that is,
one who provides the financial backing for an enterprise. The

first suggestion that the word might have been used in its present highly circumscribed sense is to be found at the end of the sixteenth century in connection with the duties of heralds. Heralds were chartered in 1483, with their duties elaborately defined in 1600 by the solicitor-general, Sir John Doddridge, as being concerned with the granting of coats of arms, the recording of pedigrees, and the supervision of funerals.[17] In discussing the heralds, Barron speaks of Garter King Sir William Dethick, who served from 1586 to 1605. Dethick, Barron narrates, was irascible, so much so that he would "brawl at funerals with the minister or the undertaker."[18] The statement contains the suggestion that while the herald supervised funerals, some one else—an "undertaker"—undertook to provide some of the funerary paraphernalia.

If such functionary existed at the date indicated his services were probably not made available to ordinary folk, or used by them. Homan's study, "English Villagers of the Thirteenth Century," shows that the church controlled all aspects of the burial of the dead except the "lychweake," or death watch—"lich" or "lych" is a Scotch or English dialect word meaning "corpse"—a folk custom according to which neighbors and friends sat up with the dead, meanwhile eating and drinking.[19]

Feudal Funerals: Long after the feudal period had passed in England, and after its rigmarole, paraphernalia, machinery and titles had ceased to have much real meaning in describing the actual social, political, economic and military relations of people, the pageantry persisted. Strangely enough, after it ceased to have real uses, during the later feudal period on through the Renaissance, heraldry and pomp reached its peak development. Significantly included in the conspicuous display which underlined and emphasized a highly stratified social order was the elaborate funeral to which the title "feudal" has since been attached. Even in a country in which social control has been as much by ceremony as by law, and in which the age old deposit of social dramaturgy is carefully husbanded for constant re-use, the elaborate feudal funeral, when compared to the ceremonies marking other human events, such as marriage and birth, seems inordinately lavish.

Originally the trappings of a feudal funeral—yards upon yards of black drapery for the chief rooms and the staircase, an elaborate black mourning bed, funeral carriages, a velvet pall, a hearse with hatchment or panel upon which the deceased person's arms were temporarily displayed, mourning clothes and mourning gifts—enough sombre materials to change the usual hearty feudal home atmosphere to one of blackest gloom, were family owned. The purchase of these goods and this equipment was enormously expensive, and as a result the cost of an upper class funeral in England, especially the funeral of a noble person, was an excessive drain upon his estate. With this fact in mind Bradford surmises that the trade of undertaker which was "unknown in England before 1688" arose in that year "from a desire to retrench the enormous expense incurred by the less wealthy families in providing their own coaches, hangings, and other furniture for every funeral."[20]

The probabilities are that Bradford's date is not early enough; that, by whatever name it might have been called, the occupational role of the undertaker had been emerging from the late sixteenth century on. The term "undertaker" in its modern sense goes back at least to 1698, at which date its present usage recorded in a parish register: "The furnishing of funerals by a small number of men called undertakers." Mencken notes that "it once had a formidable rival in *upholder*, the original meaning of which was a dealer and repairer of old furniture . . . traced by N E D (*New English Dictionary*) to 1333, but it does not seem to have come into use to designate a funeral contractor until the beginning of the 18th century."[21] At least one unidentified 17th century poet referred to the "upholder":

> Th' upholder, rueful harbinger of death,
> Waits with impatience for the dying breath;
> As vultures o'er a camp, with hovering flight,
> Snuff up the future carnage of the fight.[22]

As late as 1938 an undertaking firm in the Kensington District of London still clung to the quaint title of "funeral upholders,"[23] although the term had long since lost currency. The first appearance of "undertaker" in American colonial newspapers to designate one who undertakes to supply the funerary paraphernalia and services seems to have been in 1768.[24] However, it may have had ordinary verbal usage somewhat earlier.

Coffins, Funeral Goods and the Early Undertaker: We have seen that while the use of coffins for persons of importance extends into antiquity, the popular practice of coffined burial developed only in the last several hundred years. As late as 1820 Lord Stowell's decision in Gilbert vs. Buzzard established the point that while it is an offense to the body "to be carried in a state of naked exposure to the grave" a coffin is not "of the same necessity."[25]

"Friendly Societies," descendants of the earlier Leagues of Prayer and burial guilds, continued to arrange for the burial of the lower classes.[26] Part of the manner of operation of a burial society toward the end of the seventeenth century is revealed in an unidentified public notice quoted by Ashton:

This is to give Notice that the Office of Society for Burials, by mutual Contribution of a Halfpenny or Farthing towards a Burial, erected upon Wapping Wall, is now removed into Katherine Wheel Alley in White Chappel, near Justice Smiths, where subscriptions are taken to compleat the number, as also at the Ram in Crucifix lane in Barnaby Street, Southwark; to which places notice is to be given of the death of any Member, and where any Person may have the Printed Articles after Monday next. And this Thursday about 7 o'clock Evening will be Buried by the Undertakers the Corpse of J. S., a Glover over against the Sun Brewhouse, in Golden Lane; as also a child from the Corner of Acorn Alley in Bishopsgate Street, and another Child from the Great Maze Pond, Southwark.[27]

Ashton also lists an early 18th century undertaker's advertisement. From it clues can be gathered as to the service he and his kind rendered and the goods they provided during the reign of Queen Anne:

For the good of the Publick, I Edward Evans, at the Four Coffins in the Strand, over against Somerset House; Furnish all Necessaries for all sorts of Funerals both great and small. And all sorts of set Mourning both Black and Gray and all other furniture suitable to it, fit for any person of Quality. Which I promise to perform 2s. in the Pound cheaper than any other of the Undertakers in Town or elsewhere.[28]

The handbills of undertakers of this period were filled with decorative details indicating a morbid preoccupation with the grisly side of death—"grinning skulls and shroud clad corpses, thigh bones, mattocks and pickaxes, hearses and what not."

If some undertakers made a sideline of upholstery, some drapers made a sideline of furnishing funerary goods. A late 17th or early 18th century notice informed the public that:

. . . Mr. John Elphick, Wollen Draper, over against St. Michael's Church in Lewes, hath a good Hearse, a Velvet Pall, Mourning Cloaks, and Black hangings for Rooms to be Lett at

Reasonable Rates. He also Sells all sorts of Mourning and Half Mourning, all sorts of Black Cyprus for Scarfs and Hatbands, and White silks for Scarfs and Hoods at Funerals; Gloves of all sorts, and Burying Cloaths for the Dead . . . Prices of the Newest Fashions, and all sorts of Ribbons, Bodies and Hose, very good Penny worths.[29]

Coffined burial involved the making of wooden coffins, a skill already possessed by carpenters, cabinet-makers, joiners and other workers in wood; and thus these artisans found themselves drawn into the new and vaguely defined occupation of undertaking:

Eleazar Malory, Joiner at the coffin White Chapel, near Red Lion Street end, maketh Coffins, Shrouds, letteth Palls, Cloaks, and Furnisheth with all other things necessary for Funeral at Reasonable Rates.[30]

Eighteenth century tradesmen's cards provide additional information concerning the emerging undertaker's trade. A collection of these by Ambrose Heal[31] shows cabinet-makers, carpenters, upholsterers and undertakers, using such titles as the "Arms of the Carpenters' Company," "Chair and Tea Chest," "Four Coffins," "Royal Bed," "Three Covered Chairs and Walnut Tree," advertised their goods and services in language sometimes quaint, sometimes amusing, but always revealing:

You may be furnished with all sorts and sizes of coffins and shrouds ready made and all other conveniences belonging to funerals.

Safety for the dead. Sir William Scott has decided the right to inter in iron.

Funerals decently performed.

Velvet Palls, Hangings for rooms, large silver'd candlestick and sconces, tapers for wax lights, heraldry feathers and velvets, fine cloth cloaks and midling do. Rich silk scarves, allamode and sarsnett hat bands, burying crapes of all sorts.[32]

It is worth noting that this advertising emphasizes two points: the wide range of funerary goods made available, and the protection of the corpse.

Heal has also assembled shop signs of the late 17th and most of the 18th centuries. In them, the preoccupation with the physical and grewsome side of death is apparent. The undertaker's favorite insignia is the coffin, usually hanging vertically, and often inscribed or decorated with skeletons, skulls, crossbones, or other grim emblems. The earliest of such signboards, dating from about 1680, identified the business establishment of William Boyce, "at ye Whight Hart & Coffin in ye Grate Ould Bayley, near Newgate." Others, mostly in the early eighteenth century include such grim designations as the "Naked Boy and Coffin." "Four Coffins"; "Crown and Coffin"; "The First and Last"; and the "Three Coffins." (See Plate 18.) Other signboards told of the coffin-plate makers and the coffin-plate chasers or engravers. Carpenters likewise announced their shops, which may or may not have been undertaking establishments. It was not beyond possibility that undertakers hired cabinet-makers to make coffins in connection with their lines of furniture. An early 18th century signboard directs attention to:

George Smithson, Broker, Undertaker and Sworn Appraiser. Opposite the Bull and Gate, Holbourn, London Buys and sells all sorts of Household Goods and at Reasonable Rates. NB. Funerals Performed.[33] (See Plate 18.)

The curious assortment of vaguely related tasks joined in one establishment under the versatile George Smithson is in itself clear indication that as of date given the occupation of funeral undertaker had not emerged in England as a well defined, highly specialized trade, even though the undertaker was a recognized tradesman, at least by the end of

a) Early 18th Century English Funeral Invitation

Henry Sidgier
CARPENTER, JOYNER,
and UNDERTAKER.
At the Carpenters Arms in Great Shere Lane
near Temple Barr, LONDON.
Buys Sells and Appraises all sorts
of Household Goods, Pictures, China &c.
Likewise
Cabinet and Upholsterers Work
done and Funerals Perform'd.
Bε All sorts of Boxes & Packing Cases made

c) Part Time Undertaker, 18th Century English
Tradesman's Card

b) Corpse Lying in State, 18th Century Drawing

PLATE 17

c) Precursor to Furnishing Undertaker, Tradesman's Card of 1740

a) Trade Sign, Four Coffins and Heart, c. 1720

b) Wright Hart and Coffin

the 17th century. If, on the one hand, his occupational role grew more simple by the gradual elimination of certain tasks such as brokerage and appraisal; it grew more complex, on the other, by assimilating new and closely related tasks, such as embalming. In the round of activities of the contemporary funeral establishment embalming is so universally regarded as a legitimate function of the establishment itself, to be performed by the staff of the establishment, and so uniquely the occupational prerogative of that staff, that it is difficult even to imagine how another occupational group once could arrogate this function to itself and attempt to deny it to the tradesman undertaker. Yet, as we have seen, such was the strange fact.

Tradesman Undertaker and Medical Embalmer: With the Renaissance of lay medicine, surgery, and anatomy, in the 15th, 16th, and early 17th centuries, embalming became, as we have seen, one of the prerogatives of the surgeon or barber-surgeon, even though its funerary use was limited to the wealthy or important, and not all of these were embalmed. Whatever the reason—it may have been cost, or it may have been the lack of surgeons and anatomists to carry the load of business, or their unwillingness to give the necessary time to increased demands for their services, although this is not likely in view of their complaints—at the opening of the eighteenth century, the undertaker himself was practicing a crude form of embalming. In his earliest comedy, published in 1702, *The Funeral, or Grief a la Mode*, Sir Richard Steele, better known for his *Spectator Papers*, has the undertaker ask his hired assistants:

"Have you brought the Sawdust and Tar for embalming? Have you the hangings and the Sixpenny nails for my Lord's Coat of Arms"? (The hatchment must be put up, and mutes must be stationed at intervals from the hall door to the top of the stairs.) "Come, you that are to be Mourners in the House, put on your Sad Looks, and walk by Me that I may sort you. Ha you! a little more upon the Dismal. This fellow has a good Mortal look, place him near the Corpse; that Wanscoat face must be o' top of the Stairs: That Fellow's almost in a fright (i.e., full of some strange misery) at the Entrance of the Hall. So! but I'll fix you all myself. Let's have no Laughing now on any Provocation; Look Yonder, at that Hale, Well looking Puppy! You ungrateful scoundrel, Did not I pity you, take you out of a Great Man's Service, and show you the Pleasure of receiving Wages? Did I not give you Ten, then Fifteen and Twenty Shillings a Week to be Sorrowful? and the more I give you, I thing the glader you are."[34]

The quotation goes beyond demonstrating the absorption into the undertaker's routine of the task of embalming— "Sawdust and Tar" embalming, it is true. Also it emphasizes another role coming into the undertaker's bundle of tasks—the dramaturgic role, in which the undertaker becomes a stage manager to create an appropriate atmosphere and to move the funeral party through a drama in which social relationships are stressed and an emotional catharsis or release is provided through ceremony.[35]

The feudal period dramatized death with high ritual, it is true; yet the ceremonies were an integral part of the life of English aristocracy. In the centuries that followed others of lesser rank who had become prosperous, or those who felt it proper to do better by the dead than had been their lot when alive, sought to imitate the aristocratic funeral of the earlier period. To meet these demands the undertakers who had previously provided a limited portion of the funeral were forced to do more. They found it necessary to hire the functionaries—mutes, mourners, liverymen, and the like—to stage, or organize the funeral. Such undertakers assembled the cast—the quick and the dead, supplied the trappings to form the proper setting and create the proper atmosphere of heavy gloom, and sought to coordinate the actions of all involved. In brief, as the funeral became more of a performance, with new roles to be played, the undertaker in taking charge of these activities was shaping a new occupation, independent in its own right.

In view of the fact that surgeons and anatomists were an older occupational group, with the barber-surgeons a well organized craft, it is not surprising to find that these entrenched interests regarded the first crude efforts of the funeral undertaker to embalm as an invasion of their occupational domain. Thomas Greenhill's *Treatise on the Art of Embalming,* (see Plate 19) printed for the author in 1705, is partly dedicated to the cause of rescuing this art from the "tar and sawdust" competition of the undertaker. In this jurisdictional dispute Greenhill pleads rigorously:

. . . to see our Profession over-run by *Quacks* and *Mountebanks* and that *Valet de Chambres* are suffer'd to Bleed, dress Wounds, cut Fontanells, and perform the like Operations, is what has reduc'd *Surgery* to so low an ebb. In like manner the noble *Art of Embalming* has been intirely ruin'd by the Undertaker . . .

. . . they (the Egyptians) had these several Persons belonging to and employ'd in *Embalming* each performing a distinct and separate Office, viz. A *Designer* or *Painter*, a *Dissector* or *Anatomist*, a *Pollinctor* or *Apothecary*, and *Embalmer* or *Surgeon*, and a *Physician* or *Priest*, which last was a great Philosopher, and taught and instructed the others in these Ceremonies, as we shall shew in its proper Place.

By this means, not only the Art of *Embalming* but likewise every branch of Physic, flourish'd and came to the greatest perfection, whereas, in our Age, every Art grows the more imperfect as it incroaches on another, and the civil Wars now a Days between *Physicians*, *Surgeons*, and *Apothecaries* have been the chief occasions of reducing Physic to so low an ebb; for whilst these have been fighting for each others Countries the Monarchy was usurp'd by *Quacks* and *Undertakers*, who are the only Vultures that attend such battles, in order to prey immediately on the vanquish'd Enemy.

Is it not therefore a shame for us, who, no doubt, esteem our selves a much more polite People than these Heathens were, to suffer a sort of Men call'd *Undertakers* to monopolize the several Trades of *Glovers*, *Milliners*, *Drapers*, *Wax-Chandlers*, *Coffin-Makers*, *Herald-Painters*, *Surgeons*, *Apothecaries*, and the like . . . and 'till such Time as *Quacks* and *Undertakers*, *Hawkers*, *Pedlers* and Interlopers, and all such persons, as were not brought up in the Emploiment they profess, be remov'd we can think no otherwise but that *Art* must sink. . .

We may as well expect one, that has never seen a Campaign, should understand Military Discipline . . . as that an *Upholsterer*, a *Taylor*, a *Joyner*, or the like *Undertaker*, should be well skill'd in the misterious *Art of Embalming*.[36]

In addition to single voices of protest such as Greenhill's, the surgeons and barber-surgeons collectively protested against what they considered to be an invasion of their prerogatives. We have seen that, as early as 1604, in making application for a new charter, the barber-surgeons of London asserted their right to embalm, as against butchers, tailors, and wax-chandlers; and that in 1646 they defended that right against an apothecary. The abortive entrance of the wax-chandler into the field of embalming, through the field of funeral undertaking, merits a word of explanation. During the later Middle Ages, wax-chandlers —a "chandler" originally was a maker or seller of candles, in spite of the more common present use of the word to describe a person who deals in groceries, provisions, and small wares—had a role in the preparations for funerals, insofar as they furnished the wax candles. The volume of this business

NEKPOKHΔEIA:

OR, THE

Art of Embalming;

John ~ Wherein is shewn *Skarp*

The Right of Burial,

THE

FUNERAL CEREMONIES,

And the several Ways of

Preserving Dead Bodies

IN

Most Nations of the WORLD.

With an Account of

The particular Opinions, Experiments and Inventions
of modern Physicians, Surgeons, Chymists and Anatomists.

ALSO

Some new Matter propos'd concerning a better Method of *Embalming* than hath hitherto been discover'd.

AND

A *Pharmacopœia Galeno-Chymica, Anatomia
sicca sive incruenta,* &c.

In Three PARTS.

The whole Work adorn'd with variety of Sculptures.

By THOMAS GREENHILL, *Surgeon.*

LONDON: Printed for the Author.

**Title Page of Early Work on Embalming,
Published 1705**

PLATE 19

was considerable, due to the fact that many funeral processions were held at night, candles were used at the wake, wax was needed to seal shrouds and coffins, and pitch was sometimes required to make the coffin watertight, or for crude embalming. Perhaps it was the chandler's immediate contact with pitch or "tar and sawdust" that motivated him to enter into competition with the surgeon and anatomist, and thus made him the special target for their less-than-successful protests. In any event, there seems to have been no stopping of cheaper embalming practices offered by various kinds of special tradesmen who in one way or the other, by supplying goods and services, participated in the funeralization and burial of the dead. Because Europeans accepted embalming half-heartedly, we must turn to America to gain a clearer picture of the manner of the absorption of this and other tasks into the normal round of work now called "funeral directing." Before leaving England, however, we should examine the relationship of the undertaker to workers in two related occupational areas, the clergy and the sanitarians.

Clergy and Undertaker: While the 17th century surgeon and anatomist regarded the crude embalming of the funeral undertaker, chandler and others as wholly unacceptable from the standpoint of a decent practice in preservation, and an encroachment, to boot, on their prerogatives, opposition to the growing number and organization of burial functions taken over by the tradesman undertaker, came from another group, and for a different reason. Among the clergy, religious reformers with a social bent were wont to use the churchyard elegy not only to point the solemn lesson of the equality of all men in the grave, but to make strictures against specific evils of society as well. In his poem, "*The Grave,*" Robert Blair, an Edinburgh clergyman, summarized the mood of such pronouncements[87] by interspersing his remarks on the vanity of man's pursuits, with

a section in which he makes a very critical address to undertakers:

> But see! the well-plum'd HEARSE comes nodding on
> Stately and slow: and properly attended
> By the whole sable tribe, that painful watch
> The sick man's door, and live upon the dead,
> By letting out their persons by the hour,
> To mimic sorrow, where the heart's not sad . . .
>
> . . . But tell us, why this waste,
> Why this ado in earthing up a carcase
> That's fall'n into disgrace, and in the nostril
> Smells horrible?—Ye UNDERTAKERS, tell us,
> 'Midst all the gorgeous figures you exhibit,
> Why is the *principal* conceal'd for which
> You make this mighty stir?—'Tis wisely done:
> What would offend the eye in a good picture,
> The painter casts discretely into shades.[38]

To echo the poet's strictures the editor felt impelled to
comment:

> *Pompous funerals* are as *ridiculous* as they are *unnecessary:*
> *Ridiculous* in respect to the *living*, except in the views of those
> who reap *pecuniary* advantage from them, and unnecessary
> respecting the *dead*, who are the principal subject and occa-
> sions of them.[39]

From the Reformation to the present, representatives of
various denominations have sometimes criticized funeral
customs, funeral expenses, and the behaviour of undertakers,
comparing the funerals of more recent dates with the funerals of primitive Christianity, and alleging that some of
the pomp and majesty of the traditional feudal funeral represented a reversion to pagan worldliness and was therefore
unbefitting to Christians. The sable false front of the
post-feudal funeral, with its mummers, hired-by-the-job re-

tainers, its plumes and paraphernalia could not help but lend logic to such strictures, particularly when these goods and services were bought, rented or hired with the widow's mite. Yet, at worst, 17th 18th and 19th century undertakers, like any other tradesmen, sold people what they demanded.

Burial and Sanitary Reform: While a segment of the clergy from the early 17th century on, demanded funeral simplicity in the name of religion, equally vigorous voices demanded it in the name of sanitation. For centuries, intramural burial in England had been accumulating the dead on small plots of ground within cities, until finally the resulting sanitary problem could not longer be ignored. In the cholera years of 1831-1833 some 31,000 deaths in England and 21,000 in Ireland compelled the establishment of a public health agency, and provided an opportunity for the use of the remarkable sanitation research abilities of Edwin Chadwick.[40]

In 1839, under the auspices of the Poor Law Commissioners, Chadwick began to investigate the condition under which the urban English worker lived, worked and died; and in 1842 he summarized the findings in his famous report on the *Sanitary Condition of the Laboring Population of Great Britain,*[41] the supplement to which *The Practice of Interments in Towns,* describes the burial customs of working people and the conditions of the interment of the dead. Summing up this report Finer writes:

The Report on Intra-Mural Interments, published at the end of 1843 was of all Chadwick's Reports the most grisly and revolting. There were descriptions of such places as Russell Court, near Drury Lane, where the ground, raised several feet by continuous burials was "a mass of corruption" which poisoned air and water alike; or that place in Rotherhithe where "the interments were so numerous that the half-decomposed organic matter was often thrown up to make way for fresh graves,

exposing sights disgusting, and emitting foul effluvia." There
were horrible descriptions of corpse wakes; of dead bodies remaining days and days before burial in the one room which
served the family for dining and sleeping alike; of children
sleeping, or trying to sleep, under the eyes of the dead man.
There were descriptions of child murders committed to realize
the moneys invested in the burial club. Chadwick had also to
describe the burial of corpses under the flags of the churches,
so that however well-coffined, "sooner or later every corpse
buried in the vault of the church spreads the products of decomposition through the air which is breathed, as readily as if
it had never been enclosed.[42]

Chadwick's recommendations were far in advance of his
time. He wanted all cemeteries "municipalized," and all
"trading cemeteries" abolished. Religious rites were to be
simplified and standardized. To prevent child murder for
insurance—all too common at the time,—he recommended
that a medical officer should be required to certify before
burial as to the fact and cause of death. In 1848, five years
after Chadwick made his recommendations, many of them
were incorporated into the Public Health Bill. But his strictures did not go unchallenged. Churchyard burial was not
unprofitable to the church, and some of the clergy objected
to his efforts to set up a nationalized cemetery in London.
The large cemetery companies which had been burying up to
20,000 dead per acre led the opposition. And the mid-century
English undertaker took umbrage at his damaging bill of
particulars.[43] The charges Chadwick made against the
London undertakers were chiefly two: In the first place, although there was intense competition for dead bodies, there
was no corresponding decrease in funeral costs. Quite the
contrary, costs were so high that a death in the family was a
virtual economic disaster. As a result, in greater London
over two hundred burial clubs flourished, a clear indication
of the need felt by the poor to spread the cost of burial over

a wide number of persons. These "Friendly Societies" as they became more formally organized were the forerunners of modern "industrial" insurance. The rates charged were relatively excessive, but on the weekly collection basis the overhead was high. Yet it was the best that the poor could afford.

Not only were undertakers competing with one another to the small advantage of their clients, but, as Lewis points out there were, in and about London, "at least a thousand, and perhaps as many as three thousand, lesser tradesmen— drapers, tailors, publicans (tavern keepers), carpenters, cab-inet-makers, upholsterers, auctioneers — who displayed the undertaker's insignia in hope of catching one or two orders a year."[44] Wherever these casual undertakers found a case, they were supplied by one of the principals of the trade, and in "the last analysis it was some sixty of the leading under-takers who performed the real service, the inferior agents merely interposing their unnecessary offices and stepping up the charges to allow for their own remuneration."[45] Under-takers also sought to work in close cooperation with the operators of burial clubs; worse, it was not exceptional for an undertaker to be president of a club.

If the sanitation movement produced no direct, significant changes in the operation of funeral establishments in Eng-land during the second half of the 19th century, it made its influence felt in reforms relating to existing burial grounds, and the prohibition of new cemeteries within cities. It was impossible, moreover, to apply stringent regulation to the place of burial without involving undertakers. In passing, it should be noted that in both England and Amer-ica the sanitation movement was in part responsible for the increased practice of cremation.[46]

Yet before the 19th century ended, in spite of the

failure of the sanitation movement directly and immediately to check the excesses of the feudal funeral among the poor, and to put an end to disorganized and duplicatory services among the trades engaged in preparing and burying the dead, burial custom and usage gave evidence of bringing order into the funeral trades and of sloughing off some of the pompous display and ceremonial inherited from the previous epoch. In his *Life and Labor of the People of London,* Booth suggests the degree to which the changes had taken place by the end of the century. In discussing the trades of London he points out that under the general category of "Funeral Furnishers and Undertakers," there were the subdivisions: "Coffin and Coffin Furniture Makers." "Funeral Furniture," and "Plume Makers." An employer might be either an "Undertaker," or "Funeral Furnisher," or both.[47] Booth makes it clear that the trade of undertaker was shaping itself into definite form, with subdivisions appearing as a consequence of the need for specialization and division of labor:

The Undertaker measures the dead body (though there are some who like to be measured while still alive), makes the coffin, or has it made, arranges with the cemetery authorities, provides the carriages and men, and accompanies the funeral to the grave. In all cases it is he who is the director of the funeral.

The funeral furnisher, on the other hand, where he is not also an undertaker, has no personal connection with the conduct of the burial. He may be a wholesale manufacturer, or a job master, providing the undertaker with coffins, carriages, and all the appurtenances of a funeral, or he may be a funeral-carriage master only. In London, the usual practice seems to be for those undertakers who have not enough business to keep a stable fully employed, to make or furnish the coffins and then to apply to the carriage master, known to the trade as a "Black Master," for the hearse, etc.

Coffins are made by "coffin-makers" who belong to this industry only, and do not overlap with either carpenters or cabinet
makers. A carpenter might soon learn to make coffins, but a
coffin maker could not turn to general carpentry.[48]

While coffinmaking in England has broken cleanly with
cabinet-making and carpentry on the one hand and with
undertaking on the other and has become an independent
trade, it has also ceased to be, as it was formerly, the central
symbol of the group of tasks related to burial. In place of it
is undertaking, emerging likewise into a distinct occupational type in which the personality of the undertaker, who
is the director of the death ritual, weighs heavily.

Booth also notes:

It is more important to have a strong, presentable man, with a
good suit of black clothes of his own, than a highly skilled work-
man. And further, respectful, and if possible, sympathetic manners, are especially necessary; for future orders depend much
on the satisfaction of present customers and their consequent
recommendations.[49]

In summary, the evidence points to the development in
England of a specific trade of undertaking far removed and
different from its dispersed beginnings in the seventeenth
century among lay "Jacks of all Trades" who sold funeral
goods and services . At the close of the 19th century the
rise of the undertaker, who gathered functions formerly
scattered over several trades into a unified single occupational task, was partly to be accounted for by the inability
of the church to keep authority over all aspects of the
burial of the dead; partly by the development of new
techniques of preservation by the anatomist, the surgeon and the chemist, together with the inability of these
workers to retain complete control over the funerary uses of

their discoveries; and partly by a changing social order, in which urbanization threw aside the funerary vestiges of the feudal system, but retained the "decent funeral" as a social axiom. This new type of funeral involved the erection of a "front," usually suggestive of a social status somewhat above the actual life position of the deceased or the bereaved and required, to an increasing degree, ceremonies of disposal directed by a person who could not only take charge of other funeral tasks but with skills beyond the competence of the average person organize and direct the funeral. In answer to popular demand the funeral undertaker made such services available for a fee. Thus the modern undertaker emerged in England, in the shape of a competitive occupational service specialty engaging in a trade primarily for pecuniary purposes.

In turning from this consideration of the development of the English undertaker to that of the American funeral director it is well for us to remember that there are, as we shall see, many good reasons for asserting that while there has been considerable cultural interchange between the two English-speaking countries there also has been much independent development. The American counterpart to the English undertaker developed against a social, economic, geographical, cultural and occupational background quite different in pertinent regards from that of England. To understand the differences in the end product it is necessary to understand the differences in the development processes. For this reason the next several chapters will move to the American scene and trace the history of funeral service in America from colonial times to our own day.

CITATIONS AND REFERENCES FOR CHAPTER IV
1. See Johnson, *op. cit.*, Chapter II.
2. Huizinga, *op. cit.*, p. 128.

3. See Leonardo, *op. cit.*, pp. 126-127; Mendelsohn, *Embalming Fluids, op. cit.*, p. 12.

4. Simon Mendelsohn, "Embalming from the Medieval Period to the Present Time," *Ciba Symposia* (published by the Ciba Pharmaceutical Products, Inc., Summit, N. J., May, 1944), pp. 1805-1812.

5. Mendelsohn, *Embalming Fluids, op. cit.*, p. 12.

6. *Ibid.*

7. C. J. S. Thompson, *The Quacks of Old London* (Philadelphia: J. B. Lippincott Co., 1929), pp. 322-324.

8. Sidney Young, *Annals of the Barber-Surgeons of London* (London: Blades, East and Blades, 1890), p. 112.

9. Leonardo, *op. cit.*, pp. 118-119.

10. Bradford, *op. cit.*, p. 27 *seq.*

11. Young, *op. cit.*, p. 33.

12. *Ibid.*, pp. 111-112.

13. *Ibid.*, p. 114.

14. *Ibid.*, p. 218. Bradford states that the act of 1511 for bade anyone to practice as a surgeon in London without the approval of the Bishop of London or the Dean of St. Paul's. See Bradford, *op. cit.*, p. 29.

15. Young, *op. cit.*, p. 331. Spelling in above four references varies as to editor Young's decision to use modern English, or the language of the period.

16. Note its use in Greenhill, *op. cit.*

17. Oswald Barron, *Shakespeare's England* (Oxford: At the Clarendon Press, 1916), p. 80 *passim.*

18. *Ibid.*, p. 81.

19. George C. Homans, *English Villagers of the Thirteenth Century* (Cambridge, Mass: Harvard University Press, 1941), pp. 391-393.

20. Bradford, *op. cit.*, p. 13.

21. H. L. Mencken, *The American Language*, Supplement I (New York: Alfred A. Knopf, 1945), p. 571.

22. Quoted from *Trivia* in John Ashton, *Social Life in the Reign of Queen Anne* (New York: Charles Scribner's Sons, 1925), p. 35.

23. Mencken, *loc. cit.*

24. See Chapter VI.

25. See Wilson and Levy, *op. cit.*, pp. 80-82.

26. See J. L. and Barbara Hammond, *The Bleak Age* (New York: Peguin Books, 1934), p. 226 ff.

27. Ashton, *op. cit.*, p. 38.

28. *Ibid.*

29. *Ibid.*, p. 36.

30. *Ibid.*

31. Ambrose Heal, *London Tradesmen's Cards of the XVIII Century* (London: B. T. Batsford, Ltd., 1925).

32. *Ibid.*, pp. 22, 61-62.

33. Ambrose Heal, *The Signboards of Old London Shops* (London: B. T. Batsford, Ltd., 1947), pp. 174-175, Plate XVCVI.

34. Quoted in Ashton, *op. cit.*, pp. 35-36.

35. For a further discussion of this function of the funeral director, see Chapters X and XIII of this work.

36. Greenhill, *op. cit.*, pp. vi, 177-179.

37. Robert Blair, *The Grave: To which is added Gray's Elegy [written] In a Country Church Yard. With Notes Moral, Critical, and Explanatory*, by G. Wright (London: Scatcherd & Whitaker, 1785).

38. *Ibid.*, pp. 14-15.

39. *Ibid.*, p. 15.

40. R. A. Lewis, *Edwin Chadwick and the Public Health Movement 1832-1854* (London: Longmans, Green & Co., 1952).

41. Sir Edwin Chadwick, *Report on the Sanitary Conditions of the Labouring Population of Great Britain* (London: W. Clowes and Sons, 1843).

42. Samuel E. Finer, *The Life and Times of Sir Edwin Chadwick* (London: Methuen & Co., 1952), pp. 230-231.

43. *Ibid.*

44. Lewis, *op. cit.*, pp. 70-71.

45. *Ibid.*, p. 71.

46. For a detailed account of the relation of the sanitation movement to the practice of cremation in contemporary England and America, see Robert W. Habenstein, *A Sociological Study of the Cremation Movement in America, op. cit.*, Chapters I-IV.

47. Charles Booth (ed.), *Life and Labor of the People of London*, 9 vols. (London: Macmillan and Co., 1895), vol. V, p. 205.

48. *Ibid.*, pp. 205-206.

49. *Ibid.*, p. 206.

Part Two:
Rise of American
Funeral
Undertaking

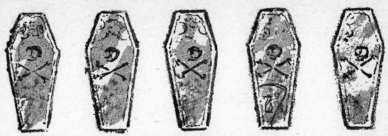

On the Death of Five young Men who was Murthered March 5th 1770. ~~~ By the 29th Regiment.

American Colonial Funeral Behavior

American Colonial Settlements were founded, in the main, by English speaking people seeking fortune, fame, freedom of religious organization, or simply, the chance to acquire a decent human existence. To this country they brought a body of beliefs and institutions, skills, arts and crafts—a social heritage which remains as basic substructure to the distinctive American mode of living.

Yet for many reasons, not the least of which was the impact of non-English speaking peoples on an emergent American culture, the New World society cannot be represented as a simple extension of the Old. Especially is this true with regard to funeral behavior, for although there are basic similarities, the modifications and developments in the organization of American funeral practices has led to a vastly different response to the problems of death and the disposal of the dead. Part of the task of developing a history of funeral service in America consists, then, in sketching out some of the more basically relevant ideological elements, socially inherited or acquired in new experience, which lie behind Colonial funeral customs.

Ideological Framework for Colonial Funeral Practices: The Virginia Colony founded in 1607 at Jamestown had as its underpinning a distinctly commercial motif; the impulse behind the Massachusetts Bay Colony, on the other hand, was primarily religious, although its charter was obtained from and underwritten by commercial interests. Interestingly enough the underwriters, in common language usage, were called "undertakers," and the commercial referent continued through most of the 17th century. Having no quarrel with the Established Church of England the Virginia Colonists incorporated it into their government where it remained, along integrated church-state lines, until after the Revolution. The Pilgrim Fathers, conversely, rejecting not only the Anglican but all other denominations and sects except their own creed, set up a theocracy which continued for well over a century. In neither case, however, was there any reason compelling the disassociation of death and the disposal of the dead from a sacred or religious context. On the contrary, as will be seen, death became one of the prime occasions for pulpit exhortations on the essential mortality of mankind and the need for more exemplary ways of living.

Although it can scarcely be argued that American funeral behavior took on distinctive characteristics through secularization, i.e., a disassociation of religious belief from the phenomenon of death, there were, nevertheless certain developments in the organization of religious beliefs which had either an immediate or eventual effect on the funeral practices of the colonists. One of these was the early Puritan disinvolvement of the *clergy* from certain ceremonial functions, including funerals. The Old World source of this usage is illustrated, for example by a section of *The Directory for the Publick Worship of God, agreed upon by the Assembly of Divines, at Westminster; examined and approved anno 1645, by the General Assembly of the Church of Scotland*, etc. presenting the following rule:

Concerning Burial of the Dead: When any person departeth this life, let the dead body, upon the day of burial, be decently attended from the house to the place appointed for public burial, and there immediately interred without any ceremony.[1]

And in an earlier instance the Independents in 1604 published at Amsterdam in *An Apologie or Defense of such true Christians as are commonly (but unjustly) called Brownists:*

. . . the celebration of marriage and burial of the dead, be not ecclesiastical actions appertaining to the ministry, but civil, and so to be performed.[2]

The general inclination of the ministry of the early New England Colonies was to avoid the "popish" error of saying prayers over the dead. Nevertheless, funeral sermons eventually were preached in church, starting about 1700, and later prayers were said in graveside ceremonies. A broader and more far-reaching development was the attempt by the colonists to shed their *legal* system of ecclesiastical law and to formalize the controls of the New World society by recourse only to common law, tempered by the inference that "if it isn't reasonable, it can't be good law."[3]

For England the story remained different. The ecclesiastical regulation of interment went unchallenged throughout the Middle Ages and the law of the clergy controlled burials and cemeteries in England without serious lay interference until the adoption of the English Burial Acts of 1855.[4] Thus, despite the fact that America had an English church for its first fourteen years, and that until the Revolution the Established Church was incorporated into the Virginia Colony, American courts at law have looked to 1607 for precedent in common law with regard to matters involving burial of the dead. Although the impulse of the colonists was generally to reject ecclesiastical law on principle, or because it did not fit all the exigencies of colonial existence, many canons specifically were brought into usage. This was the case with funeral practices. "Early American burial was in the churchyard," notes Jackson, "and though always yielding to temporal sovereignty, through the Colonial adherence to the equitable principles of the English common law, the commands of the church found their way into our law of burial."[5]

If ecclesiastical law was not in fact totally rejected by the colonists neither was it embraced in any organized, codified, or integrated form. The consequence of this avoidance seems to have been a lack of clear-cut definitions for mortuary behavior; and it is certain that the church controls of burial that existed in England were not mirrored in the colonies. The effect of this development on the rise of the American funeral undertaker will be noted later.

Two other large scale elements of Colonial ideology need to be pointed out. Both have a general reference to the rise of Protestantism: one looked to the realm of human action and was reflected in the special way of regarding one's work; the other centered around human reflection and found expression in theology and philosophy.

The terms "Protestantism" and "industriousness" have a close affinity for each other. Traditionally *hard* work, as well as good, has been an avenue of salvation for the Protestant; especially is this true in the teachings of Calvin, who interjected a commercial rationale into the theology he espoused.[6] Undoubtedly industriousness that had something more than a simple common sense basis was part of the English heritage of the early colonists. The almost compulsive nature of the industriousness of the colonists has since become legend. Hardship; disaster; decimation by plague, malaria, smallpox, or Indians; all or each of these could not keep the work of settling the New World from going on apace. Idleness was not only looked upon as a cardinal sin, it became a breach of law. For example, when the situation demanded it, Captain John Smith, the Founder of Virginia, might put men of noble birth to work in the cornfields with the humble but not ignoble hoe. The colonist was impelled by a moral, almost sacred sense of obligation to apply himself to his work. On the other hand such application yielded returns that could never be hoped for in the Old World. Three to five years bondage seems today a high cost of indenture, but to the colonist-to-be, in light of the potential *substantial* basis to the freedom he gained, the years in bondage could be almost negligible. Work, ownership, substance, and salvation all became parts of a unity of existence that made up life in the colonies, founded, as it were, upon the principle that held hard work to be akin to Godliness.

Industriousness to the New Englander, however, was a necessary but not sufficient cause for salvation. The state of one's soul was, in the end, an individualistic matter, and despite their industrious application to mundane affairs, these colonists were forced back again and again upon their own consciences in search for the righteousness of their acts. The uncertainty was no less relieved by the ministry whose sermons on hell-fire and damnation were scarcely calculated to lend peace of mind to the members of the congregation. The Southern Colonists, it might be noted, fared somewhat better. Their theology did not keep them mentally poised on the brink of a flaming abyss in which sinners were cast at death by the hands of an angry God. But to the New Englander the search for consolation in the contemplation of the Great Beyond was indeed a difficult one, and it is for this reason that the Puritans were forced into the realm of philosophical speculation and the examination of philosophical ideas.

By the turn of the 18th century urbanization and its concomitant secularization, and the rapid expansion of industry and trade had begun to weaken the theocratic organization of the New England Colonies. Theological and philosophical speculation gave way, to some extent, to the pursuit of man's worldly goods as an end in themselves. Nevertheless, until the outbreak of the Revolution, common law, industriousness, and an uncertain, fearful relation to the Almighty formed the major elements of the Puritan character. And it is against this ideological backdrop that the figures of funeral practice and the specific death customs take on comprehension and become more than items of incidental interest.

Burial Practices: Early New England recognized death as a natural, inevitable, commonplace reality. "The grave was as familiar as the cradle, and the New Englander never saw any reason to ignore or disguise it."[7]

Old New England graveyards were familiar places to the living as well as resting places for the dead. Gravestones not merely identified the bodily remains, but through inscriptions in the form of epitaphs, served as a medium of popular literary expression. As Wallis points out "The manner of expression may be ribald and ridiculous, pompous and lugubrious, eloquent, or serenely simple."[8] Yet the fact remains that the dead were not alienated from the living in Colonial times; rather, the unlettered inscriptions spun a thin thread of remembrance to the unique personalities of those who had passed on. Andrews says:

Sickness, death, and the frailties of human life were perennial subjects of conversation and correspondence, and few family letters of those days are free from allusion to them. From infancy to old age death took ample toll—so great was the colonial disregard for laws of sanitation, so little the attention paid to drainage and disinfection. The human system was dosed and physicked until it could hold no more.[9]

Death was never denied. In fact, the most persistent symbol of early New England days was probably the skull and cross bones. Shepard has offered the view that as the Colonial period advanced, the slow change from the death-skull to the winged cherub on the gravestone indicates the expulsion of the basic doubts of the early Puritan as to immortality and the development of the hope for an ascent into paradise.[10] Samuel Sewall, a ranking judge in the Massachusetts Bay Colony, kept a diary covering the last quarter of the 17th century and the early decades of the 18th. This record is regarded by American historians as one of the most revealing documents of the time, performing for the American scene much the same function that *Pepys' Diary* performs for the English. With almost punctilious morbidity Sewall notes the daily deaths in Massachusetts, and with gruesome regularity he parades Indian raids and accidents, killings, hangings, and natural deaths. But it was not these but sickness which was most feared in the small settlements. Epidemics of smallpox struck again and again. Of Sewall's prodigious family of fifteen children, more than half died in infancy or childhood. It was not unusual for a colonist to lose a wife or two or three, and remarriages were the order of the day.[11] Alice M. Earle, patient chronicler of New England social customs, sums up her studies of Colonial burial thus:

One cannot keep from being impressed, when studying almanacs, diaries and letters of the time, with the strange exaltation of spirit with which the New England Puritan regarded death. To him the thoughts of mortality were indeed cordial to the soul. Death was the event, the condition . . . of which he constantly spoke, dreamed and thought; and he rejoiced mightily in that close approach, in that sense of touch with the spiritual world. With unaffected cheerfulness he yielded himself to his own fate, with unforced resignation he bore the loss of dearly loved ones, and with eagerness and almost affection he regarded all the gloomy attributes and surroundings of death.[12]

The earliest New England burials were models of simplicity and quiet dignity. Not wishing to commit what they considered the "popish error" of saying prayers over the dead, the mourners merely followed the coffin and stood silently as the grave was filled. Lechford, describing a 17th century funeral, remarks:

At burials nothing is read nor any funeral sermon made, but all the neighborhood or a goodly company of them come together by toling the bell, and carry the dead solemnly to his grave and then stand by him while he is buried. The ministers are most commonly present.[13]

Although funeral sermons may have been preached in church *after* the burial, by the end of the 17th century the English practice of having a funeral sermon said over the body in the meeting house or in the church was again observed. Sewall notes critically the choice of text and emphasis of numerous funeral sermons, remarking that at the burial of one Goodman Pilsbury that "Mr. Richardson Preached from I Cor. 3:21, 22 going something out of 's Order by reason of the occasion, and singling out those

Words *Or Death*."[14] Following the English fashion, early New Englanders wrote laudatory verses which they attached to the bier, or hearse. The latter consisted of a framework which supported the coffin and upon which candles were placed; it had little resemblance to the modern vehicle in which the casket is transported. The early Colonial press found fruitful occupation in the printing of broadside sheets and pamphlets. Black-bordered and dismal, these were often crudely and gruesomely decorated with the macabre symbols of death: skull and crossbones, scythes, coffins, hour glasses, all seeing eyes, skeletons, and winding sheets. (See Plate 20.) Edification found rich meat in funerals. Funeral sermons for leading men of the colonies were often printed, as were the exemplary confessions made by criminals prior to their execution. It may be truthfully said that the whole social complex surrounding death and burial of the New Englanders was richly portrayed in popular verse, with imagery as grim in many ways as that of the Death Dance period of the Middle Ages. Executions of criminals were public; and ministers worked feverishly with the doomed, exhorting them to confess at the gallows. The first stammered words of repentance were greeted with cheers by the assembled citizenry.

Mourning took on an extensive social character. Rings, scarves, gloves, books, verses and products of needlecraft all were used by the colonist in the process of paying tribute to the dead. The custom of making gifts to the living to announce funerals was brought to the colonies from England where it had been part of the feudal funeral. In its new home it flourished in the late 17th century and survived through most of the 18th century. Earle remarks that "in the case of a funeral of any person prominent in State, Church or Society, vast numbers of gloves were given away."[15] The quality of those distributed at the same funeral varied with the social status or the degree of blood relationship or friendship that the recipient had with the bereaved. The excesses which developed in this funerary gift making became evident in the fact that at the funeral of Governor Belcher's wife in 1736, over 1,000 pairs of gloves were given away.[16] As towns expanded through peaceful trade and growing industry, funerals took on what seemed to many a wanton lavishness. Judge Sewall, who appreciated keenly the pleasures of funeral ceremonies and recorded carefully his gifts of rings, scarves and gloves in his diary, was led to remark on the extravagance of the early 18th century ceremonies; and, in 1721, 1724 and 1742 the General Court of Massachusetts passed laws prohibiting "Extraordinary Expense at Funerals."[17] A letter to the *Boston Evening Post*, June 20, 1737, (see Figure 2), points to sumptuary legislation passed by the General Assembly of the Province of Massachusetts as early at 1651.

For persons of importance the funeral glove collection grew to be of considerable size. When Andrew Eliot, minister of the North Church in Boston, tallied his take for thirty-two years he found that he had received two thousand nine hundred and forty pairs of funeral gloves. These were in addition to funeral rings and scarves. In less than fifty years Sewall received fifty-seven mourning rings. Earle gives other instances showing the drain which this gift expense made upon families:

We can well believe the story of Doctor Samuel Buxton, of Salem, who died in 1758, aged eighty-one years, that he left to his heirs a quart tankard full of mourning rings which he had received at funerals; and that Rev. Andrew Eliot had a mugful. At one Boston funeral in 1738, over two hundred rings were given away. At Waitstill Winthrop's funeral sixty rings, worth over a pound apiece were given to friends. The entire expense of the latter-named funeral—scutcheons, hatchments, scarves, gloves, rings, bell tolling, tailor's bills, etc., was over six hundred pounds. This amounted to one-fifth of the entire estate of the deceased gentleman.[18]

So strongly ingrained was this peculiar fashion that even pauper funerals demanded the distribution of a minimum number of pairs of gloves.

To the Publisher of the Boston Evening Post.

SIR,

I Think you cannot better serve your Country, than by publishing at this Time, the following Act, which was passed by the General Assembly of the Province in the Year 1651. against *Extravagance in Apparel*, which shews the tender Regard our Forefathers had for the People under their Care. When I consider the prodigious Excess Persons of all Ranks are run into, in Diet, Cloaths and Houshold Furniture, the vast Number of Coaches, Chairs and Chaises that are daily seen about our Streets, and flying in and out of Town, both by Day and Night, with the Expences attending such Frolicks, the pernicious and (to many) ruinating Expences at Funerals, especially among People of the lower or middling Class, together with the great Number of able bodied and healthy (tho' lazy) Artificers who are constantly employed in selling Limes, Lemons, &c. about the Town, and whose Time might be more profitably employed in some honest Labour; I say, when I consider these Things, with numberless other Extravagances, which we are run into of late, I cannot but wonder that our wise and pious Legislators have not laid us under some restraint, and made us in some measure happy and frugal even against our Wills. If you favour me with the Publication of this, I may perhaps furnish you with further Hints upon some of the above-mentioned Heads, especially that of *Funeral Expences*, which is grown to such a monstrous and pernicious height, that I may safely affirm, *it has* ruined *its thousands.* I am, Sir yours, &c.

Figure 2. Early Colonial Letter to Editor, Protesting Extravagances, Especially at Funerals.

Despite the growing concern over burial expense and the legislative attempts to curb the practice of spending a sizable portion of the estate for gifts at funerals, the colonists persisted in making the disposal of the dead an occasion for celebration. Perhaps the epitome of extravagance was reached at the funeral of Andrew Faneuil in 1738 when three thousand pairs of gloves were given away and over eleven hundred persons accompanied the funeral cortege.[19]

A typical New England town funeral at the middle of the 18th century would reveal the following basic pattern.[20] Upon death neighbors, or possibly a nurse, if the family were well to do, would wash and lay out the body. The local carpenter or cabinet-maker would build the coffin, choosing a quality of wood to fit the social position of the deceased. In special cases "Coffin furniture," i.e., metal decorations, imported from England would be added to the coffin. Relatives and friends within a few days travel would be notified immediately, for it was not customary to let the body lie in state. If the weather were warm the body, as Sewall put it, would be "embowelled and put in a Cere-Cloth" (alum, pitch, or wax-soaked sheet), and, of course rings, scarves or gloves would be distributed to all those invited to the funeral.

Funeral services would begin in the church with prayers and sermon said over the pall-covered bier. Ministers looked upon funerals as an occasion to deliver some of their most inspired remarks; it was not uncommon for their funeral sermons to be printed and circulated among the public, with the conventional black-border and with skull and cross-bones on the cover. (See Plate 21.)

The procession to the grave was on foot, with under-bearers actually carrying the coffin on the bier, while pall-bearers, men of dignity and consanguinity, held the corners of the pall. If the distance was far, fresh under-bearers were used, and in any case the procession went slowly and was marked by numerous rest stops.

Memento Mori

A Neighbour's TEARS

Sprinkled on the Duſt of the Amiable Virgin,

Mrs. **Rebekah Sewall,**

Who was born **December** 30. 1704. and dyed
ſuddenly, **Auguſt** 3. 1710. Ætatis 6.

Heav'ns only, in dark hours, can Succour ſend ;
And ſhew a Fountain, where the ciſterns end.
I ſaw this little One but t'other day
With a ſmall flock of Doves, juſt in my way :
What New-made Creature's this ſo bright ? thought I
Ah ! Pity 'tis ſuch Prettineſs ſhould die.
Madam, behold the Lamb of GOD ; for there's
Your Pretty Lamb, while you diſſolve in Tears ;
She lies infolded in her Shepherd's Arms,
Whoſe Boſom's always full of gracious Charms.
Great JESUS claim'd his own ; never begrutch
Your Jewels rare into the Hands of Such.
He, with His Righteouſneſs, has better dreſs'd
Your Babe, than e're you did, when at your breaſt.
'Tis not your caſe alone ! for thouſands have
Follow'd their ſweeteſt Comforts to the Grave.
Seeking the Plat of Immortality,
I ſaw no Place Secure ; but all muſt dy.
Death, that ſtern Officer, takes no denial ;
I'm griev'd he found your door, to make a trial.
Thus, be it on the Land, or Swelling Seas,
His Sov'raignty doth what His Wiſdom pleaſe.
Muſt then the Rulers of this World's affairs,

Portion of Colonial Broadside

PLATE 20

Broadside of Funeral Hymn, Showing Burial
Dress and Coffin

PLATE 21

In many towns there were no gravediggers; consequently neighbors supplied the necessary labor. Usually the sexton would have dug the grave and tolled the bell to announce the funeral. Unlike his English cousin the Colonial sexton exacted a fee for both services. In some towns, such as Salem, these fees were regulated by municipal ordinance. The funeral service at the grave was simple, a brief prayer, followed by the ritual commitment of the body to the earth. The filling of the grave marked the formal end of the funeral ceremonies.

Samuel Sewall gives us a word description of an upper class funeral:

Friday, Feb. 10, 1678/8. Between 4. and 5. I went to the funeral of Lady Andros, having been invited by the Clark of the South Company. Between 7. and 8. Lychus (Lynchs), [i.e., links or torches] illuminating the cloudy air. The Corps was carried into the Herse drawn by Six Horses. The Souldiers making a Guard from the Governour's House down the Prison Lane to South-meetinghouse, there taken out and carried in at the western dore, and set in the Alley before the pulpit, with Six Mourning Women by it. Was a great noise and clamor to keep people out of the House, that might not rush in too soon. I went home, where about nine a'clock I heard the Bells toll again for the Funeral. It seems Mr. Ratcliffs Text was, Cry, all flesh is Grass. The Ministers turn'd into Mr. Willards. The Meeting-House full, among whom Mr. Dudley Stoughton, Gedney, Bradstreet, &. 'Twas warm thawing wether, and the wayes extream dirty. No volley at placing the Body in the Tomb. On Satterday, Feb. 11. the mourning cloth of the Pulpit is taken off and given to Mr. Willard. My Brother Stephen was at the Funeral and lodged here.[21]

But there was more to the Colonial funeral than the ritualized disposal of the dead. Relatives and friends having travelled various distances needed to be fed and housed; the neighborhood was always involved, and in keeping with the general mood of exhilaration (undercut with latent apprehension), festivity, even frolic, was mixed with the gloom of the funeral ceremonies. The serving of liquors was as universal as it was generous. Funeral bills were often top-heavy with the expense of strong beverages. A typical example is a bill for the mortuary expenses of David Porter, of Hartford, who was drowned in 1678:[22]

By a pint of liquor for those who dived for him 1s
By a quart of liquor for those who brot him home.......... 2s
By two quarts of wine and one gallon of cyder to jury
   of inquest... 5s
By 8 gallons and 3 quarts wine for funeral...........L1-15s
By barrel cyder for funeral.............................16s
1 coffin...12s
Windeing sheet...18s

In addition to drink, food in vast quantities was supplied. At the funeral feast of Calie Dawes in Boston, 1797,[23] rum, wine, beer, gin and brandy were served along with a dinner that featured beef, ham, bacon and fowls for the funeral baked meats, supplemented by fish, oysters, 150 eggs, peas, onions and potatoes followed by cheese, fruit and sweetmeats. The total funeral cost was $844.00—a small fortune for the time, and equivalent to between five and ten thousand dollars in modern purchasing power.[24] The cost of wine at one funeral in Virginia came to more than four thousand pounds of tobacco. In the light of such expenditure it is not surprising that more than one colonial assembly passed laws designed to keep the friends of the deceased from eating and drinking the widow and orphans out of house and home.[25]

In discussing this period Hawthorne notes the expressive release which these funeral feasts gave:

They were the only class of scenes so far as my investigation has taught me, in which our ancestors were wont to steep their tough old hearts in wine and strong drink and indulge in an outbreak of grisly jollity. Look back through all the social customs of New England in the first century of her existence and read all her traits of character, and find one occasion other than a funeral feast where jollity was sanctioned by universal practice. Well, old friends! Pass on with your burden of mortality and lay it in the tomb with jolly hearts. People should be permitted to enjoy themselves in their own fashion; every man to his taste—but New England must have been a dismal abode for the man of pleasure when the only boon-companion was Death.[26]

Andrews makes the astute observation that a funeral was both a social function and a public event, and therefore drew crowds of people, children among them. These frequently acted as pallbearers. The Puritan conscience could not suffer to remain unexploited an opportunity to teach. It was hoped that the little ones "might be impressed with the significance of death as the inevitable end of a life of trial and probation."[27]

In New York and Virginia the pattern of funerals differed somewhat. Dutch funerals took place three or four days after death and were accompanied by extensive and important ceremony. The best parlor was used for funerals, prayers were said, and the pall covered coffin and bier were carried to the churchyard by twelve pallbearers. After interment the procession returned to the house where food, tobacco and drink were distributed while festivities became the occasion. A "Monkey spoon," so-called by an irreverent jest, possibly because the crudely executed Apostle intended for the handle resembled more the animal than the saint, was often given to each pallbearer. (See Plate 23.) Ceremonies were under the direction of the licensed official called "aanspreecker," and, in the main funerals were attended only by the adult males.[28]

Early Virginia funerals, like horse races and weddings, were important occasions. Bruce has pointed out the lively nature of the eating and drinking which went along with the funeral ceremonies.[29] Often a "furious fusilade" preceded the festivities, although at different times the law did not permit such waste of powder and shot. As was the case with the New Englanders, the consumption of liquor was often enormous and likely to impoverish the decedent's estate. "The expenses incurred in burying John Griggs, of York County," notes Bruce, "were estimated at sixteen hundred pounds of tobacco. The provision of food and drink for the persons present on this occasion included turkeys, geese, and other domestic poultry, a pig, several bushels of flour, twenty pounds of butter, sugar and spice, and also twelve gallons of different kinds of spirits."[30]

The excesses in eating and drinking and firing of guns were deplored by many. Some made provision in their wills for more decorous behavior at their funerals, including one Colonel Richard Cole who provided mourning clothes for all those present at his funeral, but nothing in the line of food, drink and fusilades.

Even in so solemn a matter as a funeral, informal controls served the Colonial fathers no better than they served their ancestors, who used the medieval waking of the dead as an excuse for carousing. Drinking at funerals exceeded the minimum bounds of propriety traditionally associated with Christian burial and violated the ceremonial dignity that quickly marked funerals as soon as the colonies became stable and prosperous. In order to prevent the waste of powder at drinking frolics, and to forestall false alarms, the Virginia Assembly in 1655, forty-eight years after the first settlement

An ELEGIAC
POEM,

On the DEATH of that celebrated Divine, and eminent Servant of JESUS CHRIST, the late Re:erend, and pious

GEORGE WHITEFIELD,

Chaplain to the Right Honourable the Countess of Huntingdon, &c &c.

Who made his Exit from this transitory State, to dwell in the celestial Realms of Bliss, on LORD's-Day, 30th of September, 1770, when he was seiz'd with a Fit of the Asthma, at Newbury-Port, near Boston, in New-England. In which is a Condolatory Address to His truly noble Benefactress the wor thy and pious Lady Huntingdon,—and the Orphan-Children in Georgia; who, with many Thousands, are left, by the Death of this great Man, to lament the Loss of a Father, Friend, and Benefactor.

PHILLIS, a Servant Girl of 17 Years of Age, belonging to Mr. J. Wheatley, of Boston :—And has been but 9 Years in this Country from Africa.

HAIL happy Saint on thy immortal throne !
To thee complaints of grievance are unknown ;
We hear no more the music of thy tongue,
Thy wonted auditories cease to throng.
Thy lessons in unequal'd accents flow'd !
While emulation in each bosom glow'd ;
Thou didst, in strains of eloquence refin'd,
Inflame the soul, and captivate the mind.
Unhappy we, the setting sun deplore,
Which once was splendid, but it shines no more ;
He leaves this earth for Heaven's unmeasur'd height :
And worlds unknown, receive him from our sight ;
There WHITEFIELD wings, with rapid course his way,
And sails to Zion, through vast seas of day.

When his AMERICANS were burden'd sore,
When streets were crimson'd with their guiltless gore !
Unrival'd friendship in his breast now strove :
The fruit thereof was charity and love
Towards America——couldst thou do more
Than leave thy native home, the British shore,
To cross the great Atlantic's wat'ry road,
To see America's distress'd abode ?
Thy prayers, great Saint, and thy incessant cries,
Have pierc'd the bosom of thy native skies !
Thou moon hast seen, and ye bright stars of light
Have witness been of his requests by night !
He pray'd that grace in every heart might dwell :
He long'd to see America excel ;

A greater gift not GOD himself can give :
He urg'd the need of HIM to every one ;
It was no less than GOD's co-equal SON !
Take HIM ye wretched for your only good ;
Take HIM ye starving souls, to be your food.
Ye thirsty, come to this life giving stream :
Ye Preachers, take him for your joyful theme :
Take HIM, "my dear Americans," he said,
Be your complaints in his kind bosom laid :
Take HIM ye Africans, he longs for you ;
Impartial SAVIOUR, is his title due ;
If you will chuse to walk in grace's road,
You shall be sons, and kings, and priests to GOD.

Great COUNTESS ! we Americans revere
Thy name, and thus condole thy grief sincere ;
We mourn with thee, that TOMB obscurely plac'd,
In which thy Chaplain undisturb'd doth rest.
New-England sure, doth feel the ORPHAN's smart ;
Reveals the true sensations of his heart :
Since this fair Sun, withdraws his golden rays,
No more to brighten these distressful days !
His lonely Tabernacle, sees no more
A WHITEFIELD landing on the British shore :
Then let us view him in yon azure skies :
Let every mind with this lov'd object rise :
No more can he exert his lab'ring breath,
Seiz'd by the cruel messenger of death.
What can his dear AMERICA return ?

Facsimile Portion of Broadside Elegy, Written by a Slave Girl

PLATE 22

Monkey Spoons, Used by Early Dutch Colonists

PLATE 23

in the colony, ordained that no persons should "shoot guns at drinking, marriages and funerals only excepted."[31]

Social Change in Late Colonial America: During the 18th century, Colonial society was subjected to serious upheavals resulting from two revolutions, one political and the other basically economic. The culmination of the political revolution was the war of liberation from England; yet the roots of this conflict were in the less obvious commercial and industrial revolution that gave America its urbanism, industrial manufacturing centers, and the outlines of a social class system. Both revolutions, however, had distinct consequences for Colonial modes of mortuary behavior.

Bridenbaugh makes clear the relationship between the breakdown of traditional Puritan controls and the changing standards of living which came about with increasing urbanization:

As the towns approached maturity, urban moral standards began to diverge widely from those of the countryside. Within the towns, also, wealthy aristocrats, as in other societies, increasingly pursued a manner of living radically different from that of middle and lower classes. The center of morality was shifting, and wealth and urban conditions brought about new and more elastic codes of conduct . . .

In every town the profits of peaceful trade led to great display, which seemed to many to be mere wanton extravagance. Aged Samuel Sewall observed with alarm the "Affectation and the use of Gayety, Costly Buildings, Stilled and other Strong Liquors, Palatable, though expensive Diet, Rageth with great Impetuosity, and . . . (lead) to Sensuality, Effeminateness, Unrighteousness, and Confusion." Elaborate and costly funerals were said to be ruining those who could ill afford the luxury of "gloves, scarfs, and scutcheons." . . . Similar complaints against display and declining moral standards emanated from New York and Charles Town.[32]

As commercial relations with England became strained by the Embargo Acts there was a consequent reduction of trade between the colonists and the homeland. Taking a hitch in their economy the colonists among other things began to limit themselves to what mourning paraphernalia they had on hand; when this wore out there was a noticeable diminution in the use of clothes, scarfs, gloves and other items of mourning which may have been imported. Weeden observes:

The economy enforced to avoid importations from Great Britain brought in sensible changes in the management of funerals and their attendant ceremonies. The full suits worn by all the connections were dispensed with, bands of crepe for the gentlemen and black ribbons for the ladies being substituted. The gloves, formerly being distributed generally, were now only presented to the "pall-holders."[33]

Although earlier sumptuary laws had been ineffective in curtailing extravagant display and gift-giving at funerals, these and more recent legislative measures had, in light of the seriousness of the situation, a greater urgency to them. In 1788 there appeared in the *Massachusetts Sentinel* a reminder by "The Inspectors of the Police" that a law, established before the Revolution, specifically referred to the display of mourning, and to refresh the minds of the public of Boston the law was hereby reprinted as follows:

TO PREVENT EXCESS AND VAIN EXPENSE IN MOURNING, ETC. It is hereby ordered, that in future no scarfs, gloves or rings shall be given at any funerals in this town, nor shall any wine, rum or other spirituous liquor be allowed or given at, or immediately before or after any funeral in this town, under pain that the person or persons giving, allowing or ordering the same shall respectively forfeit and pay the sum of *twenty shillings* for each offense.

And it is further ordered, that whatever male person shall appear or walk in the procession of any funeral in this town with any new mourning or new black or other new mourning coat or waistcoat or with any other new black apparel, save and except a black crepe around one arm, or shall afterwards, on account of the decease of any relation, or other person or persons, put on and wear any other mourning than such piece of black crepe around one arm, shall forfeit and shall pay the sum of *twenty shillings* for every day he shall put on and wear or appear in the same.

And no female, of whatsoever degree shall put on, or wear or appear at any funeral in this town, in any other mourning or new black clothes whatsoever other than a black hat or bonnet, black gloves, black ribbons and a black fan, on pain of forfeit and pay the sum of *twenty shillings;* and also forfeit and pay a like sum of *twenty shillings* for every day she shall at any time, or after such funeral, put on or wear or appear in such new black clothes as or for mourning, other than black hat, or bonnet, black gloves, black ribbons, and a fan as aforesaid.[34]

In 1790 the town of Salem published in the papers some regulations about funerals, among which were specific items referring to sextons and undertakers:

For each Tolling of the Bell 8 d.

The Sextons are desired to toll the bells only four strokes in a minute.

The undertakers service in borrowing Chairs, waiting upon the Pallholders and warning the Relations, etc. to attend 8.

B. Doland and B. Brown are appointed by the selectmen to see that Free Passages in the Streets are kept open.

The appearance of these and similar regulations and restrictions on matters pertaining to mourning and the conduct of funerals indicates, for one thing a gradual weakening of the theocratic tradition of government, and the early performance of specific funeral tasks in the context of secular, or non-religious activities. Concurrent with the Revolutionary War, it appears, came the shift to simpler mourning customs, the inclusion of funeral practices more specifically under legislative scrutiny, and the proliferation of funeral tasks as specialists in other occupations. The latter development will become the subject matter in the next chapter. Meanwhile, a word has to be said further about the general socio-economic trend of the 18th century, and its bearing on colonial mortuary behavior.

With the growth and prosperity of commerce and trade, the seaport towns developed into flourishing trade centers, comparable to the port cities of England. "Within these towns," Bridenbaugh notes, "merchant grandees accumulated riches so rapidly as to raise their position above that of other townsmen."[35] The upshot of this process was the formation of social classes, based not upon lineage, but upon established commercial success, occupations, and social function. Symbols of class position were sought and found in the style and size of mansion, the mode of attire, form of transportation (carriage transportation was a la mode), etiquette, manners, customs and world outlook. The beautifully appointed town house, the exquisite furniture, furs, jewels and silks, coaches, slaves, governesses, riding horses, and the like—all were combined to insure social stratification in town life of the eighteenth century colonists. As the years of peaceful prosperity deepened, so did the class barriers. Yet mobility from one class to another was never categorically blocked, as would be the case in a caste system. Laborers, seafarers, servants, even slaves could aspire to and often gain higher socio-economic class position. Likewise the *nouveau riche*, by affecting the symbols and the demeanor of the established "upper" class, might find social acceptance at a higher level, although the consolidation of such position might take several generations.

The relevance of such socio-economic development in Colonial America to the history of funeral service becomes clear when we try to make intelligible the difference between the festivities and spontaneous expression of human impulse of the early Colonial funeral, with the status of the dead *reflected* by the degree of display and the level of expense, and the later town-burials where the funerals *affected* a class position that was seldom anchored in traditional acceptance. The element of class pretension marks the significant difference between the religion-permeated but socially uproarious funeral of the 17th century Colonial America, and the status-conscious but religious-tinctured funeral of the century following.

It is evident that the early American colonies differed on the role of the Established Church of England. Massachusetts Bay Colony rejected it, to set up an independent theocracy headed by its own framework of social and political organization. Singularly enough, ecclesiastical law was generally rejected in the colonies in favor of a more flexible common law, tempered by common sense; but some canon law was brought into usage in the realm of the burial of the dead. Nevertheless, as indicated earlier, there was no consistent body of law and precedent to inform and direct Colonial funeral behavior, as was the case in England.

English industriousness, with its roots in the Protestant ethic of making a calling out of one's work, served to energize the colonists and keep them alert to the possibilities of bettering their social and economic lot—bounded of course by Puritan middle-class morality and religious humility. Although burial practices varied in different settlements, colonial funerals generally combined three functions: sociability, religiosity, and the reaffirmation of the established social status of the deceased. Although the crisis of the Revolution led to specific changes in mourning customs, the more fundamental and persisting change was toward the use of funerals as an instrumentality to express status aspirations and pretensions by the socially class-conscious members of an expanding urban society.

Although it is possible that undertakers operated in the American Colonies in the 17th century, Habenstein was able to uncover very little evidence in the operations at that time of such specialists who "made their living as funeral directors, called themselves by that name, and were popularly recognized as such, as was the case in England from about 1685 on."[36] A fragment of evidence seeming to support their claim to existence in the early 18th century is to be found in Earle, who, speaking generally of the Colonial period, remarks that "the undertakers could charge but eight shillings for borrowing chairs, waiting on pallbearers and notifying relatives to attend."[37] More likely she is referring to the funeral regulations of Salem made public in 1790.

In an effort to discover the earliest appearance of the undertaker in America as a member of a specific, recognized occupation, Habenstein examined copies of all the extant American city directories from the eighteenth century, and most of those for major cities from the first half of the 19th.[38] The earliest directory printed in America was for the city of New York in 1786.[39] Although each citizen was identified as to occupation, no one was listed in this directory as an undertaker; several sextons are designated. In a section of the same volume, captioned "Annals of New York City For the Year 1786" the funeral of the Honorable Abner Nash is described. The procession included the clerk of the church from which he was buried, sixty charity boys, clergy from other churches, his physician, pallbearers, relatives, the sexton; but no undertaker.

The evidence that funeral undertaking was emerging as a distinct occupational specialty becomes apparent in the first quarter of the 19th century when public announcements by undertakers first became common. Prior to this time the few newspaper advertisements telling of both male and female tradesmen had been scattered and infrequent. The richest data to indicate the emergence of the new occupational group were derived from the early registries and directories of New England and Atlantic Coast towns and cities.

It will be seen in the following chapter how these various factors combine to give rise to the American funeral undertaker of the 19th century—an occupational specialist—organizing within the scope of his operations the major tasks necessary to the care and disposal of the dead.

CITATIONS AND REFERENCES IN CHAPTER V

1. Massachusetts Historical Society, *Proceedings,* Vol. 17, pp. 168-169.

2. *Ibid.,* p. 169.

3. Gerald W. C. F. Johnson, *Our English Heritage* (Philadelphia and New York: J. B. Lippincott Co.), 1949. p. 156 *seq.*

4. Percival E. Jackson, *The Law of Cadavers,* 2nd ed. (New York: Prentice Hall, 1950), p. 22.

5. *Ibid.,* p. 27. Only secular law regarding burial prevails in America today.

6. The reciprocal relation of religion and commercial pursuits has been brilliantly analyzed by the German economic historian Max Weber, in *The Protestant Ethic and the Spirit of Capitalism,* trans. Talcott Parsons (London: George Unwin, 1930).

7. Zephine Humphrey, *A Book of New England* (n. p. Howell Sosken, 1947), p. 211.

8. Charles L. Wallis, *Stories on Stone; A Book of American Epitaphs* (New York: Oxford University Press), 1954, p. xi.

9. Charles M. Andrews, *Colonial Folkways,* Vol. VIII of

The Chronicle of America Series, ed. Allen Johnson, 50 Vols. (New Haven: Yale University Press, 1918), p. 92.

10. Presented by Humphrey, *op. cit.*

11. Samuel Sewall, *Sewall's Diary*, ed. by Mark Van Doren (New York: Macy-Masius, 1927).

12. Alice M. Earle, *Customs and Fashions in Old New England* (New York: Charles Scribner's Sons, 1894), p. 386.

13. Quoted by Earle, *ibid.*, p. 364.

14. Sewall, *op. cit.*, p. 39.

15. Earle, *op. cit.*, p. 374.

16. William B. Weeden, *Economic and Social History of New England 1620-1789*, 2 vols. (Boston and New York: Houghton Mifflin Company, 1890), Vol. II, p. 538.

17. See Carl Bridenbaugh, *Cities in the Wilderness*, A volume of the Ronald series in History, ed. by Robert C. Binkley and Ralph H. Gabriel (New York: The Ronald Press 1938 and Alfred A. Knopf 1955), pp. 387, 412, *passim.*

18. Earle, *op. cit.*, p. 376.

19. *Ibid.*, p. 374.

20. *Ibid*, Chapter XV. See also Andrews, *op. cit.*, pp. 92-95.

21. Sewall, *op. cit.*, pp. 54-55.

22. Earle, *op. cit.*, p. 370.

23. Somewhat fancifully reconstructed in Fairfax Downey's *Our Lusty Forefathers* (New York: Charles Scribner's Sons, 1947), pp. 209-219, based on an account given in the *Proceedings of the Massachusetts Historical Society*, vol. 54.

24. *Ibid.*

25. Habenstein, "The American Funeral Director," *op. cit.*, p. 86.

26. Andrews, *op. cit.*

27. *Op. cit.*, pp. 94-95.

28. An interesting and more complete account of early Dutch funerals is found in Mrs. John King Van Rensselaer's *The Goede Vrouw of Manan-ha-ta* (New York: Charles

Scribner's Sons, 1898), pp. 54ff.

29. Philip Alexander Bruce, *Social Life of Virginia in the Seventeenth Century* (Richmond, Va.: Whittet and Shepperson, 1907), pp. 218-222.

30. *Ibid.*, 220-221, quoted from *York County Records*, Vol. 1675-84, p. 87, Va. St. Libr.

31. Edward Eggleston, "Social Life in the Colonies," *The Century*, XXX (July 1885), p. 393.

32. Bridenbaugh, *op. cit.*, p. 387.

33. Weedon, Vol. II, *op. cit.*, p. 740.

34. Henry M. Brooks, *The Days of the Spinning Wheel in New England* (Boston: Tickner and Company, 1886), pp. 95-96.

35. Bridenbaugh, *op. cit.*, p. 411.

36. Habenstein, "The American Funeral Director," *op. cit.*, p. 95.

37. Earle, *op. cit.*, p. 380.

38. This research was undertaken at the Library of Congress, repository of the best collection of city directories and registries.

39. The New York Directory for 1786, with Description of New York in 1786 by Noah Webster (New York: Trow City Directory Co., 1786).

Early American Funeral Undertaking

If we limit the meaning of the term "funeral directing" to an occupation which 1.) provides a set of tasks for the care and disposal of the dead; 2.) takes the form of a personal service, and operates as a business enterprise, then it is clear that in this limited, modern sense funeral directing as an occupation was born in America during the 19th century. However, as with most emerging vocations, funeral directing did not spring forth full-grown, but in its earlier stages evolved by slowly adding to itself specific funeral tasks previously carried out generally and largely by other occupations. In this chapter, in dealing with the early funeral undertaker in America, we shall be concerned, then, in presenting the various classes of tradesmen who were in some way involved in the disposal of the dead at that period when "funeral undertaking," the predecessor of modern funeral directing, was emerging as a newcomer among the occupations of the early 19th century.

Tradesman Undertakers: From England, where since 1685, if not before, undertaking had been an occupation involving the furnishing of the paraphernalia of mourning in the style of an earlier feudal society, America received very few persons dedicated solely to such trade. On the frontier one man was as good as another and hereditary titles, privileges and social classes did not make much sense. The fact that such social class distinctions were less likely to be introduced into the colonies worked against transplanting the English "Dismal Trader" into America.

The only place where such persons might find root would be in the Colonial towns, but historical records do not show "undertakers," except as underwriters of commercial ventures, in the colonies until past the middle of the 18th century. One of the first of such was, somewhat surprisingly, a woman who in *The New York Journal or General Advertisers* of January 7, 1768, announced:

Blanch White, Upholsterer and Undertaker, from London, on the New-Dock, next Door but one to Alderman Livingston's; Makes all kind of Upholstery-Work, in the newest Fashions and on the most reasonable Terms; Likewise all kinds of Field Equipage, Drums, Etc. Funerals furnish'd with all things necessary and proper Attendance as in England.

Mrs. White begs leave to acquaint the Ladies and Gentlemen that she washes all sorts of Gauze Laces, caps, on the Wires; Silk Stockings, etc. in the neatest Manner, she having a proper frame and a Stove for bleaching. Flounces and Trimmings for Ladies Robes, neatly pinck'd; also Shrouds and Sheets.[1]

Another evidence of the English influence in early funeral undertaking in the New World comes not from the Colonies, but from Montreal, Canada, where in the 1820 directory of "Merchants, Traders, and Housekeepers" one finds again a woman who combined the role of upholsterer and undertaker:

> Mrs. Benjamin Birch, Funeral Undertaker,
> 20 Campeau Str. Forster & Fry
> Upholsterers & Undertakers, Cabinet
> Makers, Furniture Show Rooms

Interestingly enough the husband of Mrs. Birch is listed at the same address as "Shoemaker."

In the Colonial period, cabinet-making was often found with upholstering, and to this combination undertaking occasionally was added. Such was the case of William B. Purves, who advertised himself in a Charleston, S. C., city directory in 1835 as "Cabinet Maker, Upholsterer & Undertaker." Yet it was more frequently the case that cabinet-makers, chairmakers and the like first supplied coffins only; and then over a period of time extended the range of their functions from producer of a necessary material article, i.e. the coffin, to that of provider of non-material personal services. These craftsmen were not likely to have been English trained in the undertaker's trade; possibly only a few knew the skills of being "in attendance" and had mastered the art of furnishing all manner of funeral paraphernalia. But the rapid expansion of America and the absence of clear and uniform church regulations over funerals provided an opportunity for craftsmen to develop these skills as added specialties to their current occupations. Moreover, such actions were squarely in keeping with the spirit of industry and enterprise characteristic of colonial society.

As early as 1799, coffinmaking, as part of a cabinet-making business was combined by Michael Jenkins in Baltimore with funeral undertaking. Jenkins, already a well known

furniture maker, set up a partnership with Thomas Combs
and advertised in the *Federal Gazette and Baltimore Daily
Advertiser*, May 10, 1799:

> Cabinet and Chair Manufactory
> Combs and Jenkins
> No. 17 Water Street between
> Calvert and South Streets

At about the same time, Jenkins was apointed coroner for the
city of Baltimore; and, shortly after, he extended his activities to include undertaking.[2] Records of the business indicate
that in 1799 coffins were made and sold, with one charged to
the account of Wm. Jenkins, a brother of Michael:

                                                    L S D
Aug. 10, for a Mahogany Coffin 7 10 0

Although the partnership was dissolved in 1802, Michael
Jenkins continued cabinet and furniture making with the
undertaking business until his death September 8, 1832.[3]

The record of Jacob Knorr's establishment is a remarkable
one. In 1761 a German Quaker, Jacob Knorr, set up a two-
story joiner's shop in Germantown, Penna., and in addition
to his cabinet maker's business, and lumberyard, made coffins upon demand. (See Plate 24.) He continued to operate
in these various capacities until his death in 1804, at which
time his two sons, George and Jacob Knorr, Jr., the executors under his will,[4] sold the property, as it was unlawful
for executors to purchase property in which they were interested financially. In 1807 it was transferred back to Jacob
Knorr, Jr., and in a series of transactions the property eventually came into the hands of Samuel Nice, the nephew of
George Knorr. Until this time the owners continued the
functions which Jacob Knorr had started well before the
outbreak of the Revolutionary War. Old bills running back

before 1800 indicate the production of coffins as the major "undertaking" in providing goods and services to the bereaved. Samuel Nice continued to operate the concern until 1865 when he sold the property to B. Frank Kirk, his son-in-law, and William Johnson Nice. They in turn tore the original buildings down and set up a new undertaking establishment dedicated solely to the business of caring for the dead. Although these buildings have again been torn down and newer, more spacious ones built, the new buildings are on the same site. Likewise, though the original family name connected with the business has gone, there has been a line of kinship relation running through the operation of the coffin-shop-turned-undertaking-turned-funeral-directing establishment for the past one hundred and ninety-four years. At what point, however, the undertaking aspect of the establishment actually involved more than the making of a coffin cannot be determined. Nevertheless, as an example of the early combination of cabinet-making and coffinmaking enterprise there is very likely no similar business with such a long pedigree. (See Plate 24.)

The combination of cabinet-making with various undertaking functions appears with some frequency during the earlier half of the 19th century, these composite businesses springing up in the period of western expansion following the War of 1812. (See Plates 25, 28.) A furniture and cabinet-making business was established in Vincennes, Indiana, by Andrew Gardner in 1816, the same year that Indiana was admitted to statehood. Fourteen years later the cabinet-making firm of H. B. Deusterberg and Sons was founded in the same town; and through the course of years both these firms shifted over to funeral undertaking as their major occupational function. These firms, along with the W. D. Diuguid firm (established 1817) in Lynchburg, Virginia; J. J. Shepherd and Sons (established 1827), in Pembroke, Massachusetts; and the Boston firm of J. S. Waterman, cabinet-maker, (founded 1832) make up a partial list of early cabinet makers who added undertaking to their trade. Although the firms named do not exhaust the list of early cabinet-making and furniture business firms that began undertaking early in the 19th century, they have been included specifically to illustrate the fact of persistence of operation, as all of them in 1954, were still in business under the name of the founder.

Other cabinet-making undertakers added further services. Thomas Chartres let it be known in the 1829 Baltimore City Directory that besides selling cabinet furniture and making cabinets, "Funerals attended on the shortest notice, and Hacks and Hearse provided, if required." Obligingly, Andrew Oakes, cabinet-maker, undertaker, and coroner of Kings County, informed the public in the Brooklyn City Directory of 1843 not only of the practice of these various crafts and functions, but that lost children might safely be left with him until the parents could be found. The occupational advances made by Sherman Blair and revealed by the New Haven, Conn., city directories are instructive:

1840. . . . . Sherman Blair, Cabinet Maker
1841. . . . . Sherman Blair, Cabinet manufacturer
1846. . . . . Sherman and R. Blair, Cabinet manufacturer and undertakers
1853. . . . . Blair's Cabinet Furniture, Upholsterers and undertakers

Another tradesman-undertaker variation appears somewhat later as the "Furnishing undertaker"—an undertaker who not only offered his services on occasion at funerals, but who also furnished other undertakers with necessary supplies and paraphernalia. The appearance of the furnishing undertaker took place concurrently with the emergence of the small combination operator, the cabinet maker, carpenter, sexton, or liveryman who performed funerals as a side line and who would not be likely to have the necessary supplies and paraphernalia at hand. (See Plate 26.)

Figure 3. Trade Card of Furnishing Undertaker,
Post-Civil War Period

At the same time, once established, the furnishing undertaker served to encourage more persons to enter the field of undertaking as newcomers would no longer need be concerned about the initial outlay for the merchandise and equipment needed to start in business. Henceforth it became even more possible for individuals with limited facilities and limited business expectations to open a new establishment. The fact that all the essentials of a funeral could now be "furnished" made irrelevant the particular craft, skill, or business of the person who wanted to become an undertaker. It seems to have been the historical function of the furnishing undertaker, then, in supplying all the funeral-undertaker's material needs, to have introduced a dynamic force for change in the nature of funeral service practice. Not only was the field opened wider to new practitioners, but *personal service, unhampered by obligations to craft or trade could become a central preoccupation of the undertaker.* But before this was to happen, other classes of persons were already involved in the performance of mortuary tasks. One of these was the keeper of hacks and carriages.

As cities grew and the material resources of the townfolk increased, livery stable keepers were faced with an expanding demand for carriages for funerals. Foot processions and the carrying of coffins by hand were not only losing their appeal, but because of the increasing distances, were becoming burdensome and onerous, and the rental of carriages, buggies and other vehicles for funerals became more general. Well before 1750 those in Boston who had social class pretensions could rent coaches and black horses for funerals from Samuel Bleigh and Alexander Thorpe.[5] But by the first quarter of the 19th century, the use of carriages and horse drawn hearses began to spread more generally throughout the population. In the 1824 City Directory for Baltimore we find the proprietor of a livery stable adding funeral undertaking functions to his vocation.

Soon others were to follow, and in the following several decades certain phrases in the advertisements became standardized, especially "will attend personally and take proper measure that a decent order be preserved." (See Figure 28, Chapter 9.) When a business changed hands the new proprietor would often continue the identical advertisement of his predecessor, substituting only his own name.

a) Knorr Undertaking Establishment, Germantown, Pennsylvania, Mid-19th Century

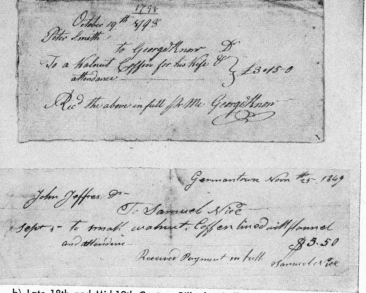

b) Late 18th and Mid-19th Century Bills, for Coffins and "Attendance"

PLATE 24

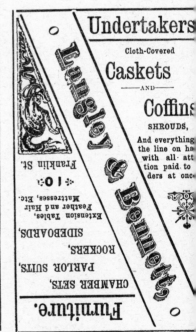
Advertisements of Mid-19th Century Tradesmen & Undertakers and Their Combination Establishments

PLATE 25

It was not unknown for a man of enterprising spirit to attempt to provide the full round of funeral services, each as a part, however, of one of the several trades he would ply. The advertisement in the Providence Directory of 1856 is instructive:

GARDNER T. SWARTZ

Livery Stable Keeper, Undertaker

Tomb Proprietor and Dealer in ready-made coffins, of all kinds and at all prices, near the corner of Pine and Dorrance—Street

Providence

Should Swartz have "tolled the bell and dug the grave" his "undertaking" would have run the gamut of all necessary functions, short of religious services, for proper mid-19th century care of the dead.

The period was not without its occupational oddities, John Dobbin rented hearses and hacks in Baltimore. (See Plate 27.) The town messengers of Charleston, Mass., in 1838, and Cambridge, Mass., in 1848, were also funeral undertakers. Moreover, if Andrew Oakes could take care of lost children as well as dead bodies, so could Z. Cotton "undertake," pull teeth, and frame pictures.

Performers of Personal Service: Well before funeral undertaking in America had evinced any positive signs of developing into a distinct occupation, the care of the dead in early America had been in the hands of those who rendered such attention as a personal service. Friends and neighbors were the first to come to the aid of the bereaved, and, as has usually been the case in small community life, certain members, quite often adult females, would develop a rough skill in laying out the dead, or, over a period of years, would have given assistance often enough to feel an informal responsibility to offer their services in cases of community or neighborhood deaths.

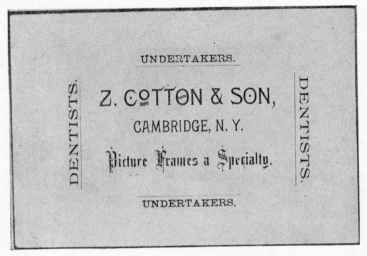

Figure 4. "Professional" Card, Mid-19th Century

The first advance toward connecting such informal personal services with a recognized occupation was seen in the tendency for the family nurse or nurse-governess to assume a slightly more formal responsibility for the preparation of the dead for burial. Judge Sewall writes in 1685:

Having read to my Wife and Nurse out of John; the fourteenth Chapter fell now in course, which I read and went to Prayer: By that time had done, could hear little Breathing, and so about Sunrise, or little after, he fell asleep, I hope in Jesus, and that a Mansion was ready for him in the Father's House. Died in Nurse Hill's Lap. *Nurse Hill washes and layes him out* . . . Thorsday, Decr. 24th 1685. We follow Little Henry to his Grave: Governour and Magistrates of the County here, 8 in all, beside my Self,

Eight Ministers, and Several Persons of note . . . I led Sam., then Cous. Savage led Mother, and Cousin Dumer led Cous. Quinsey's wife, he not well. *Midwife Weeden and Nurse Hill carried the Corps by turns,* and so by Men in its Chestnut Coffin 'twas set into a Grave (The Tomb full of water) between 4 and 5. At Lecture the 21. Psalm was Sung from 8th to the end.[6] (Italics the authors'.)

Nurses also practiced healing arts outside of particular families and cared for the sick in the small communities, and again in the case of a death they extended their personal services to include laying out the dead. Sewall notes, for example, that "This day one of my Shirts goes to lay out a Man dead at Nurse Hurds of this (small pox) distemper, being a Stranger."[7]

Although the mid-wife often shared with the nurse many of the tasks involved in burials, yet by the end of the 18th century, laying out the dead in the larger cities had become a specialty in its own right. The Philadelphia City Directory for 1810 added to the section listing occupational specialists such as "Doctors," "Mid-wives" and "Bleeders with Leeches," the category of "Layers Out of the Dead."

West Susan, 131 n. 3d   tween Vine & Race

LAYERS OUT OF THE DEAD.

Bliss Susannah, 47 Vine	January H. back 39 Arch
Bulfinch Mary, 26 Columbia avenue	Norton Rebecca, back of 17, Sterling alley
Field — 137 Spruce	Powell R. back 36 n. 3d
Fiss Deborah, 205 n. 8th	Robbins Eliz. 153 Vine
Graff Rebecca, 192 Vine	Walker Widow, 14 Sterling alley
Hutman — 4th ab. Coats'	
Heyler Catherine, 66 n. 3d	Wolbert Catherine 193 St. John
Jacobs — 22 Appletree alley	

Figure 5. Females Who Performed Undertaking Tasks, Philadelphia Directory, 1810

In 1810 three persons were listed under such heading. All were likewise listed, however, in the general registry as "nurses." Looking back through the general registry sections of directories one finds Rebecca Powell listed in 1801 as "Widow, layer-out-of-the-dead." An earlier case of a female undertaker, although this evidence is less satisfactory since there is no heading attached, finds Sarah Collister submitting a bill for different funeral tasks performed in conjunction with the burial of a Miss Mary Rynelander, Sept. 10, 1784.

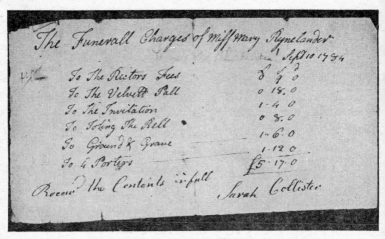

Figure 6. Late 18th Century Funeral Bill, Showing Participation by Female in Arranging for Services

Despite their early appearance in the emerging occupation of undertaking, women became less conspicuous in such endeavors as the 19th century got well under way. As the number of services expanded and funerals involved a wider range of tasks to be performed, and as undertaking began increasingly to reflect the spirit of business enterprise, other categories of tradesmen, craftsmen and functionaries came to dominate the occupation.

Religious Functionaries: Churchyard and church cemetery burial, though not universal, continued until the 19th
century to be the major mode of sepulture in America as
well as in England. Likewise the church caretaker, or sexton, has always been associated with churchyard burial
and the care of the cemetery. The sexton in America,
however, faced with incompletely defined laws of sepulture,
the growing magnitude of cemeterial care as burial grounds
expanded, and the inducements of business enterprise, found
opportunities to extend his mortuary functions far beyond
those of his British counterpart. Consequently, at the beginning of the 19th century to the conventional "toling of
the bell" and "digging of the grave" such new undertaking
tasks as laying out the body, being "in attendance," directing the procession, and, later, furnishing undertakers with
the merchandise and paraphernalia of funerals were taken
over by the sextons.

Apparently by 1800 there was an expanding market for
sextons, full or part time, in New England, and it may well
have been those who went into sexton's work from some
other trade who incorporated undertaking functions into
the bundle of tasks they were already performing. At least
the evidence of the Boston city directories points in such
direction, for by tracing back through the general registers
of earlier years from 1818 when sextons were listed separately as town officers, and forward to 1834 when "undertakers" were first listed as town officers we can build
occupational histories that follow the pattern of craftsmen to
sexton, to undertaker. Thus, Thomas Murray in 1807 was a
tobacconist; in 1818, sexton; and in 1834, an undertaker.
John Law was a cordwainer in 1796; in 1807, a sexton;
and 1817 still a sexton. Records run out at that point on
him. But nearly fifty years of occupational history are reflected in the record of Samuel Winslow who is listed first

in 1796 as housewright; in 1807 as housewright and sexton; in 1818 as sexton; in 1834 as undertaker, and in 1843 still as undertaker, although the general registry indicates he has not given up sexton's work altogether. William Cooley, sexton of Brattle Square church, took up undertaker's work in the 1840's and continued both functions, but by 1849 he had established a coffin warehouse (see Plate 27), and within a decade after had given up sexton's work to function as undertaker and proprietor of the coffin warehouse.

One of the most notable of the earlier sexton-undertakers was the Reverend Stephen Merritt who began his undertaking business in 1846, with the first entry on his books being August 1, 1846. In addition to the undertaking tasks he was cartman, assistant captain of the watch, and a lighter of the oil lamps. He was also an assitant foreman of the Mazeppa Engine Company No. 48; an assessor; and spent his evenings at the Eighteenth Street Episcopal Methodist Church where he was the sexton. Again we have an example of undertaking as a sideline or specialty, in this case along with a profusion of "specialities."[8]

Other cases of simple combination of sexton-undertaking became numerous as the 19th century gets well under way. Brooklyn in 1840 had W. B. Disbrow, sexton-undertaker; Joseph Miller of the same city three years later advertised himself in the city directory as sexton and undertaker and gave the address of his "warehouse." Before the century was half over, all the major cities of America, with the possible exception of Baltimore, had sexton-undertakers. By that time many had become large scale furnishing undertakers, such as Isaac Brown who advertised in the City Directory of New York, 1852-53:

> BROWN, ISAAC H., Sexton of Grace Church and general furnishing undertaker—coffins of all kinds and everything

requisite for funerals always on hand. Interments procured in all the public cemeteries in or out of the city . . . Orders left at his residence . . . at any hour of the day or night will be promptly attended to.

A final point on sexton-undertakers refers to the prerogative they held over burial in the churchyards under their care. Until William Ensign, one of the first "independent undertakers" of Paterson, New Jersey, shortly after 1850 took his case to the law courts, sextons had controlled the permits to bury in churchyards and church cemeteries. Such monopoly on sepulture obviously had its advantages for sexton-undertakers and may have provided another reason for their rapid expansion in numbers during the first half of the 19th century.

Municipal Officers: There is some indication that municipal concern with the burial of the dead occurred at a very early period in Colonial history. Landauer notes that one specialty connected with funerals was the "Inviter to Funerals," who actually may have called personally upon those expected to attend. In New York City in 1684, John van Gelder was "approved by the court of mayor and alderman" as "Inviter to funerals." For all who shall employ him he is to "comport himself Civally."[9] The same authority in discussing two of these public officials, notes that they were licensed, were to receive equal profits and were obliged to attend the burial of the poor without charge. By 1715 the Common Council had a specified set of charges running from "eight to eighteen shillings according to the age of the deceased." That this public monopoly of the function of inviting to funerals was not a disregarded statute is evidenced by the fact that in 1755 a suggested reform made much of the fact that violation of the ordinance was punishable by a fine of forty shillings.[10]

Early American funeral undertakers sometimes found themselves members of town officialdom, charged with duties pertaining to public health and sanitation. By the nature of his work the undertaker traditionally has been expected to have the technical skills and knowledge qualifying him for the role of coroner—and this specialty in fact has remained in close affinity to the undertaker's work for more than a century. Several of the earliest funeral undertakers, such as Michael Jenkins of Baltimore, Maryland, and Andrew Oakes of Brooklyn, New York, were coroners. Yet there were funeral undertakers in New England who as municipal officers functioned, among other things, as the *town* undertaker. The city directory of Charlestown, Massachusetts, for example in 1838 in an advertisement lists:

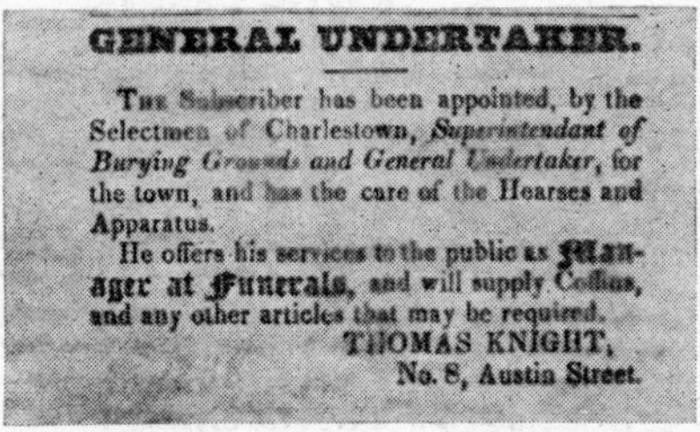

GENERAL UNDERTAKER.

THE Subscriber has been appointed, by the Selectmen of Charlestown, *Superintendant of Burying Grounds and General Undertaker,* for the town, and has the care of the Hearses and Apparatus.

He offers his services to the public as **Manager at Funerals,** and will supply Coffins, and any other articles that may be required.

THOMAS KNIGHT,
No. 8, Austin Street.

Figure 7. Charlestown, Mass.
Town Undertaker, 1838
Advertisement, City Directory

Often the undertakers would be town health officials appointed by the mayor, as in Boston in the 1830's. In different towns their status varied, however, from superintendent of all mortuary necessities, city registrar of deaths, down to city messenger. One, for example, Hollis Chaffin, at Providence, Rhode Island, who in 1856 was one of the town's official undertakers, ran an old peoples' asylum, and

CHAS. W. COMPTON,

Funeral Furnishing Rooms,

No. 148 MARKET STREET,

Opposite Insurance Buildings,

Where a large assortment of

Ready-made Coffins of various Styles and Prices

can be furnished at the shortest notice.

COFFIN PLATES NEATLY ENGRAVED.

ALSO,

BURIAL DRESSES, CAPS, &c.,

OF NEAT AND SUITABLE PATTERNS.

Having enlarged my former Stock to 16 Coaches, some the most expensive in this City, also new and elegant Hearses suitable for all ages, enables me to have the most extensive facilities in conducting the Undertaking business in a reasonable and satisfactory manner.

ALSO, MY SUPERIOR

IMPROVED PATENT CORPSE PRESERVER,

ARRANGED SO THAT BODIES CAN BE SEEN AT ALL TIMES WHILE UNDER PRESERVATION.

UNDERTAKERS SUPPLIED AT WHOLESALE.

W. V. W. VREELAND.

(Successor to TOLLES & VREELAND,)

WHOLESALE COFFIN WAREROOMS,

AND GENERAL FURNISHING

UNDERTAKER'S

ESTABLISHMENT,

125 Market Street, (up stairs.)

COFFINS OF ALL KINDS,

ALSO,

SHROUDS AND DRESSES,

AND ALL THINGS PERTAINING TO THE BUSINESS CONSTANTLY ON HAND, WHICH WILL BE SOLD AT REDUCED RATES, ALSO,

FIRST CLASS HEARSES AND COACHES

FURNISHED.

---

326   BURIAL CASKETS.

W. W. ROBERTS,

UNDERTAKER,

12 and 14 Pratt St.

Hartford, Conn.

Manufacturer and Dealer at Wholesale and Retail in

Burial Caskets,

INVENTOR and PATENTEE of the

New Round Top Rosewood Caskets,

and of several new designs in Rosewood and Walnut.

ALL KINDS OF

Caskets, Coffins, Shrouds, Caps,

and everything in my line of business furnished at low prices.

HEARSES furnished for Funerals.

All orders promptly attended to by night or day.

SAMUEL PECK,

FURNISHING

UNDERTAKER,

L. B. NEWTON, Practical Assistant.

56, 58 AND 60 HIGH ST., NEAR CHAPEL.

Burial   Caskets

Always on hand, of my own make, and of the most desirable patterns suited to all classes.

The Stein Patent

Cloth and Velvet Covered Caskets.

New and novel in construction. We have also in stock of our own manufacture

GLOBE DRAPED AND PLAIN PATENT CASKET,

Robes, Shrouds, Habits, Linings, Etc.

Mostly of our own designs, and can make at short notice any special orders with the most elaborate finish.

We are now prepared at all hours, by day or night, to furnish everything pertaining to the laying out and burial of deceased persons, giving special attention to preserving and retaining the natural appearance, with or without the use of ice. My assistant, having had long experience, cannot fail to give satisfaction to the friends of deceased persons, relieving the family as much as possible from care and anxiety.

Please call and examine new style Caskets, especially the "Elm City," (patent applied for) just completed, note prices, and see the improvements being made, then, if called upon to select for friends, you can act understandingly.

NIGHT BELL, WITH PERSON ALWAYS IN ATTENDANCE,

A share of the public patronage solicited.

MANUFACTURER AND DEALER IN

Undertakers' Goods.

THE TRADE SUPPLIED ON LIBERAL TERMS.

Telegraph dispatches promptly attended to.

Furnishing Undertakers Advertisements. Term "Coffin" Changes to Casket Between 1860 and 1870 in Many Such Ads.

PLATE 26

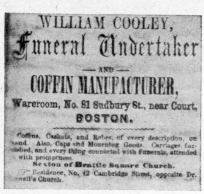

WILLIAM COOLEY,

Funeral Undertaker

— AND —

COFFIN MANUFACTURER,

Wareroom, No. 81 Sudbury St., near Court,

BOSTON.

Coffins, Caskets, and Robes, of every description, on hand. Also, Caps and Mourning Goods. Carriages furnished, and every thing connected with Funerals, attended with promptness.

Sexton of Brattle Square Church.

Residence, No. 42 Cambridge Street, opposite Dr. well's Church.

a) Undertaker, Manufacturer, and Sexton. Note Early Use (1849) of Term "Casket"

CALEB SYMMES, JR.

FUNERAL UNDERTAKER,

AND

TOWN MESSENGER,

May, 1838. **JOINER STREET.**

b) Undertaking as Part Time Work

R. FREDRICK,

UNDERTAKER OF FUNERALS

AND

CHAIR MAKER,

No. 179 NORTH GAY STREET

Opposite the Engine House, sign of Gilt Coffin

BALTIMORE.

c) Early Advertisement Indicating Use English Style Trade Sign by American Undertaker

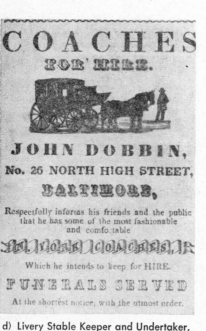

COACHES

FOR HIRE.

JOHN DOBBIN,

No. 26 NORTH HIGH STREET,

BALTIMORE,

Respectfully informs his friends and the public that he has some of the most fashionable and comfortable

Hacks, Coaches, &c.

Which he intends to keep for HIRE.

FUNERALS SERVED

At the shortest notice, with the utmost order.

d) Livery Stable Keeper and Undertaker, Baltimore, 1847

JOHN PEAK & SON,

FUNERAL UNDERTAKERS

Attend to any duty connected with their profession at the shortest notice. At their

Warerooms, 146 Friend St., and 1184 Washington St

MAY BE FOUND THE

LARGEST ASSORTMENT OF COFFINS & CASKETS

IN THE CITY.

Also, Grave Clothes, of all Sizes and Qualities

All orders left at Warerooms, or at Home, 72 Green Street, or at 36 Union Park Street, will be promptly attended to.

JOHN PEAK. JOHN H. PEAK.

e) Advertisement Showing Use of Term "Funeral Undertakers," Boston, 1873

PLATE 27

kept the city pound! In many New England towns and cities it was the practice to bring funeral undertaking under the supervision of the City Registrar whether or not he would be the town undertaker. All bills for services and merchandise would be itemized on a form provided by the city and approved by him. (See Plate 29.)

Summarizing, the *occupation* of undertaker, specifically named as such and accepted in popular usage, appeared in America in the first half of the 19th century. Although in the latter part of the 18th century one or several who had formerly been engaged in the undertaking field in England might have been practicing in the colonies, it is doubtful if the newly developing colonial society offered substantial footing for what was in England an established trade. Rather, out of the circumstances of the reformed nature of early Colonial religious values, the rudeness of the early settlements and the rise of norms that stressed community controls and the values of mutual aid, the functions of undertaking were first spread out in various ways among neighbors, relatives, clergy, craftsmen, and nurses or family attendants.

The distinctive character of American undertaking as we know it today is a consequence of a conjunction of circumstances peculiar to Colonial life, not the least important of which was the assumption of undertaking functions by other established occupations and offices. Thus the woodworker who in the earliest Colonial times made a coffin upon demand, as society and economic opportunity expanded about him, found that it made economic sense to turn a part of his shop into a wareroom or coffin warehouse. The sexton, too, found that in addition to tolling the bell and digging or supervising the digging of the grave, he could direct the funeral arrangements and provide materials and equipment which were more and more in general demand. Similarly, the proprietor of hacks and coaches found that funerals, in a land where distance was no object, often involved rather extended journeys and that the *order* of the funeral procession could not simply be left to chance or individual discretion. Thus it was a short step from furnishing a hearse or coach for funeral use to the furnishing of other funeral paraphernalia and to assuming a processional directing function. On the other hand one of the earliest functionaries to whom one of the most sacred tasks, laying out the body, was first delegated, i.e., the nurse, in a male-dominated society could find small justification for extending her function to include placing the body in a coffin, conducting the funeral ceremonies, organizing the procession and leading the last rites, Among Colonial customs there was only small precedent for female services or trade functions, although female undertakers were no novelty in England. Moreover, the "occupational jump" required to extend one's tasks from laying out the body to such functions as listed above seems far greater than was necessary to be made by sexton, cabinet-maker, and liveryman.

E. L. Devore enriches the bald summary with a few vivid details:

The burial of the dead as a distinct and separate business is of comparatively recent origin or necessity. Many of you can remember when a ready-made coffin was an unheard of thing. At that time when a death occurred, the family of the deceased called in their most intimate friend, to whom they left the arrangements for the funeral. He would go to a cabinet-maker or carpenter and together they would work all night by candlelight preparing a coffin. The ordinary one was made of pine and covered with alpaca. When something better was wanted it was made of walnut or cherry, rubbed with beeswax and polished with a hot smoothing iron.

Early Combination Business — Note Spelling of "Undertaker"

PLATE 28

Boston Jan. 26th 18__

Miss. E. A. Doe,

To N. P. WHITNEY, Undertaker, D__

For burial of Emma B. Doe aged 68 years

At Woodlawn Mass,

COFFIN
WAREHOUSE,
19 BLOSSOM STREET.
Residence, 48 Poplar Street.

COFFINS AND TRIMMINGS CONSTANTLY FOR SALE.

GRAVE CLOTHES,
OF VARIOUS QUALITIES.
Bodies preserved in ice, in the best manner possible.

Coffin Plates Engraved.

For services at the House,———	$
" placing corpse in the Coffin,	1.50
" carrying corpse and depositing the same in the Tomb or Grave, including assistance and 2 horse 5 miles,	10.00
" carrying corpse into Church,	
" opening and closing Tomb,	
" lighting Cemetery,	
" use of Pall,	.25
" digging Grave feet deep,	
" extra charge for frost,	
" disinterring and removing bodies, &c.	

Approved for $ ——

$ 11.75

City Registrar

To one coffin with handles & plate   24.20

To one black tibet robe — —   12.00

Cash for Receiveing Tomb —   15.00

$ 62.95

Receed Paym't

C. V. P. Whitney
By
W. T. W.

Boston Funeral Bill, Itemized on Form Supplied by City Registrar

PLATE 29

When the coffin was brought to the house, if the deceased was a female the ladies took charge of the preparation of such, as dressing, placing in the coffin, etc; and if a man, the men performed the same offices. The farm wagon answered for a hearse. I have heard it said that in one part of this state that the coffin containing the remains of a child was generally carried by this friend on horse-back, on a pillow placed on the front of the saddle. In one of the adjacent counties the first hearse ever seen had only two wheels. The body was about the shape of a "Boyd grave vault" and was drawn by one horse, it being led by some one riding alongside. As the country became more thickly settled the cabinet makers began to make coffins "to order" and take charge of funerals, and step by step they advanced until they became known as "undertakers" as well as furniture dealers. In the cities these men gradually limited their business to undertaking.[11]

In America, then, before 1859 we find that undertaking had taken on the characteristics of a service occupation with a set of tasks and functions organized into a pattern of behavior toward the dead that basically included the laying out, the coffining, and the transporting of the body to the grave. Around these central functions, certain auxiliary services, such as the furnishing of paraphernalia of mourning, i.e., clothing, emblems, remembrances, etc., were, to more or lesser degree, included. The role of the clergy was important; the clergyman supplied the funeral sacred ritual, and gave spiritual comfort to the bereaved. The first half of the 19th century is therefore crucially important in the evolution of the modern funeral director, because this period witnessed all the basic undertaking functions being gathered and organized under a conventionally recognized name the "funeral undertaker," or more simply and commonly, the "undertaker."

CITATIONS AND REFERENCES IN CHAPTER VI

1. *The Arts and Crafts in New York 1726-1776* (New York: Printed for the New-York Historical Society, 1938), pp. 141-142.

2. C. R. Francis, "Funeral Directors Since 1799" *The Embalmers Monthly*, July 1935 reprint, collection of the NFDA, Milwaukee, Wis.

3. *Ibid.*

4. Photostatic copy of this will is in the collection of the NFDA, Milwaukee, Wis. Other evidence was made available by Kirk & Nice, Undertakers, Germantown, Pa.

5. Bridenbaugh, *op. cit.*, p. 412.

6. Sewall, *op. cit.*, pp. 28-29.

7. Sewall, *op. cit.*, p. 96.

8. "Stephen Merritt Burial Company Memorial," pamphlet found in the Bella C. Landauer Collection of the New-York Historical Society. The firm is currently in operation.

9. Bella C. Landauer, "Some American Funeral Ephemera," *The New-York Historical Society Quarterly*, Vol. 36, April 1952, pp. 222-223.

10. *Ibid.*, pp. 223-224.

11. Speech by E. L. Devore. Archives of the NFDA, Milwaukee, Wis., n.p., n.d.

Coffins, Burial Cases and Caskets

How much time, energy, emotion, and materials a group of people, be it family, community, or nation, will spend on the funerals and disposition of their dead will vary by geographical area, historical period, and to a much lesser extent, by level of material wealth. Five thousand years before Christ the early Egyptians buried their dead in simple graves at the east end of their villages. A few thousand years later a high proportion of the energies of their elaborate civilization was taken up in the care, preservation, and disposal of the dead. Today, however, Egyptians have relatively simple burials in comparison with those of three and four thousand years ago. The mere passage of time guarantees nothing about the burial customs of peoples. Nor does geographic location. Americans spend more money on funerals than do their

Latin American neighbors, although the latter spend much more time in observing mourning ceremonies. Moreover, the money spent on funerals by Americans in different socio-economic groups does not follow any simple rule, such as that those who are poorest spend the least, and those who are wealthiest spend the most. Proportionate to their income, the situation is reversed, and courts invariably allow a greater percentage of a smaller than of a larger estate to be spent legitimately on funeral charges. Funeral directors are all aware of cases where those who could afford the most have spent the least and *vice versa*. One approaches, then, the subject of expenditure of wealth and energy in the burial of the dead with caution; few general statements can safely be offered.

Beyond the rather obvious propositions that grinding necessity, or war, famine or pestilence seldom permit a people to expend much time or wealth on funerals, and that a society which has built up a high standard of living will have the materials at hand to expend in elaborate burials—no guarantee exists as to how much will actually be expended—it must be admitted that the precise nature of the ceremonies, goods and equipment incorporated into the behavior toward the dead is always subject to the circumstances of a particular culture.

We have already seen something of the history of burial in coffins in the cultures of which America is the inheritor. In the present chapter we are concerned with the growth and transformation in America of interest in burial in coffins and in the multiplication of shapes and designs. We are also interested in the changing meaning and functions of the burial receptacle from the crude coffin of early times to the well-made and artistic casket of today.

Seventeenth and Eighteenth Century Coffined Burial in America: The great 17th century exodus from England to the American Colonies contained a large proportion of skilled craftsmen. These brought with them to the new world as part of their cultural baggage the English medieval craft tradition. A craft was a trade or occupation, the "Art and Mistery" of which was acquired only after a long period of training under a master craftsman. The household of the master craftsman sheltered one or more journeymen or apprentices. The master not only trained these, but was businessman as well, dealing with the consumer, and producing goods either upon order or on the belief that he could find a customer for them. Limited only by the willingness of the customer to purchase the goods produced, this craft system afforded adequate opportunity for the development of fine craftsmanship and individuality of product. Craft organization was not corporate—although the Europeans of the 17th century knew something of the division of labor to make quantity production possible. Although Bridenbaugh, an authority on the Colonial craftsman, does not make specific mention of coffinmakers as one of the crafts represented among the tradesmen immigrants of the 16th century it is more than likely that the cabinet-makers and carpenters knew coffinmaking as a sideline. It is also possible that coffinmakers were among those not encompassed within his study.[1]

The early colonists in America, beset by sickness, starvation, and the urgent demands made by a strange, hostile and vigorous country undoubtedly first buried their dead in the bare earth. With the growth and increasing prosperity of the settlements, however, the custom of burying in a coffin soon made its appearance. Dutch as well as New England and Virginia colonists wrapped the dead body in a shroud—a cerecloth might be used to preserve the body for short periods—and placed it in a coffin before burial. Earle

speaks of the coffin as the usual adjunct to the early colonial
burial, and in one instance, cited earlier, presents a funeral
bill for David Porter in 1678[2] which includes a "coffin"
(12 shillings) and a "windeing sheet" (18 shillings). Judge
Sewall recounts a visit to the family tomb in 1698 where:

> Twas wholly dry, and I went at noon to see in what order
> things were set; and there I was entertain'd with a view of, and
> converse with, the Coffins of my dear Father Hull, Mother
> Hull, Cousin Quinsey, and my Six Children . . . 'Twas an awfull
> yet pleasing Treat . . .[3]

From his earlier entry of 1685 we also know that the coffin
of one of Sewall's daughters was made of chestnut. The fact
that his parents had been buried in coffins would seem to
indicate that the practice was, at least among the upper
classes of a middle class society, fairly common in the second half of the 17th century. Students of funeral history have found in the burial of Roger Williams in 1683 an
early instance of the practice, although by this time the
custom may already have become fairly well established.
That the Dutch colonists of the 17th century used coffins
in their burials is amply attested by such social historians as
Mrs. John King Van Rensselaer, who in one of her tales
of the early Dutch colonists describes the funeral of a young
girl who was buried in a white coffin.[4]

The growing use of coffins is indicated in the fact that,
as early as the mid-18th century, slaves occasionally were
given coffined burial. It is recorded that Job Townsend,
Jr., of Newport, Rhode Island, who had learned joinery
under his father and set up a shop for himself in which he
fashioned furniture of every sort, on one occasion sold to
J. R. Rivera a coffin for a negro slave, and "two rolling
pins."[5]

By 1750 the development of occupations in the cities of the English colonies exhibited a subdivision of the crafts. Increasing opportunities for specialization were made possible by growing markets and a steady labor supply. Bridenbaugh points out that:

Woodworking provides an example of this breaking down or specialization within a trade, for in the city it was divided and subdivided into rough carpentry, joinery, wood turning, carving, coffin making, cabinetmaking, looking-glass making, picture framing, wagon making, coach making, and a variety of other categories to meet the constantly widening demands of the colonial population.[6]

Occasionally a craftsman in one of these restricted areas, forced by competition or tempted by a chance of increased profit, reversed the trend and supplied any article requested by a buyer. Although by the third quarter of the 18th century cabinet-making in Philadelphia had become a fairly large and flourishing business, permitting a genuine division of labor, a bill rendered by William Savery in 1774 to Joseph Pemberton included charges for mending a knifecase, globe, and hobby-horse; nailing a carpet on the stairs; putting a bottom on a rocking chair; and making a mahogany staircase and a walnut coffin with silver handles.[7]

It is highly doubtful that coffins were imported at any time during the colonial period. The ocean voyage was costly and slow, and an individual funeral, particularly in a culture that did not practice embalming, could not wait until an order had been filled from abroad. The colonists did not stockpile coffins. Importing and stockpiling would not have made sense when there were cabinet and coffinmakers available locally who on demand could and did turn out very respectable coffins. Coffin furniture—trimmings and fittings —were imported during the 18th century. The manufacture of such goods began in this country only after 1800.

Although there was plenty of ironmaking in the colonies during the 18th century—by 1775 they were producing one-seventh of the world supply—early American coffins were made of wood. Different varieties of wood revealed the economic status of the person buried. Hard woods, polished or stained, went into the more expensive coffins and served the well-to-do; while, for the most part, the lowly pine, painted with a mixture of lamp black and glue water, sufficed for the less fortunate. The shape was nearly always octagonal, a conventional Old World form, with all the sides flat. Although the coffin traditionally symbolized the trade of English undertakers, who as far back as 1680 displayed trade signs such as "The Four Coffins," and "Naked Boy and Coffin"[8] to indicate their craft, early American undertakers generally did not follow suit. An exception, found in the 1847 Baltimore City Directory, reads: "R. Frederick, Undertaker of Funerals and Chair Maker, opposite the Engine House, Sign of the Gold Coffin." (See Plate 27.) A more common sketch accompanying the advertisements of the early 19th century shows a hearse in the midst of a procession of several carriages.

Coffinmaking as a specialty in woodworking appears with the growth of an urban population in early America.[9] As noted in the chapter above, cabinet-makers and carpenters alike lent their efforts to the making of coffins when the demand was present, and nearly all earlier "undertakers" made the care of the dead only a sideline to their regular trade. Others, however, turned to coffinmaking as a full time occupation, while some of a more enterprising bent began to furnish coffins and funeral paraphernalia to those who possessed the rudiments of service skills but did not have the materials to furnish to the families of the deceased. Thus there came about the emergence of the "coffinshop," followed by "coffin warehouses" and "furnishing undertakers." As early as the mid-18th century the coffinmakers in America could buy "coffin furniture," i.e., decorations, plates, handles, etc., for their trade. In the *Boston Gazette*, May 29, 1758, there appears an advertisement:[10]

COFFIN FURNITURE to be sold by Arthur Savage Tomorrow Evening at his Vendue Room, about 50 sett of Neat Polished Coffin Furniture, consisting of Breast-plates, Angels, Flowers, etc.

Similar advertisements are found in the *Pennsylvania Pocket*, as in 1799 when John Norman is found selling:[11]

Coffin Furniture Made and Sold by the subscribers in Front Street between Market and Arch Streets, Philadelphia. Persons wanting large quantities are requested to give timely notice as materials are very scarce. The best prices are given by them for block tin, pewter, and lead. Pocket and sheet Almanacks for the year 1780 are likewise sold at the subscribers, elegantly engraved on copper, having a curious likeness of His Excellency General Washington; also, a great variety of children's books, Paper hangings, etc.

Thomas Nevell, Thomas Bedwell, John Norman.

Early Coffin Shops and Coffin Warehouses: The period of Westward expansion following the War of 1812 was marked by the rapid growth and spread of coffin shops given over exclusively to the production of burial receptacles and by the beginning of coffin warehouses. The firm of John L. Dillon, Coffin and Shroud Warehouse, of New York, founded at this time was one of the first of its kind in America. With the appearance of such small but vigorous productive enterprises, the emphasis in funerals began to shift in the direction of the *coffin*, especially with regard to price, quality and diversity of purpose.

The reproduction of the funeral bill presented by John L. Dillon to Baldwin and Spooner in 1825 carries with it more than a simple illustration of funeral service offered by an undertaker who bought his coffins from a manufacturer. The leading position of the item "Mahogany Coffin, Lined, Trim-

med, Hinged, and Mounted . . . $24.00," is especially note-
worthy when this bill is set beside David Porter's, mentioned
before in this chapter, which was rendered about a century
and a half earlier. (See also above p. 210.) In the Dillon Bill the
charge for the coffin constitutes nearly two-thirds of the entire
bill, while in the earlier specimen the twelve shilling price of
the coffin is almost inconsequential—less than one-fourth the
cost of liquors alone!

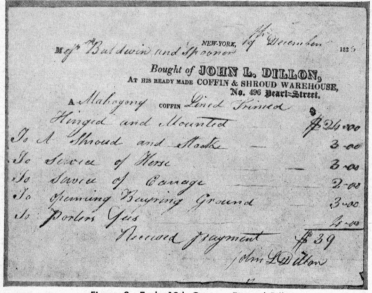

Figure 8. Early 19th Century Funeral Bill

The evidence gathered from directories, funeral bills,
newspaper and journal advertisements, and records of early
funeral establishments indicates that possibly one of the
most significant developments in the whole round of early
19th century funeral business was this growth of coffin
shops and coffin warehouses, paralleled by an increased

popular attention given to the burial receptacle as a major item in burials.

Although the pattern was not immediately established, from this period on it becomes increasingly clear that American burial, although modified by backward glances toward the late English feudal period, is beginning to build solidly upon its simple Judaeo-Christian-English foundation a pattern of its own. This pattern was in keeping with a democratic New World social system in which there were set up no well-defined social classes separated by insurmountable barriers.

Variation in Early Function and Type: Although Americans had earlier turned their increasing attention to burial in coffins in funeralizing their dead, only about 1800 did they begin to make a determined effort to improve the function, style and composition of these receptacles. Throughout the 19th century in America, by means of experimentation carried out by a considerable number of people, the old fashioned coffin slowly became transformed into the modern casket. Coffin and casket makers sensed goals which at one time or other they tried especially to reach in their improvements: their product should have increased utility; it should better indicate the importance of the dead person and his family; it should provide more protection against grave robbers, and the forces of dissolution; and finally it should be more artistic, more beautiful, the better to harmonize with the aesthetic movement in burials. The order in which these goals have been listed indicates in a rough way the sequence in which each received major emphasis from American 19th century coffin and casket makers, although some of them—such as the use of the coffin to display the wealth or importance of the dead—obviously were present throughout most of the history of Western civilization. Other themes, as will be seen in the discussion of

particular types of coffins, have waxed and waned in popularity and usage.

The practice—if not the basic idea—of burial in coffins
is part of the American inheritance from later British folkways. We have seen that by the time the American colonies
were being heavily settled many, if not the majority of Englishmen, were being buried in coffins. One function served
was purely utilitarian—a simple, unadorned wooden receptacle was used to encase the dead body before burial. For
those of higher station the coffin by its quality of materials,
workmanship, and adornment, served to indicate the social
class differences that separated their group from other
groups. Well-to-do merchants and professional people, the
aristocracy and nobility would, after death, lie in state
for an extended length of time. For these, in conjunction
with generally crude preservation methods to render the decomposing body less offensive, a lead inner-coffin was employed. Thus in Paris, on July 20, 1792, the American Naval
hero of the Revolutionary War, John Paul Jones, was buried
in a lead coffin, his limbs wrapped in tin foil. The efficacy
of the method was demonstrated when in 1905, after a six
year search, his still recognizable body was found.

With the growth of medical science in England and the
increased need for cadavers to be used in anatomical studies,
the practice of grave robbing and body snatching became
common enough to rouse the populace to a state of alarm
over the safety of their dead. British trade undertakers of
the late 18th century were aware of this concern; and advertised coffins of iron, and other ghoul-proof innovations in
burial receptacles. The trade card of one read:

IMPROVED COFFINS—The fastenings of these improved
receptacles being on such a principle as to render it impracticable for the grave robbers to open them. This security must
afford great consolation at an aera when it is a well-authenticated

fact that nearly one thousand bodies are annually appropriated for the purpose of dissection.[12]

The importance placed on iron coffins is also shown in an 1822 advertisement:

The only safe coffin is Bridgman's Patent Wrought Iron one, charged the same price as a wooden one, and is a superior substitute for lead.[13]

In America, during the first half of the 19th century when medical schools were few and far between, the theme of protection of the dead from ghouls appears to have had considerably less force in shaping the design of burial receptacles; but it did play a more important part later in the century when grave vaults were introduced into the burial complex. In strong competition with the desire to render the dead safe from human harm was the need to preserve the dead, not for eternity, but for a period of time sufficient to permit family members and relatives separated by considerable distances from the place of funeral to make the journey and attend the funeral. Conversely, the preservation of the body for a short span of time could permit its being transported back to the family burial ground from the more remote parts of the country.

Yet even before 1850 there was apparent an emerging impulse to encase the body in a receptacle whose primary claim to public acceptability lay in the fact that it was beautiful and thus suitable for use in funerals. Already under way was a gradual drift in mood from gloom to beauty. That this drift had an increasing and lasting vitality should be clear to anyone who seeks to learn the origin of the use of the casket in modern funeral practice. A corresponding development is to be found in the current emphasis on restorative art as one of the most valued aspects of the embalming process.

The key, then, to understanding the historical development of coffin styling and composition is to be found in the
dynamic interplay of five major themes in defining and fulfilling the proper function of the burial receptacle. These
themes were utility, status indication, preservation of the
body, protection, and aesthetic representation. In the illustrations of some of the more outstanding receptacle types
given below, the presence or absence, emphasis or de-em-
phasis of these various themes will be evident.

Stone and Metal Coffins: Coffins of material other than
wood make their appearance in the first half of the 19th
century, though it is possible that in very occasional
instances iron coffins might have been used in an earlier
period of American history. Although James A. Gray of
Richmond, Virginia, in 1836, received the first American
patent on a metallic coffin, a year earlier patents had been
granted to John White and Associates of Salina, New York,
for coffins made of "stone or marble" and of "hydraulic
cement." These patents were allowed to expire in 1849,
either because the coffins were hard to manufacture, or were
too heavy to be handled, or had little aesthetic appeal or
popular acceptance. Nevertheless the granting of these patents signalized a deluge of ideas in the design and composition of burial receptacles. By 1860 patents had been sought
for coffins not only of iron, cement, marble and artificial
stone; but of potter's clay; cement and wood; iron and wood;
and zinc, iron and glass combined. Before the turn of the
century the list was extended to include burial receptacles
made of elastic materials, including vulcanized rubber; fab-
ricated metals of various kinds and combinations; papier-
mâché; aluminum; cloth and wood; wood and glass; coffins
with inner-coffins. In one arresting case, a patent was granted
(1876) for "coffins or caskets and their ornaments of celluloid, which, in a dissolved or plastic state, is cast in forms or

molds, by which process the coffin or casket bodies as well as their lids are manufactured."

The Fisk Metallic Coffin: Perhaps the most remarkable coffin ever patented and put into widespread use in America was the Fisk, "An Air-tight Coffin of Cast or Raised Metal," patented in 1848. Although it was specified only as an "improvement in coffins"—metallic coffins having been patented earlier—it contained innovations in design that recalled at once the ancient Egyptian sarcophagus, the iron torpedo, and the strong box. In the original letters-patent sketch the side view shows the top half of the two shells

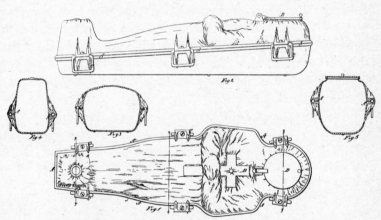

Figure 9. Fisk Metallic Burial Case, 1848, Patent Sketch

which form the coffin cast to fit the form of a man flat on his back with arms folded. A glass plate, similar to the glass in a diving helmet permitted the face to be visible. The form-fitting character reduced the weight—an important drawback of earlier metallic coffins—and at the same time reduced the air space. Its inventor, Almond D. Fisk, claimed to have created "a new and useful manner of constructing an Air-Tight Coffin of Cast or Raised Metal . . . with the least possible quantity of metal, by means of which lightness is obtained . . . (from which) . . . the air may be exhausted so completely as entirely to prevent the decay of the contained body on principles well understood; or if preferred, the coffin may be filled with any gas or fluid having the property of preventing putrefaction."

Although there is no way of determining the number of Fisk Metallic Burial Cases used in America after their introduction about 1848 or 1849, it is evident from the fact that the company continued in existence for five years before being incorporated into a more extensive manufacturing concern, that acceptance was favorable. However, the cost was considerably above that of wooden coffins, and use in most cases was undoubtedly restricted to the well-to-do. That this was the case in at least one significant instance is shown in the testimonial appearing in the *New York Tribune* in April, 1850:

FISK'S METALLIC BURIAL CASES

The entombment of John C. Calhoun in one of these cases has elicited the following letter, signed by many Hon. U. S. Senators— "Gentlemen: We witnessed the utility of your ornamental Patent Metallic Burial Case used to convey the remains of the late Hon. John C. Calhoun to the Congressional Cemetery. It impressed us with the belief that it is the best article known to us for transporting the dead to their final resting place."

The names signed were Jefferson Davis, Henry Dodge, Henry Clay, Dan'l Webster, and Lewis Cass.[14]

A year before, when ex-President James K. Polk died, his body was interred in the city cemetery of Nashville, Tennessee, wrapped with a silk winding sheet, and buried in an old-fashioned, raise-lid style coffin, which was covered with black broadcloth, and lined with copper and tightly sealed.

The Manufacture of Metallic Burial Cases: The widespread use and commercial success of the Fisk Metallic Burial Case is to a considerable extent, to be associated with the founding of a manufacturing concern capable of standardizing production on a mass basis and distributing the product in the eastern United States in large scale quantity lots. Although the Fisk case had been produced on a small scale by A. C. Barstow Co. of Providence, R. I., and the western agency has been taken by W. C. Davis and Co., stove founders, Cincinnati, Ohio, the development of metallic burial case manufacture on a significant scale begins with the purchase of the Fisk Metallic Burial Case Co. by M. H. Crane and J. R. Breed of Cincinnati. This firm was organized, August 15, 1853, under the name of Crane, Barnes and Co. Five months later it was succeeded by Crane, Breed & Co., consisting of M. H. Crane, A. D. Breed, and John Mills. In 1860 the shares of John Mills were purchased by W. J. Breed, and the firm continued under that ownership and title until 1882 when it was incorporated as the Crane and Breed Mfg. Co.

It should be noted that with the introduction of metallic burial cases into the funeral business of America at mid-century the basis of manufacture and production of burial receptacles underwent a very significant change. Although the cabinet shops and carpenter shops might still produce wood coffins in substantial numbers, the day of small coffin shops completely dominating the scene had begun to wane. Put another way, the small coffin shop, devoting most of its production to a craftsman's product, emerged at the end of the Colonial period and continued to flourish during the first half of the 19th century, but with the appearance of metallic burial cases a new mode of coffin construction, based on mass production methods, emerged, and became the leading method of manufacture in the second half of the century.

The illustration of the Crane, Breed & Co.'s manufactory in Cincinnati indicates the significance of the departure from

Figure 10. "Stoves, Hollow-ware, and Burial Cases"

the small coffin shop with its craftsmanship orientation. Stove manufacturers, instead of woodworkers, were now in the business—and a big business it was to become—of burial case production.

The success of the metallic burial case began with the demonstrable proposition that it preserved the body. "We assert," a Crane, Breed & Co. brochure of 1858 declared, "and refer to our numerous testimonials for the proof, that the bodies of the dead have been preserved in Metallic Burial Cases for months, and not unfrequently for years, without any perceptible changes." Ample time, therefore, could be given for distant relatives to journey to the home of the deceased and "behold again the features of their departed friends." Other claims calculated to commend the cast metal case to the public were advanced: protection of the body against water seepage and vermin; safeguarding against infection and contagious diseases—not a small consideration in a century noted for its plagues and epidemics; and, finally, the facilitation of removal of the body for re-burial.

The latter point was not incidental. Many of the dead did not reach their final resting place at burial; quite often, in towns and cities, the dead were deposited in public vaults "for the winter"; and already the rapid growth of towns had made the removal of graveyards to more remote or suburban areas imperative. In the older cities scarcely one of the pauper burying grounds, or "potter's fields" of the large cities was located on its original site by mid-century. And most of the cemeteries that had been already moved were to be moved again, and perhaps once again by 1900. Although regular burial grounds were less likely to be moved there was no guarantee that one would ever sleep for eternity in an urban cemetery. The large scale shipment of bodies back to family homesteads or family vaults no doubt received its greatest impetus with the mass return to their homes of the Civil War dead, and with the growth of steamboat and rail transportation. The metallic burial case thus provided an improved device for returning bodies from a distance to be buried with ancestors and other relatives.

When patented, the Fisk mummy case was far removed from the realm of art work. As first produced in 1853 by Crane, Barnes and Co., the form had been retained much like the original, with some simplification of line and design.

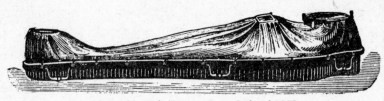

Figure 11. Fisk Mummy Case, Style of 1853

Increased public acceptance led the company to announce, in a circular dated 1854, increased facilities, stepped up production, and "new patterns, combining many important improvements in style and finish." The most important pattern changes included the new "Bronzed Case" line, i.e. cast iron with bronze finish, bedecked with highly wrought ornaments, representing drapery, flowers, emblems of mortality, etc." "Much that has hitherto contributed to shock the feelings of the sensitive and delicate,"—the brochure goes on to say—"is now dispensed with altogether. We are, therefore, warranted in saying that in all the essentials of an appropriate and befitting depository for the dead, the cases we now offer to the public surpass any that have hithertofore been in use." Two styles, the "Ornamental," and the "Cloth Covered" were offered in this line. The latter had the lower half covered with "fine French cloth, trimmed with silk fringe."

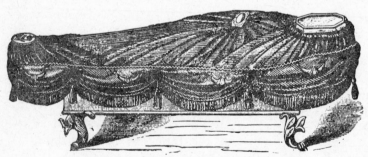

Figure 12. Cloth Covered, "Bronzed Case," 1854

Simultaneous with the issuing of the "Bronzed Case" line, in 1854 there appeared the "Plain, or Octagon" pattern, finished in imitation rosewood and polished equal to the finest furniture."

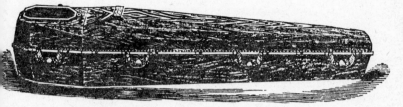

Figure 13. "Plain, or Octagon" Metallic Burial Case

A variety in sizes and depth was offered. Plain lining consisted of cambric and cotton wadding, priced separately. Those with lining cost slightly extra in the "Ornamental" line, but the refinements of the "Cloth Covered" included a substantial increase in price. In 1854 the wholesale price of a six foot "Ornamental Bronzed Case" was $20.50, with plain lining $2.00 extra. For the "Plain" or "Octagon" type of case the price was $1.75 extra. The cost of a "Cloth Covered Case," including lining with white satin and silver plated mountings, was an additional $21.00. Until the appearance of the casket, a coffin, covered or draped with fine fabric in the current European style, constituted the luxury level of burial receptacles.

Yet the "Bronzed Case" line, despite the refinement of the original Fisk "mummy case" pattern, in the words of a Crane, Breed & Co. catalog of 1862, "Repelled the sensitive, and failed, in a measure, of meeting the wants of the refined." The "Covered Case" marked the ultimate in the attempts of the company to enhance the aesthetic appeal of the original pattern, and although it fell out of favor, the idea of *beauty in burial cases* led to a new and rather distinctly American form of burial receptacle, the *casket*. The Plain, or Octagon burial case, with its enlarged glass, improved sealing flange (composition sealing was all important in metallic cases), and high degree of transportability, nevertheless continued in favor through the 1850's.

The Metallic Burial Casket: In a Specification of Letters Patent, dated April 19, 1859, A. C. Barstow, of Providence, Rhode Island, remarked on the changing sensitivities of American burial case taste:

The burial cases formerly used were adapted in shape nearly to the form of the human body, that is they tapered from the shoulders to the head, and from the shoulders to the feet. Recently, in order to obviate in some degree the disagreeable sensation produced by a coffin on many minds, the casket, or square form has been adopted; and of this kind, the metallic burial cases have for many reasons been preferred.

Barstow then goes on to note that the waste space in many of the metallic cases and the increased weight constituted serious objections to their use. His innovation was designed to improve burial cases of the square variety, i.e., caskets, by reducing the excess space through "ogee" design. (See reducing the excess space through "ogee" design. (See Plate 31.) The system of overlapping ribs has its counterpart in some form of metallic caskets currently in use.

But the origin of the American casket is difficult, if not impossible to place. Claims for the earliest straight-sided burial case have been made running back to 1830. In the popular mind the term "casket" suggests a "jewel box," or container for something valuable. When we read of "Iron Casketts" on the import lists of dutiable articles in the Colonies, the reference is to an iron box or container and not a burial receptacle. The authors' first recorded indication of the introduction of the term into American burial usage comes from the Boston City Directory of 1849 in which "William

Cooley, Funeral Undertaker and Coffin Manufacturer," advertised "Coffins, caskets and robes of every description . . ." (See Plate 27.) It is quite likely that the idea of a straight side receptacle may well have been independently conceived by several coffin manufacturers at approximately the same time. In the course of the next fifty years of experimentation in burial receptacle styles and materials such simultaneous invention was to happen many times over, as duplicating claims for something new in the way of stone, cement, glass, terra cotta and the like were to pour into the U. S. Patent Office.

Three firms, specializing in the manufacture of coffin furniture: the McGraw and Taylor Co.; a firm headed by Joseph Applegate—both companies of New York; and the William M. Smith & Co. of Meridian, Conn., might well have been involved the earliest ventures in straight-sided coffins, or "caskets," as they were later to be called. In default, however, of compelling evidence to support the claims that any of these concerns was the earliest to produce such an item, the records sustain William Cooley, Boston, Mass., as the first to offer "caskets" to the American public.

More significantly, the change in burial receptacle pat-

Figure 14. Casket, Modern Rectangular Form, About 1860

tern from the various earlier burial cases manufactured by Crane, Breed & Co., to the Crane's Patent Casket, occurring between 1858 and 1862, marks without doubt the introduction of the new style on a mass-production basis, and gives it its *popular* birthright. It might be observed that the change-over was preceded by a short-lived, in-between model, the zinc "shoulder casket" in 1857.

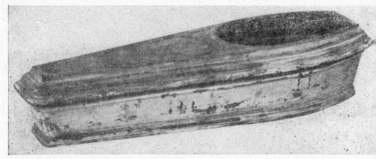

Figure 15. Zinc "Shoulder Casket" Burial Case, 1857

It can be seen that the "sarcophagus principle" of shaping the casket top to the human form had already given way, and for the modern form of casket to appear, only a "rectangularizing" of the receptacle was necessary.

In presenting the new style of burial receptacle, the manufacturer's brochure of 1862 pointed out that it possessed such advantages as being simple, "chaste", i.e., pure and simple in design, not ornate; and air-tight. The last characteristic, it was claimed, would check the spread of contagion and for a time would arrest the process of decomposition. Like the "Plain Case," it was described as "invaluable as a means of transporting the body of a deceased friend to a distant part of the land, or even to a foreign land, for sepulture." Perhaps the most radical change in the construction of this casket, as over against the burial case, was in its top, which consisted of two large sections of plate glass, between which the name plate was located. Each of the glass sections had an ornamented cap which could be screwed on before or after the funeral ceremonies. Thus the *encasing* of the body, the primary idea expressed in earlier receptacles, is modified toward the *presentation* of the dead in a receptacle designed to provide an aesthetically pleasing setting for its visually prominent and dramatically centered object of attention.

From 1862 on through the remainder of the century, improvements were made in the metallic casket and also in the wooden case. (See Plate 30.) The weight of the cast metal receptacles continued to offset other advantages, and the appearance of the lighter metal and cloth-covered wooden burial cases and caskets caused casket manufacturers for the remainder of the century to be acutely conscious of the competing principles of durability, preservation and aesthetic quality of the metallic burial cases and caskets, as opposed to the lightness and pleasing exterior of the wooden and the cloth-wooden types.

In the early 1870's the first true sheet metal casket was supplied to the trade by Crane, Breed & Co. While it retained the top of the new casket, the body was of sheet metal made over iron flanges at bottom and top. Designated the "Oriental," this casket and the earlier "New Casket," an improved version of the earlier Crane's Patent Casket, were the leading metallic receptacles on the market. In the process of shedding weight, the lighter sheet metal caskets gradually came to replace the heavier caskets of cast iron. Summarizing this development, a brochure by the Crane and Breed Casket Company states:

Increasing adaptability of steel and the ease with which it could be formed into more ornamental shapes, added to the lightness of the material, and finally displaced the heavier caskets; . . . (but) the difficulty of adopting the more durable metal zinc to these modern forms forced the abandonment of that metal for a time.[15]

The term "casket" was not destined immediately to replace either "burial case," which was sometimes used generically to designate all burial receptacles; sometimes to indicate a coffin built along Egyptian mummy case principles, or some modification or refinement thereof; or "coffin," the traditional term taken over from earlier English usage. Rather, a period of confused currency of burial receptacle terms obtained from the 1850's through the Civil War. Patent applications through this period, and later, show the highest incidence of usage for the term "coffin," in most part because this was the first category of burial receptacles used by the U. S. Patent Office. Although terms such as "burial case" and "burial casket" were to gain increasing use after 1870, it is not until the 1890's that the term "casket" came to dominate the language of burial receptacles in patent literature. In popular language the term "burial case" enjoyed a mild vogue just before and after the Civil War, but gave way to "coffin" and "casket" both of which in popular usage are interchangeable in America today for the conventional straight-lined rectangular receptacle. The wedge-shaped octagonal "coffin" no longer exists in America, but the American "casket" has yet to be popularly accepted in England and Europe. To American funeral directors "coffin," signifies the continental form of receptacle.

These statements must be made with the reservation that although "casket" is the term generally accepted in America today, a few firms still cling to the older names, probably because these have been long indentified with their businesses. Thus in the roster of firms represented at the 1955 Massachustts Conference of Casket Manufacturers, "Coffin Companies," and "Burial Case Companies" were still represented.

Examples of the Casket Makers Art, Late 19th Century.
Top Two Are Metallic, Bottom Two Wood.

PLATE 30

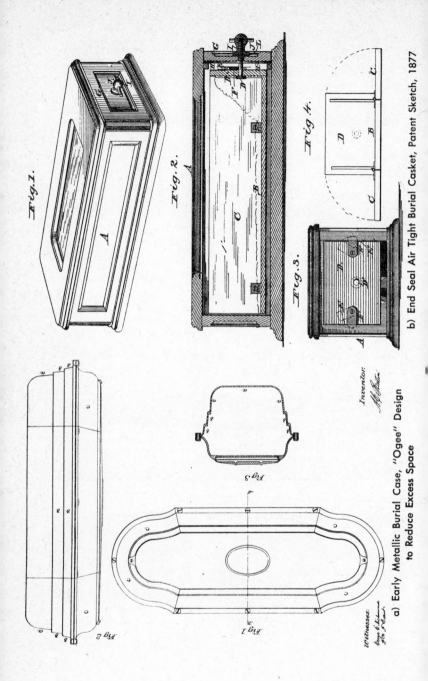

a) Early Metallic Burial Case, "Ogee" Design to Reduce Excess Space

b) End Seal Air Tight Burial Casket, Patent Sketch, 1877

Cloth Burial Cases: The success of the metallic burial case was based on the demonstrable claim of preservation of the body plus the uniqueness of design of the earliest Fisk "mummy case" innovation. Its continued acceptance was derived to a great extent from successful large scale manufacture and distribution of the product, and, also, from the willingness of its manufacturers to vary the style and materials in the direction of producing a burial receptacle that continued to please the eye. While the "metallic" never compromised its preservation function, its form, as we have noted, moved by slow development from the sarcophagus-mummy case to the rectangular casket. A somewhat different development in the manufacture of burial receptacles is found in the story of the introduction of the mass-produced wood constructed, metal reinforced, cloth-covered burial case.

Although the use of cloth to cover the more luxurious of burial receptacles had been practiced by English and Continental undertakers from the beginning of the 19th century, if not earlier, its incorporation into American burial usage, as noted before, dates closer to 1850. The development of a *line* of cloth covered burial cases as the main item of manufacture began in 1871 with Samuel Stein and his Stein Patent Burial Casket.

This man reflected all the genius of the innovator; and it is to the credit of his persistent belief in the idea of a light, strong and aesthetically pleasing cloth-covered casket that the changing pattern of American burial rapidly moved from the more ponderous type of burial receptacles. Stein, originally trained as a cabinet-maker in Austria, after a wandering career in Europe and America, settled down shortly after 1850 in Rochester, N. Y., as a builder of showcases.

Around 1870 the idea of a casket built along show-case lines with glass sides occurred to him. After experimenting for some time he actually produced a model of such a casket and secured a patent on it. However, it proved "too innovational" for the times, and he soon modified it by replacing the glass sides with wood, and covering these panels with cloth. Although the patent for this casket was granted late in 1872, Stein had already begun a small shop a year earlier to build a cloth-covered casket. His first triumph was his securing of an order for a casket to be used for the funeral of James Gordon Bennett, proprietor and editor of the *New York Herald*, who died June 1, 1872. Its appearance aroused a host of comment, and leading New York papers described its radical features in mixed tones of awe and astonishment. Said the *New York Sun:*

> The casket in which the remains of Mr. Bennett are enclosed is remarkable for its elegance. It is nearly square, and made of a species of wood said to be more durable than any metal. The side of the panels are covered with the most costly Lyons velvet. The handles, of which there are eight, are of solid silver. They represent two hands grasping a rod about eight inches long. The lid is in two parts, or panels, and made of French crystal plate glass. Two panels of Lyons velvet are made so as to cover the glass when required. The lid is hung on heavy silver hinges, and is secured by two heavy locks. The entire casket is surrounded by a massive moulding of silver, forming a framework which will survive the lapse of ages. The inside is upholstered with white satin, silk and Venetian lace, heavy silken tassels dropping from each corner.

Quite modest in its origin, the Stein Manufacturing Company had begun with a handful of workmen and a room of about one thousand feet of floor space. (See Figure 16.) As it prospered it expanded its establishment and in 1890, when it merged with the National Casket Co., it occupied nearly one hundred thousand square feet of space and was producing six hundred cloth-covered caskets weekly.

Figure 16. Workmen of the Stein Manufacturing Co. in 1873

In the early years of the concern all was not easy sailing. On the competitive side the metallic cases offered a durability which could scarcely be matched by the cloth-covered receptacle, although as early as 1874 a brochure claimed for the Stein cases that "in regard to decay they will outlast any metal casket ever placed in the ground." Also, the traditional wooden coffin, hand-made with highly polished sides, still had the favor of many undertakers who preferred to make their own. But if the specially made casket for James Gordon Bennett introduced the cloth covered casket to the country, it was the Stein casket display at the Philadelphia Centennial of 1876 that impressed the public mind with the advantages of this new form of burial receptacle. Stein decided, in what was a bold move, to make a display of modern burial receptacles as manufactured by his company available to the general public. To this end he engaged space in one of the main exhibition halls. Because of the objections of other neighboring exhibitors, however, the permission to display the Stein caskets was revoked. Stein's response was to secure the necessary permission to exhibit in a separate building of his own construction which was completed only a few hours before the Exposition opened. The success of this exhibit had the result not only of putting the Stein Manufacturing Co. on the map, but of reinforcing the fashion of placing coffins and caskets on display in coffin shops and in undertaking establishments where such receptacles were made.

In the early history of this company a third milestone was the order received in 1885 for a casket for the funeral of Ex-President U. S. Grant. The "Style E State Casket," made with the finest black broadcloth, heavy silver metal mountings, flat top, with full French plate glass, was chosen. Its inner metallic case was especially finished on the interior and set off by a pillow on which the General's initials were embroidered. The result, claimed a company brochure, was a "real triumph," adding that "another real influence on the general acceptance of the cloth covered casket was exerted." (See Plate 33.)

Figure 17. Stein "Style F State Casket," Similar to Casket for General Grant

"Also Rans" in 19th Century Burial Receptacles: During the 19th century in America three types of burial receptacles were commonly used: the traditional wooden coffin, the metallic "mummy case," and the cloth-covered metal reinforced burial case. In the course of time all three were gradually modified in an effort to improve their appearance. While these were more or less in general use, at the same time many other receptacles were dreamed of or produced which failed to receive popular favor and therefore gained no popular acceptance. These were the "also rans" of the coffin-casket industry.

Two influences were at cross purposes in this experimentation. The first was a potential market for a more artistic or more serviceable funeral receptacle, the second consisted of the "hard facts" of actual production and distribution. As a result of the operation of the latter, many innovators and inventors never managed to get their proposals beyond the "idea stage." They could not secure capital to begin production. Others found themselves owning patents, but without means of manufacturing; and still others found that they could get limited quantities of the patened funeral receptacles produced, but could find no ready market to support further operations. By the operation of economic factors a number of poorly conceived or impractically designed caskets were thus kept off the market.

Outstanding examples of such "also rans" are found in early patent files. It is interesting to note that all three patents issued in 1835—the first in America—for coffins of cement and artificial stone were not produced and expired seventeen years later without the public having had an opportunity to accept or reject the innovation. Dogged by the problem of weight, those who saw a future in coffins of some form of earth-composition continued to seek a shape or combination which would permit the production of a burial receptacle which might at least be lifted, if not carried, by the pallbearers. One variation is seen, when, in 1855, David Sholl received a letters patent for a coffin composed of *terra*

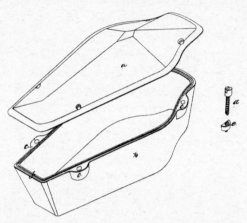

Figure 18. *Terra Cotta Coffin, 1855, Patent Sketch*

cotta, or pottery ware. Records do not show the fate of this innovation, although its lighter weight put it one step beyond the earlier cement types. Yet some sixteen years earlier, Moses Leonard of Syracuse, N.Y., had sought to perfect, and had even patented, a coffin made from a combination of wood and cement. The "cement" in this case was a mixture of rosin, bees-wax, and pulverized stone. Whether the major obstacle to the production of this type coffin developed in the mixing of the ingredients to produce a suitable cement, or of the weight once the coffin had been made, historical records do not show. In any event it failed to reach the market where wooden coffins remained the only choice available. An intermediate step between the cement coffin and its eventual form as a burial vault was the invention patented on May 1, 1880, by William H. Bachtel of Canton, Ohio, of the "coffin, burial-casket, or vault of clay or other plastic materials."

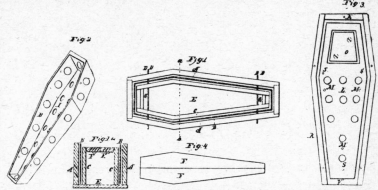

Figure 19. Wood and Cement Coffin, 1839, Patent Sketch

Most arresting, perhaps, in a review of burial receptacle forms and compositions which failed for one reason or other to gain popular acceptance in 19th century burials, is the story of glass coffins and caskets. The type first makes its appearance in the patent files in 1859, when John R. Cannon of New Albany, Indiana, received a letters patent for " . . . certain new and useful improvements in the Construction of Coffins" consisting in "coffins of glass." The coffin envisioned by Cannon was long, narrow, hexagonal, with all sides made in sections of glass. Cement was used to keep the receptacle air-tight, and iron bands, as used in a strong box, held the lid secure. A small air pump on top the coffin was used to remove a portion of the air, "so that there being less pressure of air on the outside than there is on the inside of the body, it will be caused by the air within to fill out and assume a more life like appearance—besides this by removing a portion of the air there will be less liability of the body's decaying." Other advantages claimed for this glass coffin were its non-conductive properties, durability,

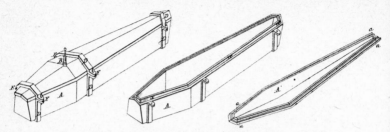

Figure 20. Coffin of Glass Plates and Iron Bands, 1859

cheapness, ease of manufacture and transparency. Its inventor claimed that "when the body within it is made to assume a more life-like appearance by removing a portion of the air, the said body may be at any time seen and observed by the friends and relatives of the deceased."

Despite the many advantages claimed by its inventor, this glass coffin did not make serious inroads into the market against other more conventional burial receptacles. But the use of glass commended itself to more than one inventive mind. Less than a year later, George W. Scollay of St. Louis had secured a patent for an improved glass coffin, built more along the rectangular casket lines, yet essentially acting as a specimen-container in that the receptacle was not to be filled with "poisonous liquour, to destroy the animalcula," but was to constitute an air-tight container "from which the air can be abstracted, (sic.), and into which can be introduced any one or more of that class of gases, which in the absence of air or oxygen, will destroy animal life, and consequently the animalcula, that develop in the body after death." The coffin was to be moulded, and had a special rib-flange construction better designed to make the receptacle air-tight. The emphasis, however, was more upon preservation than display.

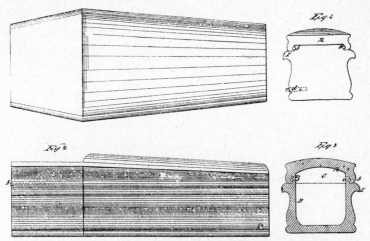

Figure 21. Glass Coffin, Air Tight, with Rib-Flange Construction

Within the decade following the Cannon and Scollay innovations, John Weaver of Baltimore and Isaac Shuler of Amsterdam, New York, had both received letters patents for coffins with glass panels, each emphasizing the display function. Likewise in the two decades between 1870 and 1890 the profusion of patents granted for coffins and caskets incorporating glass into their structure indicated a growing concern with the transparency feature of glass, as over against other physical properties.

Nevertheless, the casket made wholly of glass was not destined to be retained as part of the fashion of modern burial, although two offshoots, the glass panel and the glass liner, are in use today. The experience, which we have already mentioned, of Samuel Stein and his early (about 1870) "Showcase-casket" is indicative of an imminent desire on the part of the late 19th century burying public not only to display a body in its physical entirety, but to place it in a handsome setting part of which is comprised by the casket. Thus, although some of the glass cases were undoubtedly fine pieces of casket construction, their artistry and work-manship on the whole went unrewarded by the public.

Figure 22. Glass Casket, Late 19th Century

Glass caskets might be one of the great failures in the 19th century burial receptacles; yet it is evident that the use of some glass in modern caskets persists. Likewise, cement and stone, although never feasible as the major substances for burial receptacles, eventually did find use in the construction of burial vaults. Many other new ideas and new substances had a less fortunate life history. Such, for example, was the case with celluloid, offered to the American public in 1876 by Aaron Pitman of Matawan, New Jersey; likewise with papier mâché patented as "a substance which is positively imperishable," by Jefferson Evarts of Madison, Conn., in 1868; and with caoutchouc, or India rubber, "air-tight and very light" patented a year later by Cornelius Hurlburt of Springfield, Mass.

Additionally among the "also-rans" were innovations such as the willow coffin, made of basketry or wicker-work, sug-gested by protagonists of burial reform, but never patented, and as far as can be determined by historical record never produced for actual use. Again, a remarkable form of casket which did not survive the 19th century was the cruciform, or cross-shaped, burial case manufactured specifically by the Oswego Cruciform Casket Co. of Oswego, New York, whose popularity ran a relatively short course a decade before the turn of the current century. Another failure for

PATENT CRUCIFORM CASKET

The Patent being on the design of a Casket having plenty of room for the shoulders and wide part of the body, and being narrower above and below, which necessarily assumes the form of a cross.

All religious denominations pronounce it the most appropriate form of Casket made, and Undertakers who have used them say there need be no more crowding of the shoulders, and that the Cruciform will be known as the "Common Sense Casket."

Figure 23. Cross-shaped Casket, 1877

what might logically seem to have been a sure winner was the burial casket of John Homrighous of Royalton, Ohio, patented in 1878. This receptacle had what the inventor claimed was the answer to the undertaker's most pressing need—an adjustable casket, suitable for the largest and smallest cases. Again, no records exist to show this model ever got into production.

Life Signals: An interesting, somewhat bizarre, but nevertheless important image in the minds of many people during the 19th century was the horrifying prospect of being buried alive. The foundation for such morbid pre-occupation stems from an earlier period of the great plagues and epidemics when in the frenzied haste of disposing of the dead the stricken might well be mistaken for the dead. Even in classical antiquity there were customary acts performed by the bereaved which functioned as crude tests of death, such as the Roman *conclamatio*, the Greek washing of the body with warm water, and the Hebrew wake, or watch, in the sepulcher. In America this concern might be expressed in prose and poetry, but with the focus of popular attention on the burial receptacle, during this period there was a corresponding increase in inventions designed to indicate to the living whether life still existed in the grave.

The earliest of these "life signals" to be patented came from the drawing board of Christian Eisenbrandt, of Baltimore, Md., who in a specification of letters patent dated November 15, 1843, claimed a "new and useful improvement in coffins" which he termed "a life-preserving coffin in case of doubtful death." His invention (see Plate 32) was designed, by an arrangement of wires and pins and a spring lid to enable the occupant of the coffin by the slightest movement of hand or head to cause the coffin lid to spring open.

While Eisenbrandt's life-preserving coffin obviously had utility only before the coffin was buried in the earth, the next four similar devices to appear in the patent files were designed to operate even after the body was interred. First of these, invented in 1868 by Franz Vester of Newark, New Jersey, consisted of a square tube, containing a ladder and a cord, one end of which was to be placed in the hand of the person laid in the coffin, while the other extended up to a bell on the top of the tube which was attached to the head of the coffin. (See Plate 32.) A very similar idea is expressed in the invention of Theodore Schroeder and Hermann Wuest of Hoboken, New Jersey, whose "Improvement in Life-Detectors for Coffins," patented in 1871, consisted of a narrow round tube, similar to a speaking tube, which was to be attached to the head end of the coffin in such manner that the rope within it might be pulled by the

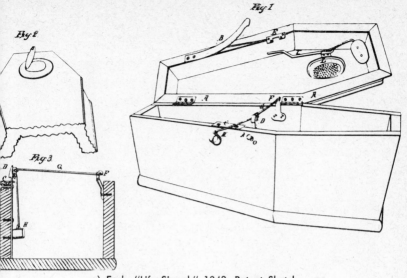

a) Early "Life Signal," 1843, Patent Sketch

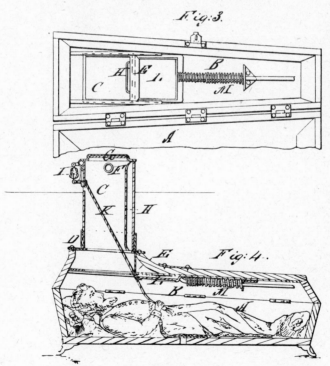

b) Life Signal to be Used with Electrical Alarm, Patent Sketch

PLATE 32

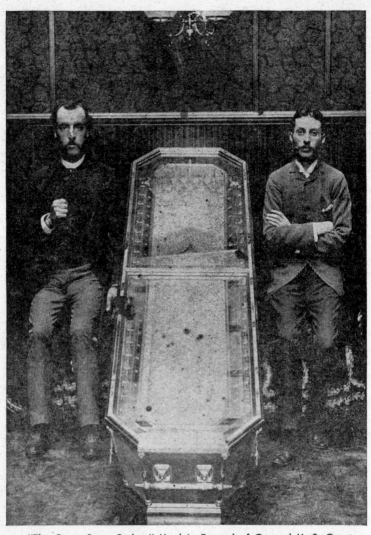

"The Grant State Casket," Used in Funeral of General U. S. Grant

PLATE 33

buried person, releasing an air opening in the mouth of the tube and simultaneously setting off an electrical alarm. (See Plate 34.) If the name of the inventor could be considered a recommendation, the invention of Albert Fearnaught of Indianapolis, Indiana, should have had instantaneous public acceptance. His "Grave-Signal," patented in 1882 (see Plate 35), consisted of a rather elaborate device to release a flag through the end of a tube which projected up from the foot of the grave, if its occupant were to move a hand. A final example of life signal is offered in the invention of John Krichbaum of Youngstown, Ohio, whose "Device for Indicating Life in Buried Persons," patented likewise in 1882, consisted of a rather formidable arrangement of (see Plate 36) pipes, bars, tubes and cross-pins, which would, upon a movement of the hands of "persons being buried in a trance," open an air vent and at the same time give indication that there was life in the coffin below.

As far as present research has been able to ascertain these inventions did not provoke more than a ripple of attention from the world of undertaking and funeral service, and it is doubtful if any were marketed. And yet the mere fact that this number and possibly more were brought to a patentable stage indicates a fear of being buried alive, widespread at the time. Stories of people buried alive are legendary and whether fact or fiction always attract much attention. Newspapers of today seldom fail to publicize the occasional reports of persons who "come alive" after being thought dead. One of the effects of embalming by chemical injection, however, has been to dispel fears of live burial.

Another creation of the inventive mind applied to the problem of protecting the grave from prowlers, "resurrectionists,"—a "resurrectionist," by a grisly joke, was one who stole bodies from graves to sell to anatomists, a "body snatcher"—ghouls, or grave robbers was the coffin torpedo.

This device, made of iron, about an inch in diameter and six inches long, contained a charge of explosive and a mechanism set to go off with the tampering of any coffin which had properly been prepared. One such type of coffin torpedo was actually put on the market by the Clover Coffin Torpedo Manufacturing Company of Columbus, Ohio, and described fully in 1878 in an issue of *The Casket*.

Burial Vaults and Outside Boxes: Although the use of the burial vault has not been solely an American burial practice, the growth and development of the vault as an item of manufacture, and the thinking behind its popular usage cannot be divorced from the general picture of changing American taste in funeral service and interment. It is, of course, true that the basic idea of permanent protection of the body from ghouls and the elements has persisted in various cultures and civilizations extending back before antiquity. The Egyptians customarily enclosed their mummies in a case which at times might best be described as a coffin, decorated, and inscribed with its renowned "coffin texts." At other periods the crudeness of the outside case and its obviously utilitarian purposes makes the term "vault" seemingly more appropriate. The stone coffins of the Greeks and Romans were more likely to be simply stone slabs laid together to form a crude protective box or vault. Also, English barrows often have been noted to contain a similar type slab vault, especially where chalk, a favored material for use in such cases, might be found.

Throughout the 19th century occasional attempts were made to put into the grave linings of rock, stone, or brick, cut or laid in such fashion that the body was to some extent separated from the earth about it. Later, concrete slabs were used, and before the century had ended one form of lining consisted of "sectionals," i.e., concrete slabs sealed together with a sand-cement mortar.[16] As early as

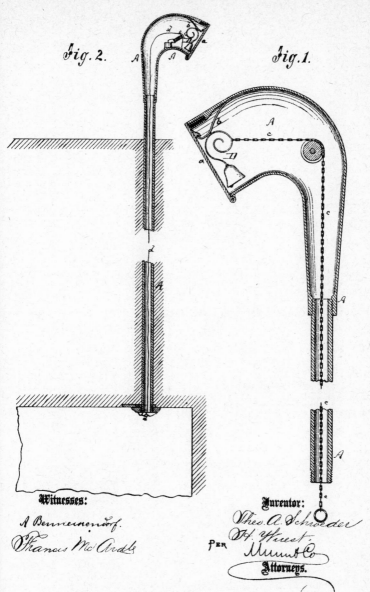

Fig. 2.

Fig. 1.

Witnesses:

A Bennenendorf.

Francis McArdle

Inventor:

Theo. A. Schroeder

H. Wrest.

PER Munn & Co

Attorneys.

Life Detector, Mechanical Principle, 1871, Patent Sketch

PLATE 34

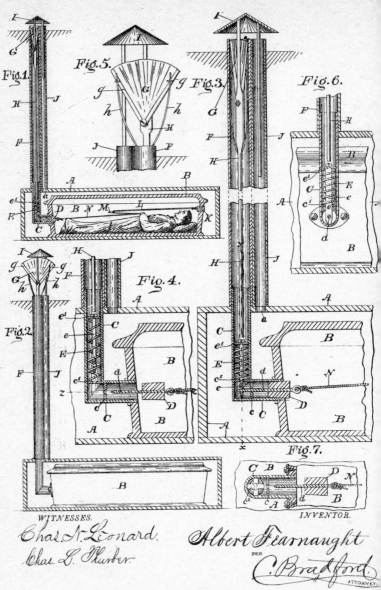

Fig.1. Fig.5. Fig.3. Fig.6. Fig.4. Fig.2. Fig.7.

INVENTOR.

Albert Fearnaught
PER
C. Bradford.
ATTORNEY.

Grave Signal of Albert Fearnaught, 1882, Patent Sketch

PLATE 35

1872, however, Jacob Weidenmann of Hartford, Conn., commenting that "various costly expedients have been resorted to (to preserve the dead) such as building brick-graves, covering coffins with a large body of cement, and the like," in his specification forming part of a letters patent, offered a "cheap, effective, and durable impermeable covering for coffins and caskets." His improvement in burial cases, he claimed, was a common coffin-box of wood, used ordinarily to encase a coffin, but so designed as to permit cement to be poured into it and around the coffin to form a vault. The term "vault," however, was not specifically used; nor does it seem to have come into popular usage until later in the same decade.

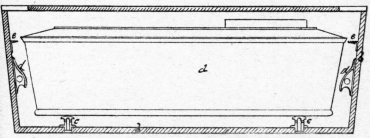

Figure 24. Cement Mold Type of Burial Case, 1872, Patent Sketch

The "burial-safe," an example of which is represented by the invention of Andrew Van Bibber of Cincinnati, Ohio, in 1878 (see Plate 37), was specifically designed to protect the body from ghouls and marauders. The theme of protection of body and casket from the earth and the elements in the design of such "mort-safes" is virtually ignored.

Another form of earth material, slate, was brought into use for grave lining somewhat later in the century, and grooved and bolted slate vaults were marketed before the more easily manufactured concrete vaults appeared and eventually dominated the stone and stone-composition portion of the burial vault industry. Yet despite the early appearance of cement mixtures in burial receptacles and coffins, the concrete vault, as it is known today, did not come into prominence until shortly after 1900. Many firms, particularly in the Great Lakes area, had their beginning in that period. Some of these had been making other concrete products, and many of them had been engaged in concrete construction work.[17]

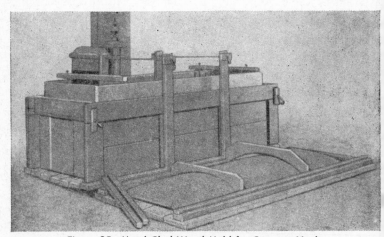

Figure 25. Metal Clad Wood Mold for Concrete Vaults

The number of patents granted in connection with concrete burial vaults is greatest during the period 1900-1920. This development, it has been noted, brought about an active trade in molds and territories for vaults of uniform design to be sold under a trade name. Where gravel, sand and cement are available, concrete vault-making can and usually does occur. Even though the size of a business may not be

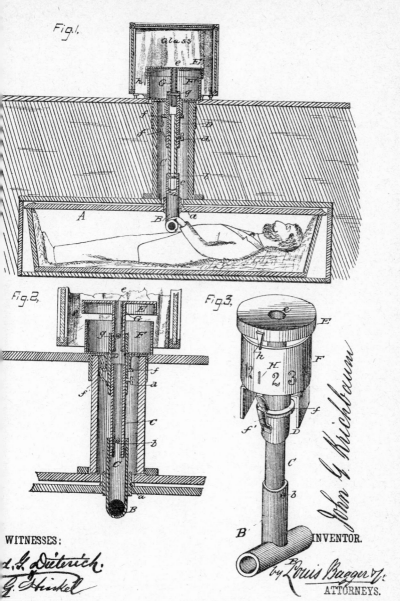

Fig.1.

Glass

Fig.2.

Fig.3.

John G. Krichbaum

INVENTOR.

by Louis Bagger & Co.
ATTORNEYS.

"All Weather" Device for Indicating Life in Buried Persons, 1882, Patent Sketch

PLATE 36

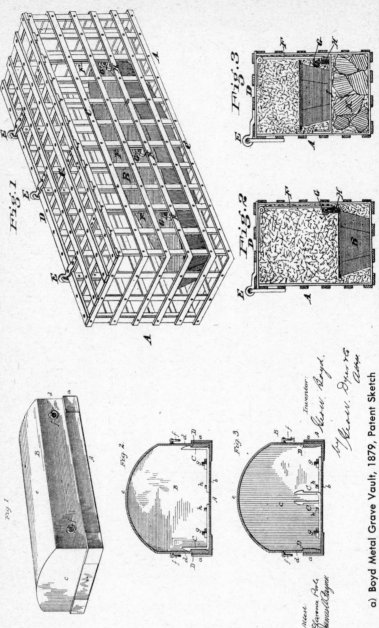

a) Boyd Metal Grave Vault, 1879, Patent Sketch

b) Burial-Safe, to be lowered into the Grave, 1878, Patent Sketch

great, the competitive advantage of lower shipping cost may permit profitable operations. Thus, the weight and bulk of vaults has militated against the concentration of their manufacture into a few large companies.

On the other hand, the metal vault shows a more clear-cut continuity in its development. Metallic coffins of the mummy-case type, the prototype of which is to be seen in the Fisk Metallic Burial-Case, in the course of several decades of use and improvement established the fact that metal sheets of one sort or another could be sealed together in such fashion as to provide relatively permanent protection of the body from the earth and elements. As this burial receptacle was changed so that it was better appearing, there arose a popular repugnance against placing an object of such beauty directly in the ground.

Since Colonial times *some* box or container to enclose and protect both body and casket seems to have been demanded by those burying their dead; consequently, as the term "casket" and the kind of receptacle it implied came into popular use, the "burial case," originally thought of as a form of coffin, was now extended in terminology and as a physical object to mean a type of protecting container for the coffin or casket. In rough fashion, then, the terminological sequence starting in the late 1840's ran "mummy-case," "burial-case," "coffin-case," "casket-case" or "casket-burial case," and finally, somewhere in the late 1870's "grave vault." Still, as pointed out earlier, there was considerable overlap, both in term and conceived function, of the case used to protect the receptacle which held the body. William H. Bachtel of Canton, Ohio, in offering "Coffins of Clay or Other Plastic Material," patented 1881, claimed by his improvements "to produce a coffin, burial casket, or vault that will be much lighter, more easily handled than those composed simply of baked or burned clay." His would have a vitreous surface. Jacob Coover, of Chambersburg, Pennsylvania, on the other hand, offered in 1883 a grave vault which upon examination turned out to be a mode of reinforcing wooden outside boxes in such way that they could sustain a cover of iron, which if desired could in turn be covered with cement—an early application of the idea of iron-reinforced concrete which was to prove fruitful in the 20th century construction of large buildings.

The final stage for setting the type of metal grave vault which today remains substantially in the same form and function begins with the famous "burial-case" (see Plate 37) patented in 1879 by George W. Boyd of Springfield, Ohio. This outer receptacle consisted of the conventional two parts, cover and bottom, both made of "wrought-metal plates riveted together like boiler-plates" which could, if desired be "nickel-plated, bronzed, or otherwise ornamented." The cover actually comprised most of the vault, and the bottom consisted of a narrow iron frame into which the former was locked. The crux of the invention was to be found in the "manner of securing the ring-catches which lock the two parts of the vault together, enabling them to be transported in one piece without locking . . ." Summing up the purpose Boyd stated further in his specification that his object was:

. . . to prevent the resurrection of human bodies, by providing a case or vault for containing the burial-casket, coffin, or other case in which the body may be put, which will be burglar-proof, so that it cannot be opened after being once closed, and will be made of such strong material that it cannot be broken into at any point, and at the same time will be portable and easily conveyed from place to place, and will be cheap to manufacture when compared with other devices for the same purpose.

Mr. Paul Pence, an officer in The Champion Company for many years, relates the story of the Boyd Vault in this manner:

In 1879, a man by the name of Boyd was running a machine shop in Springfield. Mr. Boyd was impressed by the number of grave robberies which were going on at that time. He conceived the idea of a burglar-proof vault which would be a defense against grave robbing. The result was the Boyd Vault which was originally aimed at protection against grave robbing. However, the principle of the Boyd Vault, unknowingly to Mr. Boyd, was the air seal type. Thus, the Boyd Vault was originally made to sell for protection against grave robbing, but developed into the present air sealed burial vault.

After Mr. Boyd had developed the burglar-proof metal burial vault, he found that he had a good idea, but no way to exploit it. He contacted Mr. Scipio Baker, who was then developing a sales organization to distribute embalming fluid for The Champion Company and sold Mr. Baker the original Boyd patent. Mr. Baker had a sales organization but no manufacturing facilities, so he made arrangements with the Springfield Metallic Casket Company to make this vault for him and the Champion Company salesmen sold the vaults. Later the Champion Company provided manufacturing facilities and started to produce the Boyd Metal Burial Vault which they have done to this time.

In 1900, shortly after The Champion Company began manufacturing its own vaults, the Springfield Metallic Casket Company began producing vaults patterned somewhat after the Boyd, which they called The New Baker Patent Burglar-Proof Grave Vault, also made of cold rolled steel. It is interesting to note that the air seal principle, operating on the principle of the diving bell, was not recognized for its function in keeping interiors of vaults air-tight until many decades later, and that Baker's "improvements" included putting the cover for the vault near the top, thereby losing the air seal advantage. The Champion Company also put out the Baker type vault through the first decade of the present century. These two companies dominated the production and distribution of grave vaults through the rest of the century, and, along with other concrete and metal vault producers established somewhat later, shared and continue to share in the production and distribution of the burial vault as an important item in the American funeral bill of goods.

Another variant of the burglar-proof vault, known as the "end sealer," was made like a safe-deposit box with a hinged door. The casket was placed inside this vault, necessarily, either alongside of the grave, or on planks or a lowering device which was set up over the grave, and then it was all lowered as one after the vault had been sealed. These vaults were known as "burglar-proof," and were made specifically for that purpose. It was felt that their construction and the difficulty of raising the entire vault would prevent ghouls from robbing the graves.[18]

Yet the sale of vaults based on the need of protection from ghouls and burglars was slow. By 1915 five to ten percent of all funerals included vaults, nearly all of metal. As the fear of grave robbing gradually diminished, the basic function of the vault became that of protection of the casket and its contents; and eventually the aesthetic principle which had been so efficacious in changing the form of burial receptacles made itself felt in regard to vaults, so that today these receptacles are designed for eye appeal as well as for their basic protective purpose.

A final mention of the wooden "outside," or "rough" box is needed. From the time that the coffin became more than a utilitarian receptacle for the corpse, some sort of outside container or protective arrangement has been put into use as a part of burial procedure. That this container should often be of wood is not surprising, especially during times when wood was cheap and plentiful. In fact, up to about 1875 the ordinary unfinished outside, or "rough," box was buried simply to get rid of it. Yet the growing and insistent demand for protection from man, beast, or elements, quite generally outmoded the wooden outside box, although never

a) Hand Made Glass Caskets, Built About 1900, Found in Bozeman, Montana

b) Casket After 65 Years Underground, Showing Protection of Metal Vault

PLATE 38

Catalogs of Coffin and Casket Manufacturers, Late 19th Century

completely so since a receptacle is nearly always used to encase the modern casket, and such a container need not necessarily be concrete, metal, or a combination of both. Probably the peak use of wooden boxes came after the introduction of the metallic vault, but before the rise of the concrete burial vault industry early in the present century. As early as the late 1870's or early 1880's the Stein Manufacturing Company was producing fine cedar, chestnut, oak, and mahogany outside boxes. Prices ranged from $25.00 to $30.00 for adult sizes, depending upon quality of wood,

Figure 26. Finished Outside Boxes, Used in Late 19th Century

metal hardware, and workmanship. Even in outside boxes, woodworkers displayed much ingenuity in their product. In the *Western Undertaker* of December 1889, J. Wittig of Marinette, Wisconsin, advertised a skillfully contrived burial box that displayed the craftsmanship of a cabinet-maker. He described his creation as the "Undertaker's Friend." In spite of a well-made product, however, the wooden container for the coffin or casket could not, apparently, continue to fulfill the demand of the American public for an outer container or vault that would provide substantial and enduring protection for a sacred body encased in an inner, aesthetically pleasing receptacle.

An equally important factor was the resistance of the cemetery managers and authorities to the wooden box, due to problems of grave upkeep, especially in perpetual care cemeteries. Many cemeteries today demand the use of either a metal or concrete vault in burials.

Balance Sheet on Wood, Cloth, and Metal: It would be erroneous to assume that metal, and wooden, cloth-covered caskets had made a clean sweep of the market for burial receptacles during the second half of the 19th century. The number of large-sized manufacturers producing these items during this period was never great. In 1886 *The Casket Directory of Manufacturers and Jobbers of Funeral Supplies* listed thirteen concerns dealing with cloth caskets and covered work, six dealing with metallic cases and caskets, and four with composition caskets. At the same time an association of makers of wood coffins claimed some twenty large manufacturers as members. Again, there were more shops producing casket hardware and trimmings than were those manufacturing the three kinds of coffins listed in the *Directory*.

Yet the field of manufacturing and wholesaling burial goods was much larger than any directory would indicate. In point of fact there were in 1879 seven hundred and sixty-nine establishments engaged in such ventures. When the U. S. Census Bureau in 1889 redefined factories to exclude "hand and neighborhood shops" the figure dropped that year to one hundred and ninety-four.[19]

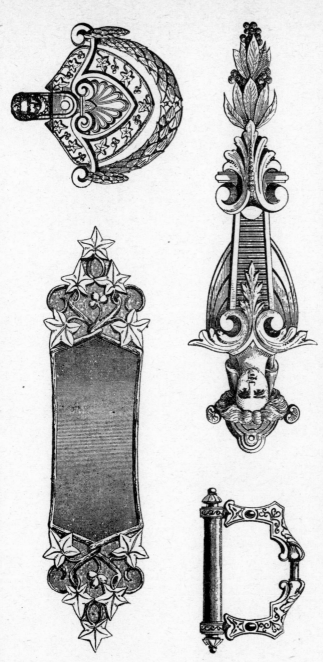

Ornamental Casket Trim and Hardware, From a Manufacturer's Catalog, Late 19th Century

PLATE 40

It seems clear that since most hand shops produced coffins as their main item of funeral goods manufacture—usually in the context of furniture manufacture and cabinet-making or carpentry, and since the hand shops outnumbered the factories by a tremendous margin, and finally, since cloth-covered and metallic cases were produced in only a handful of factories—probably less than two dozen—a majority of the coffins and caskets made and used must have been of wood. The balance, moreover, has favored wood up through the current period. In the last analysis the acceptance of metallic and wooden, cloth-covered cases and caskets reflects the tendency of Americans to express themselves through the material objects they use. The basic appeal of the new types and patterns has been to the sense of beauty, and the varieties of materials used singly or combined attest to the willingness of Americans to bring the area of mourning behaviour under canons of taste set not by ancient and venerable traditions, but by popular fashion, and by seeking objects not only different but improved.

CITATIONS AND REFERENCES IN CHAPTER VII

1. See Carl Bridenbaugh, *The Colonial Craftsman* (New York: New York University Press, 1950), p. 3 *seq.*

2. Earle, *op. cit.*, p. 370.

3. Sewall, *op. cit.*, p. 138.

4. Van Rensselaer, *op. cit.*, pp. 63-66.

5. Bridenbaugh, *The Colonial Craftsman, op. cit.*, p. 82.

6. *Ibid.*, p. 75.

7. *Ibid.*, pp. 80-81.

8. Sir Ambrose Heal, *The Signboards of Old London Shops* (London: B. T. Batsford Ltd., 1947).

9. Bridenbaugh, *The Colonial Craftsman, op. cit.*, pp. 65-96.

10. Quoted in George F. Dow, *Everyday Life in Massachusetts Bay Colony* (Boston: The Society for the Preservation of New England Antiquities, 1935), p. 128.

11. From the Collection of the Massachusetts Historical Society.

12. Sir Ambrose Heal, *London Tradesmen's Cards of the XVIII Century* (London: B. T. Batsford Ltd., 1925), p. 22.

13. James M. Ball, "Resurrection Days" in *Lectures of the History of Medicine* (Philadelphia: W. B. Saunders Co., 1933), p. 114. Iron coffins were first patented in England in 1796.

14. *Reader's Digest*, Jan. 1953.

15. *The Evolution of the Modern Casket*, brochure, ms. photostat, Collection of NFDA, Milwaukee, Wis., n.p.

16. Cf *The First Fifty Years Were the Hardest: A Brief History of the Concrete Burial Vault Business* (Columbus, Ohio: National Concrete Burial Vault Association, 1953), p. 3 ff.

17. *Ibid.*, p. 3.

18. Personal communication to Howard C. Raether, April 8, 1955, from Harry J. Gilligan.

19. Gebhart, *op. cit.*, pp. 223-224.

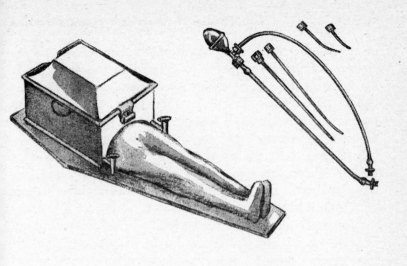

Through the Ice-Age in Embalming

In its treatment of the body after death mankind has run a gamut of procedures which might well startle the imagination of the uninformed. The data of the ethnographer and anthropologist are rich with variations in death customs the world around. One of the major decisions a society must make about its dead is whether or not the corpse should be preserved. The answer to this, as well as to other questions related to major crises in the lives of human beings, tends to be phrased by custom and tradition.

When attention is turned, however, to the role of preservation of the dead in an emerging 19th century American society, the outstanding phenomenon appears to be the rapid rise, spread and acceptance of a felt need for the body to be preserved as a necessary preliminary to its proper interment. Another interesting aspect of this development is the attention, ingenuity, and effort directed to the preservation of the dead by many persons who acted independently of and often unknown to one another. However, in puzzling out an interpretation of the facts of changing embalming practices in America, the historian finds himself first looking backward to tradition and custom for clues, and in default of adequate explanation based on tradition and custom, looking to the "situational" or immediate circumstances of the change.

Customary Aspects of Preserving the Dead: The growth of methods and the limitations on the practices of embalming the dead on the European Continent before the American Colonial times have been presented in earlier chapters. Briefly, in looking for an explanation underlying these early developments it is to be noted that the practice of letting the nobility and persons of substantial rank and status lie in state for a period of about a week, reaches back into classical antiquity. Also, if this custom did not at first find acceptance and support in Christian belief and practice, it nevertheless reappeared in the Christian care of the dead through the Middle Ages; and was reinforced indirectly by the practice, at the close of this period, of the preservation and distribution of portions of the bodies of religious leaders to churches, shrines and other places to be hallowed by the presence of such relics.

Likewise, as the pretentious medieval funeral of an earlier feudal period became an object of imitation and emulation by the socially mobile merchant and commercial classes in Renaissance times, the preservation of the dead, as crudely performed by physicians, surgeons, and barber-surgeons for nobility and important clergy, was arrogated to themselves by various classes of tradesmen and artisans who "undertook" the organization of funeral obsequies and provided the paraphernalia for funerals for those to whom elaborate mourning behavior in the fashion of the nobility, to which class they did not belong, was primarily an affectation. Body preservation techniques, in the light of this development, tended to deteriorate by the turn of the 18th century to the "sawdust and tar" level, and was lost as a prerogative reserved for branches of the healing arts.

The growth of cities and the organization of funeral service within the context of the tradesman's service in 18th and 19th century England also gave rise to a need for preservation of the dead along lines totally different from those reflected in the desire to have the body, as a mark of social status, lie "in state." This "need" appeared as a consequence of the inability of the poorest urban classes to pay funeral expenses; the corpse necessarily remained unburied and without the benefit of funeral ceremonies until the requisite amount of money could be raised. The impulse to give the dead a "decent Christian burial" has always been strong in Western society. These factors underlay the early appearance of burial associations and burial societies, and remain today as a social element in the structure of modern institutionalized insurance.

In sketching out the background for the rise of embalming in America, as an integral part of the funeral service, it is probably fair to state that the influence exerted by cultural extension from Europe and the tradition of the Western world were both instructive, in that the practice of letting bodies of important personages lie in state, as well as the custom, dictated by need rather than tradition, of the poorer classes to delay burial, provided cues for the funeral behavior of the early colonists. There is little, however, to suggest that these usages were of a compelling nature; rather the search for a more complete and satisfying explanation for the rapid and virtually universal spread of embalming in America needs to be extended to the particular circumstances of a new way of living in a new world, and as an important aspect of the emergence of new social forms emphasizing *taste* in American funeral behavior.

An earlier chapter, discussing Colonial funeral customs, offered several clues to the genesis of embalming as a widespread practice in America. On the one hand, the small settlements fostered a community spirit which, among other ways, was expressed in either church or family graveyards. Thus the family plot has always been a common element of cemetery organization in America. From the middle of the 17th century on, the well-to-do were likely to have family tombs in which the various generations were buried. Much importance was attached to being gathered not only *to* but *with* the fathers. Whether relatives gravitated toward urban centers, edged toward the frontier, or merely took up residence in other parts of the Colonies, the traditional impulse to gather beside the bier of the departed relative was apparently no whit diminished by the distance separating one from the other. Upon the death of a dear friend or relative, colonists would set out on what might be several day's journey to participate in the funeral, comfort the immediately bereaved, and share in the social gatherings which automatically followed the get-together of scattered relatives and friends who seldom met except on an occasion such as this. In order for such gatherings to take place it became necessary, in many instances, to use whatever preservative methods were available at the time to restrain the putrefaction of the corpse while the funeral was delayed, since a funeral lost much of its significance without a corpse as the central figure. Several crude methods—disembowelling, filling its cavity with charcoal, immersing the body in alcohol, or wrapping the body in a cloth soaked in alum, or "sere sheet," were used by the early colonists.

In 1773 in a letter to Barber Dubourg, Benjamin Franklin speculated on the possibility of embalming in wine. "I wish it were possible from this instance to invent a method of embalming drowned persons, in such a manner that they may be recalled to life, however distant."[1] Lord Nelson, according to some of his biographers was returned to England from Trafalgar in a barrel of rum.[2] A felt need for preservation produced a number of ingenious efforts to find a satisfactory preservative. The stories that tell of the embalming of persons in beverage alcohol are not a few. When a young woman, Nancy Martin, died at sea, in 1857 at the age of 27, her father did not wish her buried at sea, and so he had her body thrust into a cask of alcohol and returned to this country. The cask and its contents were buried in Oakdale Cemetery, Wilmington, North Carolina.[3] Even in less dramatic circumstances, upon occasion, when the body was sent elsewhere for burial, it was encased in a metal container, usually of lead, soldered air-tight, and again encased in an outside coffin of wood.

In the decades that marked the expansion of America following upon the War of 1812, the American people found themselves more and more separated from one another, both as members of kinship groups and of communities. The village life of the Colonial period to some extent was founded upon mutual aid and protection. The towns in Colonial America were likely to be patterned after the European model in which people did not live on their farms, but went out from towns to work on their fields. The pattern of defense was to live together, rather than to attempt to fortify each dwelling. But the first half of the 19th century found pioneers giving over small settlements in which houses huddled together in favor of scattered and often isolated homesteads. The compact village did not appear as commonly west of the Appalachians as it did in New England.[4] After the first great danger of Indian raids had passed it was safe for rural people to live scattered over a farming community.

In many cases expediency dictated the place, and to a certain extent the mode of burial. Yet the impulse to be buried in the same earth as one's ancestors persisted, as did the tradition of the family burial plot. Thus the need for more adequate and reliable methods of body preservation was generated in intensity just to that extent that the desire to be buried "home" called for transportation of the body for increased distances. In a period marked by the rise of individualism and the spirit of enterprise, American ingenuity met this demand in a host of different fashions and usually without reference to the state of technological advance in other geographic regions or, for that matter, in other countries. Thus while in England and France the utility of chemical embalming had long since been demonstrated, though without any appreciable popular acceptance, American methods of preserving the dead well into the Civil War period were based on the simple rudiments of refrigeration. Following this period, with considerable overlap, was the attempt to preserve bodies by using air-tight burial cases as described in the previous chapter. Not until shortly before the Civil War was the contemporary principle of chemical embalming by injection brought into the American funeral complex.

Corpse Coolers and Cooling Boards: In May, 1846, two years before the appearance of the Fisk Metallic Burial Case, two Baltimore undertakers, Robert Frederick and C. A. Trump, received a patent for a "Refrigerator for Corpses." Three years earlier, the first "corpse preserver," based on the principle of ice refrigeration, had been granted to John Good of Philadelphia. It did not find its way into the commercial market, however, and the patent was allowed to lapse in 1850. In their specification, Frederick and Trump indicated that their invention was an innovation which rested upon a conventional principle:

Various devices have from time to time been essayed for preserving bodies after death by the application of ice; but where applied directly to the body it was troublesome and ineffectual, wetting it and thereby rendering it more subject to decomposition. Another process has been to place the body in a coffin shaped case, said case being surrounded with ice, but this method was objectionable on account of the space that must intervene between the ice and those parts of the body most desirable to congeal. Experience has proved that it is not only necessary to freeze the trunk or abdomen and the chest; but no apparatus has heretofore been made that would with any degree of certainty effect this object on all sized persons without an immense expenditure of ice . . . By our invention we effect this, and with a very small quantity of ice we freeze the corpse as much as is necessary, while at the same time, our apparatus is portable and convenient.

Their "corpse cooler" consisted of a common cooling board on which the body was laid out, and a concave, metal, ice-filled box which fit the torso, and was equipped with lid, spigot and handles. (See Plates 41, 42.)

The Frederick and Trump corpse cooler not only was patented, but successfully marketed to a substantial number of undertakers who were happy to find a cooling device that was portable and economical. Moreover, it could be used *after* the body was dressed, so that shortly before the funeral the body could be lifted, fully dressed from the corpse cooler and placed in the coffin. Such was its obvious utility that no other type of cooler could seriously challenge its dominance for the next two decades. The predecessor for the cooler of the type likely to be found in early city morgues was patented in 1868 by Charles Kimball, of Quincy, Massachusetts. This consisted of a large refrigerator with two compartments, one for the body and the other for ice. This

Kimball cooler had an early competitor in the corpse preserver of Howard V. Griffith, of Altoona, Pennsylvania, patented in 1870. (See Plate 42.) In the same year R. C. Andrus of Poughkeepsie, New York, patented a corpse preserver, shown below, which consisted of a set of ice-cases, all built along the Frederick-Trump principle, one to encase the head, and another for the chest. A case for the limbs was optional. The cases were to be made of zinc or wood.

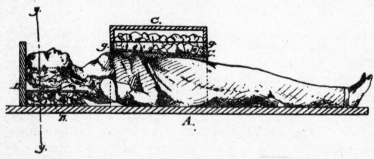

Figure 27. Corpse Cooler Consisting of Several Ice Cases, 1870, Patent Sketch

Corpse coolers continued to be patented until the start of the last quarter of the 19th century, and for many undertakers ice cooling became so much a part of their services that they persisted in using coolers and cooling boards until the dawn of the present century. By then, however, the "cooling board" had taken on the function of an embalming table. For some time after the cooling operation had ceased to be a part of it, the embalming table was still called a "cooling board."

The "Air-Tight" Receptacle: Early, metallic burial cases, described in some detail in the previous chapter, were presumed to have both preservative and protective properties. In the cycle of their development from crude "mummy-cases" to aesthetically pleasing metal caskets, the preservative func-

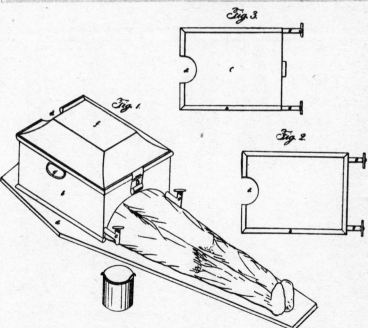

Corpse Cooler of Frederick and Trump, 1846. Top, an Actual Cooler,
Bottom, Patent Sketch

PLATE 41

ROBERT FREDERICK,

Would inform his friends and the public generally, that he continues the business of manufacturing

FURNITURE,

As well as repairing and painting, in superior
style and at cheap rates.

At his warehouse an assortment of various sizes

COFFINS

are constatly kept, and those requiring would do
well to call before purchasing elsewhere, as they
will be sold very cheap for cash.

THE CORPS PRESERVER

Can be had by applying to
the advertiser or any of the
Undertakers on moderate
terms.

All concerned are invited
to give a call at my place of
business.

CORNER OF MONUMENT AND ENSOR
STREET.

a) Advertisement of Co-Inventor of
Corpse Cooler, 1847

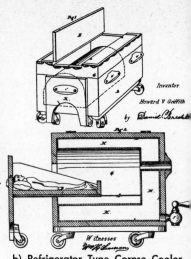

b) Refrigerator Type Corpse Cooler,
1870, Patent Sketch

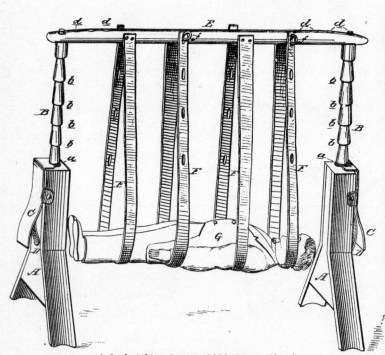

c) Body Lifting Device, 1880, Patent Sketch

PLATE 42

tion came to play a role of somewhat lesser importance. Nevertheless there were some receptacles made available to 19th century funeral service which had as their basic virtue the preservation of the body by keeping it enclosed in an "Air-tight" manner. Others operated on the principles of introducing or creating within the case a gas which would have the power of preservation. Still others attempted to keep the body from decay by immersing it in a container filled with some composition which, upon hardening, would render its contents impervious to all forces of decomposition. Most arresting of all, possibly, outside of a proposal (never patented) to preserve the body by electroplating, was an oval shaped elastic receptacle, portable, having a funnel-like top, handles at the side, a grooved back, and a tube for deodorizing purposes, patented in 1863 by Dr. Thomas Holmes, a resident of the District of Columbia. (See Plate 43.) This invention, by no means Holmes' first, though one of the few he got around to patenting, was designed specifically for battle use in "the carrying of badly-wounded dead bodies hurriedly away that could not otherwise be quickly removed for want of proper conveyances . . . " Deodorizing substances were introduced by way of the aperture and tube for the purpose of preserving the body for a short time. After the body was inserted a large drawstring drew the opening together, and what amounted to an early version of the modern flexible rubberized body carrier was ready to be borne away.

Chemical Embalming by Injection and Its Innovators: In conjunction with the aesthetic and material upgrading of burial receptacles, and especially the casket with its "jewel-box" emphasis, there followed a corresponding disposition to keep the body on display for a longer period. Although the corpse-cooling devices which depended upon the principle of ice-refrigeration undoubtedly predominated from the

1830's through the 1870's, if not later, the problems attending this method of preservation, including the difficulty of keeping the corpse on display, were sufficiently pressing to induce a certain amount of receptiveness by undertakers for a better mode of delaying the onset of bodily putrefaction. At the same time two other parallel developments, one in sanitation and the other in medical pathology, coalesced to give an added impetus to the search for better methods of preserving the dead.

The first of these traces back to the early popular concern over the ravages of pestilence and plagues in American cities. From the time of the earliest Colonial settlers the ravages of sickness and disease had contributed a tragic overtone to an otherwise heroic tale.[5] Smallpox, diphtheria, scarlet fever, yellow fever, and lesser infectious diseases had again and again swept the settlements and towns. By the beginning of the 19th century attention had begun to turn, albeit very slowly, from medical treatment toward the general bettering of health and the prevention of disease through improvement of sanitary conditions.

The progress made on the Continent arrested the attention of those who were constructively concerned about the recurrence of epidemics in America. One consequence in the early thirties was a trip to Europe by Dr. Richard Harlan, to study methods of plague control. There he became acquainted with some of the leading figures in medical and sanitary science, including several pioneers in the development of techniques and fluids for the preservation of the dead. Embalming as a sanitary measure apparently impressed Harlan. Upon his return he translated from the French Gannal's *History of Embalming*, and had it published in Philadelphia in 1840. Although there is no evidence that he actually engaged in further research on the subject, or that he actually practiced or attempted embalming in America, it cannot be doubted that through his efforts a substantial interest in the subject was awakened in this country, not only in medical and sanitary circles, but among undertakers as well. For the remainder of the century this book was the standard reference on matters pertaining to the preservation of the human body. It also provided the inspiration and material basis for numerous articles in early mortuary trade journals.

Turning specifically to developments in the production of embalming fluids, one has good reason to believe that in the two decades between 1840 and 1860 experiments in their production were being carried on more or less independently by physicians, anatomists, chemists and other persons interested in embalming as an adjunct to the field of funeral service. On the medical side, the preservation of anatomical specimen material in American medical schools demanded a working knowledge of chemical preservatives. Gannal significantly was a chemist. One of the lesser heralded accomplishments occurred in 1846 when Ellerslie Wallace, demonstrator in anatomy at Jefferson Medical College, originated a zinc chloride-based compound for the preservation of dead flesh. It is quite possible that this substance had already been in use abroad, as had arsenical and mercurical compounds. Notable in this latter respect are the facts that in England in 1836 an embalming process involving arterial injection of an arsenic compound was patented—thirty years before the first embalming process patent using arsenic was granted in America; and that in 1846, poisonous embalming compounds based on arsenic and other metallic salts were outlawed in France—better than a half century before the same was done by the states in America.

The claims of the above mentioned Dr. Thomas Holmes to be the "father of modern embalming" have been accepted

by many writers. Our studies do not support these claims.[6]
The stories of Dr. Holmes follow these lines:

Thomas H. Holmes was born in 1817 in New York, the son
of a merchant who wanted a medical career for his offspring.
Young Holmes, gifted with many talents and an insatiable
desire for experimentation matriculated early at the New York
University's School of Medicine. Between 1840 and 1846 he
worked as an assistant to the coroner of New York County
where an earlier interest in preservation of human flesh re-
expressed itself in his analyses of the shortcomings of the brine
pickling of cadavers for dissection purposes. Resigning his post
as coroner's assistant he moved to Brooklyn to set up a combined practice as physician and pharmacist, still interested,
however, in the preservation of dead bodies. After experimenting with numerous methods and different chemicals he began
to offer his services to his clients as an embalmer of the dead
whose fluid would preserve bodies "forever, or at least as long
as stone." (It is generally believed in mortuary circles that
this fluid was a compound of zinc-chloride and arsenic.) When
the Civil War broke out Holmes received a captain's commission in the Army Medical Corps, and was assigned to Washington, D. C., where his talents were put to use in embalming Army
officers killed in battle, whose bodies would then be shipped
home.

In Washington and environs Holmes embalmed many famous
war officers, including Colonel Elmer Ellsworth of the New
York Fire Zouaves, killed in Alexandria on May 24th, 1861. No
funeral during the war attracted more attention than that of
Ellsworth, who was a popular hero, and was shot down when
an individual death was still national news.

Sensing the commercial opportunity provided by the desire
of families of the dead to have the bodies of their loved ones
returned in a good state of preservation Holmes resigned his
commission and set up practice in 1863 in Washington as an
embalmer of the dead. Charging an average of $100.00 per case,
Holmes became both well known and well off from his work
with the war dead. His enormous success became a legend;

and, in a letter of March 23rd, 1893, he claimed to have "embalmed 4,028 soldiers and officers, field and staff." If the war was providing the opportunity for Holmes to perfect his embalming techniques, it also provided occasion for America at large to hear about the new process for embalming the dead. As a result, popular acceptance of the practices was given remarkable impetus.

Returning to Brooklyn after the war, his fortune somehow or other spent, Holmes resumed practice as physician, druggist, embalmer, concocter of various fluids, including a tasty root beer, and experimenter. As years passed he became eccentric and somewhat embittered by the publicity which accrued to others, besides himself, in the field of embalming. He engaged in occasional arguments about his position as "father of modern embalming" and, as a parting gesture of contempt for the competence of other embalmers expressed a dying wish that he should not be embalmed after death. Thus passed America's colorful pioneer, the "father of modern chemical embalming."

Though sketched in very general outline, the above "accepted version" of Thomas H. Holmes, upon assessment of available research data, reveals many inaccuracies. For one, there is disagreement as to whether Holmes had actually completed medical training and was certified as a physician, or whether he arrogated the title to himself after going to work for the county coroner. That he embalmed Civil War casualties cannot be doubted; yet the Division of Military and Naval Affairs of the Executive Department of the State of New York, after exhaustive research through voluminous records, was unable to identify a Thomas H. Holmes of New York State who served in the Civil War in the grade of captain. In point of fact, the only Thomas H. Holmes found was mustered in as a private in 1863 from Hempstead, and died a year later. Five other Holmes, four privates and one corporal, do not in any way match the characteristics of America's Pioneer Embalmer. Moreover, according to a letter of July 11, 1945, from the Division office, "A search under the headings, embalmers, undertakers, etc., on the official records of the War of the Rebellion, yields nothing. A search under 'Interment' yields nothing. A search under 'Burials' shows the following General Order (No. 33) issued from the War Department in 1862 and is the only mention made of the subject of the disposition of the bodies in the entire work of about two hundred volumes:

'In order to secure, as far as possible, the decent interment of those who have fallen, or may fall in battle, it is made the duty of commanding generals to lay off lots of ground in some suitable spot near every battlefield, so soon as it may be in their power and to cause the remains of those killed, to be interred with headboards to the graves bearing numbers, and, where practicable, the names of the persons buried in them. A register of each burial ground will be preserved, in which will be noted and marks corresponding with the headboards.' "

From the above it seems evident that when Holmes wrote that he "went to the front" he did not go as a member of the U. S. Army. As to that version which has Holmes as a member of the "27th Brooklyn Fire Zouaves," military records reveal no such organization having ever existed. As far as having embalmed more than 4,000 soldiers and officers, (some writers put the figure as high as 6,000) with the crude instruments and complicated process of preparation, the physical labor involved would have had him embalming night and day throughout the whole course of the war. Yet, the name of Holmes does not appear in the Washington, D. C. Directory until 1863. It *does* appear on a Letters Patent dated December 10, 1861; but the application lists "Thomas Holmes M.D. of Williamsburg, New York." The four hundred thousand dollar income he would have received for this work has never been accounted for, although Holmes later admitted "having lost a fortune."

Undoubtedly, careful, dedicated research, covering years of effort would be necessary to establish Holmes' true contribution to the introduction of embalming in America. In view of the stories that surround the man and his work it is questionable whether any *definitive* statement at this time can be made beyond pointing out the inadmissibility of many of his own claims and the inaccuracies of those who have written about him.

In point of fact, while Holmes was experimenting in the basement of his Brooklyn pharmacy, others interested in the preservation of flesh whether for food, for use as anatomical specimens, or in conjunction with the burial of the dead, were conducting similar research. It is interesting to note that until 1885 at least, the Patent Ofice included devices and compounds for preserving animal flesh for food under the general heading of "Embalming."

In 1856 the first patent (No. 15972) for a process of embalming the body by a method depending primarily, but not wholly, on injection of a chemical compound, went to J. Anthony Gaussardia of Washington, D. C. The process involved injection of an arsenic-alcohol mixture, electrically charging the body, successive washings with various chemical compounds, anointing with oils and placing the body in a coffin filled with "an alcoholic mixture of arsenic." Notable in this case is the lesser importance of display of the body. Permanence of preservation may have been assured; but beyond the utility for transportation there was little to this mode of preparing the dead that would commend itself to the funeral director. A chemical laboratory would have been required in which to do the embalming; and the funeral director would have been restricted in his choice to hermetically sealed metallic coffins. (See Plate 44.)

Undoubtedly Holmes had been compounding embalming fluids at least a decade earlier than the date of Gaussardia's patent, but such compounds as he was able to produce before the Civil War never got to the patent office.

One of the reasons, seemingly, was that the basic ingredients, comprising arsenates and various poisonous metallic salts, chlorides, and the like were fairly commonly known; and had been in use for preserving flesh, as indicated above, in England and on the Continent, for many decades before. In order to market an embalming fluid made of such derivatives it was better for him to keep the formula secret, and manufacture it himself. This, precisely is what Holmes did, for although he manufactured and sold a prepared fluid, "Inominata," at $3.00 per gallon, he did not patent it. His three major patents were two for embalming by exposure of the body to disinfectant gases, 1877 and 1891, and the other mentioned above, in 1861, for an "Apparatus for Filling Blood Vessels of Dead Bodies." (See Plate 43.) The latter was by far the most significant, and it was Holmes' intention to sell the apparatus to undertakers for $100.00 and the "right" to use them for an additional $200.00. Although the success of this venture is unknown, the principle of the force pump was familiar enough; and, from later accounts of undertakers concerning their initial ventures into chemical embalming by injection, it appears that many, including John Epply and Hudson Samson, made, or had made, their own.

Between 1856 and 1869 inclusive, a total of eleven patents were granted for embalming fluids, related media and processes, as noted in the following table:

EMBALMING PATENTS IN AMERICA: 1856-1870[7]

Date	Patent Number	Patentees
	ARSENATED COMPOSITIONS	
1856	15,972	Gaussardia, J. A.
1860	30,576	Iddings, Warren
1868	81,755	Crane, Elliot N.

SULPHUROUS ACID AND SULPHITES

1863	38,749	Hutton, Franklin A.
1867	67,170	Granja, Edward
1868	75,992	Sickel, James C.

OTHER DISINFECTANT GASES

| 1867 | 61,472 | Scollay, G. W. |

MISCELLANEOUS NON-FORMALIN COMPOSITIONS

1864	44,495	Morgan, John
1867	69,312	Brunetti, L.
1868	74,607	Seely, C. A., & Eames, C. J.

INNOVATIONAL

| 1867 | 67,145 | St. Clair, Colin C. |

it is obvious that a diversity of approaches to the problem of preservation of the dead characterizes this thirteen year period. The two earliest patents specified arsenic as the basic element in the embalming compound; and the third, sulphurous acid. John Morgan's compound, patented in 1864, called for common salt, potassium nitrate, and powdered alum. All these were mixed with water. St. Clair's patent, on the other hand, required the immersing of the corpse in a mixture of plaster of paris and hydraulic cement, with parts of the cadaver temporarily perforated with tubes to permit the escape of gases. (See Plate 43.)

The listing of these patents during this short span, not only serves to indicate the multiplicity of innovations and inventions for preserving the dead, but to some extent underscores the *futility* of attempting to determine "the first embalmer," or "the first embalming fluid," or other equivalent "firsts." What seems to be more important is the fact that the earliest center of embalming in America gravitated to Washington, D. C., at the onset of the Civil War—if it was not there already. The great number of casualties in and around the Capitol, including those who died of sickness and fever, provided an occasion for those interested or proficient in embalming to convert their inclinations into profitable ventures. In 1862 the Washington, D. C., City Directory lists an advertisement by "Joseph Gawler, Undertaker" offering all conventional funeral items and "bodies embalmed if required."[8] Although the person who actually did the embalming for Gawler may be lost to history it would be a safe guess that he was in some way connected with the medical profession. By the following year the Washington Directory had added three more "embalmers of the dead": Brown and Alexander, Surgeons and Embalmers, 523 D St., North; the above mentioned Holmes, Thomas, 80 Louisiana Ave.; and Hutton, F. A., Dr., 451 Pennsylvania Ave.[9] This Hutton is the same as the inventor of the 1863 variety of "improved embalming fluid," and undoubtedly the competition he and others provided Holmes was substantial, in spite of Holmes' statement that he had more work than he could perform. In the 1863 Directory, Hutton took a full-page advertisement announcing that Dr. Hutton & Co. had established themselves in the city. The advertisment was designed to convince the public that their method of embalming "exceeds any thing of like nature in the world."

Bodies Embalmed by Us
NEVER TURN BLACK!

But retain their natural color and appearance; indeed, the method having the power of preserving bodies, with all their parts, both internal and external,

WITHOUT ANY MUTILATION OR EXTRACTION,

and so as to admit of contemplation of the person Embalmed, with the countenance of a one asleep . . . Surgeons and all interested are cordially invited to call and examine specimens after Embalmed . . .[10]

N. B. Particular attention paid to obtaining bodies of those who have fallen on the Battle Field.

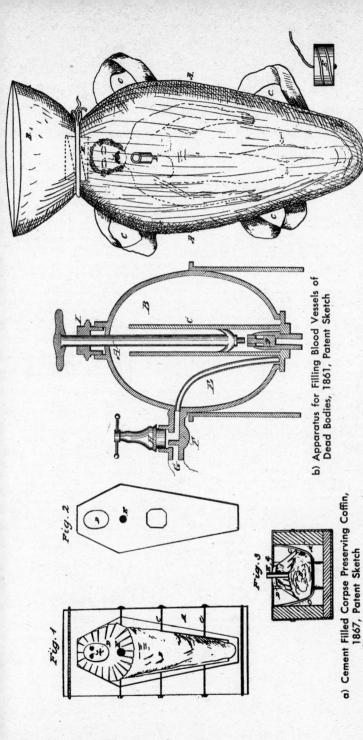

Fig. 1

Fig. 2

Fig. 3

a) Cement Filled Corpse Preserving Coffin, 1867, Patent Sketch

b) Apparatus for Filling Blood Vessels of Dead Bodies, 1861, Patent Sketch

c) Portable Elastic Receptacle for Shipping Body, 1863, Patent Sketch

PLATE 43

UNITED STATES PATENT OFFICE.

J. ANTHONY GAUSSARDIA, OF WASHINGTON, DISTRICT OF COLUMBIA.

METHOD OF PRESERVING DEAD BODIES.

Specification forming part of Letters Patent No. **15,972**, dated October 28, 1856.

To all whom it may concern:

Be it known that I, JOHN ANTHONY GAUSSARDIA, of the city and county of Washington, in the District of Columbia, have invented a new and Improved Method of Preserving Dead Bodies, of which the following is a full, clear, and exact description.

The body or subject to be preserved is first placed upon a table or other suitable place in a horizontal position and then injected with a strong mixture of acidum pyroligneum arsenicalis, a gallon of the mixture being sufficient for a grown person of ordinary size, this mixture being prepared by the addition of four ounces of white arsenic to one gallon of pyroligneous acid. The body thus prepared is then gradually charged with electricity from an electric machine until the liquid matters and humors have become congealed or coagulated, this being ascertained by the body becoming firmer or more solid to the touch or pressure of the hand, this part of the process, as a general thing, being effected in the course of from two and one-half to five hours, according to the condition of the body, one of the conductors of the machine being applied to the mouth and the other to the anus. The body is next washed in a strong mixture of arsenic, nitrate of potash, chloride of lime, and alchohol, this mixture being composed of about four ounces each of the arsenic and nitrate of potash, with two ounces of the chloride of lime to one gallon of alcohol, three successive times, a few hours being allowed to intervene between each to permit the mixture upon the body to become thoroughly dry, after which it may be anointed with aromatic oils and placed in a metallic coffin so constructed as to be capable of being hermetically sealed. In this condition the coffin is then filled with an alcoholic mixture of arsenic. The specific gravity of the alcohol in no case should be greater than .285, the quantity of arsenic required for this purpose being about the one-fiftieth part of the whole weight of the body thus treated, or at the rate of about two ounces of white arsenic to the gallon of alcohol, about eight ounces of the oils of cicuta and caryophyllus aromaticus being then added, after which the coffin is hermetically sealed and the process complete.

It may be here observed that the quantity of the mixture of the acid pyroligneum arsenicalis is increased or diminished according to the condition of the body being preserved. If partially decomposed, then a greater quantity is required than if it were in a good condition. Such being also the case where it is large and gross, these conditions being also dependent upon the age of the person whose body is being prepared and the season of the year in which the operation is being performed; but bodies once prepared in this manner will keep in all climates and for almost any length of time.

Bodies can, if desired, be so prepared as to preserve them but for a short time to enable them to be transported from the place where death intervened to the spot where their friends may wish to have them interred, this being effected by merely lessening the quantity of acidum pyroligneum arsenicalis to be administered and the quantity of electricity.

Having thus described my improved mode of preserving dead bodies, what I claim as new, and desire to secure by Letters Patent, is—

Injecting the body with a mixture of arsenical pyroligneous acid and then charging it with a current of electricity for the purposes described, and then filling the coffin in which the body is placed, and which is afterward hermetically sealed, with an alcoholic mixture of arsenic, together with the oils of cicuta and caryophyllus aromaticus, substantially as described.

J. A. GAUSSARDIA.

Witnesses:
P. HANNAY,
ARTHUR C. WATKINS.

Facsimile of First Patent for Embalming Process, 1856

PLATE 44

Below this advertisement is listed the undertaker, Mr. E. A. Williams, associated with Dr. Hutton. In his portion he offers both his services and a line of metallic, zinc, rosewood, and mahogany coffins. The final line gives the key to the whole operation and the picture at this juncture comes into focus. Although the U. S. Government did not establish the office of embalmer within the Army Medical Corps, nor in any other branch of the armed services, civilian undertakers were contracted to bury fallen or stricken soldiers, and many of these were embalmed preliminary to shipment home to relatives.

In point of fact several of the best known undertakers of the late 19th century established themselves in the business of caring for the dead directly as a result of receiving army contracts for soldier burial. Among these were Collins H. Jordan of Chicago who contracted for the burial of soldiers who died in the vicinity of that city; Lewis Jones, engaged by the government for the same services in and around Boston; John C. Rulon who handled the dead at Gettysburg; and John P. Epply, Cincinnati, who buried many of the soldiers who fell in the Shenandoah Valley, and E. A. Williams of Washington, D. C., and others. Jacob Gish, who was engaged as coffinmaker by the Quartermaster Corps during the War, returned afterwards to Omaha to enter the undertaking business. Still others, such as George W. Murphy of Quincy, Illinois; John Reade of Milford, Massachusetts; and Robert F. Atkins of Buffalo, served as soldiers in the army and returned to set up undertaking establishments at the close of hostilities.

If undertakers were engaged to bury the war dead by the government, embalming of bodies was not apparently specified in such official actions, or by official order. Whatever embalming had been done previous to the Civil War seems to have taken place within the context of medical pathology, and was based on such non-aesthetic considerations as sanitation, specimen-preservation, and other uses in connection with anatomical studies. Coroners whose background and orientation were medical likewise had reasons to seek better methods of preserving bodies. It should not be considered unusual, then, that at the outbreak of the Civil War chemical embalming by injection would at first be performed by men of medical training, since only they were familiar with the process. Their operations in the care of the dead consequently were technical and specific. Undertakers, in traditional fashion *undertook* the multiple tasks of removing, transporting, and "funeralizing" the dead, whilst medical embalmers either associated themselves with the undertakers in establishing the business of dealing with the dead, or, as was more likely the case, offered their special embalming techniques professionally for a fee. Holmes, apparently, had no scruples about advertising his services, yet it also must be noted that his operations were carried out in the parlors of established undertakers. Writing about this period later on, he explains:

When the war broke out, I want to Washington, had thousands of circulars distributed among the soldiers who were then protecting that city, and embalmed bodies free of charge—amongst whom was Col. Ellsworth. I exhibited bodies at Mr. Buckley's undertaker store, 304 Penn. Ave; at George Burch's Main Street, Georgetown, D. C., and at Benjamin Wheatley's King Street, Alexandria, Va.

The second year of the war, there was a large number of spurious embalmers in the army and around Washington. Some styled themselves "Government embalmers." A complaint was made to General Grant by the railroad companies of offensive odor from bodies on trains going North. An order was issued to Jacob Weaver, Undertaker at Baltimore to board every train and remove all bodies that were offensive, put them into a vault, or enclose them in tight zinc boxes and notify their friends, and every embalmer at City Point was ordered to leave the army. Large numbers of bodies which had been dead only two or three days were taken from the trains.[11]

While many of Holmes' statements and claims have been shown to be false or exaggerated, his remarks about the influx of embalmers into Washington, D. C., and environs seem well substantiated. There is no indication by Holmes in this correspondence that he was either a "Government embalmer," or a member of the armed forces acting in any capacity; likewise no record of such order dealing with the shipment of bodies has been found. Nevertheless, in the decades to follow, the problem of improperly prepared shipping cases became an important issue involving railroads, railwaymen's associations and funeral directors.

A series of closely grouped events that undoubtedly "triggered-off" a run of attention and gave an avenue of expression to a slowly generating desire to preserve the body in its natural state was the embalming of military officers, governmental officials, and other prominent Civil War figures. Col. Ellsworth was the earliest of such to be embalmed by Holmes according to his own list of important military embalmings. The case provided an occasion for widespread comment concerning chemical embalming by injection. Holmes is further credited with embalming the bodies of Colonel Bailey, Major Generals Buford and Sedgwick, and Brigadier Generals Farnsworth, Rice and Stevenson.[12] One of his students, Dr. E. C. Lewis, assisted the successful Nashville undertaker, W. P. Cornelius. Otherwise Holmes did not function as a teacher or professor of embalming. Although no important military embalmings seem to have gone to Dr. Hutton, nor to Dr. Chamberlain, the Civil War embalmers and surgeons, Brown and Alexander, prepared the body of young Willie Lincoln who died in 1863; and two years later embalmed Lincoln himself.[13] It is from these notable examples that the public in general first became aware of the most recent innovations in the preservation of the dead. Additionally, those who were able to have the bodies of their relatives returned from the war theaters—there seems no way to estimate their number—could give testimony to the effectiveness and desirability of chemical embalming by injection.

"Schools," Fluid Houses, and the Spread of Embalming: From the Civil War to the end of the century the story of embalming in America is best seen in three dimensions: first, the resistance to chemical preservatives; second, the rise and decline of the medical specialist as embalmer; and third, the development of a commercial enterprise in the compounding and distribution of embalming fluids, with the attendant rise of the "embalming school."

Resistance to the use of embalming fluids came from two sources, the public, and the undertakers themselves. Preservation by ice, "conserving the remains" as was usually the phrase, was somewhat awkward, but it had the virtue of simplicity and it yielded a modest profit. Ten dollars was not an unusual charge for such a service. Earliest chemical embalming was the specialty of the physician and the fee was high—Holmes averaged $100.00 per case for an embalmed Union soldier—and it was a simpler matter to use the conventional ice cooling than to bring in the "expert," whose skill was often suspect, and whose finished product was not always satisfactory. Public resistance to the mutilation of the remains, moreover, had the sanction of the Christian tradition that the body is the temple of God, and that the remains are always sacred and must in every case be treated with reverence. In an attempt to dispel this objection, advertisements such as Dr. Hutton's, stressed the "humaneness" of the new process.

Important also, the need to embalm chemically without evisceration was met by the invention of an injection pump with an elongated, hollow needle. This pump and needle device was used both for aspiration of body cavities and for the injection of embalming fluids, without the necessity of making major bodily incisions. The needle, later called the "trocar," was patented in 1878, the year that embalming fluid was first compounded commercially on a substantial scale. By 1890 this important instrument was universally a part of all standard embalming equipment. The injection into body cavities of embalming fluid is, however, antecedent to the use of the arterial system as the medium of chemical embalming.

If the opening of the Civil War found embalming and the compounding of embalming fluids monopolized by physicians, surgeons, physiologists, anatomists, chemists, pharmacists, druggists, and other persons connected with the rising medical profession, its close saw changes which would eventually bring these processes and preparations almost completely under the control of pharmacists, undertakers, and wholesale chemical compounding concerns. Although undertakers in particular had virtually no experience in chemical embalming by injection before the outbreak of the war, it was almost inevitable, if they handled the dead through government contract, that bodily preservation would become increasingly a problem, especially as transportation facilities grew and the desire to have the dead returned home for burial remained strong. The "air-tight" metallic burial case offered one solution, although the case never was completely satisfactory, since the gases generated by the decomposing body developed great pressures and often burst the sides of the receptacle. Embalming by injection of preservative fluids offered another. This latter method had the drawback that it was a newcomer in America, and very much within the province of the physician. Ice preservation obviously had extreme disadvantages for undertakers shipping bodies any distance.

Undertakers with government contracts for the handling
of the war dead were faced periodically after every battle with
the problem of time and of shipping many of the bodies
for considerable distances. Since embalming was beyond the
routine procedures of many undertakers, some of them retained surgeon-embalmers on a fee basis, or took them into
partnership. Others, unable or unwilling to operate through
specialists, found themselves in the role of innovators and
experimenters. The case of W. H. Devore, a Pittsburgh
undertaker, illustrates the point. Writing in *The Casket* in
October, 1895, he remarks:

At the commencement of the Civil War I secured the government contract for embalming and burial of all bodies from
camps and hospitals then located in the section of the country
around Pittsburgh; also the contract for the city, Allegheny
County, and all railroads centering in Pittsburgh. These contracts were over and above my regular business. So it is readily
seen that a multitude of opportunities were presented for experiment. My first experiments were during the early part of
the military encampments here and were continued with increasing success for many years, both as to the fluid used and
manner of operating.

Although it is highly doubtful that embalming was officially stipulated in such contracts, the demands of these
situations made it one of the ready solutions. For many
undertakers the war presented an opportunity for them to
develop and henceforth to put to use a new mortuary skill.
While this statement does not mean, of course, that embalming by injection of chemical fluids dominated the picture of
body preservation at the war's close, it seems clear that, by
the time the last shot had been fired, this mode of preservation had secured for itself a permanent place in the American
funeral customs.

The decade following the war found the surgeon-embalmer
playing a less important role. He was less eager to make a ca-

reer out of embalming than were certain others outside of or peripheral to the medical arts. While Holmes returned to New York and practiced medicine, compounded drugs, and sold his own fluid, pump and process, other medical practitioners dropped out of sight in the mortuary field, or in a few notable cases shifted to the compounding and sale of fluids, or the teaching of embalming techniques, or to a combination of merchandising and teaching. As medical practitioners retreated from the field, undertakers advanced into it; until, as has been noticed, the period became for them one of great opportunity, in which they experimented with new practices and ideas, and reviewed the developments in the funeral field as they had been augmented and accentuated by the war. Men like Thomas W. Bothick of New Orleans, Robert Atkins of Buffalo, George W. Murphy of Quincy, Illinois, James Taylor of Trenton, New Jersey, and Jacob Gish of Omaha, Nebraska, to mention only a few, could, as a result of Civil War experience found undertaking establishments, or shift to undertaking as a full time occupation. Embalming, no longer unknown and untried, had already gained its toehold; and these men and many others were willing, along with those who had known, or learned the rudiments of embalming during the war, to add this technique to their services. One of the foremost of those inspired was Hudson Samson of Pittsburgh, who as early as 1870 had embalmed the dead as part of his funeral services. (See Plate 45.)

The receptiveness of many undertakers to this innovation had its counterpart in the willingness of druggists and pharmacist-physicians to experiment in the compounding of various fluids. We noted earlier that between 1855 and 1870 a dozen or so patents were granted for various kinds of embalming fluids and processes emphasizing chemical embalming by injection. Other concoctions, such as Holmes' and Hill's, were marketed but not patented. It is interesting also to note that the earliest compounders of embalming fluids, whether medically trained or not, chose to call themselves "professors." Although this term had somewhat more validity later, when "schools" of embalming first got under way, it is likely that its original use was due to the inspiration of undertakers and other non-medically trained individuals who felt the need to legitimate their interests and experiments in embalming techniques, the compounding of fluids, and the building of embalming apparatus.

Thus a good decade before the appearance of any type of formal instruction, Prof. E. H. Crane, who had embalmed Civil War soldiers, had patented in 1868 and sold "Crane's Electro-Dynamic Mummifier," a preparation composed mostly of salts of heavy metals, to be forced into all bodily cavities. His customers were undertakers in and around Michigan. By 1878 Prof. George M. Rhodes, bought the rights to this or a similar compound from Crane and marketed it as "Professor Rhodes' Electric Balm." By 1880 at least four concerns were compounding embalming fluids commercially: The Hill Chemical Company of Springfield, Ohio, which had started in 1878 and shortly afterward became The Champion Chemical Company; The Clarke Chemical Works; and Mills and Lacey, of Grand Rapids, Michigan, who were compounding Prof. Rhodes' formula. The fourth company emerged when Crane went to Kalamazoo, and interested O. M. Allen, Sr., in a similar enterprise. "Crane's Excelsior Preservation" was prepared and sold as a sideline by the Globe Casket Manufacturing Company.[14]

The Champion Chemical Company (now The Champion Company) was the first organized to make and sell embalming materials. The formula was provided by Mr. Ed. Hill, a druggist in Springfield, who had developed it in connection with his interest in the funeral industry. Although Hill did

September 1870

John G...
Walnut Casket & box.   20.00   March 1
    name Plate   3.00
13½ yards of Crape   8.10   April
18 "   " Ribbon   4.50
4 pairs " Gloves   1.00
Merino Rapper   6.00
10 Carriages   50.00   98 60
    & Hearse   6.00
                       $98.60 $98 60

20 Estate of Hannah
To fine O.G Rosewood coffin 80.00 July 28
    name Plate   3.00
14½ yards of Crape   7.25   100.00
25 "   " Ribbon   6.25   Cr with
13 pairs " Gloves   2.50   May
20 Carriages   120.00   Jan
    Hearse   9.00
1 Carr all day   4.00
                          $230.00 $230.00

20 Estate of Hon. G.L.
To fine Rosewood Casket   154.00
    name Plate   5.00   Oct 8/70
12 yards of Crape   7.20
2 Bolts " Ribbon   6.00
14 pairs " Gloves   8.40   244.60
Embalming & Services   30.00
                          $210.60 $211.60

20 Harper & Co
    Mary
    7 yds crape   3   50   Sept
    12 yds Ribbon   3   00   April
    4 Pairs Gloves   1   00
                        5   00   13 50

from Ledger of Hudson Samson, 1870, Showing Charge for "Embalming and Services."

PLATE 45

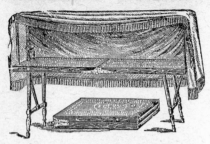

Cooling Boards and Improved Ice Caskets, Late 19th Century

PLATE 46

not have the aptitude for making and selling embalming fluid on a commercial scale, he interested Dr. A. A. Baker, a physician in Springfield, and his son Scipio Baker, in developing his formula and presenting it to the funeral industry. Actually the operation of the company fell to the son, who remained its chief executive well into the present century.

The multiplication of chemical compounding concerns in the early '80's created the need for wider markets, and expanded distribution. Salesmen were sent on the road, some of them also representing lines of caskets, fluids, and other funeral paraphernalia; others promoted the sale of fluids alone. The sale of embalming fluid was assisted by the wave of humanitarianism that was sweeping over the country. Here, they claimed, was an answer to the mutilation of the body, to freezing the corpse with ice, or to encasing it in a heavy metal receptacle wherein decomposition might be arrested but not necessarily stopped. In an article on the history of embalming appearing in *The Casket* for April, 1892, N. T. Shaw traces out in his own experience a typical case involving the transition from ice-cooling to embalming:

> In the first place I will state, I am now sixty-two years old and have been engaged in the undertaking business all my life, until the departure from the ice to the fluids, and from the huge ice-casket to the nicely draped cooling board.

> My first experience in embalming was when in the army. There I found but few who made a success of it. Two of those who were successful were Dr. Holmes, of Brooklyn, and W. P. Cornelius, who is now a prominent undertaker of Nashville, Tenn. So, on my return from the army, to my business of undertaking, I determined to do away with the cumbersome ice-casket, and in order to further perfect my plans I invented and patented a canopy-top cooling board (as I then called it, and by the way this was the first ever patented.) which I substituted in place of ice-caskets. This I soon found to be a grand success in my business in Newark, Ohio, and went on the road to try and introduce this new reform.

The first two years I met with rather poor success; partially on account of the poor knowledge of embalming and partially on account of my imperfect board. It soon became apparent to Prof. Clarke that the time had come for a reformation in this line; so he prepared himself for the work; and with Dr. Lukens, and Charles M. Eppley (a prominent undertaker in Cincinnati) they organized what was then called the Cincinnati School of Embalming, which I claim, was the perfecting of the reform.

Clarke's pioneer role in setting up the early—possibly earliest—embalming "schools" or "institutes" is interesting, because it reveals the interdependence of the early selling and promoting function with instruction in embalming techniques. Brought up to be a druggist, Clarke as a young man first became interested in the preservation of dead animal tissue. Later he studied medicine privately, and was in medical school when the Civil War broke out. His only war service was as a civilian assistant hospital steward. With the return of peace, he became a "house and road" salesman for the White Water Valley Coffin Company, or Connersville, Indiana. While on the road he met the erstwhile Professor Rhodes, who sold Clarke six bottles of embalming fluid, and gave him a modicum of advice on arterial and cavity embalming. Using the cadavers of his casket-buying clientele Clarke experimented with the art of chemical embalming by injection, and soon satisfied himself that this skill would not only add a new dimension to the service of the undertaker, but also held out promise for commercial exploitation.

In the fall of 1881 Clarke suggested to Dr. C. M. Lukens, a demonstrator of anatomy in Pulte Medical College, Cincinnati, Ohio, that an embalming school should be set up at that institution. Agreement was reached in March, 1882; and the first session opened in the ampitheatre March 8, and ended March 31. This brief course marks the beginning of *established* embalming schools carried out under institutional, or quasi-institutional auspices. Although the

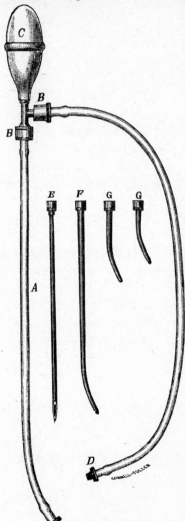
Advertisement for Embalming Supplies, 1880, *The Casket*

PLATE 47

When Your Fluid Fails
Who Pays the Damage?

The forfeit of the price of one or two gallons of fluid will not atone for the damage. You pay for the failure by loss of prestige and loss of business. Isn't that so?

The safest and cheapest way is to use a fluid that can't fail—a fluid that has the

=== STRENGTH ===

to successfully overcome every condition that can be found in a dead body.

It is the strong fluid that carries few worries—it is the strong fluid that thoroughly preserves when the case is a difficult one, when ammoniacal gases exist and in hot, sultry weather—it is the strong fluid that establishes the embalmer's reputation for good work—and the fluids which have shown conspicuous strength in successfully preserving every kind of a case, no matter how difficult or what the conditions, and have demonstrated that they are entitled to the name "Strong Fluids" are

THE NON-POISONOUS BIG FOUR

ESCO-RADIUM, N. P., ESCO, N. P., UPTIMUM AND BESTCON, (Best Concentrated Fuid.)

It needs something more than the ordinary formaldehyde fluid to successfully overcome ammoniacal gases and hold Dropsy, Typhoid Fever cases, and stop purging in hot, sultry weather. But there is no case so difficult, no condition so bad that these fluids will not overcome every time.

They will preserve indefinitely, not only for three days, but for three years if you want it; they preserve the life-like appearance, not a putty colored, or shriveled up mummy. They are successful every time because they contain the right kind of chemicals for overcoming every kind of condition that the embalmer meets.

25 years manufacturing nothing else but embalming fluids and embalmers' supplies, a life-time of study of what is needed for the proper preservation of a body, are what have made these fluids what they are—safe and sure fluids in every instance.

Every undertaker, every embalmer, every manager, who wants positive results in all cases should send for a supply of these never-failing hot weather fluids for hot weather work and important cases.

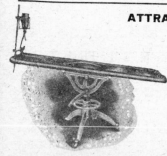

ATTRACTIVE PARLORS

impress the public and bring business.

Nothing so adds to the attractiveness of an undertaker's establishment as an ESCO BRASS RIM MORGUE TABLE. Nothing has ever awakened so much interest in the profession as this extremely attractive business-bringer. Hundreds of shrewd, far-seeing business men have equipped their places with these tables, because they realized that they were business-bringers and are exceedingly good advertisements to their place.

THE EMBALMERS' SUPPLY CO.
WESTPORT, CONN.
CHICAGO, and LOS ANGELES, CAL.

Originators of Formalhyde and Concentrated Embalming Fluids and Manufacturers of the Celebrated Non-Corrosive Esco Instruments, Sundries, Disinfectants and Disinfecting Appliances.

Early Advertisement for Non-Poisonous Embalming Fluid, 1909, *Western Undertaker*

PLATE 48

Champion College of Embalming traces back to 1878, it had a nebulous institutional existence; the Rochester School of Embalming, conducted by Auguste Renouard, who had instructed privately in the art of embalming for several years previously, also opened in 1882, somewhat later than Clarke's, and lasted only two years. Renouard, however, continued to be a prominent figure in mortuary education.

The first year of the Cincinnati School of Embalming, as it became known, saw six classes given in Cincinnati in medical schools and in Dr. Lukens' office; and four others in Philadelphia, Boston, and New York, respectively. These ten classes graduated approximately one hundred and twenty-two undertakers, many of them well known in the field. Dr. Lukens acted as principal, while Clarke and C. M. Epply, son of John Epply, assisted as lecturers and demonstrators. Although Lukens and Clarke attended strictly to matters pertaining to embalming, Epply instructed and demonstrated lining and trimming caskets, funeral conduct, and practical undertaking. When circumstances permitted, students were given cadavers to embalm; and at the close of a week's instruction had usually mastered the rudiments of the embalming process. Clarke tells of one student who ran and hid in a closet at the sight of two dead bodies, but "was brought out of his hiding place, put to work and became a good student and operator."[15]

The proponents of preservation by ice were not always easily convinced. Among the doubters was Major Hulfish, of Hulfish and Crans, Newark undertakers. According to Clarke:

(Hulfish) . . . told me I was a fraud and humbug to . . . say I could teach anyone not a physician how to embalm and preserve dead bodies without ice, and invited me to leave the office, which I did not do until I had an interview with his partner, Mr. Crans, who invited me to call again and have another talk with the

major, which I did on my next visit to Newark, and Mr. Crans
saw me embalm the body of a lady for Mr. Ormsby, and knew
the body kept beautifully without the aid of ice for several
days and was convinced. In our next trip east Mr. Crans
came to New York to be humbugged, and said that ten times
the cost of tuition had been received during the course.[16]

The early tours of Clarke and his associates occasionally
met with disbelief and misgivings. In one instance there
was doubt voiced that an embalmed body would ever get to
heaven; in many others the demand for the use of ice was
strong. However the demonstrations almost always were
convincing, the thirty dollar fee was usually considered money
well spent, and the certificates were prized by their recipients.

By the end of the 1880's numerous embalming fluid companies had entered the commercial field. In 1886, a manufacturers' directory published in *The Casket* listed ten
companies as manufacturers of embalming supplies. Most
companies hired demonstrators for classes, or "schools" of
embalming. One of the foremost teachers of his day, and
undoubtedly one of the best embalmers of this period, was
Dr. Auguste Renouard, a competitor of Clarke. Each represented a different brand of fluid, Clarke his own, and Renouard, for some time that of the Brooklyn Embalming Fluid
Company. Likewise Dr. Eliab Meyers demonstrated for the
Champion Company.

It is interesting to review some of the names of the
various fluids. An identification with the past, especially with
Egypt, is noticeable: the Egyptian Chemical Company;
the Egyptian Embalmer Company; and such fluids as
"Utopia," "The Oriental," "Egyptian," and the like. More
recently embalming fluid terminology has tended in the
direction of pseudo-scientific imagery, with combinations
drawn from the symbol storehouse of modern chemistry.

Techniques of embalming rapidly improved; before 1882

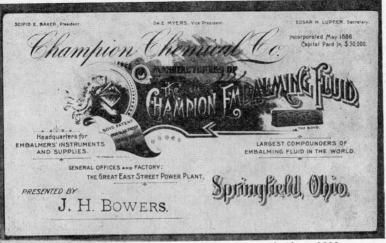

a) Embalming Supplies Salesman's Business Card, About 1900

b) Advertisement of Pioneer in Embalming, Auguste Renouard

PLATE 49

most embalming was done through the use of injection of fluid into body cavities. The spreading use of arterial embalming coincides with the increased commercialization of fluids and their promotion by the demonstrators of the "schools" and classes. By 1886 there was only one company, J. C. Taylor, listed in *The Casket* directory under the category of "Cold Air Preservers."[17] By the end of the succeeding decade the battle of "ice vs. arsenic" was definitely over, and arterial and cavity embalming, promoted and popularized by manufacturers of divers embalming fluids, not only had won over the resistance of undertakers but had allayed the fears of the public as to such questions as mutilation and other forms of man's inhumanity to man on the embalming table.

CITATIONS AND REFERENCES IN CHAPTER VIII

1. Charles L. Wallis, *Stories on Stone* (New York: Oxford University Press, 1954), p. 240.

2. *Ibid.*

3. *Ibid.*

4. Ralph H. Gabriel, *The Course of American Democratic Thought* (New York: The Ronald Press Co., 1940), p. 4.

5. For an excellent study of epidemic sickness in this period see John Duffy, *Epidemics in Colonial America* (Baton Rouge, La.: Louisiana State University Press, 1953).

6. Among the many sketches of "Dr." Holmes, one of the more entertaining is "The First Embalmer" by Trentwell M. White and Ivan Sandrof in the November 7, 1942, issue of the *New Yorker*. Somewhat more critical is Seabury Quinn's "Who Was the Father of Modern Embalming?", in *The American Funeral Director*, May, 1944, pp. 27-30.

7. Adapted from Mendlesohn, *Embalming Fluids, op. cit.*, pp. 110-111.

8. Quoted in Quinn, *op. cit.*, p. 28.

9. *Ibid.*

10. *Ibid.*, p. 29.

11. *The Casket*, May, 1892.

12. Quinn, *op. cit.*, pp. 28-29.

13. *Ibid.*, p. 29.

14. Joseph H. Clarke, *Reminiscences of Early Embalming* (New York: The Sunnyside, 1917), pp. 3-5. This is one of the most important references dealing with the rise of mortuary science education in America.

15. *Ibid.*, pp. 11-12.

16. *Ibid.*, pp. 13-14.

17. *The Casket Directory of Manufacturers and Jobbers of Funeral Supplies, 1886.*

~ Transportation: Carriage to Gas Buggy

The death of a human being universally interrupts ordinary routines and calls for new modes of physical and emotional behavior. One of the most inescapable needs created by death in an organized society arises from the fact that the corpse must be moved from the point of death to other places for preparation and disposal. Those who are involved with the dead are therefore faced with a transportation problem that broadens itself to include the mourners and others connected with funeralization. Additionally, with the social, physical, and economic development of society, transportation is likely to assume new functions and forms and to take on new meanings and importance.

Although in our funeral history we have generally moved forward to the end of the 19th century, this chapter will begin with a brief retrospective glance at early American transportation usages and paraphernalia. Special attention will be directed to the changing meaning and form of some of the *terms* which have now become associated with funeral transportation.

Funeral Processions and the Hearse: Whether the point of sepulture be a grave, tomb, pyre, or as an extreme example, a coffin-laden boat to be set afire and set adrift on the outgoing tide, the procession to it is a solemn social act that imparts importance, dignity, and profundity to the ceremonial disposal of the dead. Whether it takes the form of pageantry; of mournful, simple silence; of noise and expressive behavior; of mock gaiety or real gloom, the funeral procession is a dramatic movement involving many actors. Although the performance may have its basis in an indispensable physical act, social participation in it cannot help but produce significant ceremonial overtones. So important is the collective act of bearing the dead to the place of sepulture that it has tended historically either to be incorporated into religious organization, or to come under religious control. Even when the inspiration for them is secular, parades have the power to stir; and when a parade is joined to the intrinsic solemnity of death and burial, that power is increased. "Of all processions," says Rech, "the funeral procession is the oldest. It starts at a period antedating wheeled vehicles, and it has continued down to the present. The character and form of the procession, or to use the modern term, the funeral, varies widely in different countries. Regardless of variety, it is one of the most universal human acts."[1] It might also be noticed that the word "funeral" is derived from *funeralis*, the Latin for "torchlight procession."

One of the standard pieces of equipment and the most common symbol of the funeral procession has been the hearse. This term has its origin in the French word *herse*, which in turn is taken from the Latin *hirpex*, meaning a rake or harrow. The resemblance that originally existed is clear when it is considered that the first hearse was a stationary framework of wood to hold lighted tapers and decorations placed on a bier or coffin. In this form it must have looked much like a huge, rectangular rake lying with its teeth or prongs pointed upward. This early simple frame later developed into an elaborate, pagoda-shaped erection of wood or metalwork for the funerals of royal or other distinguished persons. It held banners, candles, armorial bearings, and other heraldic devices. Complimentary verses or epitaphs were often attached to the hearse.[2]

Hearses were also used to enclose the tomb or grave. This type varied from the simple iron stand over which the pall might be draped during the ceremony to highly stylistic devices resembling miniature gothic churches with many iron or brass spikes on which candles were impaled. (See Plate 50.)

A simple forerunner of the hearse, in the conventional sense in which we use the term today, was a bier or "bear" in the form of a hand-stretcher on which the uncoffined body was carried to the grave. (See Plate 50.) As coffins were brought into popular use they were likewise borne on the bier; but the additional weight, especially in the case of lined or multiple coffins, necessitated an adaptation to the problem of long carries. One solution was to have two sets of bearers. Four of the oldest or most prominent men were called the "bearers"; another four, whose duty it was to relieve the bearers, were called "under-bearers."[3]

As long as bodies were buried in churches, the stationary nature of early hearses is understandable. Once intramural burial became limited or restricted, and cemeteries were established outside of cities, the need for some better form of transportation than that provided by "bearing," or by hand or shoulder carrying became urgent. As burial grounds were laid out at a greater distance from thickly populated districts, carrying the body on a hand-bier grew to be too laborious, and some sort of a horse-drawn vehicle became necessary.[4] Rech notes that the first instance of a hearse on wheels is found in the burial of Colonel Rainsborowe in 1648, and that in 1673, Anthony Walker, a preacher, said, "More friends attend a hearse to the Town-end than will drive through with it the whole journey." Also, by 1690 the hearse had become a necessity in England, and advertisements appeared in the *London Gazette* offering hearses for hire.[5] Yet the term "bier" also continued in use in connection with conveyances strictly limited to carrying the dead, and as late as the mid-19th century "hearse" and "bier" were commonly interchangeable.

Because the roads leading out from early towns and villages were often narrow, rough, and muddy, and sometimes little more than paths, the earliest moveable hearses were of necessity much smaller than the stationary hearse that preceded them. In some instances these hearses were so short that the coffin would come up under the seat of the driver who would either have to straddle it, or sit to one side of it. To increase maneuverability, the wheels would cut under the body of the vehicle. Later the carriage part was made a distinct unit.

Colonial Hearses: In early Colonial times rural and village funerals undoubtedly lacked the convenience of the hearse, or horse drawn bier specifically intended for funeral purposes. Bodies might be transported simply by wagon, although the funeral procession, whether to the family grave, or the community churchyard, would more likely be on foot and the body borne by hand. As cities appeared along the seaboard and in the wilderness behind it, commercial successes fostered more elaborate forms of social organization, and funerals for prosperous and important people often took on a character reminiscent of upper-class English usage. As early as 1687 Judge Sewall wrote in his diary that at the funeral of Lady Andros (a Church of England woman, not a Puritan), "The corps was carried (from the church) into the Hearse drawn by Six Horses . . ."[6]

When in 1697 Colonel Shrimpton died of apoplexy and was given a military funeral, Sewall noted cryptically, "Ten companies, No Herse nor Trumpet, but a horse led. Mourning coach also & Horses in Mourning, Scutcheons on their sides with Death Heads on their foreheads."[7] Some twenty-seven years later Judge Sewall noted the surviving use of escutcheons on the hearse carrying the body of Mrs. Katherine Winthrop.

Nearly a century before the Revolutionary War a few horse drawn hearses were in use by several of the richer families in towns in New England and the Middle Colonies. Although well-appointed livery was relatively scarce before 1700, and most funeral processions were on foot, the use of carriages and coaches in making the journey to the grave was no novelty. "Glass coaches" had already made their appearance in England; and until the colonial craftsmen of a later period could assemble the materials, men, and know-how, carriages, coaches, and chaises were necessarily imported.[8]

The making of gentlemen's coaches such as were used in funeral processions involved considerable skill. Bridenbaugh points out that coachmaking was an urban luxury craft:

One of the most spectacular symbols of colonial affluence and gentility was a gentlemen's carriage, and as men grew richer in town and country the business of coachmaking prospered. It was a trade requiring the careful combining of talents of wood and metal workers, as well as the skills of other artisans; the blacksmith and the ornamental iron worker assisted the joiner or coachmaker, the carver, the upholsterer, and the leather worker in building a vehicle upon which the painter, japanner, and perhaps the heraldic-device liner placed the finishing touches. An elaborate industry such as this, moreover, demanded a large investment of capital, and not until after the middle of the century (18th) did American coaches begin to compete with carriages imported from London and Dublin.[9]

Another category of persons also became involved as problems of transportation expanded along with the growth of towns and cities. These were the liverymen who imported and sold hearses to the well-to-do, or rented to the less well-off who desired the prestige of a coach-and-four. Bridenbaugh again notes:

Most of the Boston gentry kept coaches, and carriage makers like John Lucas had orders enough to keep them constantly at work. Gentlemen and their "virtuous consorts" reclined on cane seats or sank comfortably into the green plush of their equipages, while Negro coachmen drove them to church or to social gatherings, for all to see and for laborers and tradesmen to envy. Those with pretensions, but without the means, could hire of George Hewes "a Handsome Chair Chaise on Reasonable terms," while Samuel Bleigh and Alexander Thorpe kept coaches and black horses to rent for funerals.[10]

In the New England Colonies the preliminary steps by which the role of undertaker came into being usually involved work as sexton, cabinet-maker, or coffinmaker. In the Middle Colonies the carriage master or livery stable operator was more likely to extend his function beyond merely supplying hearses and carriages to that of *service* in the care and disposal of the dead. One short step from providing transportation would be the directing of the funeral procession and the taking charge of the order of the proceedings. In Baltimore, where the move of the carriage master toward the undertaker had an early start, we find in an 1824 City Directory this announcement:

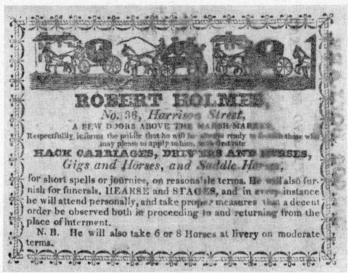

Figure 28. Early 19th Century Ad of the Liveryman-Undertaker

The drawing above shows three types of conveyances, one of them definitely a hearse. Examples of American funeral hearses, much earlier than those found in livery stable advertisements, exist, however. One such conveyance still in good condition (see Plate 50), although reputed to have been built in 1787, has glass panels, ornate exterior cabinet work, a narrow lined interior, and drapes on either side. Another fine, substantial example of an early pioneer hearse (see Plate 51), shows simplicity itself: large hind wheels; smaller front wheels that turn under the body; a narrow body with the coffin fitting up under the driver's seat; and the only non-functional objects, six wooden-turned "urns" spaced across the top of the vehicle.

Hearses with Horses: 1850-1910: Until the Civil War the field of hearse manufacture was a somewhat stable sideline for several carriage manufacturers. A few concerns such as the Merts and Riddle Coach and Hearse Co. of Ravenna, Ohio, established in 1831; The James Cunningham, Son & Co., carriage and hearse manufacturers of Rochester, N. Y., established in 1838; and Brownell's Hearse Repository, founded in New Bedford, Mass., about 1843, engaged in the manufacture of these transportation specialties. The stability of this sideline arose from the fact that until the War, fashion had little effect upon hearse design or materials. Advertisements in directories show that from 1825 to 1850 hearses changed only slightly, although it is possible that in the largest cities, the demands of undertakers for improved vehicles were beginning to make headway among hearse manufacturers. The slowness of change in the next fifteen years is evident in the fact that with only slight modification the hearse already in use in 1853 appeared in the advertisement of Lockhart and Seelye, Coffin Manufacturers, in the Cambridge, Mass., City Directory for the year 1866.

In spite of the conservatism that carried the styles and materials of hearse-making from year to year with little change, by the outbreak of the War in the spring of 1861 fashion was beginning to play a more important role in funeral equipage, and by the end of the War the styles had changed so that the older hearses were rapidly becoming outmoded.

The hearse of the 1840's and 1850's might linger in use during the 1860's, but from that period on styles in hearses changed with cyclical regularity at intervals of about 15 years. Reasonably enough, fashion seemed to have joined hands with the amount of use a manufacturer built into his hearses, for in this period the wear and tear occasioned by hard driving, frequent trips, and constant washing, made it necessary either to replace a hearse or to have it substantially rebuilt. As explained by a "Cincinnati Expert"[11] in an

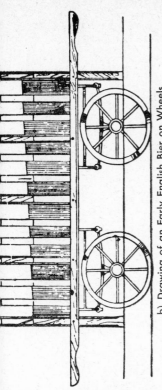

b) Drawing of an Early English Bier on Wheels

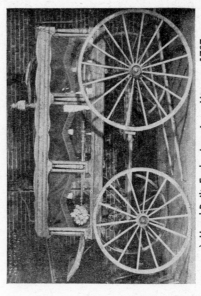

c) Hand-Built Early American Hearse, 1787

PLATE 50

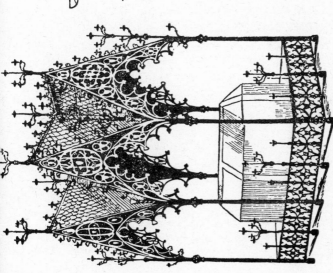

a) Wrought Iron Hearse of Renaissance Times

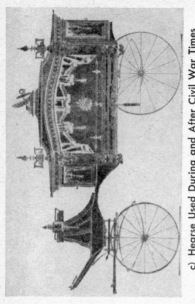

a) A Pioneer Hearse

c) Hearse Used During and After Civil War Times

b) American Hearse of the 1850's

d) Return to Severe Design About 1884

unsigned article reviewing the history of style changes in hearses:

> After about fifteen years . . . the owner thinks it time for a change; time to have a new hearse, and something as different as possible, in order that its newness be apparent for purposes of advertising.
>
> So the undertaker buys a new one . . . (which) creates a sensation; so altogether different; so bright, sparkling and new; and with a new team—a fine pair of young horses, most likely, and with a new livery for the driver, a new silk hat, etc. Everybody notices it. There is a "write-up" in the newspapers, probably, and, all else being right as it should be, there is an increase in business. Competitors "sit-up and take notice." Their own hearses now appear to be a little out of date, not to say back numbers, and pretty soon there is another hearse in town . . . (In) about eight or ten years there is not one of the previous styles of hearses in town; neither in that town nor other towns, for the new style has spread all over the country.[12]

After all local undertakers had put new hearses into use there followed a period of a few years when the hearse style remained relatively unchanged. Then the earliest to make the change found his hearse the oldest of the new but now aging style. As before, he wanted something so different that it would be quite evident that he had made another change. Perhaps he had thought of a few innovations of his own, which he would be able to persuade the carriage maker to incorporate into the newly ordered hearse. Or, perhaps, the carriage maker himself modified his product in order to keep and enlarge his market. "Another copy, the style spreads—and the change in style again gradually takes place all over the country."

Although the fifteen year style cycle naturally operated to their advantage it does not follow that this cycle was a simple creation of the manufacturers of hearses. Had they been able to control the style change, obviously it would have been profitable to exploit annual models, as does the modern automobile industry. But the spread of a new style was slow, and the decision to change by undertakers was a product of a calculation in which the utility of the old vehicle was balanced against the advantages to be gained by getting ahead of competition or keeping up with it by purchasing a new vehicle. For this reason the style cycle in hearses operated seemingly in terms of a number of distinctly economic and social factors reflective of forces and conditions, many of which were outside the control of hearse manufacturers. Hence the "Cincinnati Expert" notes:

It is not true, as a rule, that the factories get up the new styles and start them on their way faster than buyers can be expected to purchase them. It does not pay them to do so. The factories do not wish radical changes to come too often. They prefer that the changes come just about as they have come—gradually, and in cycles of about fifteen years.[18]

The hearse of the 1850's (see Plate 51), was basically a long, rectangular box, with windows along the side of double thick French glass, and skimped curtains. Shafts usually were for one horse only and the driver's seat was on top. By the time of the Civil War the style had already changed, (see Plate 51), and the hearse had become longer and higher, with full plate glass sides, fancy scroll-work along the top, metal columns, and a scrolled iron neck—a "goose neck"—that connected a fancy seat for the driver with the body. Some hearses of this type had plated metal Corinthian columns. Although this style was roomier than its immediate predecessor its inner dimensions were only such as to afford space for an extra-size casket, and it was still called a "hearse," as against a "funeral car." The latter title did not come into use until the conveyance was later considerably increased in size.

At the close of the War, in response to general change in fashion which touched many items of living, there was a call for something different, something more imposing, finally resulting in the building of the really large and massive, bent glass, full circle end, or Clarence front, hearses. These remained in style for a little more than 15 years, until the New Orleans Cotton Exposition, about 1884.[14]

At least until 1875 no hearse was considered completely trimmed without plumes waving from the urns that usually decorated the top of the body. After this period the plumes were replaced by deck ornaments and emblems; and later, these were cleared away and smooth, undecorated tops became the fashion.

The James Cunningham, Son & Co. exhibit at the New Orleans Cotton Exposition in 1884 featured a "funeral car," radically different from the prevailing style. (See Plate 51.) It was rectangular—falling back to an earlier form—and had a hip roof, five urns, and at each corner a gilded column "around which there climbed an ivy vine in green." Shortly after the War hearses for children came into use and the beautiful white child's hearse of this company sold by The Stein Patent Burial Casket Works met with immediate popular approval. Throughout the last quarter of the 19th century children's hearses were standard equipment for all undertakers and funeral directors. (See Plate 52.) In 1884 the rectangular "four poster" fairly revolutionized the hearse building industry. As a result for a few years and in certain restricted localities the term "hearse" soon became almost an epithet to be applied to an out-of-style funeral vehicle. Undertakers bought "funeral cars," or admitted hearses were out of date. The word "hearse" has since returned to accepted standard usage for the vehicle used to transport the dead at funerals.

In 1889 Hudson Samson's special eight-poster, oval-decked, funeral car, and a similar vehicle but with six columns, ordered by James Lowrie and Sons of Allegheny, Pa., sounded the warning bell for the new style and a death knell, after a quarter century or more, of the ornamented deck. By 1898 all funeral directors of any pretension had an eight-column, oval-decked funeral car, no matter what the price.

At the Chicago World's Fair in 1893, Crane & Breed Mfg. Co. exhibited the most elaborate and outstanding funeral car of the 19th century. (See Plate 54.) Designed for West Indian and South American trade, its features included extraordinary size; churchlike design; massive carvings in bold relief; gildings; heavy gold fringes and tassels; and lamps of gold. Weighing 2400 lbs. as against a standard weight of about 1600 lbs., it was laden with golden angels and cherubs; crucifixes and statues; a processional scene over the middle glass in which the Saviour was depicted bearing the cross and preceded by the two thieves, the two Marys, a throng of Roman soldiers and others. Other sculpture over the quarter lights showed the adoration of the Christ child and the Ascension.

This awe-inspiring vehicle, designed to be drawn by eight horses, was not intended for use in America. But by happenstance, it was available immediately after the close of the Fair for the funeral of Chicago's assissinated mayor, Carter H. Harrison. On this occasion the temporary axles with which this funeral car was equipped sustained the load, although they later bent under the heavy weight of the load. Probably no other American funeral of state has been featured by so imposing a funeral car. Certainly no similar vehicle was ever adorned with an equal profusion of religious scenes and symbols. Instead of being shipped as intended, directly to South America, this equipage was sold to M. Raoul Bonnot of New Orleans for $5,000. A year later

a) Hand Carved Wooden Drape Hearse, About 1898

b) Model of Ornate Child's Hearse, Late 19th Century

PLATE 52

a) "Ready for the Funeral," A Well Appointed Hearse of the Late 19th Century

b) Mosque Deck Style Popular Through the 1900's

c) Chicago Funeral Trolley Car, World War I Period

PLATE 53

it was resold by him to Messrs. Infanson and Sons, of Havana, Cuba, where for many years it was used for state funerals.

Although by 1898 the eight column, oval-decked funeral car definitely dominated the style-cycle, in that year Hudson Samson, one of America's most famous innovators in funeral fashions, proposed the most radical change in funeral car design ever to find its way into actual general use. His idea was a funeral car, the body of which should be *entirely obscured* by gracefully draped imitation of cloth—an immense pall, held up in place by cords and tassels so as to form the draperies, the whole to be carved out of solid wood. (See Plate 52.) It was finished in February, 1898, at a cost of $4,000 and from the builder's standpoint, it was the greatest triumph ever achieved in the art of hearse making.[15]

Despite the fact that in three years Samson tired of this creation and moved on to other specially designed funeral cars, the seed had been planted for the development of the style of closed, columned hearses with carved wood draperies; and within a decade, these represented the dominant vogue. Other changes meanwhile had taken place. During the 1890's the funeral car with squared ends and oval or "mosque deck," (see Plate 53), which had been in vogue since 1884, began to lose favor, and undertakers demanded a return to the elliptical ended vehicle, or to modified versions thereof. By the early 1900's this feature had been combined with Samson's wood carved drapery to produce a style that again was quite different from that which it gradually displaced. Summing up the style cycle pattern the chronicler of hearse patterns remarks:

Thus, in 1853 the style was for very small and inferior square hearses with plumes, that were gradually and greatly

improved upon until 1867, when the full circle end, or Clarence fronts, came in. From 1867 the style was for full circle
ends, with large plumes, gradually improving and substituting
deck ornaments for plumes, until 1884, when the square end,
4-columned "funeral car" came in. From 1884 the style called
for a strictly square end, with hip-roof, four columns and five
urns, gradually improving, until 1893, 94, and 95 (the Chicago
World's Fair period) when eight columns and the oval or
mosque, deck came in. From 1895 to 1910 the best style was the
Mosque deck without any urns at all; 6 columns or 8 columns,
but finally settling down to 8 columns, and gradually improving to the beautiful carved-wood draperies, carved woodhammer-
cloth seat, and other styles of ornamented seats.[16]

In 1909, to the question, "What next in hearse style?" the
answer would have to take into account a major technological
development having results for funeral car designs far beyond simple variations in body style. Already the gas buggy
had become more than a mechanical curiosity, and the broad
field of human transportation was experiencing the effects of
advances in technology which eventually would set a whole
nation on fast rolling wheels. Electric cars meanwhile had
been coursing through city streets and plying the interurban
expanses since 1885, when the first electric street railway
in the United States was christened in Baltimore. Four years
later the street railway company of Atchison, Kansas, began
operation of a trolley funeral car to nearby Mt. Vernon
cemetery. The car was only eight feet long with a table
in the center fitted to hold the casket. Extending lengthwise
through the car were seats for the undertaker and the bearers, while at the back one large folding door opened wide
enough to permit casket entry and egress. Above the side
panels were plate glass windows, and at the end were movable windows. The car was finished in black and gold within,
and cherry without. Fees ranged from eight to ten dollars,
varying according to the distance traveled and the time con-

sumed. Additional cars for mourners were available; these however were of the conventional trolley car variety.

The use of funeral trolley cars, most of which were of conventional trolley car size, spread through the '90's and into the early years of the current century. Most of the major cities put them into use, and many were operated on a regular schedule to the larger cemeteries. As late as the 1920's the sombre funeral car could have been seen in Cleveland and Chicago, carrying casket, flowers, and mournful passengers out to suburban cemeteries. (See Plate 53.)

Yet the use of funeral trolleys was limited to the larger cities, and even there public acceptance was short of enthusiastic. The cortege or funeral procession seemingly lost some of its dignity as iron wheels creaked and screeched on turns and rumbled over intersections, and the public seemed unable to repress a feeling of repugnance at the spectacle of a funeral "shooting through the streets at a high rate of speed."

In 1896 the first gasoline powered automobile laboriously and slowly felt its way through the streets of Detroit. Some dozen years later, Fred Hulberg of New York City, specified in a letters patent eight innovations which joined to form a "new and improved combined hearse and passenger vehicle." (See Plate 55.) The drawings displayed a large, boxlike passenger section of a truck-like vehicle, in front of which and directly above the motor was a rectangular container for the casket. The driver sat in the open, much like the driver of a fire truck. This compound vehicle amounted to a combination of a horse-drawn hearse, a funeral trolley car, and an automobile power plant. Sixteen feet long, selling for about $6,000, Hulberg's invention was designed to replace three carriages and a hearse. No records exist to show how this innovation fared. It is doubtful if any were actually produced and placed in operation.

It is quite probable that within the next ten years, individual funeral directors with a mechanical bent and a flair for innovations made, or had made for themselves, combination carriage and gas buggy hearses. Mobile-minded funeral directors had for many years been concerned with problems of getting around more rapidly. An editorial in the October, 1894, issue of *The Casket,* anticipating the advent of rapid transportation, raised the question of the possibilities of the bicycle in the undertaking profession and wondered editorially if it might ever be considered proper for an undertaker to head a funeral procession on such a vehicle? By 1905 at least one member of the profession had an "undertaker's auto" (see Plate 56), used for business purposes, and within the next few years more than one auto chassis had its crudely mounted hearse body. (See Plate 57.) In 1909 at least two companies were producing motorized vehicles for funeral service. From Rochester, N.Y., early that year, came news that the Cunningham factory had produced a model motor ambulance fully equipped with a 32 horse power motor, rubber tires, a heater, and a gong. The interior consisted of one suspended cot, two seats for attendants, and a system of electric lighting. Inside trimmings were stained mahogany, and the outside was painted silver-grey, striped with gold. First displayed at the local auto show early that spring, the Cunningham Motor Ambulance (see Plate 56), was first advertised for sale in December, 1909, in *The Western Undertaker.* By this time the Crane & Breed Mfg. Co. already had their first auto-hearse (see plate 56) in production. This equipage was put on the market in June, 1909, and was followed in two months by a more ornate model. (See Plate 56.) Their first advertisement of this innovation remarked rightly concerning the revolution which would take place in funeral service as a consequence of the introduction of the automobile hearse. The public had

Processional Hearse, Exhibited at Chicago World's Fair, 1893

PLATE 54

F. HULBERG.

COMBINED HEARSE AND PASSENGER VEHICLE.

APPLICATION FILED OCT. 16, 1908.

919,868.

Patented Apr. 27, 1909.

2 SHEETS—SHEET 1.

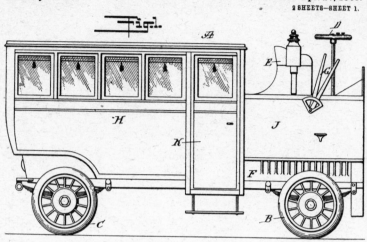

Fig. 1.

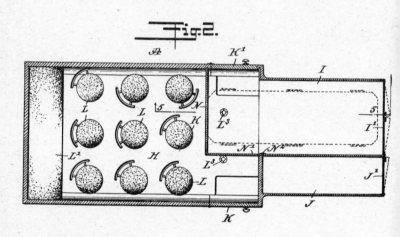

Fig. 2.

WITNESSES

F. G. Hackenberg.

Thos. Hoover

INVENTOR

Fred Hulberg

BY

ATTORNEYS

Patent Sketch of an Early Auto Hearse-Passenger Vehicle

PLATE 55

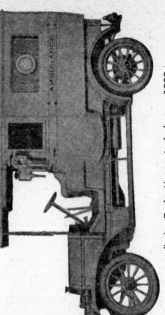

c) Undertaker's Auto Built in 1905

d) An Early Motor Ambulance, 1909

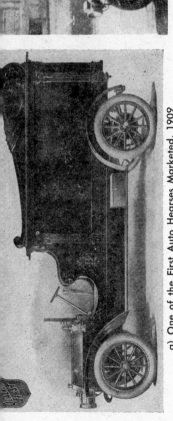

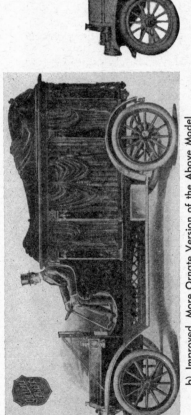

a) One of the First Auto Hearses Marketed, 1909

b) Improved, More Ornate Version of the Above Model

PLATE 56

a) Rear Loading Funeral Car of the Early Twenties

b) Two Tone Finish Funeral Car of 1922, Lighter Colors Gain Favor in the Succeeding Decades

c) Hearse Body on Auto Chassis, 1908

d) Post World War I Hearse Showing Persistence of Black in Funeral Vehicles

already become used to riding in automobiles, and were beginning, the advertisement pointed out, to object to the long and (to them) uncomfortably close and slow carriage journey. They wanted speed—the smooth glide to the cemetery, same as down-town or anywhere else—especially in the larger cities.

The first commercially produced auto-hearse was enclosed, painted black, with little decoration to it except a rather grotesque replica of the famous tomb of Scipio carved in wood atop the otherwise flat roof of the rectangular coach. The second model reverted somewhat to the prevailing style of conventional four-posted, wood-carved, draped-window, horse drawn funeral car, still keeping, however, the "Scipio" motif. By November, Crane & Breed Mfg. Co. had added an auto ambulance to their rolling stock.

Emil W. Hess, a veteran hearse manufacturer, in a personal communication suggests:

With the advent of automobiles, the first or early motor hearses were bodies from old horse-drawn hearses mounted on lengthened passenger car chassis, or on truck chassis. This was done before hearse and ambulance bodies, suitable for automobiles, could be designed and built.

It may also be of interest to note that the principal demand and sale of our motor ambulances and motor hearses did not come from the larger cities, but from the better class medium-sized cities. This was due to the fact that in the big cities, some of the largest Funeral Directors had a large investment in horse-drawn equipment and they were naturally slower to change to motorized equipment.

For your information, I would like to cite a case in New York City where we had a customer who was a livery man and served some 30 or more funeral directors. This man had both horse-drawn and motor hearses. On one occasion when I visited this customer, he told me he was buying used carriages very cheap (including harness) and he said he was buying these carriages for less than what he formerly paid for the harness alone. I told him at the time that I thought he should not invest any more money in horse-drawn equipment as the demand everywhere was increasing for motorized equipment, and that his business in horse-drawn funerals may suddenly discontinue. When I called on this customer a few months later, he said I was right. He further stated that he had over 75 horses to feed and no work for horse drawn equipment. He was shipping his carriages to Cuba and selling them for any price he could get.

It will no doubt be of interest to know that New York City had horse-drawn funerals for sometime after most of the country had adopted motorized equipment.[17]

Public response to these additions to funeral service was at first mixed, and many arguments were put forward to indicate the non-feasibility or undesireability of automobile transportation for funerals. "Timber Awl," a constant contributor to the "Letter to the Editor" section of mortuary journals, enumerated, at the same time that ambulances and auto hearses were going into commercial production, five compelling reasons why the "auto funeral" would be slow in coming: first, auto hearses would involve a high outlay of cash, $4,000-6,000 apiece for vehicles that would be lucky to last three years, as against an average of $1,500 for a longer-lived horse drawn coach; second, auto hearses could go no faster than horse-drawn carriages, so if speed were wanted there would necessarily have to be auto-carriages as well; third, upkeep and the cost of trained chauffeurs would be excessively expensive; fourth, the cost of operation would be so high that undertakers would have to cut costs on some other item—most likely the casket; and, lastly, sentiment militated against rushing people to their grave; and old people would still prefer the slow, leisurely, and more dignified trip to the cemetery. Thus it would take a new, speed-minded generation to give acceptance to the use of the automobile for funeral purposes.

Timber Awl made no mention of ambulances, a type of transportation in which the principle of speed had been accepted if not demanded by people. Events, however, soon settled the argument and proved Awl unduly pessimistic, for in the decade between 1910 and 1920 the automobile came to dominate the field of funeral transportation, and eventually replaced all other types of vehicles used in funeral service. Not only was the hearse replaced; but casket wagons, casket and ambulance wagons, embalmer's buggies and other service vehicles were superseded in short order by gasoline-powered conveyances serving similar functions. Through World War I auto hearses tended to become increasingly ornate. Martin notes that the peak in elaborate adornment was reached in 1920, when one company marketed a hearse on the body of which was a statue of Gabriel blowing his horn.[18]

Although patents were granted as early as 1909, it was not until after World War I, that limousine hearses made their appearance. Apparently tiring of ornately carved vehicles, funeral directors and the public turned toward the longer, smoother lines of the limousine, first conceived as an automobile having an enclosed compartment for passengers and a driver's seat outside but covered by a roof—which was beginning to set a new standard in style and luxury for passenger vehicles. Reduced height in the new style also made loading and unloading easier.

Limousine hearses consequently mark the beginning of the tendency toward the blending of hearse and other conveyances in the funeral procession in uniform, harmonious, and aesthetically pleasing style. (See Plate 58.) Along this line the invalid car, as distinct from the emergency-suggesting ambulance, was developed in the early '20's, and followed the limousine pattern. (See Plate 58.) In like manner passenger limousines, specially built to carry eight passengers,

came into use by funeral directors and were rented out for
the pallbearers or as a family car. The larger funeral home
might rent these cars to competitors.

The side-servicing feature for hearses was introduced in
1926. This innovation has added much to the convenience
and dignity of the funeral service as it makes possible loading
the vehicle without the necessity of the pall-bearers' walking out into the street, and, as sometimes was the case, into
the mud.[19]

Chassis: The first motor-driven hearses were generally
mounted on truck chassis which in many cases were of the
open driver's cab type. The next change was to use heavy-
duty passenger car chassis, usually of the seven-passenger
variety, in which case the wheelbase was generally lengthened to accommodate the longer hearse body requirements.

The extended spliced chassis have been used intermittently
over a great number of years. However, no manufacturer
has ever achieved any great degree of success in merchandising the extended chassis cars because of high upkeep
and poor handling characteristics of the final product. Because of the unsatisfactory operation of the extended chassis,
it soon became apparent that a full-length commercial chassis, designed specifically for the purpose for which it was to be
used, was the final answer. In regard to this development
Mr. Hess remarks:

Through the efforts of the body builders in the ambulance
and funeral car industry, we finally prevailed upon the large
manufacturers to engineer and build these commercial, specialized units, and as a result today, the spliced frame or converted
passenger car chassis has dropped to a low of only about 3%
to 5% of the total volume of the industry.

Down through the years, there were other types of conver-
sions that proved unsatisfactory because of the fact that they
were not designed specifically for the service requirements of
the funeral car. Among these were the deluxe panel delivery,

a) Funeral Limousine, c. 1922

b) Funeral Hearse, Used by Chinese in America

c) Matched Funeral Vehicle Procession, Early Twenties

PLATE 58

a) Side Service Funeral Used in 1946

b) An Ambulance Used in 1934

c) A Side Servicing Car of the Twenties

d) Style Setting Funeral Car, 1932

PLATE 59.

the station wagon, and the common suburban type vehicle.

Because of the necessity of keeping a commercial vehicle for a greater number of years than the average passenger car, it was found that the larger, higher prestige-type of car was a better overall investment because of its low depreciation over its life span.[20]

Hearse Sizes and Colors: Until the Civil War, hearses were nearly always painted black. After the War as they increased slowly in length and width, they began to exhibit some variation in color. Children's hearses, which were introduced within a decade after the War, were nearly always white; while the larger funeral cars kept to the darker colors. The most popular color combinations were the basic black with fine lines of silver or gold. Light gray, however, became a favorite for carved hearses, and during their vogue possibly one-half of all funeral cars were finished in some shade of this color. A light purple hearse was exhibited at the Chicago World's Fair in 1893, but the popular consensus was that this color was too delicate, too likely to fade or show wear and tear. Motor hearses were first black and later, around the time of World War I, were also offered in various shades of gray. (See Plate 57.)

Because hearses were always scrubbed and polished after each funeral the problem of maintaining a fine finish was a real one. To meet it, some companies included in the purchase of a new hearse a repainting service every six months over a stipulated period of time. Changing fashions provided another solution. It was not unusual for an undertaker to tire of his hearse long before it became unserviceable. In the classified section of the March, 1909, edition, of *The Western Undertaker* the following advertisement indicates the variety of types of funeral vehicles then in use, their different styles and their inevitable depreciation:

FOR SALE—Fine 5-glass landau in maroon leather. Very light weight. $650. Fine full leather landau, almost new, drab cloth, $700. Four passenger broughams, $350 to $700. Embalmers buggy, $275. Panel wagons $300 and $400. Very elegant Crane & Breed car, cost $2,500 and not hurt, for $1,200. Six column white car, 6x4 table by Cunningham, $500. Four column white hearse by Cunningham, $450. Side door 6-passenger pall bearer's coach, like perfect order, $475. Ambulance, silver gray, full size, complete $500. Address William Seymour, 381-387 Wabash Ave., Chicago, Ill.

The transportation of flowers to the grave called for special arrangement or separate vehicles. Earlier, flowers were transported in regular hearses equipped with special trays or receptacles attached to the side walls of the hearse body above the casket. When it was necessary to handle an extra large quantity of flowers, an extra or second car was put into use to transport them. With the advent of the automobile, the first flower cars put into service were the large seven-passenger phaeton type, or open touring cars on which the top was let down. After this type had been in vogue for a few years, an entirely new style "flower car" was designed and built. (See Plate 76, Chapter 13.) These new cars were and are used principally in the larger cities.

Just as the automobile effected a great change in the life of the individual, so has the development of the motor hearse, with its constant technological improvements, helped to revolutionize the burial of the dead. For one thing, as the journey to the grave became longer, the provision of transportation for corpse and mourners became an integral and necessary part of a developing modern funeral service. Thus while the undertaker who entered coffin and casket production on a mass scale found himself farther removed from the bereaved, the funeral director who gave up production of burial receptacles and turned toward his clients, taking over transportation responsibilities, found himself in closer professional interaction with those he served. Although of and by themselves inter-personal relations do not guarantee that services will be of a professional character, one of the requisites for professional service is that the special form of interaction between the professional and his clients is based on an understanding of the clients' personal needs.

The involvement of the funeral director with problems of transportation did more than increase the number and closeness of his contacts with the bereaved. It added to the complexity of his task, and further helped to shift that task toward a professional status. As funerals became more involved and the process of funeralization was carried with the procession to greater and greater distances, the task of *directing* this extended service, of arranging the procession and successfully moving it, of leading it to the burial ground, and assisting in the committal service, naturally fell to the funeral director.[21] One of the more important concepts called to mind by the term "funeral director," defines him as a person skilled in the management of the funeral procession. It should be pointed out, too, that the funeral director's responsibilities to the mourners, in terms of both safety and sentiment, likewise grew apace with the growth of his function in directing transportation. To produce a coffin or a casket upon demand involved a relatively simple business transaction with responsibilities attuned to the ethics of a tradesman-customer relationship. To move people about in a vehicle is a service relationship. But to organize and direct a procession which must be profoundly ceremonial, which cannot be rehearsed or repeated, and in which mistakes are always magnified by

a high level of emotional intensity, defines and fixes a responsibility which by conventional standards of occupational
recognition elevates the funeral director's work beyond and
above that of the craftsman, tradesman, or purveyor of petty
personal services.

CITATIONS AND REFERENCES FOR CHAPTER IX

1. Edward H. Rech, "Glimpses Into Funeral History,"
unpublished ms., prepared under the auspices of The Hess
& Eisenhardt Co. of Cincinnati, Ohio, n.d., n.p.

2. *Ibid.*

3. Edward Martin, "Hearses and Funeral Cars" unpubished ms., 1947, Archives of the NFDA, Milwaukee, Wis.,
n.d., n.p.

4. *Funeral Customs Through the Ages, op. cit.,* n.p.

5. Rech, *op. cit., passim.*

6. Sewall, *op. cit.,* p. 54.

7. *Ibid.,* p. 147.

8. See Bridenbaugh, *The Colonial Craftsman, op. cit.*

9. Bridenbaugh, *Cities in the Wilderness, op. cit.,* p. 90.

10. *Ibid.,* p. 412.

11. "Concerning the Evolution of Styles in Hearses," *Sunnyside,* March 15, 1913, pp. 14-15. The writers have followed this excellent sketch in their discussion of the influence
of fashion in hearses.

12. *Ibid.*

13. *Ibid.*

14. *Ibid.*

15. *Ibid.*

16. *Ibid.*

17. Personal correspondence to Howard C. Raether, from

Emil W. Hess, President, The Hess & Eisenhardt Co., April 29, 1955.

18. Martin, *op. cit.*

19. *Ibid.*

20. Personal correspondence to Howard C. Raether, from Emil W. Hess, Oct. 9, 1953.

21. Cf. Martin, *op. cit.*

The Pattern of Late 19th Century Funerals

In examining in separate chapters the functions, mortuary goods and paraphernalia of the 19th century undertaker and funeral director, it was unavoidable that a certain amount of discontinuity should result in the narration. The present chapter represents an effort to bring together into a balanced, continuous account, the items scattered in the previous chapters and to add to them such additional material as will provide a typical illustration of funeral service and care of the dead in the last portion of the 19th century,

389

centering around 1880. The actual time span of the example will be brief, covering only the few days beginning with death and ending with burial. Because, particularly at this time, America showed wide variations in funeral thoughts and customs between the rural areas—frontier, farm, village, town—on one hand, and the urban areas—the larger cities—on the other, the characteristic problems of death behavior of these two social groups will be compared.

As the Preface pointed out, it is necessary at times to survey a field in which there is some uniformity in the midst of many variations. Moreover, it is useful to collect these common elements into broad generalizations. This is hazardous, especially when one deals with nearly contemporary or contemporary society. If the practices of funeral directors at any period exhibited complete uniformity, if statutory law or some necessity defined and regularized the practices, it would be a simple matter to describe these patterns accurately. But here is a field in which there is still room for many variations, and in which there are some contrasts set by custom and law. For instance, in Catholic funerals in some cities in Ohio (among them Cincinnati, Cleveland and Youngstown), it has been long customary to seat the mourners on the right or the "Epistle" side of the church. However, in Brown County, Ohio, only thirty or forty miles from Cincinnati, they seat them on the left or "Gospel" side.

No comprehensive survey of the practices of funeral directors was made in the 1880's. There is none available which carefully describes practices today. As we approach the nearly contemporary or contemporary scene, the likelihood increases sharply that for every general statement, someone, somewhere, will be able to point out exceptions he knows of by his own experience or by hearsay. From region to region, place to place, and man to man there are differences. In spite of such variations, the limited evidence available indicates that there are broad patterns. These can and will be described.

First Responses to Death: In an American home in 1880 the coming of death brought with it the same shattering of human bonds and the resulting confusion that in any society everywhere and at all times have attended the death of a human being. In addition to this fundamental, universal reaction, the atmosphere of anxiety and emotional strain was heightened by the general tone which character-ized the death customs of the period. The frontier was passing, and some new and challenging or traditional but satisfying theme of social existence was needed to give mean-ing and support to a way of life that was in rapid transition from being fundamentally rural and agricultural to being predominantly industrial and commercial. Large numbers of immigrants were continuing to pour into the country in what historians have since named the "Great Migration." These new arrivals brought with them diverse backgrounds of race, religion, language, manners, customs, ways to make a living. In the great cities, and to a lesser extent across the whole country, they were thrown into the melting pot to-gether with the descendants of earlier arrivals, without ben-efit of a common and unifying basis in tradition, culture, or morality, except in the most general terms. Under such con-ditions, a society in the sense of an enduring and competently cooperating social group firmly held together by custom or tradition, could not be built overnight; nor could a young na-tion making astonishing growth even while it was being assem-bled out of highly diverse elements be expected to do so.

The prevailing funeral mood of the time was one of stiff formality overlaid heavily with gloom. This mood, strangely enough, did not originate in this lusty period of brawling American growth, nor did it express the irreverent matter-of-fact spirit of the day. It was borrowed from abroad, from England, and was a backward glance toward an earlier period and a different type of social organization. The pompous, elaborate, rigidly prescribed, prolonged, morbid, feudal-type funeral of the 1880's was a transplant in America.

Yet the sense of rugged individuality generated in frontier living, and the pre-occupation of the early 19th century American with his fellow man as a person could not help but leave its mark on the developing and changing pattern of American mourning behavior. Something of the simple sincerity, the primitive neighborliness of the frontier was never lost in the folkways of American funerals no matter what imported fashions were mixed with it.

Looking back on her mother's girlhood in Delaware County, Ohio, in the 1810's and 1820's, Mrs. A. Baldwin, chronicler of the Mid-West, reckoned that although her father and mother did not like funerals they always went to them.

In those days, every man within ten miles was a neighbor and every neighbor was a friend and when anyone died, a boy was sent on horseback from house to house to tell the sad tidings. On the day of the funeral, all the men and women in the country round laid aside their work, however important, and attended it. Rough wagons, with boards across for seats, perhaps with a chair for some old grandmother, formed the procession, followed often by men on horseback with their wives behind them. They had no hearse and the best wagon of the settlement held the coffin, and a homespun blanket answered for a pall. I have seen many grand processions since then. Once I saw a city hung with mourning and thousands of soldiers marching with muffled drums and all the people mourning a great man. But I have never seen anything that seemed to me so solemn as those wagons winding through the forests and over rough roads to the half-cleared graveyard of that new country.[1]

Beneath the external pomp and show which marked late 19th century funeral customs, the practice of giving way to grief and anguish—a reaction well supported in earliest Hebrew and Christian funeral behavior—is indication that the Americans of the period were modifying the imported fashion. This element of unfiltered emotional release, by the same token became more pronounced as one moved from the cities to the towns and villages, from the urbanity of the metropolis to the expressiveness of the frontier.

A final contribution to a developing pattern of mourning behavior in late 19th century America, was a growing, popular desire to provide for the facts of death and burial a setting that was beautiful to see and feel. This all-pervasive tendency was in strong contrast to the mood of gloom and sombreness which had been imported from the mourning style of feudal times. It is this tendency, many times alluded to, which in its unfolding has done most to set apart American from other funeral behavior in Western Civilization.

The composite form of response to the operation of these and possibly other social forces, does not, as possibly might be gathered from the following sketches, crystallize into a uniform and enduring set of conventions. For every point designated it is necessary to make exceptions and qualifications, but such variations must not obscure the single, simple conclusion that toward the end of the 19th century a conflict took place in America between the two great themes of death, gloom and formality, and beauty and expressiveness; and that the latter won out. In a period of activity, bustle, great opportunity, free competition, Americans did not choose to maintain an attitude toward death and certain archaic practices that had come down to them from a feudal society which had flourished a half thousand years before.

At the House: In late 19th century America, when a person died, the anxiety and nervous strain which attended the care of the sick or injured might be dissolved in the tears of the immediately bereaved. Most deaths then occurred in the home; if outside, the body was quickly returned there, so that the home was for most people the central point of mourning. A hush fell over the household, the blinds were drawn and people walked about on tiptoe and spoke in restrained tones. The first gestures toward the dead would be made by the women of the home, who closed the eyes and straightened the limbs. In cities, the undertaker, as he was called (although a few were already calling themselves "funeral directors") would be summoned to come and take charge. The decision as to whom to call might already have been made, as it would be natural to look to the same man who had laid out and buried other members of the family.

In the city the arrival of the undertaker released the family and friends of the dead person from many responsibilities which rural folk traditionally accepted as their own. Instead of proceeding with the actual preparation of the dead for burial (this presupposed no embalming) the men of the family decided what plans should be followed for the funeral or burial. In such deliberations the undertaker played an important advisory role. Although by far the greater majority of funerals were held in the home, as early as 1880 the choice of a home funeral or the undertaking parlor service was available in some places. As late as the 1910's it was many times virtually impossible to get permission to remove a body from the home. Indeed when death occurred in a hospital or other place outside of the home the family was most insistent upon bringing it to the house as soon as possible. Funeral parlors even then were used for people who had no home of their own or had no relatives or friends who would offer the facilities of their quarters. While sentiment and custom at that time dictated home funerals, the impulse to delegate both the care and custody of the body to the undertaker, reinforced by the desire of the latter to do his work, particularly embalming, in more functional surroundings, made the decision of some importance and difficulty. In addition to agreeing upon the place of the funeral it was necessary to decide how much time would elapse before burial took place. If the answer was more than one day, preservative measures would be needed. Again the choices were two. Until the funeral, the body could either be kept in a cooler or "corpse preserver," surrounded with ice (see Plates 41, 42), or the undertaker could embalm it with chemicals. Although the latter method had been widely talked about since the Civil War and had recently become popularized by the fact that certain great personages, including several presidents, had been chemically embalmed, there still remained a popular fear based on Christian and humanitarian concerns that the process involved mutilation of the body. Much of the opposition was based on a fear of the unknown. People did not understand the nature of embalming; many embalmers could not or did not explain it very clearly, and the mutilation question was dragged in by some persons who were seeking an argument to defend a position.

In rural areas and small towns the news of death spread rapidly, and many people, relatives, neighbors and friends, found themselves in one way or another involved in the care and disposition of the body. The body was laid out either by the bereaved or by persons in the neighborhood who had had experience in these matters. Washed, dressed in the best or favorite suit or dress, the deceased was moved from the bedroom to the parlor, to be viewed even before a casket was obtained. The mourning behavior of small town midwesterners during this period is well described by Atherton, who emphasizes the social participation of the whole community:

Friends began pouring in to the bereaved home as soon as the news reached them, and the members of the family, seated in the living room, received their condolences. Each caller tiptoed into the parlor to see the corpse, as everyone was expected to perform that rite, and all commented on how natural and peaceful it looked. Cakes and pies and meats began to appear in the kitchen in profusion, the gifts of friends and neighbors.[2]

If the undertaker had training in chemical embalming he undoubtedly protested its "humaneness" and pointed to all its obvious advantages over ice-cooling: sanitation, duration, reliability, and simplicity. The possibility of an ice-cooled corpse decomposing rapidly once taken out of the "preserver," and exploding the casket during the funeral ceremonies could not be ignored; nor would the astute embalmer-undertaker fail to mention it. Prices either way did not vary greatly; chemical embalming, on the whole, tended at the time to be a little more expensive, unless the amount of ice used in keeping the body cool was excessive. Some twenty years earlier Holmes had charged as high as a hundred dollars for chemical embalming; in 1870, a prominent undertaker, Hudson Samson, charged as little as fifteen. By the 1880's there was little variance in practice, $10 being a usual charge. (See Figure 29.) The books of a well known Cincinnati establishment show that subsequent to this time additional charges were made in the case of men for "washing, shaving and dressing," and for women for "casketing and dressing." Having settled these matters, the undertaker would defer consideration of other details until the body had been properly "laid out."

Assuming that the body would be chemically embalmed, the undertaker would have brought with him a portable cooling board and an embalming cabinet and dressing case containing essentially a hard rubber pump with check valve, arterial tubes, trocar, needles, forceps, scalpel, scissors, eye caps, razor, granite cup for shaving, combs, brushes, shaving soap, chin supporters, surgeon's silk, a piece of oiled muslin, a package of court-plaster, a paper of pins, a dozen collar buttons, cotton sheet, whisk broom, and two one-half gallon bottles. In addition, he carried several bottles of concentrated embalming fluid, and an assortment of door badges.

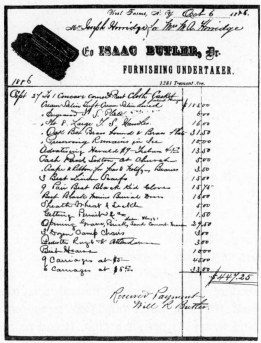

Figure 29. Itemized Luxury Funeral Bill, 1886.
Note "Preserving Remains in Ice."

On his first call the undertaker would select the appropriate door crepe or badge and attach it in such manner that the door bell or knocker was covered. Custom decreed black as the color for the old, white for the young, and black with white rosette and ribbon for the young adults. Before the end of the decade 1880-1890 combinations of purple, lavender and grey were used in connection with mourning, and the door badges often reflected this changing choice in color. (See Figure 30.) Later when the majority of funerals were

Figure 30. Door Badges, Late 19th Century

still being conducted from the homes of the decedents, and floral wreaths had taken the place of door crepes, the florist in the city often failed to attach the flowers until several hours later. In rural districts the funeral director carried with him artificial flower door badges.

Embalming the dead in the home presented 19th century undertakers with problems, both physical and social, which have long since been relegated to the realm of historical anecdote among modern funeral directors. If the family raised the mutilation objection strenuously it was sometimes necessary to permit a close friend or male member of the family to watch the process. Many people had the erroneous idea that embalming necessitated the removal of all or the majority of the internal organs. When the observer saw the size of the small incision made to raise a major artery, he was generally satisfied, and seldom remained to witness the balance of the embalming procedure unless he was curious as to its operation and developing results. The body was undressed, washed on the bed, the orifices were plugged, and the entire body was swabbed with embalming fluid and then placed on the embalming table. After moving the body into the best light in the room, it was shaved (if a man), the eyes were closed over eye-caps, the mouth closed, and if necessary the lips were lightly sewn together. If the dead person wore false teeth, these would always be inserted and a chin support might be used to keep the jaws closed. An early attempt at "restorative art" might be tried with the new liquid flesh tint recently marketed by the fluid companies.

Having finished the preliminary work, the undertaker then embalmed the body. If he followed recent advances in the field he employed arterial injection, supplemented by cavity injection, with the trocar inserted in the umbilicus and in the corner of the eye, where in neither case would an incision be noticeable. Having injected the body sufficiently with fluid—being careful to get none on his hands or parts of his body—he tied off the vessels and sewed up the incision. Some embalmers wore rubber gloves; others embalmed with their bare hands. Next, he dressed the body, placing a clean sheet under it, dusted the face with powder, placed a small pillow under the head, draped another sheet over the body, and placed a small square of white cotton material or a handkerchief over the face. The net effect was the impression of a reclining form. Additionally, he might attach a canopy to the cooling board. In either case the body was ready to be placed in whatever room was chosen for it to be viewed, and the first call was completed. The undertaker's next step was a conference with the family to complete the arrangements for funeral ceremonies.

Funeral Arrangements: Although in the 1880's as now, there were standard services which the undertaker was called upon to perform for the dead and the living, in actual practice many variations appeared. While the following statement makes mention of only a few of these, in a general way the practices it details are quite typically those of the time. Before the undertaker departed from his first call, he inquired regarding local notification and asked what telegrams should be sent, and on a printed blank made a brief record of the earthly career of the departed. Another blank provided for the names of the clergymen who were to officiate and the singers who were to compose the choir. These persons were promptly notified. As soon as possible, the following day preferably, the arrangements were completed. Important items were the choice of the casket, the elaborateness of the ceremonies, the selection of the pallbearers, the number of relatives and friends for whom carriages should be provided, and the order of precedence of mourners in the procession. In case the funeral was to be held from a church, the proper authorities and the sexton would have to be notified. Even the floral pieces, if any, were ordered through the undertaker. At this time the battle of flowers versus drapes had been well under way for more than a decade.

The casket was chosen either from a catalogue, the undertaker's display room or stockroom, or in some cases, from the casket showrooms which manufacturers were beginning to set up in the larger cities and to which undertakers might take their clients. Selections in any case ranged widely in style, composition and price, although polished hardwoods —caskets of oak, mahogany, walnut or rosewood—were long since the traditional favorite, the big bulk of sales was in less expensive caskets. Metallic burial cases and caskets formerly finished in imitation rosewood were now offered in a distinctive bronze finish, a few styles of metallic-glass combinations were available, and a substantial line of cloth-covered wooden caskets in a somewhat cheaper price range completed the conventional list of alternatives.

As early as 1875 the Stein Patent Burial Casket Works had published a striking catalogue of pictures to be shown customers. (See Plate 39.) In addition to the conventional black for adults and white for children, this company made available broadcloth and velvet-covered caskets in combinations of royal purple, aniline blue and lavender, with ornaments and trim in gold, silver and black enamel. The catalogue of Chappel, Chase, Maxwell & Company for the years 1881-1882 contained a line of cloth-covered caskets featuring a variety of color combinations equal to that furnished by the Stein Company. While the variety of styles, color and material was not as wide in the 1880's as it is today, it still gave people a chance to exercise some refinement of choice. We have already discussed how at this time fashions and taste were beginning to intrude themselves into areas of life that long had been under the canons of custom and traditions.

The selection of a casket from a catalogue, and its delivery in time for the funeral were made possible by improved techniques of body preservation and by developments in communication and transportation. If the family selected a casket which the funeral director did not have in stock, or made a selection from a catalogue, then the question of delivery became an important problem. There were many instances in which the desired casket could not be secured in time for the hour of the funeral without curtailing the hours of visiting; and other instances, when it could not arrive for the original date of the funeral itself. The hours between placing an order for a casket and its delivery, and then its subsequent inspection to see that the order had been carried out in every detail, were always harrowing the funeral director. Nor did the fact that this situation occurred again and again relieve his anxiety. He was always conscious that there was a whole array of contingencies that might disarrange his careful schedule. Once the choice had been made, the undertaker immediately dispatched a coded telegram to the factory. When first manufactured in job and mass lots, caskets and burial cases were given names to designate particular styles. These names might indicate a style or form designed or suggested by an undertaker, or, on occasion by his wife. Such was the "Emma." Likewise, the "Peltier," "Hogan," and "Curtis" styles of caskets were named for the undertakers who designed them or suggested the style. Others, especially the more expensive, had names descriptive either of important phenomena—"The State," (see Figure 17 and Plate 33), "Imperial"—or of important persons—"Monarch," "Princess," and "Grand Duke." As early as 1876 the Stein Company was already using letters and numbers to code their caskets, and as the century came to a close, descriptive terms and personal names were replaced by impersonal and colorless code words and numbers.

Once the telegram reached the factory or warehouse, the casket asked for was immediately boxed and rushed to the express office for shipment, if it was available. An undertaker in New York City could expect a casket from the Stein factory at Rochester twenty hours after his telegram had been received; to Chicago it would take thirty hours; and to St. Louis, thirty-eight hours. Even "the State" casket, "only made to order," was guaranteed delivery at any point within a thousand miles from the factory within sixty hours or less. This company claimed to have shipped over three thousand telegraph-ordered caskets in the twelve months ending June, 1876.

On the other hand, in rural and village areas the selection of a casket was a fairly simple matter. Either the local cabinet-maker was called upon to build one for the occasion, or a ready-made receptacle was purchased from the furniture store. In the latter case, the casket might not yet be lined, or "trimmed," and the furniture dealer, who might also advertise on his signboards that he did undertaking, would, with the aid of his wife, often complete the trimming.

In 1880 the undertaker was not licensed either to practice or to embalm; another fifteen years were to elapse before states began to pass licensing legislation. But with the establishment of Bureaus or Departments of Vital Statistics, it became incumbent upon the undertaker to meet certain legal requirements before arranging for the burial or cremation of the human dead. Certificates authorizing burial or cremation had to be secured from the city or township officials. Physicians were obliged to notify these authorities of the deaths of patients they had attended, and the approximate time of death and the causes thereof. Without such notice the registrar, town clerk, or other official authorized to issue burial certificates, would not do so. Consequently, to facilitate matters the undertaker would take a death certificate to a physician for his statement and signature, and then secure the burial permit. This is still the accepted practice. In like manner, burial within a cemetery required sanction from cemetery officials. Burial on a particular lot or in a particular location necessitated some evidence of ownership and right of sepulture. This once again became a self-imposed responsibility of the funeral director. Often he accompanied members of the mourning family to the cemetery to give suggestions regarding the location of the burying place and made arrangements with the superintendent for the bricking up of the walls, if not the bottom of the grave, or the building of a vault of sandstone slabs to receive the casket. Sprigs of evergreen might be used to trim the grave and soften the harshness of the freshly turned clay. For a child's burial fresh flowers would be used instead.

The Funeral: In the rural and village areas of America, during the late 19th century, the role of the funeral director was considerably different from what it was in the city, and he played a smaller part in the funeralization of the dead.

H. J. Blanton, dean of American small town newspaper editors, in his engaging reminiscences of youth in the small town notes the "modest part" of the undertaker who did not "lay out" the corpse, but ordered the casket made by the local furniture factory, helped place the body in it, and generally arranged things so that the preacher could play the dominating role.[3]

News of death travelled fast in small communities and often most of the people of the town or village, in one way or another, were involved and, in keeping with the Christian tradition, shared the sorrows of the bereaved. In cities, people received notice of death first by special courier— indeed the position of "Inviter to Funerals" in New York City goes back to the late 17th century—who delivered funeral notices, invitations and mourning cards. (See Plates 60, 61.) But from the middle of the 19th century the invitations in many cases were sent out by the undertaker as one of the many personal services that were coming under his direction. Hill's *Manual of Social and Business Forms*, 1879, under "Etiquette of the Funeral" recommended the more traditional usage of sending out invitations to friends of the deceased by private messenger, but, as noted by Landauer, the contemporary *Gaskell's Compendium of Forms* stated that newspaper announcements might "meet the requirements of distant friends."[4] Before 1900 the mourning card for personal communication had changed into the "letter edged in black," (see Plate 62), while for those less touched by the event, the newspaper announcement sufficed.

Before the turn of the century, funerals were most likely held in the home of the deceased, sometimes in the church, and only very seldom in a funeral parlor. In the city the undertaker generally arrived at least an hour before the service. The body in its casket was in view. Taking leave of the remains had already become a custom toward which the undertaker could develop little enthusiasm, but the wishes of the family traditionally governed the procedure. Otherwise the undertaker tended to regard his role as one of general supervisor of the funeral, having slowly moved in his occupational duties from a supplier of objects, and an arranger of paraphernalia, to a director or supervisor of a complex set of practical and ceremonial actions.

By the time of his arrival his assistant would have distributed folding chairs and arranged furniture so that an assembly could take place. As friends came into the house they were directed to seats, some of which would be assigned to close relatives. Fraternal orders often participated in the funerals of the time, and it was incumbent upon the undertaker to make arrangements so that participation functioned smoothly, integrating itself with the ceremonies performed by the clergyman.

"Abide With Me," "Thy Will Be Done," or "Over The Stars There is Rest," and "Christian Hope Beyond" were favorite selections of the time. The arrangements for the several component parts of the funeral service were generally gone over in advance, with the funeral director acting as prompter, if one were needed, and standing by to smooth over any last minute hitches.

Services at the home were invariably long and delivered in a mixed context of religious awe, hope, fear and gloom. After an opening prayer of some four to five minutes at a Protestant funeral, the minister would in many cases read the Twenty-Third Psalm, and possibly short passages from the Seventh Chapter of Revelations. Following this would be the remarks on the mystery of life and death, the suffering on earth as a prelude to a more glorious life to come, and then would come the eulogy in which the character of the deceased would be thoroughly reviewed. Often a short life history would be included, in some cases delivered by a close friend of the deceased and couched in terms of personal reminiscence. After a closing prayer, and the singing of one or several songs, or possibly the recitation of a favorite piece of verse, the funeral service was completed. The total time consumed was seldom less than an hour.

Home services over, the undertaker would take charge of the pallbearers. Funerals held from an upper floor always posed a special problem. A long strap or length of webbing was frequently used to lower the casket, step by step down the stairs. Doors often were so constructed that egress was impossible without removing the hinges, and in some cases a part of the framework. In one of the earlier manuals of funeral management the undertaker is advised in extreme cases of blocked passageways to consult with a safe-mover!

Hearses were seldom backed to a curb unless the mud was prohibitively deep. While the body was being loaded into the hearse, the assistant busied himself gathering up the flowers to be transported ahead of the procession to the church or cemetery where they would be properly rearranged. The occupants of the carriages next were seated in rough order of their closeness of kinship to the bereaved. Here skill in human relations was necessary, for then as now, some relatives might not be on speaking terms with others, and it was necessary at all costs for the undertaker to keep harmony among the participants. Immediate consideration, of course, went to the family, and they were loaded first. To fill a dozen or more carriages and bring them into proper order unavoidably produced a certain amount of delay. To the majority of participants, however, the factor of time was negligible; funerals were neither rushed to, rushed through, nor rushed from. The logistics of funeral service were only just beginning to become a matter of concern to the undertaker, yet as his function of *direction* took on a depth it was inevitable that a smooth, well-ordered funeral in which little motion was wasted should come to be his goal.

Once the procession got under way, its direction was in the hands of the undertaker. Sometimes he rode with the driver on the hearse, or sometimes, but less frequently, he left the procession in the hands of an assistant and drove to the cemetery to make sure that everything was in readiness there. If the undertaker stayed with the procession, he rode with the minister in the front carriage. In cases of very large funerals his position was in a carriage of his own at the head of the line of march.

As the funeral left the private home, an assistant immediately began to restore order. Folding chairs, rugs, pedestals, and door scarf were taken away. Furniture was moved back so that the family upon return found nothing to remind them that a funeral ceremony had taken place there only a few hours before.

To retrace steps, while ordinarily the body was kept in the family home, in some cases, especially in the larger cities, the undertaker might have a "morgue" in his establishment in which the body could be kept until the time for the funeral or it might be "in state" in the funeral parlor. In 1880 the funeral home, in the sense given to the term today, was just beginning to appear, and for every funeral undertaker operating an independent establishment, four or five others carried on the trade in connection with some other business.

Thus, the common alternative to a home funeral was a funeral which began in the home with the viewing of the body, was followed by a procession to the church for the main ceremony, and completed by the conventional trip to the cemetery and the committal service. Should the family decide upon a church funeral, then a new complication was added to the work of the undertaker. A church funeral called for further expenditure of time, effort, and paraphernalia, and added such problems as were involved in organizing and directing a group of persons in a performance for which there could be no rehearsal and whose complete success could not be guaranteed in advance. The introduction of the chapel into the funeral home at the close of the 19th century marks no lessening of religious involvement in the funeral ceremonies of the time. Instead it points up a natural reaction to the problems of transportation, time involvement, and the difficulty of directing the performance of group ceremonial and ritual in physical areas over which the undertaker had little control.

In the typical church ceremony, the undertaker was met in the vestibule by the clergyman who preceded him up the aisle. The body was placed at the head of the center aisle, and flowers which had been sent in advance or were brought with it were arranged about it in stands or on tables. In the Catholic ceremony, three candles were placed at each side of the bier. During the rest of the ceremony, the undertaker assumed a point of vantage from which he could assist if and as needed, and assume his duties when they arose. Fraternal escorts were given a special position so that in leaving they would occupy the same places as on entering.

The custom of opening the casket in church for a final view of the body persisted strongly during the 19th century despite objection by clergymen and undertakers alike. When such practice was observed, the mourners filed silently by and passed outside to the waiting carriages. Finally, the pallbearers carried the casket to the hearse and the procession moved slowly toward the cemetery.

Undertakers preferred to have the drivers of their hearses and carriages dressed in livery. In keeping with the sombre-toned tradition, throughout most of the century the dress followed the gloomy motif: well-dressed liverymen were garbed in black broadcloth or doe-skin coats, pantaloons and vest. The coat and vest were single-breasted and buttoned up completely to the neck. With these garments they wore a white linen garotte shirt collar and black silk tie, black kid gloves and black top hat. (See Figure 31.) Since the

Figure 31. Professional Dress, Left, Coachman; Center, Undertaker; Right, Undertaker's Liveried Assistant

independent undertaker of the time could scarcely afford to keep a dozen drivers as part of his hired personnel he faced an almost universal problem of trying to get drivers from carriage stables to appear in respectable, uniform livery. This problem, in point of fact, was one of the earliest taken up for consideration in the first undertakers' trade journals.

The Funeral Cortege: The long line of coaches and carriages moving slowly toward the cemetery not only presented an imposing spectacle, but helped generate a sense of the importance that the social group attached to the matter of the demise of one of its own. The hearse invariably dominated the procession by its beauty and magnificence, decorated with the classical symbols of grief, the drooping cypress, the reversed and extinguished torch, the cere, and "black plumes awaving."

During late 19th century the role played by the plumes atop the hearse was of great importance, for by their number and color the station of the deceased was revealed. An absence of plumes indicated that the deceased was poor; two plumes that he was of moderate circumstances; three or four plumes, fairly well-to-do; five or six, well-off; and seven or eight, rich.[5] For children the undertaker supplied a miniature hearse, usually white, which would be drawn by one horse. (See Plate 52.)

As flowers came more generally into use, a special carriage was added to the cortege solely to transport them. Customarily it preceded the pallbearers' carriage, yet was not too far from the hearse so that the association of flowers with the body and casket would be lost.

A common arrangement of the procession was as follows: clergymen, flower carriage, honorary pallbearers, active pallbearers, hearse, immediate family and relatives, and finally friends. Societies of fraternal orders, if they formed part of the procession, always took the lead. In the funeral procession of a well known funeral director in 1890 there were in line:

> Ballston Spa Brass Band
> Morning Star Encampment, I.O.O.F.
> Odd Fellows Lodges
> Knights of Pythias
> Ancient Order of United Workmen
> Rechabites
> Union Fire Company #2
> Wheeler Post, G.A.R.
> McKittrick Post, G.A.R.
> Minister
> Bearers and gun squad
> The Hearse
> Relatives and mourners in Carriages

In cases such as this, fraternal and other organizations would precede the carriages on foot. If the cemetery were too far, these marching groups would drop out after several blocks, or, possibly at the city limit. The number of carriages, in some cases the grandeur of the hearse, the appointments and the size of escort served as visible index not only of the social status or position of the deceased, but of his sociability, because they depended in a large measure upon the friendships and social connections he had developed in the course of his lifetime. The bereaved felt they had an obligation to insure that the funeral provided the fullest measure of respect for the dead; and in a time when the measure of things was becoming increasingly worldly they were likely to translate this respect into material objects and display.

At the Cemetery: The working relationship of the clergyman and the undertaker was compounded at the cemetery by the presence of another functionary, the sexton, or cemetery superintendent. A portion of the directing function was relinquished by the undertaker as either of the latter would direct the procession to the grave. While the undertaker directed the activities of the pallbearers, the clergyman prepared to lead the way. The pallbearers then deposited the casket over the grave, the clergyman took his position facing the family and began the committal service. At his words, "Earth to earth . . . ", either he or the undertaker sprinkled a handful of fine dirt over the casket. Under the supervision of the undertaker, the casket was lowered into the grave, either by the pallbearers—not an easy task for the unskilled—or by trained cemetery attendants. Filling the grave nearly always awaited the departure of the bereaved.

Rural Variations: Although for rural and village funerals of the period the treatment of the dead bore a basic similarity to funerals in cities, definite variations were evident. For example, the family of the deceased underwent more severe emotional strain, generated in part by the ceremonies and in part by the fact that a funeral tended not only to involve more people but because of their participation to touch them more deeply. On the other hand there was more opportunity for emotional release.

At the home or church, men, women and children turned out in numbers. Atherton remarks that "while the bereaved family would not have had things otherwise, they were in for a rough hour. A long eulogy by the preacher and doleful hymns by a quartette only served to weaken those closest to the deceased and to leave them defenseless for the final ordeal at the grave."[6] The funeral sermon provided the minister with a choice opportunity to appeal to the unsaved and to remind others of the fires of damnation awaiting unrepentant sinners: "The time to make peace with God is now." Special attention was given the family of the deceased. In his remarks on the life of the departed member, a minister would spare no sector of human sentiment, and until all the members were wracked in uncontrollable grief, minister and community alike could not pronounce the funeral successful. Blanton notes that in Paris, Missouri, well before the turn of the century the filling of the grave took the form of a contest with the masculine friends vying with each other in their ability to manipulate a shovel. Nobody thought of leaving until the grave was filled.[7]

Late 19th Century Mourning Symbols: In major part the symbols of mourning during this period expressed the gloom and formality, the solemnity and lugubriousness of the feudal funeral of the late Middle Ages and Early Renaissance. That such a pattern of death-response should be incorporated into the mourning of a rapidly growing, ever increasingly industrialized American society is a puzzle for social and cultural historians. For decades Americans had been enthusiastically writing and reading romantic fiction; certainly the wave of Romanticism—a backward looking philosophy—would have supported such turning back from the simplicity and realism of American funeral customs of a century before. Whatever the basic reasons, the solemnity and gloom was obvious enough. The house in which the death had struck not only had its scarf or "crepe" on the door, but it was not unknown for the bereaved to drape the room in which the dead lay, or possibly, the whole downstairs of the house, in black or deep shades of grey. Deeply colored veils were often hung in the doorway; servants attired in mourning livery were stationed at the doorway to attend the callers. If the household contained a maid, she would wear black, with apron, collars and cuffs of white, with black ribbons attached to her white cap. For the bereaved, black was considered the color most suitable for the trappings of woe. Its sombre effect was reflected not only in the mourning garb but in the dress of the functionaries, the shroud, the hearse and its plumes, the pall spread over the casket, and even the horses used in the funeral cortege.[8]

Of the fabrics employed, funeral crepe was considered most effective; although black and blue-black bombazines, alpacas, black silks, black kid, and black cotton were used in the making of mourning garments and accessories. The combination of the shrouding folds of the major garment, the black mourning bonnet with streamers reaching "well below the waist line," and the black crepe of the widow's veil made her mourning garb the most distinctive and lugubrious of any. Following a death mourning wear was used to indicate not only degrees of kinship with the dead, but the several defined periods of mourning. The widow, for example, was clearly labeled by the white ruche that showed as an inner lining along the front of the bonnet. For the first year the widow was expected to wear everything with a dull black finish. Her gloves, purse, handkerchief border, ornaments and gown were to show no lustre, as if a lack of lustre in her appointments declared the lack of lustre brought into her entire being by death.

In the first six months of the second year of mourning the crepe gave way to less funereal materials, such as black silk or crepe-de-chine, and for the remainder of the year the use of both white and violet was permissible. After two years the widow again could wear ordinary clothes. Should a woman lose her husband late in life she might commonly wear mourning for the remainder of her days. As the 19th century drew to an end, the fashion of wearing all white for summer mourning made its appearance, although white never became a dominant mourning theme as it had been in classical antiquity. For women, the loss of a loved one— husband, child, boy or girl, or grown offspring, brother, sister, or parent, even grandparent—mourning garb was varied enough to indicate the nature of the bereavement.

The widower customarily wore a suit entirely of black cloth with plain white linen. Any other coloring was prohibited. Shoes, gloves, cuff-links, and hat were all of dull black. A conspicuous crepe mourning band adorned the hat. For the widower, mourning might last for a year with a period of secondary mourning in which he was permitted to relieve his black garb by grey. The wearing of a mourning band on the sleeve of the coat was not generally approved, unless the ordinary costume was in the form of a uniform which might not be changed. With some latitude allowed for special cases of attachment, mourning was not generally prescribed or approved for kinfolk living apart from the immediate family, such as uncles, aunts, nephews, cousins and other collateral relatives.

In any event, the first six months after a death, commonly known as the period of "deep mourning," carried with it a proscription against participation in any social or recreational affairs. As the mourning colors during the mourning period grew progressively lighter, so in parallel fashion did the social and personal contacts of the mourners, and by the time all mourning garb was dispensed with, so were all restrictions as to movement and social contact. For the woman this was more definitely the case; for the man, social activity was resumed somewhat more quickly. Another phase of social contact, correspondence, fell under the regulation of mourning custom. Stationery was prescribed as to color: for the widow, white or grey with black border, a quarter inch wide for the first year of mourning, an eighth inch for the next six months, and a sixteenth for the remainder of the second year. (See Plate 62.) Colored crests were prohibited, as was perfume. Simplicity in the lettering and even the containment of scrawling handwriting were advised.

Calling cards were likewise edged in black, the width of the edging indicating the degree of relationship to the deceased, the thinner the edge the more distant the relationship. Propriety and decorum were to be observed in all correspondence, as in all behavior involving other persons and in all actions, perceived or private, of the person in mourning. Post cards were decidedly not permissible.

Other classes of people participated in the symbolization of the mourning gloom. Not only was the undertaker's garb of the traditional black, but so generally was the garb of all those who figured importantly in the funeral, minister, pall-bearers, drivers and other functionaries, as well as the bereaved. Friends would don either black or their darkest or most subdued dress to attend the ceremony. Other symbols were affected. It was still fashionable in 1880 to wear a funeral sash, or a linen scarf. These were worn along with gloves, ribbons and badges. An 1878 *The Casket* ad for badges lists, "black, white or black-white combination lettered in gold or silver, 'Pall Bearer,' 'Bearer,' 'Undertaker,' or with

Masonic, IOOF, Catholic or other society emblems as may be desired." (See Plate 63.)

Music likewise symbolized solemnity, if not gloom. It was considered singularly appropriate at the time to have a brass band precede the funeral procession, and the strains of the "Dead March," from "Saul" with musicians marching in broken ranks, were as much in keeping with the tenor of the occasion as are the strains of "Lead Kindly Light" on the church organ for the funeral of today. The songs mentioned above were designed to be sung on such occasions. Other intensely religious songs, or, perhaps, the favorite numbers of the deceased might be included. In all cases, the emotional character of the situation was enhanced, reserves were further broken down, and feelings were given an opportunity to find full expression. The church bell tolling to mark the arrival of the funeral procession at the church has been a customary feature of village and city life in America since colonial days. In rural areas, the church bell played a communicative role in that by the different modes of tolling the age and sex of the deceased were indicated. In some sections of the country, a trombone choir was used to announce the death of a fellow member of the church. The musicians assembled in the belfry and played certain selections which were codes for the members. One piece was used for married adults and another for children.[9]

Aesthetically Pleasant Mourning Symbols: Despite the overwhelming tone of gloom, formality, and solemnity with which it was characterized, it would be a mistake to think of the late 19th century funeral as entirely governed by the pattern of the feudal system of mourning behavior as developed in the late Middle Ages. The chapter on burial cases, coffins and caskets supplies us with an illustration of the breaking away from this pattern. Well before the Civil War, people were demanding that the receptacle for the dead should do more than indicate social status by its expensiveness—as was the case after the Revolutionary War—or serve as an object of mere utility. The very term "casket" signified box or container for something precious, and the preciousness of the human body was felt to be best expressed to the world *symbolically* by the aesthetic luxury of the casket, and *dramatically* to the world by the funeral ceremony. From about 1850 on, the casket found its meaning more and more in the realm of popular tastes where sweeps of fad and fashion played across the appetites and dispositions of the 19th century American mind. The appearance of the casket, its form and composition both subject to the prevailing canons of taste, signalized the beginnings of the breakdown of a system of mourning which was yet to reach its own peak several generations later.

By 1880 the enterprising town or city undertaker, selling caskets out of the catalogs of three or four large casket companies could present a customer with at least a hundred different choices of casket styles, embracing such materials as wood, wood-cloth combination, metal, wood and metal, and metal and glass combinations. As noted earlier, colors ranged from the conventional black to varieties of silver, bronze, aniline blue and lavender, in many variations. Yet these caskets had a standard form, and came in a highly limited range of standard sizes. The discriminations in style which could be made covered a broad range, but the variations were minor; one chose from a great variety of styles, but seldom were the choices radically different.

The second major breakthrough of the funeral gloom of late 19th century mourning came in the area of the setting, or backdrop for the casket. Just as the casket became more an object of beauty, or evocative of aesthetically pleasant feelings or imagery, so eventually did the setting change, and the heavy black folds of the casket drape were replaced by the colorful, warmer, or more striking colors of the casket lining, which by the end of the century had come to dominate the casket exterior, especially in the "couch" types.[10] (See Figure 32.) With the remarkable changes in the burial receptacle and the increasing emphasis upon its aesthetic effect, the

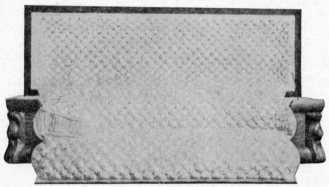

Figure 32. Couch Style Casket

traditional "props" of the draped pedestal and, possibly the bedraped room, could only produce an ambiguous or disharmonious effect. A more appropriate setting commended itself in the form of the floral backdrop. Starting with the placing of a small bouquet on a table beside the casket—a custom lost in its origins—from the middle of the century on, there was a slowly increasing sentiment in favor of matching the color, beauty, and aesthetic appeal of the casket and its striking colored, or white lining, with the natural beauty and color of flowers. During the time when this new fashion was becoming popular or at least gaining acceptance, some question arose as to whether or not funeral flowers had pagan associations, and whether a wealth of floral tributes might not be an indefensible waste of money.

Although opposition to the use of flowers was never organized, church officials were not loath to criticize excesses in display as a departure from Christian custom. Another form of religious criticism appeared as early as 1878 when the Bishop of Rochester, New York, in a letter to the *Catholic Times* remarked that:

Whatever of sentiment may have been in the use of flowers on and around a corpse when, at first, loving hands placed a few near it was killed by usage demanding that such tributes should be repaid on the first occasion available. Thus, in time, floral tributes for the house of mourning became a question of give and expect: a compliment to a friend with a marketable value attached. No wonder that some families deprecate the invasion of their homes with such tributes and cry out, "Omit the flowers."[11]

It is interesting to note that in the same city and in a catalogue dated the same year, the Stein Patent Burial Casket Works advertised for order by funeral directors floral offerings, in fresh flowers or "immortelles" in twenty different designs, most of them carrying four or five sizes, and ranging in wholesale price from a dollar-and-a-half to twenty-five dollars. "Immortelles"—non-perishable, artificial, dried, or prepared natural flowers and leaves—generally were fifty-percent cheaper. Those wishing to order funeral decorations through their undertaker had a choice of set pieces: the Plain Wreath; Cross, flat or standing; Anchor, or Anchor Cross, flat or standing; Faith, Hope and Charity (anchor, cross and heart in one piece); Harp or Lyre, standing; Square and Compass; Crown, flat or standing; Star; Heart; Maltese Cross; monograms, sold by the letter; Three Links; Combinations of Wreath and Cross, Harp, Anchor, Crown, and Star; Crescent; Crescent and Star Combined; Broken Column; Monument; Shield; Sickle; and, finally, Lamb and Cross.

The fact that there was opposition to the use of flowers on the ground that they were pagan; to their extensive use on the score that it was wasteful; and to the sense of reciprocal necessity because it was worldly, indicates that the usage must have been growing. The broad choice of styles, forms, sizes and motifs, gives further proof, if such were needed, that a shift in popular taste was making heavy inroads upon the tradition of feudal gloom at the very time that the pompous and solemnly formal funeral seemed to be enjoying its greatest vogue.

Victory of flowers over crepe was given striking support by the flower burial of the controversial, widely popular Anti-Slavery clergyman, Henry Ward Beecher, in connection with whose death in 1887 a virtual "flower funeral" was held. Beecher had always been of the mind that flowers were more appropriate at funerals than black crepe. Hence, when he died a basket of flowers was fixed at the door of his residence in Brooklyn, instead of the conventional black emblem. Likewise, the floral theme dominated all the church decorations. The old reading desk, placed to the right of the pulpit platform, was covered with asparagus ferns and pink and white roses. Beecher's chair was lost in a sea of white carnations, pink roses, smilax, and eucharist lillies. Behind the dais where the coffin rested, extending to the ceiling, was a solid bank of flowers, formed of azaleas, calla lillies and other blooms. Each post around the face of the gallery was surrounded with clusters of plants, and the ledge of the gallery was covered with a continuous bank of flowers. Between the pillars were wreaths of laurel; from the chandelier in the center of the church ropes of laurel were stretched in every direction to the cornice, where they were met with clusters of evergreen fastened against the walls. Underneath the gallery the walls themselves were hung with wreaths of evergreens, and the ceiling was completely concealed by hangings of smilax, caught up with bunches of bright flowers. From each gas bracket in the church were hung baskets filled with cut roses, azaleas, chrysanthemums, and other bright and fragrant flowers. On the Bible stand was a design of ferns in which there were three doves; to the right was a floral cross bearing the words "Our Chaplain," while nearby was a large pillow of white flowers with the letter "B" formed of pink roses in the center. To complete the flower motif the front of the church was decked with ropings of smilax and evergreen.[12]

In the year before the Beecher funeral, the principal floral offering at the funeral of a fire chief was a large floral fire engine, nine feet high and six feet long, patterned after the old Red Rover #3, and covered with smilax, carnations and roses. Lettered in violets on the boiler were the words, "Our Chief." Another floral piece was fashioned after a fire alarm box. It bore the number "4," in memory of the last fire to which the Chief had responded. During the same year the custom of writing with white ink on the leaves of natural flowers became popular. In 1888 the IFDA—International Funeral Directors' Association, the title used by the present NFDA during its affiliation with the Canadian Funeral Directors' Association—encouraged its members to use flowers instead of crepe. Inscriptions were the vogue in funeral flowers. It is recorded that a gentleman of New York who had been entertaining a Cuban friend sent the office boy to get flowers for the friend's stateroom on the steamer home. The boy returned with two broken columns inscribed, "We mourn your loss" and "Gone to another shore." When the Secretary of the New England Funeral Directors Association died he was honored with a floral offering of a closed book on a mound of smilax on which was laid his secretarial pen surmounted by a wreath of roses. Above these symbols was poised a floral crown.

Artificial flowers were being widely sold in the 1890's because the distribution of natural flowers was spotty, and they could not be obtained in some areas and at some times.

By 1892, it was recorded that floral pieces containing sentiments and descriptions were going out of fashion. Three years later some concern was expressed over the stereotyped patterns of floral offerings, and the suggestion was made that supporting bouquets or greens could better be employed than the endless repetitions of "Gates Ajar," "The Broken Column," or the "Unstrung Harp," with its gold or silver wires. But the fashions were too well established to be terminated by a little criticism. When the elaborate pieces of the Philadelphia Immortelle Co. was criticized, it answered that the business of all florists had increased, and that one florist with a $10,000.00 annual gross had made 50% of his sales in dried flowers and wheat sheaves. The floral vogue did not reach Jewish funerals during this period.

Sepulture and Memorialization: In the 1880's, in urban communities, burial would most likely take place in a "central" cemetery, that is, in a large burial tract on or beyond the outskirts, in which many families drawn from a wide area of the community owned private lots. Single grave spaces could be purchased also. Although a large number of such cemeteries were denominational, some were sponsored by non-religious corporations. Most of them contained remains transferred from older, smaller cemeteries that had been crowded out by the rapid expansion of American cities. In some cases, graves had been so removed several times. Under the changing fashion which sought beauty in death and burial, cemeteries during this period began taking on the aspect of a park. Perpetual care plans were still uncommon. The breaking away from the custom of burying in the church graveyard or in scattered small public or private lots had been going on for three-quarters of a century.

A movement for burial outside the corporate limits of cities arose in the United States in the opening years of the 19th century. The example of France proved a strong influence in the matter. A report of the New York City Board of Health in 1806 advised the removal of all graveyards from the city and recommended that burial places should be made public works. In that same year a law was passed authorizing the Corporation of the City of New York to prohibit interment within the city limits. No effort was made to enforce it until the following year. Nor did anyone show much interest in the problem of intramural burial until epidemics of yellow fever and cholera convinced the public that there was need for cemeteries outside the city.[13] The condition of some of these city graveyards became apparent from the fact that in 1822 quick lime was placed over them to kill the summer odors arising from them.[14]

The first of the new extramural cemeteries was Mt. Auburn at Boston, established in 1831; Laurel Hill in Pennsylvania was opened soon after; and Greenwood in New York City in 1837.[15] A treatise by Dr. John H. Rauch of Chicago seems to have been influential in later cemetery development. New York State passed a Rural Cemetery Act in 1847, providing for the founding of cemetery associations and granting certain privileges such as freedom from taxes, the right to make rules and regulations, to distribute payment for land purchased for such cemetery uses over the life of the cemetery.[16]

While each town or city had its own cemetery experiences, in a general way the problems were common, and they were therefore likely to find more or less common solutions. Chicago offers a case in point. An 1830 map of Fort Dearborn, Illinois, shows a cemetery on the edge of the small military reservation or garrison. In 1832 a ship sailing into Chicago was ravaged by cholera. The first dead were weighted and buried at sea. Eighteen others were interred on land not far from the place where the American Temple House was later erected at the intersection of Lake and

Wabash. The burial was primitive, without coffins or shrouds, and with blankets for winding sheets, the earth removed to cover one corpse hollowing a grave to receive the next that died. By 1835 the village authorities were facing the cemetery problem, and the trustees ordered the surveyor to lay out sixteen acres on the South Side near the foot of 23rd Street for Catholics and ten acres on the North Side —on what is now Chicago Avenue just east of Clark Street —for Protestants. Burial in any other part of the town was forbidden.

The first recorded grave digger, a Prussian immigrant by the name of Henry Gherkin, arrived in Chicago in 1836. The laying out of the two cemeteries, Catholic and Protestant, apparently left unsolved certain of Chicago's burial problems, as can be inferred from the fact that only two years later the city's charter was amended in the interest of public health to permit the establishment of a city burial grounds. The amendment also gave Chicago the right to regulate the burial of the dead. By 1840 the sprawling town was again in cemetery trouble, and the Council decreed the abandonment of the early cemeteries and the establishment of a burial ground further out. The new location was on the site of Lincoln Park. Three years after this action, the city passed an ordinance providing penalties for burial in the old cemeteries.

In the meantime, in 1842, Greenwood Cemetery was established. Oakwood Cemetery, at what is now 107th and Greenwood, had its first burials eleven years later. But the growing pains still continued, and in 1865 the Chicago Council decided to vacate the Lincoln Park Cemetery, as it could not establish clear title to this property. Lot owners were given titles to lots in newer cemeteries. The moving of the bodies took several years.[17]

The celebrated Mt. Auburn Cemetery, where many Boston notables are buried, illustrates some of the influences at work which changed the American pattern from interment in the church graveyard or the privately owned plot to the central cemetery. In 1825 Dr. Jacob Bigelow expressed the belief that a country cemetery should be established to put an end to what he believed were the dangers to the public health resulting from church vault and church yard burial. To put his ideas into practice, he called a meeting of his friends.

Strangely enough, in order to gain for itself a place in which to conduct experiments, the Massachusetts Horticultural Society decided to lend a hand with the project, and a Boston citizen, George W. Brimmer, at no profit to himself, sold "Stone's Woods" to the Society. To gain support, public meetings were called and the newspapers were supplied with announcements and articles. Distinguished Bostonians and others, among the group Supreme Court Justice Joseph Story, the great Daniel Webster, the eminent statesman and orator, Edward Everett, Abbott Lawrence, Samuel Appleton, and Henry A. S. Dearborn, President of the Horticultural Society, lent their names and active support to the project. On June 23, 1831, an act was passed authorizing the Horticultural Society to dedicate real estate for a rural cemetery. Consecration services, with Justice Story providing the oration, were held on September 24th of the same year. It was soon discovered that an experimental garden and a cemetery were two distinct enterprises, and so by act of March 31, 1835, the cemetery was placed under separate management.

In 1881, six central cemeteries were available to the citizens of Milwaukee which city was probably fairly typical. The largest of these, Forest Home Cemetery, was established in 1850 by the vestry of St. Paul's Episcopal Church. Thirty years later the property consisted of 188 acres. "Thousands of dollars have been expended in cutting

and smoothing wide gravelled roadways, maintaining beautiful flower beds, planting trees, erecting a fine fountain and
otherwise making it a Forest Home—a restful city of the
dead. For beauty of natural location and taste in artificial
adornment, it has not a superior in the West."[18] Three
members of St. Paul's vestry served, without pay, as a
Management Committee. In 1864, under authority of the
Wisconsin State Legislature, about 1,200 bodies interred in
Milwaukee Cemetery, then being surrounded by the growing young city, were transferred to Forest Home. In 1880
"several lot owners are considering the propriety of be-
queathing certain sums of money in trust for the purpose
of perpetually providing for the care and maintenance of
their lots. The corporation would gladly take charge of such
trusts." By 1880 recorded interments reached about 14,000.

Catholics could find burial either in Calvary or Trinity
cemeteries. Like Forest Home, Calvary cemetery, a 55-
acre tract, established in 1857, was the inheritor plot for
several earlier graveyards. In very early days within the
original boundaries of the city, a small non-sectarian fenced-
in cemetery was developed. Later this became a Catholic
cemetery, and in 1844 Bishop Henni purchased the "Old
Catholic Cemetery," a ten acre tract on Grand Avenue—now
Wisconsin Avenue—in the very heart of the present city. As
the city developed, the First Ward Cemetery was no longer
used for burial, and the bodies interred therein were transferred to the "Old Cemetery." First interments at Calvary
were remains transferred from the "Old Cemetery," which in
turn was being abandoned as the city closed in upon it. In the
twenty-three years from 1857 to 1880 Calvary Cemetery received 10,307 remains. Holy Trinity was a smaller Catholic
cemetery originally purchased to provide burial grounds for
a single Catholic parish. The graveyard was three or four
miles removed from Holy Trinity Church.

Union and Pilgrim's Rest Cemeteries accepted Protestant burials. Greenwood Cemetery, adjoining Forest Home, was "devoted exclusively to the use of Israelites."

Frederick S. Frantz, a third generation Pennsylvania funeral director, traces, in most general outlines, the history of cemetery development in the Middle Atlantic region:

In Grandfather's time, there was no cemetery as we know it today. In fact, it was not called a cemetery—it was a "graveyard" or "churchyard" or "God's acre." As our forefathers settled this section of the country, they set aside part of their own land for their own families. It was God's acre, and kept as such. This little tract of ground so hallowed, was convenient and necessary—but later it often became a handicap in the sale of property, for the next owner would not wish the first party's burial lot, and the original owner would not wish to be separated from the dead. One can easily see the complications that would arise from this transaction. The churchyard then became the logical place for burial and this ground was placed in the hands of the church officers, who in turn had authority over the permits. No lots were sold and space was opened for graves as needed. This often meant that husband and wife were separated by as many graves as were used between the two deaths. We have some records where these graveyards were divided into the following groups: married section, single adults, choir, children, and those who were outside the church—not members.

About this time, the duty of grave digging fell upon the shoulders of the pallbearers. They assisted the family and undertaker from the time of the first call to the very end—the closing of the open grave.

The church "graveyard" had its limitations in growing sections, for in many towns of 1,500 people there were at least 15 "graveyards." Ground became valuable and the boundaries of the lot were limited by houses that had been built on the four sides. Therefore, the central cemetery was the logical growth, and the burial lot passed from the hands of the church to organized and chartered groups who developed the beautiful memorial parks of today.[19]

The effort to beautify the surroundings of death had further expression in the memorialization of the dead.

In their designs and materials, the gravestones themselves responded to the changing funeral mood of the day. Instead of the earlier simple marble or limestone slab, the sculptor went to work industriously to add cornices, fancy caps, arabesques, scrolls, imitation tree trunks, statuary. Sometimes he combined several types or shades of stone. The peculiar bad taste of the romantic period which produced Main Street mansions faintly reminiscent of German castles or Italian palaces, and furniture that looked to the jig-saw and lathe rather than to the carver's bench, filled cemeteries with a minor vertical forest of petrified and very indifferent art. But here again the impulse to create beauty even in death was strong, although the effect is not always happy to the modern eye which prefers simplicity and harmony. It has been well said however that with the passing of such ornateness, something has been lost as well as gained. The "uncouth lines and shapeless sculpture" of which Thomas Gray once spoke are no longer in fashion. The present tendency toward uniformity and simplicity may add a sense of dignity to cemeteries, but graveyards lack somewhat the intriguing personality of an earlier day.[20]

Something of the changing mood toward death and funerals can be learned from a reading of grave inscriptions. Wallis remarks:

On these stone silhouettes of bygone days, we may read the hopes and despairs, the joys and frustrations of Everyman. The manner of expression may be ribald and ridiculous, pompous and lugubrious, eloquent, or serenely simple.

The common grave slab probably originated as an effort to safeguard a new grave from wild beasts. Names and dates were inscribed for purposes of identification. An epitaph, representing pious sentiments consistent with a person's life, or words of advice or caution for the instruction of the living, later made one stone distinctive from another. Quotations from the Bible have long seemed singularly appropriate.[21]

Inscriptions and decorations on tombstones provide additional clues to popular attitudes toward life and death at any period. Early American epitaphs had minced no words, used no sweetened or softened expressions to veil or sugar the hard natural facts. Through the 18th century and before, and well into the 19th, they spelled out the reality of death. When they told biography it was unvarnished. They called sinners, sinners; saints, saints. They did not shun to tell what lay beneath them; not infrequently they spelled out the message with skull and cross-bones to illustrate the point. After having looked into the face of death, some survivors were not beyond making a crude jest or a merry pun. Although the endless variety tempts one to halt at length here, a few illustrations must suffice. There is the harsh New Hampshire epitaph, written in simplest imagery, which reads:

> This rose was sweet a while,
> But now is odour vile.[22]

Some forgotten necrophile uses an undated, nameless Massachusetts tombstone to express his frustration:

> Oh would that I could lift the lid and peer
> within the grave and watch the greedy worms
> that eat away the dead.[23]

Or the terse:

> Soon ripe
> Soon rotten
> Soon gone
> But not forgotten.[24]

Or the pathetic couplet to the eight-year old boy who in 1795 was buried in Milford, Connecticut:

> Christ called at midnight as I lay
> In thirty hours was turned to. clay.[25]

No one has ever written better "The short and simple annals" of a young wife and mother who died in childbirth:

> Eighteen years a maiden,
> One year a wife
> One day a mother
> Then I lost my life.[26]

Details concerning the manner of death were badly and boldly written:

> Killed by a kick of a colt
> in his bowells.[27]

When a four-year old boy died of burns from an overturned coffee pot, his tombstone commented:

> The boiling coffee on me did fall,
> And by it I was slain,
> But Christ has brought my liberty
> And in Him I'll rise again.[28]

Friends of Thomas Mulvaney were reminded:

> Old Thomas Mulvaney lies here,
> His mouth ran from ear to ear,
> Reader, tread lightly on this wonder,
> For if he yawns, you're going to thunder.[29]

In many old graveyards are found inscriptions and other reminders of the sicknesses that caused untimely and even timely deaths. Dropsy, heart disease, consumption, St. Vitus dance are not uncommonly mentioned. Nor are inscriptions wanting which describe the suffering brought on by the several maladies: "severest pains," "body affliction," "painful illness." Sermons in stone can be found on many an older monument in an old graveyard at the side of a church or next to the village green.

While there is no sharp cleavage, it is noticeable that after 1850 monument prose, verse and art more and more softened the hard facts, grew less didactic, less blunt, less inclined to roar with rude laughter. The skull and cross bones gave way to the winged cherub and to other symbols of faith and hope. By 1865 it was not deemed inappropriate as it would have been a half century before to write:

> 'Tis but the casket that lies here
> The gem that fills it sparkles yet.[30]

And, by 1880 a wife would comment:

> Stranger call this not a place
> Of fear and gloom,
> To me it is a pleasant spot
> It is my husband's tomb.[31]

Sentiments such as those adorning tombstones in the 1880's conform in mood to that of the four-by-six-inch gilt-edged, gilt-printed "mourning" cards of the period. These were distributed to friends. (See Plate 61.) The card of Thomas Ardron, who died April 19, 1891, at the age of 76 years, two months and eight days, has a dove at the top holding a streamer which bears the legend "In Loving Remembrance." Upon the outline of the Holy Bible are printed the Masonic symbols and the name of the departed. Below, on a scroll, is the elegiac verse:

> How slender is life's silver cord.
> How soon 'tis broken here!
> Each moment brings a parting word,
> And many a falling tear.

> And though these years, to mortals given
> Are filled with grief and pain,
> There is a hope—the hope of heaven,
> Where loved ones meet again.[32]

When James S. Pilling died on March 14, 1889, at the age of eight, his card, "In Loving Remembrance," carried two separate poems: the first reminded the bereaved that:

> "There is no death." What seems so is transition;
>   This life of mortal breath
> Is but the suburb of the life elysian,
>   Whose portal we call Death.[33]

The second dealt with the small boy himself:

> Sleep on in thy beauty,
>   Thou sweet angel child,
> By sorrow unslighted,
>   By sin undefiled.

> Like the dove to the ark,
>   Thou hast flown to thy rest,
> From the wild sea of strife,
>   To the home of the blest.[34]

The impulse to memorialize in verse and the willingness of verse makers to provide copy for such memorials have both persisted to our day. Even though mourning cards have long gone out of fashion, the reminders of death and anniversaries of death occasionally appear in the daily newspapers.

The Changing Functions of the Undertaker: We have seen that in the early years of the 18th century the role and duties of the undertaker were changed by the new emphasis placed upon the coffin as the major item in the funeral, together with the resultant development of the coffin-warehouse, or wareroom. Later, toward mid-century, other changes were produced by the emergence of the "furnishing undertaker," whose concentration of necessary funeral paraphernalia in one establishment made it possible for the undertaker to give increased attention to the rendering of

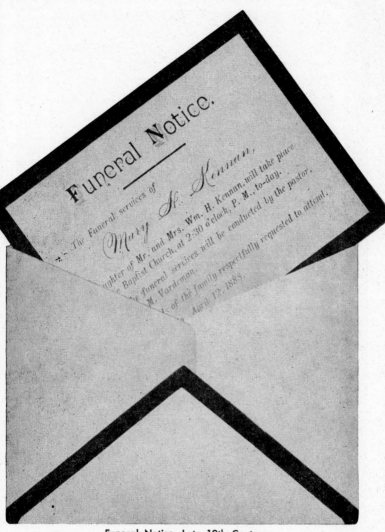

Funeral Notice.

The Funeral services of

Mary H. Kennan,

daughter of Mr. and Mrs. Wm. H. Kennan, will take place
at the Baptist Church at 2:30 o'clock, P. M., to-day.

The funeral services will be conducted by the pastor,
Rev. M. Vardeman.

The friends of the family respectfully requested to attend.

April 12, 1888.

Funeral Notice, Late 19th Century

PLATE 60

In loving remembrance

Thomas Ardron,
Died April 19, 1891.
Aged 76 Yrs. 2 Mos. 8 Days.

Holy Bible

How slender is life's silver cord.
How soon 'tis broken here!
Each moment brings a parting word,
And many a falling tear.

And though these years, to mortals given
Are filled with grief and pain,
There is a hope—the hope of heaven,
Where loved ones meet again.

Mourning Card, Memento of the Deceased

PLATE 61

personal service to the bereaved. Such changes in an occupation would suggest that it was in a state of transition, and that the last twenty or thirty years of the century would produce further change. The facts well warrant the assumption.

As early as 1862 the furnishing undertakers were issuing professional cards. (See Figure 3.) While it is true that many of these establishments carried lines of other wares, such as furniture and household necessities of many sorts (see Plate 25), there is a noticeable change in emphasis away from undertaking as an incidental or auxiliary service, or from the furnishing of undertakers' supplies as a mere side line. True, undertaking in 1875 to 1900 had not as yet crystallized out into a clear-cut occupational role (funeral directing still has its ambiguities), yet the outlines were clear enough, and the general image of the modern funeral director was coming into clearer focus all the time. There were yet activities which he must lose, slough off, or delegate to others. And there were new functions such as counseling the survivors which were still in the future. Despite the hazards of interrupting the process of narrative for a circumspective glance at a period which was marked by transition rather than stability, it seems worthwhile at this point to pause around 1880 and in keeping with the general sense of the chapter to take a cross sectional view of the occupational role of the undertaker.

In the first place, he had probably reached a peak in supplying material objects, or funeral paraphernalia, for the care and disposal of the dead. At this time not only did he provide major items such as casket and carriage, but such mourning materials as drapery, door badges or scarfs, items of clothing, caps and neckerchiefs for such participants as pallbearers, ministers, honor guards, and others as well. He also kept on hand a variety of memorial cards, announcement forms, and other stationery upon which he arranged to have pertinent information printed such as names, dates and places. He provided flowers, stocking immortelles or other imitations, or ordering such from dealers by telegraph. He also made arrangements with the local florist to supply tributes made of either fresh or imitation flowers. He provided, likewise, chairs, robes, pillows, nets, gauze, candle sticks and crucifixes, kid gloves and ornaments. In short, he generally furnished any material object that was likely to be used specifically for funerals.

Yet at the same time that the peak in furnishing material goods was reached there were already seeds germinating for the appearance of the new role of the funeral director, so that by the end of the century the undertaker, as dominantly a furnisher of goods, represented an occupation that was fast becoming obsolete.

The new fact in late 19th century undertaking was the great increase in control which the undertaker was beginning to exert over the whole matter of the funeralization of the dead. Spelled out in detail, this meant that he moved from a merchant who first provided goods needed by the bereaved in their burying activities; to a seller of service who actually took part in the preparation of the dead, performing a portion of all of the laying out of the body in the home—"conserving the remains"—and transporting body and mourners to places of worship and sepulture; and finally to a director who took charge of the body and of the proceedings involved in its ceremonial disposition.

Funeral direction as we find the occupation today, grew out of three needs, which also were at the root of the modern funeral home. First, embalming by chemical injection carried with it the need of a special working laboratory, constructed and equipped along clinical lines.

Newtown Shaw
Dec. 20th 84

Dear Cousins
I write a few
lines hoping to find
all well I am verry
sorry to inform you
of the Death of my
Mother who Died on
the 5th inst with a few
hours Sickness we
was not escpecting it
the Docter called it
Pleurisy and inflam
ation but it was

Harbinger of Death, the Letter Edged in Black

PLATE 62

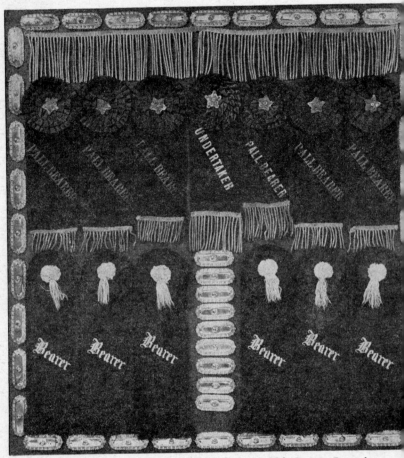

Funeral Badges, Indispensable to the Late 19th Century Funeral

PLATE 63

Second, the crowding of cities, the development of small living units in apartment and other buildings, created a need for the establishment of the funeral "home" or "parlor" especially designed for the ceremonial disposal of the dead. Third, in urban communities, the problems attendant upon the transportation of both the dead and living to places of worship added a need for the development of a chapel in such establishments which could be used by those desiring such use, as a setting for the religious ceremonialization of the dead. As the 19th century drew to a close, consolidation of these three functional areas, the clinic, the home, and the chapel, into a single operational unit gave rise to the modern funeral home, and provided the cues for the emergence of the funeral director as we know him today.

Yet, funeral directing in the sense of managing a complex series of activities, designed, among other matters, to create and sustain a mood, was still in an unformed state. Basically, in 1880, the American funeral undertaker was a merchant, selling goods to customers, but at the same time he was becoming more and more involved in taking charge of the management aspects of the care and disposal of the dead. Thus, he still tendered bills which itemized goods and services without discrimination. (See Figure 29.)

As a matter of fact, many of the services such as the opening and the bricking up of the sides of the grave, the arrangements made with sextons and cemetery superintendents, the securing of permits, extra ice for coolers, the provision for carriages and the like were profitable, even if small transactions. The undertaker had as yet to conceive of the value of personal services offered professionally for a fee, legitimately claimed. Being "in attendance" was as far as he would concede his services as worthy of such fee. The charge for this item was very minimal, usually only a few dollars, while the profit from the sale of the casket was substantial, and the undertaker sometimes realized his greatest return from providing a number of carriages. On the other hand, the making of cash advances, one of the more obviously non-service functions in a private enterprise economy, was clearly more of a personal accommodation than a financial transaction. This practice had its origin about the middle of the century. Although undertakers may have been merchants they were never commercial money-lenders. Had they assumed this function as one of their occupational specialties, it is doubtful if the personal serv-ice element, involving professional judgment of what are appropriate actions in funeral service, would ever have evolved out of 19th century undertaking.

In a word, at the end of the last century the undertaker was a supplier of funeral necessities who was at the same time on the threshold of becoming a provider of directions, definitions, and ideas for appropriate ceremonial actions. To provide humane treatment of the dead, he could or soon would be able to take the body from the home, and in the same physical structure, render it innocuous to the health of the community, preserve it, and make it available for appropriate viewing as custom dictated, and provide when and as desired a religious setting where, with the aid of a clergyman, the body could be made ready for burial. Al-though the furnishing of goods and paraphernalia has always been part of the business of the funeral undertaker, and continues to be one among a number of functions of the funeral director, its relative importance began to decline before 1900, and it has long since been relegated to one of the numerous specialties of a profession-oriented occupation, centrally based in the performance of personal service.

63.—All wool cream merino.

No. 65.—All wool cream merino, puffed
satin front, knife plaiting, and
crepe lisse trimmed, cream satin
sash.

No. 68.—White cashmere; puffed satin front,
double point box plaiting.

Burial Robes Sold by Undertakers, 1880

PLATE 64

CITATIONS AND REFERENCES FOR CHAPTER X

1. Mrs. A. Baldwin, *When Our Mother Was a Little Girl* (1888), p. 2. From the Collection of the NFDA, Milwaukee, Wisconsin.

2. Lewis Atherton, *Main Street on the Middle Border* (Bloomington, Indiana: Indiana University Press, 1954), p. 191.

3. H. J. Blanton, *When I Was a Boy* (Columbia, Mo.: E. W. Stephens Publishing Company, 2 vols., 1952). See especially, "When the Undertaker Had a Modest Part," Vol. 1, pp. 1-3.

4. Landauer, *op. cit.*, p. 226.

5. Harry A. Weisbord, "Time Stays—We Go," *Hobbies*, August, 1940, pp. 10-11.

6. Atherton, *op. cit.*, p. 192.

7. Blanton, *op. cit.*, p. 1.

8. See, for example, Marvin Dana, *The American Encyclopedia of Etiquette and Culture* 1922, n.p., Part Six.

9. Frederick S. Frantz, "The Funeral Director in Grandpa's Time," in *Clinical Topics*, p. 6.

10. See George S. Herrick, "The Facts About Casket Textiles," *Casket and Sunnyside*, reprint contained in a brochure entitled *Casket Manufacturing*, n.d.

11. *The Casket*, July 1878.

12. Adapted from the document "The Beecher Flowers" in the Collection of the NFDA, Milwaukee, Wisconsin, n.p., n.d.

13. Wilson and Levy, *op. cit.*, p. 21.

14. See F. D. Allen, *Documents and Facts, showing the Fatal Effects of interments in Populous Cities* (New York: publisher unknown, 1822).

15. C. F. Perkinson to Maynard C. Weller, February 7,

1944. Letter in the Collection of the NFDA, Milwaukee, Wisconsin.

16. *Ibid.*

17. See Paul Gilbert and Charles L. Bryson, *Chicago and its Makers* (Chicago: Felix Mendelsohn, 1929). Also Bessie L. Pierce, *History of Chicago (1673-1848)*, Vol. I (New York: Alfred Knopf, 1937).

18. *History of Milwaukee* (Chicago: Western Historical Company, 1881), pp. 953-957.

19. Frederick S. Frantz, *op. cit.*, p. 6

20. Charles L. Wallis, *Stories on Stone* (New York: Oxford University Press, 1954), p. xv.

21. *Ibid.*, p. xi.

22. *Ibid.*, p. 185.

23. *Ibid.*

24. *Ibid.*, p. 181.

25. *Ibid.*, p. 182.

26. *Ibid.*, p. 173.

27. *Ibid.*, p. 116.

28. *Ibid.*, p. 119.

29. *The American Funeral Director;* loose clipping, Collection of the NFDA, Milwaukee, Wisconsin, n.p., n.d.

30. Wallis, *op. cit.*, p. 185.

31. Charles L. Wallis, "Their Last Words Had a Punch." *Saturday Evening Post*, April 17, 1954, p. 44.

32. Mourning card in Collection of NFDA, Milwaukee, Wisconsin.

33. *Ibid.*

34. *Ibid.*

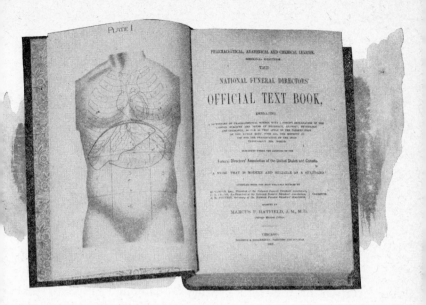

Plate I

The Associational Impulse

The 19th century produced an economic revolution which shifted the economy of the nation from one based predominantly upon an agrarian society to one increasingly characterized by industry, manufacture, urbanism, and corporate business.[1] In the social and cultural realm this process was paralleled by the emergence of new social movements, some seeking to set the world aright by harking back to the venerable ways of the past, others with bold ideas hoping to chart new programs of human action. As the century rolled by there were few important areas of American occupational life left untouched by these changes and developments. One of the most significant effects of these social and economic forces was the appearance of large scale *associational* activity—the gathering together and organ-

445

izing of significant numbers of people around a limited set
of interests and objectives. Thus in the world of industry
the laboring man formed his trade union; the industrialist
found strength in his trade association; and the practitioner
sought colleagueship in his professional organization. It is
the problem of the formal organization of funeral directors
into various limited-objective types of associations, and the
growth, prosperity, problems, issues, and changing forms
and functions of these associations that will form the burden
of the following chapter.

BACKGROUND FACTORS

Occupational Organization: The modern concept of an
occupational or professional association was almost entirely
a creation of the 19th century.[2] Although prior to that
time professional organization had been limited to the
fields of medicine and law, this period witnessed an astonishing extension of occupational organization among a vast
number of vocations and organized forms of personal services. A partial explanation of this extension is to be found
in the progress of science and technology, which gave rise
to numerous new professions such as engineering, architec-
ture, chemistry and dentistry. In addition, the consequent
social and cultural revolutions created a demand for all
types of specialists trained to cope with the increasingly
complicated machinery of changing patterns in government,
business, and education; as a result we had the burgeoning of
new occupations, such as various types of public adminis-
trators, accountants, secretaries, realtors, surveyors, patent
attorneys, nurses, librarians, and the like.[3] In consequence
of these developments, there appeared a growing occupational self-consciousness among these and various personal
and service occupations, and in vocations bordering upon
the traditional or established professions. Two not unrelated

models of association commended themselves—professional and trade. The one was exemplified by the organizations of medical practitioners, and lawyers; the other, although less distinct in form functioned basically to define and help attain the interests of businessmen.

While the ends of these forms of collective association were not necessarily opposed, neither were they in any sense identical. Professional associations sought not only to formulate standards, control membership, and enforce an inspectional system, but most of all to assure the several clienteles of the high personal character and the good moral standards of their members. While in many ways seeking somewhat allied goals, trade associations subscribed to the proposition that the buyer-seller, or market relationship, is impersonal and calls for an awareness of both parties of values given and received. The trade association thus turned its attention primarily to the material interests of its own special membership; other matters, such as standards of character and the adequacy of training were held as definitely secondary in nature.

In those vocations where personal service was emphasized, it was a natural occurrence for associational activities to look to the model of the professions; for vocations involving merchandising transactions, on the other hand, the trade association, by the same token, offered the greatest potential. It will be seen that in the case of 19th century funeral direction no one of these two associational models commended itself forcefully, to the exclusion of the other. Also, to create further complexity, the funeral establishments themselves were often patterned after the guilds, with master, journeyman, and apprentice relationships featuring their internal personnel organization.

To assist associations, and particularly those of a professional and semi-professional nature to attain their ends, two instruments have been available. The first of these is the use of educational prerequisites and training institutions in the indoctrination of new recruits in the professions. The system of educational requirements has been used by the occupation to control the supply of new members.

The second, which will be described below, is the regulatory system developed by the state as an outgrowth of its police powers. Systems of this type generally are incorporated into small bodies or boards empowered by law to set standards for admission to practice, to license, to establish codes, and in these and other ways to exert a significant measure of control over certain vocations.

Internally, the primary method for achieving vocation-wide definitions of relationships of the professional man with others in his field as well as with the community has been the ethical code of the profession. The licensing system marks the next step toward protection of professional status by giving legal status to the codes of ethics and by establishing a legal register of "qualified" practitioners.[4]

Until the Civil War the established professions could scarcely be termed organized in terms of associational structure; and at that time in the service vocations and quasi-professions associational activities were virtually nil. In the remainder of the century, state, local, and national associations representing a wide range of vocations with professional aspirations were formed, and as a matter of immediate concern, pressed for the passage of state licensing statutes. By 1900, of thirty-eight professional and technical vocations, twenty-one had been touched by at least one piece of statutory legislation, with a total of nearly two hundred statutes passed since 1870.[5] In the first quarter of the present century occupational licensing reached its peak; since then with rules fairly well set, the rate of enacting new legislation has naturally declined, although the number of different occupations licensed by one or more states continues to increase.[6] Of the two hundred pieces of legislation mentioned, at least nineteen dealt with the funeral director and embalmer, since by 1900 that number of states had passed laws licensing one or the other of these occupations. Although we will return to the subject of licensing and state regulation of funeral direction and embalming, with emphasis on the latter, in a later section of the chapter, it suffices to point out at this time that the quarter century from 1875-1900 was marked by a tremendous growth of professional and trade associations, and that the impulse to professionalize seems to have diffused rapidly though many occupations whose earlier status was something less than that shared by such established professions as law, medicine, and the ministry.

Such then, is a portion of the backdrop of social and economic forces which have impinged upon the groping efforts of undertakers attempting to rise above the traditional status of providers of funeral paraphernalia and factotums of burial. One other set of broad-gauge social factors needs to be explored before the specific associational efforts and gestures of these individuals can be taken up directly. We turn, then, to the area of socio-cultural movements, examining two in particular; the general Public Health Movement, and the specific movement in America for Burial Reform.

Socio-Cultural Movements: a) **The General Public Health Movement:** The general awakening in social reform, humanitarianism, and philanthropy of the middle 19th century had its basis in the cardinal tenet of the dignity and worth of man. Being unique by virtue of his capacity for rational thought, man can discover the natural order of things and the laws that govern their behavior. Once having discovered these laws he may initiate action calculated to better himself and his society. Armed with such knowledge, when necessary, he may reorganize political and social institutions with the end in view of creating the kind of society which will best realize the worth of man.

This was the underlying political philosophy for late 19th century social reform. It was supported by religious philosophies of disinterested benevolence which turned the mind toward society and away from introspection and concern with self. It was supported also, in less philosophical fashion, by the exigencies which made themselves drastically felt as America in this period experienced a rapid industrial growth, a flood of immigrants, the rise of cities, and the breakdown of customary modes of behavior. In default of clear-cut and universally accepted traditional rules for handling them, behavior problems were solved by everyday, catch-as-catch-can methods, pragmatically, with little thought of more than making the best of the immediate situation.

Yet the social problems attending the burgeoning of a new industrial society called for more than the simple, pragmatic approach. Themes for organizing human endeavor and responses in terms of large problem areas emerged at this time. For this study one of the more significant of these is the general social movement for the betterment of the nation's health by the use primarily of preventive sanitation measures.

The Public Health Movement in America was formally launched in 1850 by the publication of the "Report of the Massachusetts Sanitary Commission," which body recommended the establishment of a system of sanitary police, with state and local health departments, and a careful collection and analysis of vital statistics. No effective action was taken upon this report until 1869 when the Massachusetts State Board of Health, the first of its kind in the nation, was established. By 1878 sixteen other states had set up similar boards, and by 1900, the total had swelled to thirty. It will be noted later that the several associations of funeral directors brought strong pressures to bear for the establishment of such state boards of health and for the setting within their framework of special boards to examine and license the members of their own occupational group.

Since 1789 when John Adams, the second American president, began his second annual message to Congress with a reference to the yellow fever pestilence and urged the passage of federal laws to promote the health of persons in the several states there has been an awareness by the federal government of the need for national health legislation. Quarantine legislation demanded the attention of Jefferson and Monroe. Martin Van Buren, John Tyler, and Franklin Pierce, between the years 1837 and 1853 sent messages to Congress regarding plans and sites for marine hospitals.[7] Both Andrew Johnson and Ulysses S. Grant transmitted to Congress papers relative to an international conference on cholera. Recognizing the importance of quarantine as a means of controlling the epidemics of cholera and yellow fever which plagued the country, Rutherford B. Hayes recommended to Congress in 1878 that the administration of quarantine be brought under federal jurisdiction, and in April of that year a weak quarantine law was passed. Shortly afterwards, following a severe epidemic of yellow fever, Congress proceeded to establish a National Board of Health with a term of four years. Although this board did not become a continuing part of the federal government, the Marine Hospital Service, which succeeded it, grew into the United States Public Health Service, which today is the principal, though not the only health agency of the Federal Government.[8]

At the same time state governments continued to put reliance upon their own health organizations in meeting problems of epidemics and plagues. Yet in spite of their independent efforts it became increasingly evident that the magnitude of some of these visitations was too great for individual states to meet. When the need for federal jurisdiction over matters of quarantine became apparent, the Quarantine Act was passed by Congress in 1893 and amended in 1901. This act forms the basis for present federal authority in this field.

But there were other pressures and forces coalescing to bring public attention, effort, and organized action to the matter of the nation's health. Cities such as New York had been the scene of citizens' organizations, or "Sanitary Associations," pledged to bring under municipal control the sanitation problems which sorely beset them. The "Metropolitan Health Bill" passed by the State of New York created a Metropolitan Board which was not subject to judicial review. It was submitted to the legislature in 1866, just as cholera was raging in Europe and seemed certain to visit American shores. With its passage New York was given the most comprehensive and powerful piece of state sanitary legislation in the country.

From the religious leaders of the country came added pressures for better health measures in the name of sanitary reform. Among the New England clergy literally a score of those best known preached a gospel of health and sanitation; and their words and work were given concrete expression in their efforts during the Civil War, particularly with the Sanitary Commission, a great philanthropic movement organized during the Civil War by Dr. Henry Bellows, minister of the All Soul's Church in New York City.[9] The Commission rendered innumerable services to men in the armed forces of the North, and to their dependents. It set better mental and physical health as its great aim, and to promote these it launched a campaign of education in personal health and spiritual guidance. Most of the influential positions in this organization were held by ministers or by prominent laymen or laywomen. Through its activities, by the end of the War a precedent had been set for wide-reaching efforts to better the nation's health, and the spirit in which these were carried forth was the spirit of social reform. From this concern with the public health in general the problem of the disposal of the dead and the menace of the overcrowded urban graveyard emerges as an area of specific focus for those with a social and reformistic bent.

b) The Specific Movement for the Cremation of the Dead: Although articles had appeared in American journals and newspapers on the subject of burial reform as early as 1737 when the *Boston Post* published a letter protesting the extravagance in dress and gift-giving at funerals (see Figure 2), and from time to time, as we have seen, legislative bodies in the American Colonies had acted to restrict funeral expenses, the first organization to seek a specific program of funeral reform precipitated out of a movement to introduce cremation of the dead into American funeral customs.

In New York in 1873 the subject was first discussed at occasional assemblages, but no organization was set up. There was interest, however, among physicians and sanitarians, and by 1876 nine articles had been written on the subject, seven of them from the pens of men of medicine and health.[10] In 1876 Dr. F. Julius LeMoyne, prominent Washington, Pennsylvania, physician, erected in his home town America's first crematory, constructed primarily for the incineration of his own body and those of his friends. In the same year the body of Baron de Palm, eccentric elderly German Theosophist, was the first cremated in a building dedicated solely to that purpose. In the next several years other cremations were performed for the remains of some rather well-known persons, including the wife of the well-known Cincinnati phonographer, Ben Pitman, brother of Sir Isaac Pitman, inventor of a shorthand system, and for the founder, Dr. LeMoyne, as well. Quite a variety of religious beliefs held by those cremated is noted, including Presbyterian, Free Thinker, Theosophist, Swedenborgian, and Lutheran.

Augustus Cobb, early historian of cremation, notes the blossoming of collective action for cremation in the early eighties:

Between 1881 and 1885 a number of cremation societies were organized in different cities in the United States, and many lectures were delivered, and pamphlets and articles published advocating the reform. Efforts made during the preceding years had met with very little success, and it was only during the years above that a general popular interest became manifest. The work by the different societies was almost entirely educational. The object of all of them was about the same. As expressed in the by-laws of the New York Cremation Society, it was "to disseminate sound and enlightened views with respect to the incineration of the dead; to advocate and promote, in every proper and legitimate way, the substitution of this method for burial; and to advance the public good for affording facilities for carrying cremation into operation." The steady, unobtrusive work of these societies was destined to produce good results, although as late as the spring of 1884, there was but one crematory in the entire country.[11]

The New York Cremation Society was established in 1881, and as a separate but complementary unit, the United States Cremation Company was organized to build and operate a crematory, although it was not until 1885, that the latter went into operation at Fresh Pond, Long Island. Meanwhile a second cremation retort had made its appearance in Lancaster, Pennsylvania, built by Dr. M. L. Davis, with the support of the cremation-minded citizens of that town.

As the number of crematories increased so did the number of cremations. Between 1876 and 1884 there were 41 cremations in America; in the next five years there were 731; the total number of cremations for the five years preceding 1894 was 2,898; in 1899 the five year total was 7,197 and with the addition of the year 1900 the grand total for the fifteen years was 13,281.[12] Although the rate of increase obviously was rapid, the percentage of cremations to total deaths did not reach one percent before the turn of the century. Yet by this point 24 crematories were operating in 15 different states, including California, where retorts had been established in both Los Angeles and San Francisco.

Meanwhile, the same number of cremation societies had sprung into existence, with notable organizations in New York City; Buffalo, N. Y.; Lancaster, Pa., where in 1886 the local founder of the society, Dr. M. L. Davis, edited and published the first cremation journal, *The Modern Crematist*; San Francisco, Calif.; Davenport, Iowa; Detroit, Mich.; Milwaukee, Wis.; Philadelphia, Pa.; Boston, Mass.; and New Orleans, La. Personnel making up these societies were of several distinct sorts. In many of the larger cities German ethnic groups established among themselves burial "assurance" societies, and some of these groups, whose cultural history included acceptance of "flame burial" as a legitimate mode of disposal of the dead, adopted the practice of cremation. In San Francisco the cremation society was originated by a group of German Freethinkers. In New England, Protestant clergymen, basically interested in burial reforms, organized several cremation societies. A third major supporting group was composed largely of members of the medical profession and sanitarians. It is interesting to note the increasing number of articles written on the subject during the last twenty-five years of the 19th century, the peak being reached in the five year period 1884-1889 when 61 pieces of literature appeared. More than half, 35, were written by men of the medical, public health and sanitation professions. By the 1904-1908 period the figure had dropped to four, and since then these groups have produced very few articles on cremation.

While leadership for a burial reform movement in the East was scattered, among New England leaders those most active were the Rev. John Storer Cobb; Rev. Paul R. Frothingham; and Charles W. Eliot, president of Harvard. In 1874 in New York the Rev. O. B. Frothingham was the first to preach on the subject of cremation. In his twenty-eight page sermon on "The Disposal of Our Dead," from the religious-rationalist approach, he strongly advocated cremation, protesting that "Its significance is in its simple humanity."[18] Two decades later, in 1894, Bishop Henry C. Potter organized the Burial Reform Association of New York. Yet the spark of leadership that eventually led, in 1913, to the formation of the Cremation Society of America was produced by Dr. Hugo Erichsen, indefatigable cremation enthusiast, who from 1876, when at the age of sixteen he read the accounts of the first American cremation, until his death in 1942 devoted much of his time and energies to its propagation as an instrument of social and sanitary reform. It was Erichsen's idea to form a national association which would embrace all who favored cremation. In 1886 he organized one of the first state cremation associations in the Midwest, at Detroit, Michigan. It was not until 1913, however, that his dream of the National Association was realized. At the initial meeting of the Cremation Association of America on August 27 and 28, 1913, in Detroit, the great majority in attendance were operators of the forty-odd crematories in the country under business management, or their representatives. Under such sponsorship the question of burial reform received scant consideration.

When Hugo Erichsen was elected the first president of the C.A.A. at the Detroit meeting his first remarks to the fledgling organization emphasized reform:

Every crematist must be a missionary for the cause, and embrace every suitable occasion to spread its gospel, the glad tidings of a more sanitary and more aesthetic method of disposing of our beloved dead.[14]

He was not speaking to his audience but to the memory of a social reform movement which was already in a process of rapid change. What was emerging to take its place was simply a trade organization made up of persons connected with cremation as a business enterprise. The progress of cremation in America will be touched upon in a later chapter, so it is sufficient at this point to note that, although cremation was an integral part of the "burial reform" movement in the latter part of the 19th century, by the time a national organization was formed, the "reform" elements were a definite minority.

NINETEENTH CENTURY ASSOCIATIONAL DEVELOPMENT AMONG FUNERAL DIRECTORS

As indicated in earlier chapters, the close of the 19th century witnessed major changes in the role and function of the undertaker. From an enterprising furnisher of goods, paraphernalia, and, occasionally, the rudiments of personal "services" along with his items of merchandise, he moved in the direction of becoming a seller of personal services. This new role involved him closely with the bereaved, whom he now conceived of as distraught human beings rather than as customers for his wares. In carrying out this new role he was called upon to exercise not only technical skills in preparing the bodies of the dead, but administrative skills in the direction and organization of funeral proceedings, and logistic skills in arranging the order and sequence in the transport of both the living and the dead. Beyond this enrichment of function, 19th century funeral directing had another major achievement to its credit. This was the development of strong occupational groups at local, state, and national levels. As we discuss these it is well for us to bear in mind that funeral directors, as well as members of other occupations that were becoming self-conscious and occupationally mobile at the time, had before them the two associational models—trade and profession—from which to choose.

Origins and Early Developments: Insofar as available records indicate, the first formal organization of undertakers occurred in Philadelphia, when in January, 1864, the Undertakers' Mutual Protective Association of Philadelphia was formed. This group adopted a constitution which among other provisions called for the establishment of a "Black Book, to keep a register of objectionable and delinquent customers, for use and inspection of members only . . ."[15] (See Plate 65.) Four years later Chicago undertakers organized and sustained a city association which functioned in a much broader capacity than the Philadelphia group. It is probable that in most of the major cities during the period 1865-1880 undertakers founded associations for the purposes of mutual protection, dispensing information and setting of preliminary standards for operation of their trade. In New York City at this time the church sextons tended to dominate the undertaking scene. Thus one of the earliest organizations of undertakers in that city was designed primarily to harmonize the relations between sexton-undertakers and those who made undertaking a more or less full time occupational pursuit.

While these early local organizations performed many useful services, association on a wider scale commended itself to many undertakers and to the editors of the trade journals as well. The role of the latter is stressed, possibly overstressed, by an early funeral director-historian, George L. Thomas of Milwaukee, who, in an address at the twenty-eighth annual convention of the National Funeral Directors Association stated:

The beginning of the association movement in the undertaking and embalming profession dates back to 1879; and the first faint inklings of a desire for united efforts on the part of those engaged in caring for the dead were apparent in the columns of trade journals, which constituted a definite medium through which the voices of all who were anxious for better things might be heard. The trade journal was undoubtedly the alma mater of the association movement, and due honor and credit must in every history be given to Albert H. Nirdlinger and Thomas Gliddon (editors of *The Casket*), who early recognized the value of associated effort in other lines, and who, always having the best interests of our profession at heart, fostered and encouraged the early growth of the association movement.[16]

In considering the various forces affecting the undertakers of the time and motivating the impulse to form associations discussed below it would be fairer to state that the progress of association was certainly accelerated by the actions Mr. Thomas credits to the trade journals, and that the point of their being used as a medium for the expression of opinion of practicing undertakers is well taken. But the associational impulse came from leaders among the funeral directors themselves.

An instance of such initiative developing within the occupational group itself is to be found in a letter in which Mr. William J. Camp of Covington, Kentucky, proposed a "Southern Undertakers' Union." In response to his proposal many favorable letters reached Mr. Camp. When he read an article on the "Etiquette of Undertakers" written for *The Casket* by Mr. Silvanus Hawley of Wyoming, New

York, Mr. Camp repeated his proposal, adding the hope that "at no distant day would there be organized a grand undertakers' union upon plans similar to those of the 'Knights of Honor' or 'The Ancient Order of United Workmen.' "[17]

Although the idea of a fraternal, benevolent, and insurance organization did not fit the undertaking trade, the proposal was not without some effect, because it led Messrs. Nirdlinger and Gliddon to editorialize: "The desire for a more satisfactory understanding between the profession in various towns and cities should promote an immediate convention, even though it should impress those of only a small territory. Who will lead in this movement and carry it to success?" At this moment leadership among undertakers themselves seemed to be in the hands of Mr. Hawley, who perspicaciously pointed to the need for the formation of legitimate associations, "such as are for the improvement and protection of the interests of any profession or trade." These he maintained, "are good and worthy . . . whilst the clan or league for selfish ends is reprehensible . . ."[18] Hawley then suggested that the representatives of the profession be communicated with, in the hope that a sufficiently favorable response would warrant holding a national convention in the middle of August, 1879. The next six months found the editorial pages of *The Casket* filled with comments on this scheme, including many letters written by undertakers from various states pointing out the obvious need for such a convention. Despite this strong support, the plan for a national organization at this time never reached the point of actuality, and it remained for the state groups to form first their own organizations before a coast to coast organization could be launched.

In November, 1879, Allen Durfee, well known Grand Rapids undertaker and compounder of embalming fluid, inserted a circular letter in *The Casket* asking Michigan undertakers for an expression of opinion on the possibility of holding a "State Convention of Undertakers at some central point, say Grand Rapids, Jackson, or Lansing, for the purpose of forming an Undertakers' State Association, which the rapid advancement in the science of undertaking seems to demand." Response was immediate and so favorable that an *ad hoc* committee, composed of Allen Durfee, E. A. Tompkins, C. A. Conklin, Charles L. Benjamin, T. H. Roberts, and the Messrs. Sammons and Quincy, all prominent Michigan undertakers, was successful in arranging the first state convention of undertakers at Jackson, Michigan, January 14, 1880.

In his opening address, Mr. Thomas Gliddon, editor of *The Casket*, who had been invited to help with organizational matters, recommended the appointment of several committees. One of these was to look to the formation of a permanent organization; another to draw up and submit resolutions; and a third to gather, edit, and publish the convention proceedings, disseminate information regarding professional duties, agree on rules to govern ethical advertising, indicate a policy to be applied to distributing price lists, and finally memorialize (*sic*) the legislature. Mr. Durfee, later elected first president, outlined the possibilities of the gathering and presented arguments for a permanent association. He hoped, moreover, that from the state association there might be born a national organization "as broad as the United States and as imperishable as our national union."[19] His words were prophetic, and the Michigan Association did serve as the prototype not only of other state organizations soon to follow, but in many respects for the national association, still two years from its birth.

In the preamble of the Michigan constitution, the models of both trade and professional organizations were accepted, as the undertakers pledged themselves to form "into an

association for the purpose of mutually disseminating the
most correct principles of business management, the best
methods of protecting our own interests in professional
practice, and the general good of all recognized legitimate
undertakers."[20]

The year 1881 was prolific in the formation of associations.
Iowa, under the leadership of Mr. Will Hohenschuh of
Iowa City, later to become an authority in the field of
funeral directing and mortuary education, organized early
in that year; Ohio led by Mr. John H. Sharer of Alliance
was next; then Indiana, with S. R. Lippincott of Richmond
playing an active role; and before the year was out undertakers had organized state associations in Georgia, Illinois,
Kentucky, and Pennsylvania. California followed suit the
next year, along with Wisconsin; while Nebraska, Missouri,
Tennessee, Kansas, and Minnesota were all organized in
1883.

By the middle of 1882, even while state organizations
were being rapidly formed, leaders of the several groups
were becoming increasingly conscious of the need for a
national organization. The matter emerged from discussion
into action when in January, 1882, at the insistence of
President Allen Durfee, the Michigan Association passed
a resolution stating:

. . . the time has come for the calling of a National Convention,
for the purpose of forming a National Association, and the op-
portune time would be the third week in June next, and the
place in the City of Rochester, in connection with the New York
State Funeral Directors' annual meeting, and the National Fair
of Funeral Goods, which is to be held there at the same time,
and that the association appoint three delegates, with three al-
ternates, whose necessary travelling expenses shall be borne by
this association.[21]

This call was circulated among the various states, and one hundred and five undertakers, many of them leaders in their state associations, signed. Mr. Thomas Gliddon volunteered as Secretary, Pro Tem.

The next issue of *The Casket* contained, in large headlines, the following announcement:

1882

THE DAWN OF PROGRESS
NATIONAL FUNEREAL INDUSTRIAL EXPOSITION
Commingling of Inventors, Manufacturers and Professionals

A NATIONAL MEETING
Special Session of all the Embalming Experts

TWELVE PRACTICAL LECTURES
And Operating Lessons in a Special Amphitheater,
Under the immediate charge of

AUGUSTE RENOUARD, at Rochester, N. Y.
Beginning Monday, June 20th and continuing six days
To close with a
Grand Complimentary Banquet at Niagara Falls,
ON SATURDAY, JUNE 24.
Instruction, Recreation, and a Great Reunion

On June 22, 1882, two hundred and forty-one persons appeared at the City Hall of Rochester, were welcomed by the mayor, and addressed briefly by Mr. Allen Durfee. Mr. Durfee reviewed the steps that led to the calling of the convention, remarking significantly, "The desire for a more rapid educational improvement, led me to believe that through meetings and associations much good might be accomplished, which could not be obtained in any other way." Mr. Robert Atkins, of Buffalo, N. Y., was elected temporary chairman and the business of organizing the association got under way.

Three significant events took place at this first national convention. One related to the composition of the body, and after rather heated discussion it was decided that at this, the first gathering, all undertakers present were to be entitled to votes in the convention, but that in future conventions three delegates only from each state were to have a voice. Opposition to this procedure came heaviest from the delegates of the Chicago Association—a strong city organization which had been continuously operating longer than any other association, state or city. This decision set a pattern for the National Association which in effect meant that it should function as a parent organization for state associations, and that henceforth organization at the state level would necessarily take precedence over organizations at the local level among undertakers in states not yet featured by such associations.

A second development that had significant consequences, not so much for direct action as for the development of a new self-conception by undertakers, was the decision to name the organization "The Funeral Directors' National Association of The United States" (later the NFDA). This decision was reached only after lively argument, with many present favoring the traditional term "undertaker," and a few the less familiar, less frequently used "funeral manager." One delegate, Thomas Blood, had been advertising his services as a "mortorion," but he did not suggest this term as an associational title. No one offered the term "mortician" —later to come into currency as an alternative to "undertaker" and "funeral director." The emphasis in the title of the national organization was on funeral directing; and henceforth the use of the designation, "funeral director," was, as defined by the association, a mark of progress.[22]

The third feature that marked the first convention was the close relationship manifested between the national convention and the manufacturers of morticians' goods. A precedent was set at this meeting when a complimentary banquet was given jointly by James Cunningham, Son & Co.; Chappel, Chase, Maxwell & Co.; Stein Mfg. Co.; Egyptian Embalming Co.; and the editors of *The Casket*. The meetings of the New York State Funeral Directors Association held simultaneously with the holding of the National Fair for Funeral Goods likewise tended to make the exposition of merchandise and paraphernalia integrally a part of the national meetings and thus underscore their associational aspects.

Pressures, Interests, and Motives: While in no sense detracting from the important role played by the trade journals in fostering associational activities among funeral directors, it should be noted that the social and economic pressures generating in and around the occupation were such that some form of collective action was almost inevitable. As indicated in the first section of the chapter, the late 19th century was a period marked by a proliferation and tremendous expansion of associations, both trade and professional or semi-professional. The associational impulse was strong and growing. Physicians and surgeons, pharmacists, civil engineers, architects, dentists, and veterinarians had all organized their national societies and associations before 1870, and other similar groups were in the process of formation at the time.

In closer relation to the subject at hand one notes that before 1880 there had been formed the Carriage Builders' National Association; the Coffin Manufacturers' Association of the East and West; the National Burial Case Association (later referred to by funeral directors as the "Manufacturers' Association"); as well as the National Association of General Baggage Agents—whose importance will be discussed later. In the decade following the list extends to include the Eastern Burial Case Association; the National Cloth Casket Association; the Metallic Burial Case Association; the New England Burial Case Association; the Casket Hardware Manufacturers' Association; the American Association of Cemetery Superintendents; and the Casket Salesmen's Protective Association.

A further impetus to group action, and therefore organization, developed out of the fact that other associations and agencies were looking to funeral directors for spokesmen or representatives with whom to transact necessary business on a state or national level. The problem of the transportation of the dead is typical. This problem reached a crisis during the Civil War, demanding general regulations when it became necessary to inspect trains at depots for improperly embalmed bodies, broken shipping cases, bodies bearing the germs of infectious diseases and the like. The powers of the National Board of Health being severely restricted, regulation of the transportation of the dead fell to states and smaller governmental agencies. The chaos of uncodified and non-articulatory rules and regulations dealing with this problem is well described by one exasperated funeral director:

By the laws of one city the certificate of death is pasted on the coffin or case, there to remain till its destination is reached; but before that, they are stopped just outside of another city with the order to detach it and bring it to their health office, and in return they will issue one. With this a State is traversed, and reaching a third city in the evening, they find though the entrance is easy, exit is denied until a third certificate is obtained, and as it is late there is nothing to do but remain all night, breaking all connections and involving perhaps from twelve to twenty-four hours' delay.[23]

It should be stressed that when railroad officials went to funeral directors—as was natural—for advice concerning the proper methods of handling and shipping dead bodies, they wanted—and their want created a need among funeral directors—a single, collectively-made answer, that would provide them with a uniform or standard practice. To supply such answer, it was necessary that the occupation itself should be organized to a point where agreement could be reached and declared. To repeat: until such single answer was made, and practice set up nationally in accord with it, funeral directors themselves experienced difficulty in shipping bodies.

While it could be easy to exaggerate the influence of these and similar needs upon the development of the associational impulse among funeral directors, the fact remains that to some extent occupational associations tend to create situations calling for other occupational associations, although much more compelling than these collective factors were two basic motivating forces impelling funeral directors into associational action. One was the need to protect themselves from excessive and therefore harmful competition from within their own ranks, and from destructive business practices by manufacturers and jobbers. The other was the urge to bring a sense of professionalism to what had formerly been for many a mere trade or sideline.

The need for protection from unfair, even though legal, competition within the occupation itself was quite evident. Protection was especially needed by funeral directors in Eastern and Mid-Western states where nearly any merchant who sold furniture could include a line of caskets in his wares, and thus threaten the very existence of recognized establishments.

In the year 1888, the first for which statistics are reliable, for every funeral director, that is, for almost every funeral establishment, there were about 4,700 inhabitants. In the above-mentioned Eastern and Mid-Western states, however, the proportion was smaller. Thus in New York the ratio was one funeral director for every 3,200 persons; in Vermont, 1—2,000; Pennsylvania, 1—3,000; Michigan, 1—3,800; and Illinois, 1—3,600.[24] Despite the fact that death rates were about twice as high as at present, infant mortality was greater, and, while the gross average of deaths per funeral director country-wide was about 87, significantly, for the states in which the first state associations were formed, the figure was lower. Michigan had about 77 deaths per funeral director; New York, about 70; and Pennsylvania, about 60. In these areas competition was keen from fellow undertakers, a majority of whom, or nearly eighty per cent of the total number of establishments, were engaged in combination operations in which sale of coffins and caskets was a sideline. Thus from within the occupation, the established funeral director with aspirations toward becoming an independent seller of personal services and funeral merchandise exclusively—apart from any ideas about professionality—frequently found the going rough. That irresponsible, marginal, or unsound competition may have kept within the law, as it then existed, could have been small consolation to a responsible operator facing it.

From without, the pressures, threats, and forces were enough to provide ample material for a speech delivered in 1884 before the Illinois Association and later read to the National Association, in which the burden of the argument was that the National Association must take immediate steps "in regard to the multitude of jobbers, drummers, quack professors, professional embalmers, or more properly speaking, embalming-fluid fiends, and the thousand and one other frauds that hang on to and suck the very life blood out of this profession."

The practice of "jobbing" lots of caskets to the funeral director, ostensibly to permit him to buy more economically in light of larger purchases, was an outgrowth of conditions in the casket manufacturing industry itself. In 1888 although there were about 700 coffin shops and casket manufacturing houses, less than 175 of these were companies of any considerable size, and perhaps some two dozen were what might be called large scale producing units. While less than half of those in existence could easily have supplied the funeral directors of the land with a sufficient number of good burial receptacles, yet with the field so crowded it was almost inevitable that competition would produce less than the best product. Often cheap, shoddy, competitively priced coffins and caskets were literally dumped upon the funeral director. Curiously enough, because of the necessity of maintaining standards, the larger companies, despite their ability to mass produce, could not undersell and drive out the smaller, uneconomically organized coffin shops. The latter, through the "jobbing" system of sending out high pressure "drummers," could either cut prices to obtain an account, or would try to induce anyone with the desire to become an undertaker to lay in a stock of coffins "on consignment." Thus one of the most important *trade* problems of the funeral director of the late 19th century was protection from the kind of competition that would eventually ruin whatever community goodwill and social acceptance he already had earned.

At mid-20th century, about one-fifth of all funeral establishments are combination operations, and these, it should be noted, are more likely to be found in the rural and small town areas of the country. In 1888, however, even in the more densely populated areas the ratio of single purpose to combination establishments was scarcely better than one to five; Pennsylvania had about 23 per cent of its funeral directors operating independently of any other business; Georgia, 21 per cent; Vermont, 24 per cent; and Illinois, about 25 per cent. Of all the funeral directors in the country in 1888 about 23 per cent held membership in the National Funeral Directors Association. Many in combination businesses did not belong to funeral director groups because to them the funeral portion of their work was only a sideline. While many of these part time operators were men of excellent business and personal character and represented a transitional stage in the emergence of a trade into a profession, the degree of commercialization at which a few combination undertakers occasionally operated is illustrated by the advertisement reprinted from a country newspaper "in one of the Middle States" by *The Casket* in 1879.

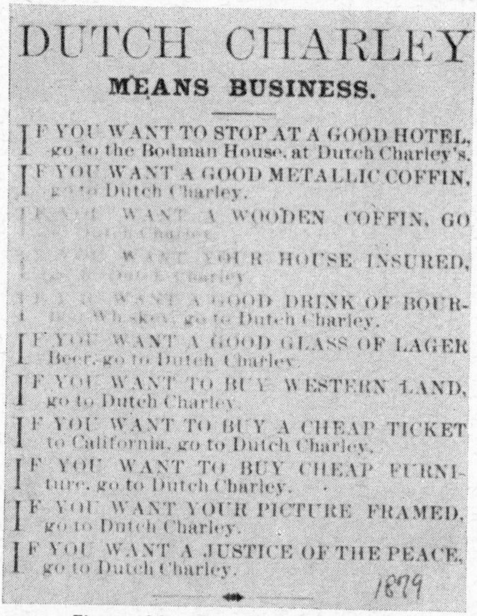

DUTCH CHARLEY

MEANS BUSINESS.

IF YOU WANT TO STOP AT A GOOD HOTEL, go to the Bodman House, at Dutch Charley's.

IF YOU WANT A GOOD METALLIC COFFIN, go to Dutch Charley.

IF YOU WANT A WOODEN COFFIN, GO to Charley.

IF YOU WANT YOUR HOUSE INSURED, go to Charley.

IF YOU WANT A GOOD DRINK OF BOUR-bon Whiskey, go to Dutch Charley.

IF YOU WANT A GOOD GLASS OF LAGER Beer, go to Dutch Charley.

IF YOU WANT TO BUY WESTERN LAND, go to Dutch Charley.

IF YOU WANT TO BUY A CHEAP TICKET to California, go to Dutch Charley.

IF YOU WANT TO BUY CHEAP FURNI-ture, go to Dutch Charley.

IF YOU WANT YOUR PICTURE FRAMED, go to Dutch Charley.

IF YOU WANT A JUSTICE OF THE PEACE, go to Dutch Charley.

1879

Figure 33. The Many Businesses
of Dutch Charley

Another major factor motivating funeral directors to organize into an association was the desire on the part of certain outstanding and farsighted members of the group to professionalize their occupation, thus gaining for it and for themselves as well, a higher degree of social estimation. In a period when sanitary reform and the general social movement embracing public health had gained widespread attention, and with this interest reinforced by terrible epidemics and plagues, many funeral directors found it natural to associate their functions with those of the sanitarian. This concept seems to have been present at the very inception of the National Association, at least among the acknowledged leaders of the group, and in more or less degree has been incorporated into the self-conceptions of funeral directors ever since.

Again, in arrogating to themselves the function of embalming, funeral directors were inevitably drawn into the company of the surgeon, the physician, and the physiologist. At first physicians were solely the ones to perform embalming. Later, as these two groups were drawn into closer association while embalming skills and techniques were being learned by funeral directors, the men of medical and biological science became the instructors, if not the founders of schools of embalming. Thus the association between the two continued. Even today, due to the demands of modern schools of mortuary science for cadavers, there continues to be a tendency for them to be located near medical centers; and in many cases, physiologists, pathologists and other categories of medical scientists are brought into the schools as instructors.

It seems a fair statement, then, that the association of funeral directors with members of the medical profession, sanitarians, and public health officials tended to contribute toward the development of the self image of the progressive funeral director of the late 19th century as a sanitarian. His role as "sanitary embalmer," in a period when epidemics and plagues had the whole society fearful, conceivably enhanced the public estimation of his work, and consequently his own. This image, it should be remarked, like the image in other professional groups, was not equally appropriated to themselves by all funeral directors. As with other occupations, all funeral directors did not share an equal sense of the high social importance of the round of tasks, nor were they equally prepared to make the personal sacrifices needed, to translate the high ideal into a daily way of working.

The terms "professional" and "profession" were seized upon at the first National Association meeting and were used repeatedly. As will be pointed out below, the leadership of the Association during the period was highly dedicated to the proposition that a program of action was essential to bring professional status to funeral directors and that words alone would not suffice. Nowhere is this better shown, perhaps, than in the 1886 presidential address of Hudson Samson, one of the most influential, and incidentally, best-educated, of the leaders of the Association. In blueprinting future policy he noted the failures of the past and then reiterated some suggestions which were to bear fruit in the succeeding decades:

We have to decide whether we will follow in the wake of the broom makers', box and basket-makers', bakers', . . . and butchers' associations. (They) . . . are intended to benefit men who work at manual labor; they resort to the boycott and the strike to carry their cause through, right or wrong. I will mention a few who take a different view of the realities of citizenship: the members of National, State, County, and City Medical Societies . . . the legal profession . . . clergymen . . . educators and Civil and Mining Engineers (have societies which) . . . assist one another across the hard places.

I would advise (funeral directors) . . . to convince our state Board of Health of the necessity of having a law passed that will compel all who have not been a certain number of years serving as Funeral Directors to pass an examination, and to serve a given time as an apprentice. I would have a Board of Examination appointed by the Governor whose duty it shall be to determine the fitness of applicants for license to serve as

Funeral Director: the Board should make such arrangements with the County Boards of Health as will best serve the purpose of keeping a complete register of all Funeral Directors. . . .

I would have a law regulating the care and burial of the dead the same as there is for the practice of medicine—the same as you will find in the several States to insure the better education of practitioners in dental surgery . . . I would advise an active step be taken in some State to have an act passed regulating the burial of the dead and we, as a National Association, to help, aid and assist in bringing about such legislation.

Do not think that we can get the public to RECEIVE US AS PROFESSIONAL MEN by simply meeting in convention and making constitutions and by-laws, by adopting a code of ethics, or getting our State Legislature to pass an act governing the burial of the dead, or by getting the National Burial Case Association to do what will be of as much advantage to themselves as to us, guarding against funeral reform, building crematories, or having a report on our trade journals, or providing a text-book that will assist you in beating the Egyptians.

All of these are means toward the desired end. One thing that will do more to bring about a professional feeling among the Funeral Directors is for us to act and talk as though our competitors were gentlemen; if we gain professional fame it will be by us as individuals leading pure, upright, professional lives.[25]

Characteristics of Early Leadership: Among the funeral directors of the latter part of the 19th century leadership was in the hands of fairly well-to-do and fairly well-educated middle-class persons who leaned in the direction of creating a profession out of their trade. A check of the social characteristics of forty-two better-known morticians of the day, whose biographies appeared in *The Casket* from 1876-1880 and who played an active leadership role in associations, reveals several interesting facts: most of these men were born in America and a preponderant number resided and operated their establishments in the Middle Atlantic and New England states. Investigation of the occupational backgrounds of the fathers of these men indicates that with few exceptions they were *not* sons of practicing undertakers. Of the 42, 14 had fathers who were farmers, 6 professional men, 4 manufacturers and executives, and the rest, with the exception of 4 undertakers (all operating combination shops), were engaged in small businesses, skilled and unskilled trades, or clerical and sales work.[26] By no stretch of the imagination could funeral direction be conceived of as a "family" occupation during this period, as it justifiably could in the first quarter of the present century. In many cases, then, funeral directors were farm born, self-made men.

With respect to the occupational background of the forty-two directors themselves, the pattern indicates that the greater number of them entered the trade through some traditionally related occupation, such as cabinet or furniture making, or, through the carriage or livery business. In other words, funeral directors of the period *worked* their way into the trade and did not merely succeed their fathers. Consequently they were less likely to be rigorously bound by occupational traditions than their sons who succeeded them. Moreover, there were at the time few legal and quasi-legal restrictions to regulate the manner in which they might operate. It is not surprising then that during the period under discussion a high degree of independence and individualism became characteristic of the occupation and its practitioners. Some of this mood developed in the period under discussion has persisted into modern times.

Code of Ethics: The drive toward a professional status made by State, Local, and National Associations during the late 19th century took the form of a series of efforts, some of which, such as getting railway agencies and baggage agents to recognize their embalming techniques as standard, professional operations, and the constant, eventually successful

pressure applied to state legislatures to secure licensing legislation, have already been discussed.

Other efforts to achieve professional recognition—some
alluded to above—were based on the recognition of the
need to develop a sense of inner-cohesion or colleagueship
among funeral directors; to establish a sense of responsibility; to provide formal instruction in the special skills and
techniques of the occupation along with increased backgrounds in general éducation; to develop lines and media
of disseminating information to funeral directors themselves,
their business associates, and the general public, and to indoc-
trinate all these groups with the new concepts. Simply talking
about professionality, however, as Hudson Samson wisely
pointed out before the infant National Association, would
lead nowhere.

A major early step toward developing honor and colleagueship among funeral directors was taken in the establishment
of a Code of Ethics, at the third meeting of the National
Association, at Chicago, October 2, 1884. About six hundred
words in length, this Code was patterned after other professional codes of the times, alternating between statements
of a general type indicating the character and occupational
morality aimed at and injunctions against specific kinds of
actions. Beginning, "A funeral director, on entering the
profession . . . " it went on to posit the necessity of obeying
the law, and of maintaining a high standard of conduct and
propriety at all times. This was imperative, since, it said:

> The nature of our calling takes us to the inner circle of the
> families that are afflicted. Secrecy and delicacy, when required
> by peculiar circumstances, should be strictly observed. The
> obligation of secrecy extends beyond the period of our profes-
> sional services. None of the privacies of personal and domestic
> life should ever be divulged.[27]

Advertising was dealt with in a negative vein, and, among other things, advertising in the "daily prints" was prohibited. Proper procedure and protocol in the case of two directors being called at the same time was indicated, along with the injunction to the profession to carry on in times of epidemic and contagious diseases. Also outlined were the correct methods for dealing with shipping and removal cases. The first Code of Ethics closed with the statement:

There is, perhaps, no profession, after that of the sacred ministry, in which a high-toned morality is more imperatively necessary than that of a funeral director's. High moral principles are his only safe guide.[28]

The Code appeared in the appendix of all subsequent printed proceedings and was broadcast among the various trade papers and journals. The most controversial section, as it turned out, was that dealing with advertising. Undertakers had traditionally printed and distributed private cards, handbills, and in the daily papers had invited the attention of the public to their wares. (See Plates 25, 26.) Although the Code was reaffirmed "as law" at the Toronto meeting in 1889, it was evident that the tradition of advertising had not been erased, and that, instead some concessions to the practice eventually might have to be made, since in cities many if not most funeral directors were continuing to advertise. A related problem, foreseeable in the not too distant future, and more difficult to make rules for and to dispose of was the mass operation type of funeral home, whose business was based on a large volume of cases attracted by cut-throat advertising and other highly questionable promotion methods. But these were developments that were to come to a focus shortly before World War I. As the century closed the Code of Ethics remained in precisely the same form as when created and adopted by the National Association in 1884.

Communication Within the Trade: In a rapidly growing country such as America during the 19th century the expansion and proliferation of industries and businesses posed many problems of organization, not the least of which was the building up of an effective system of liaison and communication among and within related vocations, businesses, and between these and the general public. For funeral directors this problem was complicated by their dispersion, highly fluctuating number, and diversification—nearly four-fifths were operating their establishments in combination with other businesses, or practiced undertaking as a side-line to other services offered the public.

One of the first agents of communication to the funeral directors was the casket salesman, or "drummer." Casket salesmen and jobbers covered extensive territories, competed briskly, and were not without some self-consciousness as to the out-of-the-ordinary nature of the products they were distributing. The itinerant nature of the occupation was put to verse by "Timber Awl" whose "The Song of the Coffin Drummer" appeared in one of the trade papers, the first stanza of which sets the theme of itineracy:

> From Illinois, Iowa
> Nebraska and Dakota,
> To Michigan, Wisconsin too,
> And lovely Minnesota.
> From Lake Superior's Copper mines
> Through Hoosier Indiana,
> To Mississippi's cotton field,
> And Low Louisiana,
> I furnish wooden overcoats
> To many an Undertaker;
> For Banker, beggar, one and all,
> The Butcher and the baker—
>   Baker—
> Butcher and the baker.[29]

These commercial knights of the road could be expected to bring with them news of the trade and interesting information concerning other funeral directors. Their importance in this respect declined somewhat with the appearance of trade papers and journals dedicated to different, often many, sectors of the field of funeral service.

In 1871 Henry E. Taylor, funeral goods manufacturer of New York, published the first trade paper, "A Monthly Paper Dedicated to the Interests of the Undertaker and to the Discussion of Grave (sic) Matters" which he chose to call *The Undertaker*. Possibly the subtitle contained only an inadvertent play on words, yet this trade paper as well as those which came after it—reflective apparently of the desire to dispel the dismal and gloomy public image traditionally held of undertakers and the trade—followed a definite policy of spicing up the copy with jokes, puns and anecdotes, some connected with the subject at hand, others drawn from various sources. *The Undertaker* continued under the original title only until the following year, when it was changed to *Sunnyside*. Taylor continued to publish it until 1885 at which time it passed into the hands of independent publishers, although he continued to show his interest in the enterprise by bringing news and information to the trade through its columns. In 1876 the most pretentious morticians' trade paper of the 19th century, *The Casket*, began publication at Rochester, N. Y. Some fifty years later its publisher was to buy *Sunnyside;* henceforth the journal appeared as *Casket and Sunnyside*.

Subsidized heavily by the Stein Patent Burial Casket Works, and James Cunningham, Son & Co., hearse and carriage builders and sub-titled "A Monthly Journal devoted to and officially treating on all subjects of vital importance to UNDERTAKERS AND KINDRED PROFESSIONS," *The Casket* was sent *gratis* to funeral directors everywhere for the first year.

After that the subscription was one dollar per year. In the "Salutatory" the editors protested the need for such a journal, noting, with some historical inaccuracy concerning the sexton as the sole progenitor of the undertaker:

Over six thousand men are rated at this date in this country "Undertakers." From the menial obscure church-yard sexton, there has within a quarter of a century been developed a recognized professional—represented by men of means, intelligence, taste and refinement; reading and thinking men, who have elevated their profession; therefore, why should they not be represented by a Journal and control an organ devoted solely to their interests; an official authority, in which they can interchange their professional views?[30]

And indeed such views were expressed in its pages. One of its most significant services to the field was the publication of a long series of articles by the celebrated embalmer, Auguste Renouard, on all aspects of the embalmer's work, the proper conduct of the funeral, and the necessary demeanor for those aspiring to be truly professional. One of the less "professional" services of the journal over a period of years was the effort to establish clearly by editorial comment the fact that cloth-covered burial cases and caskets need not be cheap, shoddy imitations of wood or metal, and that the Stein Co. could be relied upon to produce an artistically conceived, aesthetically pleasing cloth casket suitable even for the President of the United States. (In point of fact, several Stein caskets were later so used.)

Following *The Casket* in 1879 came *The Western Undertaker* (to become *The American Funeral Director*), and in 1880 *The Shroud*, a journal edited and published independently by Richard McGowan, a colorful figure among casket salesmen, which continued long enough to be accredited in 1884, along with *The Casket*, as one of the official journals of the American Funeral Directors' National Association. Shortly thereafter it expired. Others were not long in taking its place, and the decade 1885-1895 was prolific with trade papers and journals, which appeared, ran for a few issues and then passed out of existence. By 1894 not only had *The Shroud* ceased publication, but *The Embalmer; Our Paper; Shadyside; Progression*—a competitor to *The Casket*— *The Canadian Casket;* and *The National Undertaker* had all become casualties to the rough road of early trade journalism. (See Plates 66-69.)

The Embalmers' Monthly was a notable exception. Launched auspiciously at Sioux City, Iowa, in April, 1892, it appealed directly to the embalming side of funeral service, and stayed strong through the years following. It is still in print (1955) under the same title. Captain A. J. Millard, the first publisher, and W. W. Harris, editor, banked on an increasingly bright future for what they saw to be an important profession in the making, and as their contribution to this development brought before the field the names and knowledge of early American leaders in embalming: Hohenschuh, Barnes, Carpenter, Worsham, Dhonau, and others. In 1903 the *American Undertaker* was merged with the *Embalmers' Monthly*, and as a consequence the range of subject matter covered by the journal was increased.

These journals, whether they were designated "official" or not by The National Funeral Directors Association (Hereinafter NFDA), played an important, if not clearly assessable role, as media of communication in the field of funeral service, and as an instrumentality for placing before the public at large the claims of professionality that funeral directors felt justifiably should be made. (A list of present journals is in the Appendix.)

Growth, Problems and Change: In the last two decades of the 19th century, associational activities on the part of funeral directors covered a broad range of interests and problems some of which had been pressing since the Civil War, while others were growing out of the changing times.

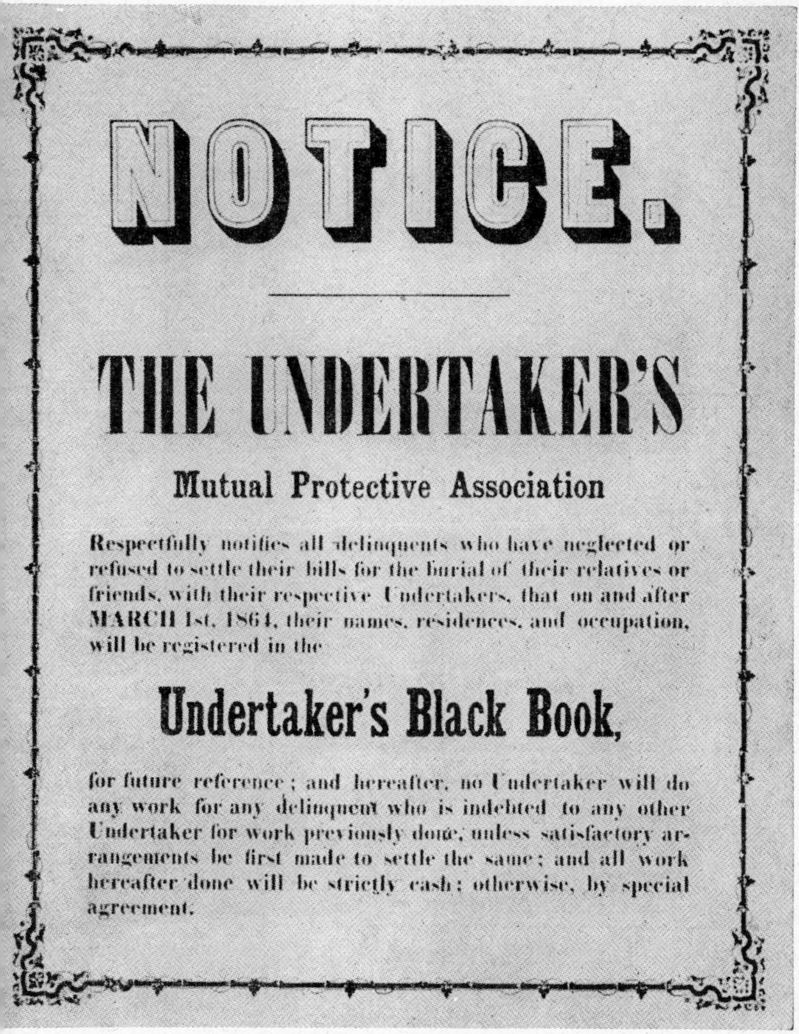

NOTICE.

THE UNDERTAKER'S

Mutual Protective Association

Respectfully notifies all delinquents who have neglected or refused to settle their bills for the burial of their relatives or friends, with their respective Undertakers, that on and after MARCH 1st, 1864, their names, residences, and occupation, will be registered in the

Undertaker's Black Book,

for future reference; and hereafter, no Undertaker will do any work for any delinquent who is indebted to any other Undertaker for work previously done, unless satisfactory arrangements be first made to settle the same; and all work hereafter done will be strictly cash; otherwise, by special agreement.

"Black Book" Notice of Early Philadelphia Undertakers Association

PLATE 65

THE CASKET

A JOURNAL DEVOTED TO THE INTEREST OF UNDERTAKERS.

VOL. I.　　　　　ROCHESTER, N. Y., MAY 1, 1876.　　　　　NO. 1.

The Casket.

A Monthly Journal, devoted to and officially treating on all subjects of vital importance to Undertakers and kindred professions.

SUBSCRIPTION (including postage), $1 PER YEAR, payable in advance.

ALBERT H. NIRDLINGER & CO., Editors and Publishers.

OFFICE OF PUBLICATION—Cor. Court and Exchange Sts. ROCHESTER, N. Y.

Rates of Advertising made known on application. Address all communications to

THE CASKET, Cor. Court and Exchange Sts. ROCHESTER, N. Y.

Salutatory.

Biography of the Self-made Men of the Day connected with this Trade and Profession.

SAMUEL STEIN, INVENTOR.

UNDERTAKING.

Front Cover of First Issue of *The Casket*

Plate 66

Although the activities dealt with below to some degree impinge upon one another and even intermingle, they will in part be discussed separately. Among these interests and problems are the relationships of funeral directors' associations with individual manufacturers and with manufacturers' associations, with the general baggage agents of the nation's railways and health agencies in the matter of the transportation of the dead, and with public health agencies generally. Other matters of moment at the time were mortuary education and training, communication within the occupation itself, and professionality.

Some indication of the state of business affairs involving funeral directors and casket manufacturers was given above. The rapid growth in number of casket manufacturers, the lack of organization and standardization of their business practices, and the free-wheeling sales activities of the casket jobbers and drummers, left the average funeral director of the 1870's and '80's with little assurance that he was being dealt with fairly and would receive satisfactory funeral merchandise. "The time is at hand," one irate undertaker wrote to the editor of *The Casket* in 1879, "when the undertakers must form a union to protect themselves and their trade on account of the many different frauds that are practiced by some of the wholesale coffin and casket as well as undertakers' hardware and trimming manufacturers." In his presidential address of 1883 the first president of the National Association, Charles S. Benjamin of Saginaw, Michigan, spoke directly to the funeral goods manufacturers, calling for their cooperation, deploring the resolution passed in the Association's first meeting asking for an exposition subsidized by them, and lecturing them to let the "Strife between them not be who shall sell the cheapest goods, but who shall sell the best finished and most desirable at the price."

In keeping with the conviction, expressed or implicit, that their Association could address itself equally well to trade and professional problems, the membership called for rather stringently defined, restrictive trade practices. In terms of these, State or Local Associations would be party to an agreement with the Manufacturers' Association whereby members of the funeral directors' associations would trade only with recognized and accredited members of the Manufacturers' Association, and the latter would guarantee that its manufacturer members would sell their funeral goods only to funeral director members in good standing with their respective associations. This proposed relationship was generated at the local, or grass-roots level, and found formal expression in the report of the first Committee on Resolutions in the second (1883) meeting of the National Association:

Resolved, That we request every manufacturer or jobber of funeral goods or supplies not to sell, six months after this date, any individual or firm wishing to establish a new business without a certificate of consent from the Executive Committee of the State or Local Association under whose jurisdiction they may be, or a committee appointed for the purpose of examining the field they propose to occupy, the probabilities for their success, the reputation for honesty and integrity, and the financial and professional ability of the new firm.

Resolved, That we request all manufacturers and jobbers after this date not to sell or to supply goods to any person or persons, who shall be reported to the Secretary of the Manufacturers' Association by the proper authority of a local, district, or state association, for having violated the Constitution or By-Laws of the Association under whose jurisdiction they may be.

Resolved, That we respectfully request the manufacturers not to supply any jobber who shall be complained of by the Secretary of the National Association as supplying any person or firm who may have been condemned by the Grievance Committee for violating the Constitution and By-Laws of any State Association.

APRIL, 1892

THE

EMBALMERS'

MONTHLY.

A MAGAZINE

DEVOTED TO THE

SCIENCE OF EMBALMING

AND THE INTERESTS OF

EMBALMERS

— AND —

FUNERAL DIRECTORS.

Front Cover of First Issue of *Embalmers' Monthly*, April, 1892

PLATE 67

Portions of Front Covers of Early Undertaking Trade Journals

PLATE 68

Entered April 17, 1903, at South Bend, Ind., as Second-class Matter, Under Act of Congress, March 3, 1879.

Vol. XXVIII. SEPTEMBER, 1905. No. 9

Additional Front Cover Titles. Note Changed Format on *Sunnyside*

PLATE 69

Resolved, That we, as funeral directors, condemn the manufacture of covered caskets at a less price than fifteen dollars for an adult size; and that we would be pleased to see the manufacturers of covered work form an association similar to that of the National Burial Case Association, and pledge ourselves to support them in a movement of this kind.

Respectfully submitted,

Chas. T. Whitsett, Indiana

A. C. Burpee, Illinois

L. A. Jeffreys, New York[31]

On the same day a Committee on Manufacturers was appointed, which drafted a resolution calling for the creation of a standing committee to meet with a Committee of the National Burial Case Association "for the purpose of considering any and all questions that may arise between manufacturers and dealers." This resolution was adopted, and a Committee on Manufacturers, at times slightly altered in title, continued to function throughout the remainder of the decade.

At the third annual meeting, in 1884, the subject was brought up again by the Secretary, Samuel Lippincott, who related the problem of non-compliance on the part of manufacturers, along with the burden of correspondence occasioned by members of state associations writing him to protest the sale of funeral goods by members of the National Burial Case Manufacturers' Association to non-members of funeral directors' associations. President Robert R. Bringhust later submitted the report of the Committee on Secretary's Report in which the matter of restrictive agreements was proposed to be standardized for all funeral directors. The instrumentality would be a formal contract, or compact, signed by funeral director and funeral goods manufacturer alike. It read as follows:

This is to certify that I, _____, of the firm of_____
_____, of the City of_____, do hereby covenant and agree,

for said firm, that we will not sell, loan, advance or consign our goods to any undertaker or funeral director not a member of a local organization under state jurisdiction, when such local organization exists, pledging ourselves to the bearer thereof, to forfeit to him the sum of ten (10) dollars, if, by legal proof—proof sufficient to convict in law—we fail to carry out such compact; provided, that the holder thereof, _____, of the city, _____, State of _____, doing business as a funeral director therein, party of the second part, does in return, guarantee that he will not buy, receive on consignment or otherwise, for sale, any goods, directly or indirectly, from any firm or jobber of coffins and caskets known in the trade as wooden goods, or dealer therein, who is not a member or authorized jobber of the National Burial Case Association, does not further pledge himself yearly to submit his account and books to a member of the National Burial Case Association, for examination, and does further agree to freely testify, under oath, on demand, as to his business affairs, so far as this compact is concerned.[32]

When brought up for vote this section of the report was tabled. There were two important reasons for this action: The first was that many funeral directors felt that the "combination" of manufacturers into what was popularly becoming known as the "coffin trust" had served only to increase prices without noticeably standardizing quality at a reasonable level; the second was that many "old line" undertakers were still in business. Some of these maintained their own cabinet and woodworking shops, while others were coffin-shop proprietors. The objection of this group to such contracts is self-evident.

Nevertheless, contracts between various burial case manufacturers' associations—there were four by 1888—were entered into by members of state and local funeral directors' associations. It should be pointed out that these agreements were *never* entered into at the national associational level. The results were so highly mixed that the relations of associations of funeral directors with manufacturers' associations, were seldom satisfactory to either of the contracting parties. Such agreements were nullified in 1890 when Congress passed the Sherman Anti-Trust Law, "An Act to Protect Trade and Commerce against Unlawful Restraints and Monopolies." While the contracts lasted, each side apparently was lax in enforcing its part. As a result, some members of the various funeral directors' associations bought indiscriminately from organized and unorganized case manufacturers alike, while certain members of the Manufacturers' Association sold indiscriminately to funeral directors, without regard as to whether they were members of one of their associations.

In Canada, however, similar agreements made between the Province Associations and the Dominion Burial Case Association operated with singular effectiveness, although complaint was made to the National Association that American casket manufacturers were shipping their merchandise into Canada, and, by so doing, were breaking down the structure of restrictive trade practices.[33] In 1889 these agreements were mutually abrogated in consequence of legislation passed in Canada prohibiting written agreements between manufacturers and associations, in restraint of trade. Meanwhile, in 1888, the Canadian Provincial Association was brought into the National Association, with the result that the name of the latter was changed to the "International Funeral Directors Association." After several years, cooperation between the two groups began to grow less close, until, in 1893, the affiliation was discontinued and the American group adopted the title it still bears, "The National Funeral Directors Association of the United States." As the experiments in trade restriction and international organization failed or proved less than entirely successful, other problems, many of them present in the background for decades, assumed new importance and claimed the attention of the funeral directors' association.

One of these was the matter of transporting the dead. As pointed out above, in default of any set of comprehensive federal regulations or of a codification of rules and restrictions laid down by the several states, municipalities and other governmental agencies, funeral directors were faced with exasperating and time-consuming red-tape and delays in their efforts to secure needed transport for the dead. To further complicate this problem there were no general rules governing the practices of railway baggagemen in this matter. Under these conditions it became apparent to funeral directors that collective action was necessary to provide solutions for these and related problems to be worked out cooperatively not only with governmental agencies but with other organizations concerned. The relationships with the railway baggagemen's union was as wide as the group's jurisdiction among the railroads.

Because the problems were national in scope, the answers could not be local, state, or even regional, but must be national; and to provide national answers, an effective national association was a *sine qua non*. The need for concerted action on the problem of railway transportation of bodies was first brought to the attention of the National Association in 1888 when a special committee of the National Association of General Baggage Agents listed seven suggested rules with the recommendation that they be laid before the several State Boards of Health, the National Conference of State Boards of Health, and the National Association of "Undertakers," with a view toward "establishing some simple, effective rules which could be the guide for all Railroads and other Transportation Companies in the United States and Canada." The response of the National Association was to send a committee to meet with the baggagemen at their next regular meeting, and the eventual result of the subsequent conference was a list of rules adopted by the baggage agents' association and sent to the various boards of health with the recommendation that they become universally adopted and put into effect.

In the majority of cases the health boards were highly receptive to these recommendations, and incorporated them into their own growing body of health and sanitation rules and regulations. Impetus was given to this reception by the decision of the Conference of Officers of the State Boards of Health at Nashville, Tennessee, in 1897, to accept virtually unchanged the suggested rules as they had been worked out by the railway baggage agents and the funeral directors. The committee deliberations of the latter two groups lasted almost a decade and turned out to be well worth the time inasmuch as the resulting joint decisions could be clearly, authoritatively, and decisively stated at the Conference of State Health Officers, somewhat to the surprise of the "distinguished physicians present" who "conceded to the funeral directors who were present superior knowledge of the subject in hand."[34]

The rules, in brief, prohibited transportation of bodies dead of certain deadly and contagious diseases; permitted the transportation of others dead of less virulent diseases only when thorough embalming and disinfecting had been completed; specified conditions under which bodies dead of non-contagious diseases might be transported; dealt with the problem of persons accompanying the dead body; and listed the steps in securing transit permits, applying pasters, and the like. These rules, finally, were approved by the National Board of Health.

The importance of this development becomes clear only in light of its effects. Funeral directors could henceforth look forward to increased standardization of public health

rules regarding transportation of the dead. For the first time
they were able to convince somewhat skeptical baggage
agents—who after all over-saw the handling of these dead in
transport—and the even more skeptical physicians and public health officers, that embalming could render a corpse
germ-free and innocuous to the living. Finally, they gained
professional recognition for their work in embalming; that
is, the affidavit of a funeral director that he had embalmed
a body was accepted at face value henceforth by baggage
agents and public health functionaries alike. Little wonder
that the NFDA's meeting in 1897 was carried out in an
atmosphere of jubilant excitement, and that in addition to
the formal report they received, the delegates insisted on
informal recitations by all the committee members of the
inside story of the "victory at Nashville."

All problems of transportation were not solved in this one
success, however, and with the development of checking
systems and the increase of transfer companies, new issues
were brought before the Association with the result that the
major point of discussion of the National Convention of
1907 centered around new transportation problems as
brought up in an address by Mr. A. Traynor, General Baggage
Agent, Union Pacific Railway Co., on the subject of "The
Silent Passenger."

Problems relating to health and sanitation, however, were
not exhausted by the work accomplished by the funeral
directors on rules and regulations for transportation of the
dead. For the past quarter of the 19th century the
most important concern in this area, and one that had
involved both trade and professional aspects, centered on
the setting up of licensing apparatus to regulate and control
the practice of embalming, along with an extension of effort
to bring about other health-related legislation in the mutual
interests of both the public and of funeral directors. As early

as 1884 a Committee on Resolutions in the National Association stressed the need for uniformity in death certificates in order that "a great many important facts might be obtained, and tables of vital statistics prepared that would be of use to our National Board of Health."[35] In the same year the evils of the quack professors of embalming were brought to the attention of the National Association by the Association of Undertakers of the State of Illinois, who asked that it "recommend that the several State Associations in their respective States, charter such schools as would be above reproach; recommend a course of instruction, to embrace anatomy, chemistry and a thorough course on disinfectants, and to last at least three months." In light of the fact that the so-called "schools" often were conducted for periods of three days to a week, this proposal sounded only slightly less than revolutionary. Another delegate, a Mr. Russ of Chicago, hoped for a form of State or Federal control of the occupation in such manner that any man who put up his name as an undertaker would be "compelled by the State, and indorsed by the United States, that he should be a man of good integrity, sober, industrious, and truthful in every respect." Oscar N. Crane, second president of the National Association, stressed the same point in his presidential address, in 1885, when he remarked:

It seems to me that the time is not far distant, if not already dawning on us, that there should be a legal standard; some qualifications; some governing laws; some moral fitness; necessary, which should be required and regulated by Statute both of State and Nation; a standard of ability, and morals which on strict examination, the applicant should be, must be, found to possess.

And then, and not till then, will he be permitted to engage in a calling so solemn and at the same time, so full of professional responsibility.[36]

Later in the same meeting a resolution was passed encouraging members and trade journals to urge legislatures to create State Boards of Health in order to further better sanitary measures and to facilitate and expedite the transportation of bodies in and through their respective states.

It was also pointed out by Hudson Samson in his presidential address of 1886 that two universities—Michigan at Ann Arbor and Pennsylvania at Philadelphia—and a medical college in Chicago—had already "manifested a willingness to provide a course of study that would be desired by a student preparing for the Funeral Directorship."[37] In this speech, printed in part earlier in this chapter, he also stressed the need for legislation setting up training and education requirements for a license to enter into the profession of funeral directing and regulatory requirements for remaining a funeral director.[38]

Samson also urged all members to join the American Public Health Association, which had among its various committees one on the burial of the dead, to participate in its activities, and to write and present papers on sanitation and the funeral director at its annual meetings.

Following his own advice within the year and with the aid of several of his outstanding colleagues, Samson prepared a model legislative act designed to insure the better education of funeral directors. This document was distributed to the executive committees of the various State Associations. It was entitled "An Act Pertaining to the Care, Preparation and Disposition of the Dead, and to Insure the Better Education of the Funeral Directors," and from it were drawn many of the features and provisions that went into the first licensing legislation of the states.

But state legislatures were not readily convinced, either of the public welfare aspects of such legislation or of the quality of the practitioners who pressed for it. Despite the example of the Province of Ontario in setting up a Board of Examiners in 1887, nearly eight years elapsed before the passage of a law by a state legislature, regulating the practice of embalming. Virginia led the way when on March 5, 1894, the Governor signed the regulatory bill. In the year following three additional states, Alabama, Missouri, and Pennsylvania passed like legislation, setting up a board of embalmers, or its equivalent, and laying down certain regulations as to educational and technical preparation necessary to enter and practice the art of embalming. Before the turn of the century the ranks of regulating states had been swelled by twenty names to make a total of twenty-four in all having passed *some* sort of embalming legislation.[39]

One might fairly observe that for all their traditional gayety the nineties were a period in which the efforts of funeral directors to achieve occupational licensing, and thereby to underscore their claim to be practitioners in a profession rendering necessary, important, personal services legitimated by the community, slowly began to bear fruit.

Traces of Professionalism at the Turn of the Century: In spite of much spade work it could be said at the turn of the century that while funeral directing in America had managed to organize, to establish itself, and to gain public recognition as a distinct occupation, it still had a very long distance to go in becoming a full-fledged profession. For one thing, even among its own practitioners, its aims and interests were by no means universally agreed upon. For another, the procedures or controls whereby any profession secures its aims and brings its members into conformity by social and legal pressures, were only partially developed.

Many problems faced the emerging profession of funeral directing as 1900 came to a close. Some of these arose out of the processes, equipment and materials available for use in its practice. Embalming procedures, techniques, and fluids—

especially the last—had by no means been perfected. Adequate controls over the quality of embalming fluids were lacking, and, as a result, side by side with standard brands produced by reputable companies, the market was flooded with an incredible variety of untested and uncertain compounds, produced both by fluid houses and by individual compounders.

Other problems were posed by a lack of a firm, universal definition of what constituted proper training to enter the occupation. Most undertakers by 1900 felt that a diploma from some kind of embalming school was sufficient evidence of proficiency to qualify a candidate. As with medical schools of the day, however, there was no general agreement as to what should be the educational requirements for admission to the course, what the course content should be, how long the training should last, and what qualifications schools should meet in faculty and physical equipment.

A diploma from an embalming school could mean anything from exposure to three days of demonstration made by an itinerant "professor," whose real purpose might be to sell a particular brand of embalming fluid, to graduation from a several months' course offered by a well established formal school of embalming.

The lack of state laws for licensing constituted another problem to challenge the movement of the occupation toward a profession. While the states of Washington, Oregon, Nevada, Texas, California, Arizona, Arkansas, Louisiana, Mississippi, Wisconsin, Michigan, Ohio, Kentucky, Tennessee, North Carolina, Florida, Vermont, Maine, Massachusetts, Connecticut, New Jersey, Rhode Island, and Maryland; and Indian Territory all had scattered bits of legislation regarding embalming and burial of the dead, they lacked formal licensing laws. The viewpoint held by some members of state legislatures that funeral service legislation was passed only to secure the benefit of the funeral director, and therefore as wholly a favor to him, constituted a serious impediment to the development of much needed licensing and regulatory law.

Unsavory advertising and cut throat competition had not yet reached its peak in 1900, but the lack of an unequivocal and general definition of what constituted legitimate promotional practice led later to grave abuses. This issue remains partly unsettled a half century later.

Even though the term "public relations" was unfamiliar in 1900, and the felt need for them probably much less than it is today, then as now good public relations constituted another problem for the profession. The successful efforts of funeral directors to reach an agreement with funeral goods manufacturers, and the resultant practices in restraint of trade, did little to reassure the public of the *service* bases of the funeral director's work. If the medical profession looked askance at funeral directors, so also did the American press, which sustained the stereotype of the funeral director as the traditional undertaker, the "dismal trader" of doubtful character and indifferent feelings.

These and similar problems were not then and are not now unique to the occupation of funeral directing. They are the problems that in a general sort of way every profession met with at its emergence, and from time to time is called upon to solve again.

Perhaps the most difficult problem still facing the funeral director at the turn of the century was the all-encompassing question of professionalization itself. How far should the effort to professionalize the group be carried? By its very nature the occupation could have swung sharply and far toward one or the other of opposites, or remained in some intermediate position. It faced the choice of becoming either an out-and-out trade or business, or a profession, or of compromising these extremes. It merits repeating that the *personal service* elements in funeral directing have a natural "professional" orientation; the *impersonal service or merchandizing elements* a natural "trade" orientation. Up to 1901, the great decision had been straddled, although the movement was toward professionalization. But it was apparent that in order to create a cleavage in the public mind between the undertaker who furnished merchandise and rendered services, and all other undertakers, a strong element in the occupational group, using the NFDA as its chief instrument, was successfully building a set of standards or measuring sticks, which could be incorporated into a licensing procedure. In order to eliminate the competition of merchants and others, who sold caskets but did not furnish service and, later, "facilities," both professional-minded and trade-minded groups endeavored, as we have seen, by means of trade agreements with manufacturers and supply houses, to restrict opportunities for buying such merchandise. Further, they attempted to penalize competing manufacturer-merchants by not buying from them, and by encouraging other funeral directors to buy only from recognized manufacturers who were not engaged in or directly supporting the service end of the business.

In 1900, in the minds of most undertakers or funeral directors, *both* forms of conducting one's occupation and thus serving self and mankind were merged into a concept of a vocation. And, like most of those occupations which during the 19th century had become self-conscious and sought to improve their economic and social status, funeral directing had achieved some kind of organization and internal order among its members but by no means had fully accomplished its aims. Meanwhile, it was not considered necessary to make the choice of being professional men *or* tradesmen as the point of self-designation for funeral directors. The impulse to associate, however, provided the impelling motive for directing and molding the desires of men who would better the status of their occupation, and thereby elevate the condition of their work, their security and legitimate rewards, the good opinion in which they were held by other occupations and by the public at large, and finally, their own self-esteem.

CITATIONS AND REFERENCES FOR CHAPTER XI

1. *Occupational Licensing in the States* (Chicago: The Council of State Governments, 1952), pp. 16-17.

2. *Ibid.*

3. *Ibid.*, p. 18, quoting from A. M. Carr-Saunders and P. W. Wilson, "Professions," in the *Encyclopedia of Social Sciences*, vol. VI, p. 477.

4. *Ibid.*, p. 21, *passim.*

5. *Ibid.* Figures taken from Table A, p. 23.

6. See *ibid.*, p. 22.

7. James A. Tobey, *The National Government and Public Health* (Baltimore: The Johns Hopkins Press, 1926), pp. 21, ff.

8. James A. Tobey, *Riders of the Plague* (New York: Charles Scribner's Sons, 1930), p. 78.

9. For a more complete account of the activities of the Sanitary Commission, see George W. Cooke, *Unitarianism in America* (Boston: American Unitarian Association, 1902), pp. 180-184.

10. Habenstein, "A Study of the Cremation Movement in the United States," *op. cit.*, p. 82.

11. Augustus Cobb, *Earth Burial and Cremation* (New York: Putnam, 1892), p. 136.

12. Adapted from the table on page 117 of John Storer Cobb's *A Quarter Century of Cremation in North America* (Boston: Knight and Millett, 1901).

13. O. B. Frothingham, *The Disposal of Our Dead* (New York: D. G. Francis, 1874).

14. *Proceedings of the First National Convention* (Detroit: Cremation Association of America, 1913), p. 4.

15. *The Keystone State Echo,* Golden Jubilee Number, June, 1931, p. 97, ff.

16. *Proceedings,* National Funeral Directors Association (hereinafter NFDA), 1909, p. 49.

17. *Ibid.,* p. 50

18. *Ibid.*

19. *Ibid.,* p. 52.

20. *Ibid.*

21. *Ibid.,* pp. 56-57.

22. *Proceedings,* American Funeral Directors' National Association, 1882, p. 22

23. *Ibid.,* 1884, p. 76.

24. *Proceedings,* International Funeral Directors' Association, 1888, p. 14, *passim.*

25. *Proceedings,* American Funeral Directors' National Association, 1886, pp. 5-10, *passim.*

26. Habenstein, *"The American Funeral Director,"* *op. cit.,* p. 173 ff.

27. *Proceedings,* FDA, 1884, p. 11.

28. *Ibid.,* p. 12.

29. From *The Casket,* 1886, Archives of the NFDA, Milwaukee, Wis., *op. cit.,* no month, n.p.

30. *The Casket,* May 1, 1876.

31. *Proceedings,* American Funeral Directors' National Association, 1883, pp. 31-32.

32. *Proceedings, op. cit.,* 1884, p. 53.

33. *Proceedings, op. cit.,* 1888, p. 29 ff.

34. "Rules Governing Transportation of Dead Bodies, Adopted by the National Board of Health" in *Proceedings,* NFDA, 1897, *op. cit.,* pp. 147-149.

35. *Proceedings, op. cit.,* 1884, p. 75, ff.

36. *Proceedings,* American Funeral Directors' National Association, 1885, pp. 14-15.

37. *Proceedings, op. cit.,* 1886, p. 7.

38. *Ibid.,* pp. 7-8.

39. *Proceedings,* NFDA, 1900, p. 53.

Part Three:
Organization of Modern
Funeral Service

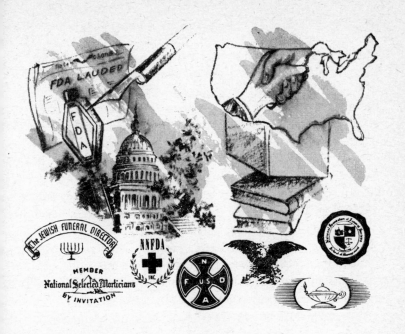

Institutional Growth and Modern Associational Developments

In the conditions of their emergence and change occupations differ considerably. Some grow slowly, adding new workers and, possibly, new functions to the basic work or service performed. Others, especially in modern times, appear almost overnight, born of technical innovations and inventions. Yet no matter what the specific conditions of appearance, all occupations face a general problem of institutionalization, that is, of putting order, harmony, and certainty in the minds of those who work in them. One of the major functions of an occupational association is to create a definite image of the occupation in the minds of those who engage in it, and to impress this image as the true representation of the occupation in the minds of the public.

We turn, then, in this chapter to a description of some of the recent historical developments in funeral directing as they reflect the problems and actions of men trying to introduce order, harmony and certainty of mind into a rapidly growing field. The path is not entirely new, since in many ways Chapter 11, dealing with the associational impulse, has already cast light on the organizing activities of men striving to build an orderly vocation. In dealing with recent institutional growth and associational developments in funeral directing we will consider five related matters: mortuary education, developments in mortuary law, multiplication of associations, economic growth and expansion, and, finally, evidences of integration and stabilization.   .

Mortuary Education: In the process of becoming instituted as one of the more important sectors of present day funeral service, mortuary education developed four identifiable areas. These consist of: 1) the schools of mortuary science, as they have come to be known; 2) the agencies controlling the activities of these schools and setting their standards of content and instruction; 3) the committees which represent the various interests in the general field of mortuary education and which advise and recommend action to the agencies; and, finally, 4) the body of legislative actions and the rules and usages laid down by the boards of the several states. Although these divisions overlap somewhat they will be taken up in the order listed.

(1) Schools: As we know from brief references in Chapter 8, which dealt with embalming, schools of mortuary science before 1900 were more notable for the men who conducted them and the products they used and supported than for the quality and thoroughness of the instruction they provided and the range of subject matter their courses

covered. Included in this group are such men as Dr. Auguste Renouard, who as early as 1874 independently instructed a small number of undertakers in the back room of a furniture store in Denver, and whose *Undertaker's Manual*, written in 1876 and published in 1878, marked a first; his son, Charles A. Renouard, one of the first to establish an independent, non-commercial-house-connected school of embalming in 1894; Will Hohenschuh, later to become an authority in the field of funeral service generally; that showman, Dr. Carl Lewis Barnes, founder of many schools of embalming and compounder of several varieties of fluids; C. B. Dolge, founder of the United States School of Embalming in 1887, and president of the Brooklyn Embalming Fluid Co.; Felix A. Sullivan, itinerant teacher of embalming and founder of schools, whose embalming of well known persons led him to be referred to as "the dean of embalmers of the English speaking peoples"; Joseph H. Clarke, described earlier; and the scholarly physician, text-writer, and embalming school pedagogue, Dr. William S. Carpenter. These make up only a partial list of the pioneers in the field of mortuary education.[1]

"In the beginning," remarks Charles O. Dhonau, the generally accepted "dean" of mortuary education today, "the training of individuals to be practical operators was largely promoted by those who were either associated then, or later, with concerns whose business it was, or is, to produce and to distribute embalmers' supplies."[2] Yet the commercial support of these early schools was not an unmixed evil, since there was probably no other way at the time by which the practice of embalming, crude as it might be, could be diffused so rapidly through the field. To this point Dhonau states:

In all fairness to commercially operated "schools" of that early period, they were quite successful in enrolling students from existing "undertaking establishments," "livery stables," "furniture stores," and "cabinet makers," as well as from the ranks of that one-out-of-ten-thousand individuals who had a natural bent toward rendering what was then the service of an "undertaker." Many of the leading members of our profession "graduated" from these commercially motivated schools . . . Their "professional education" did not end with their short school term, but they improved themselves, their knowledge, their conduct, their personalities, through that agency we may call the "university of hard knocks," to the point where their success was unbounded.[3]

Non-commercial schools of embalming before 1900 were rare mainly for two reasons: the limited demand for embalmers, as contrasted with the demand for physicians or dentists; and the relatively high cost of instruction. In addition to the Renouards' school—both father and son operated it until 1912—there were the Illinois School of Embalming, opened in Chicago in 1884 under the sponsorship of the Chicago Association of Undertakers; and the Iowa School of Embalming, founded about 1890. These constituted three of the more lasting "independents" before 1900.

A feature of many of the other early embalming schools was their itineracy. It was customary for a team of demonstrators to start out on tour, going from city to city, holding sessions each of which lasted from three or four days to a week. School diplomas were granted at the end of each session. Occasionally examinations would be given. After 1894, with the introduction of embalming legislation in the several states, these schools were forced to perform an added function, the preparation of the student who expected to take the examination prepared by the State Board of Embalming.

Other innovations at the turn of the century were the "quiz compend" (a list of questions commonly used by the State Boards, together with the correct answers to be memorized), and the mortuary correspondence schools. At this time the course prepared by H. S. Eckels was perhaps the most popular. Again the emphasis was upon preparation for the State Board examination.

Instruction in all the "formal" schools was limited in the main to lectures and demonstrations in anatomy, bacteriology, practical embalming, disinfectants, and the study of contagious diseases. Memorization, again, was one of the ends of instruction and demonstration. By 1900, courses at the more reputable schools—there were no formal standards or grading systems at the time—lasted about three weeks. Literature on the subject was scanty, and often the founder of the school would find it necessary to prepare his own texts as well as to lecture and handle administrative matters. In the twenty years between 1874 and 1893 only seven items of literature dealing directly with embalming were written in America, according to a list drawn up by Charles O. Dhonau. In the next two decades the figure had tripled. In comparison with the amount of literature being produced in the last few decades, the period 1895-1914 may be looked upon as prolific from the standpoint of works in the field of embalming. Many of the basic texts and reference works written during this period were substantial products written by men trained in anatomy, physiology, and chemistry, whose theoretical knowledge was amplified by practical experience in the field.

The quarter century of growth in embalming schools after 1900 produced some rather striking developments, most notable of which, perhaps, was the rise of the proprietary school with the beginnings of a standardized curriculum, and the lengthening of the term of instruction. If, for example, one wished to study embalming in Chicago at the Barnes School of Anatomy, Sanitary Science, and Embalming around 1905, he would have no trouble enrolling any day of the year—Sundays included.[4] In 1910 the average length of courses in embalming schools was about six weeks; fifteen years later in 1925 it was increased to eight weeks; in 1928 to three months; in 1930 to six months, and in 1934 the nine months' course was originated at Eckels College of Mortuary Science.[5] At present, in 1955, courses range from nine months to a year, to meet state law requirements.

At least eleven schools of mortuary education were founded between 1900 and 1920: The Simmons School of Embalming, in 1902; the American College of Embalming in 1903; the Indiana School of Embalming in 1905; the Columbus Training School for Embalmers, the Cleveland College of Embalming, and the Boston School of Anatomy and Embalming, all in 1909; the Worsham College of Embalming, in 1911; the University of Minnesota, Course in Embalming and Sanitary Science, 1914; the Los Angeles College of Anatomy, Embalming and Sanitation, 1918; and the Gupton-Jones School of Embalming in 1920. With the exception of the University of Minnesota these schools were proprietary, in the sense that they represented private ownership of an educational enterprise by an individual or set of individuals—as over against the eleemosynary, or non-profit, public-serving institutions. Although the tendency was to operate these schools without outside help from the fluid and other morticians' goods companies—the reorganized Cincinnati School of Embalming was an outstanding example in this case—such was not always possible. Some schools unabashedly continued to operate with commercial support.

The next phase in the development of schools of mortuary education took place in the late twenties and early thirties after many pioneer founders died or retired, and the institutions were faced with the problem of survival without the personal guidance, inspiration, and often the unstinted time of their founders. In numerous cases these schools, never more than twenty-five at any one time, were faced with crucial problems of reorganization. One solution was to reincorporate along non-profit lines, with the faculty assuming responsibility for administration of the school itself.

The current phase of these schools started with the establishment of the Wisconsin Institute of Mortuary Science in 1936. For the first time the term "Mortuary Science" appeared in the title of a school of mortuary education. By 1955, most of the old, and practically all of the newly-established schools, had adopted this term. Many of the present schools of mortuary science came into existence through mergers and combinations, and it was often the case that at one of these junctures a change in title would occur which would reflect the changing emphasis in mortuary education. For example, the Hohenschuh-Carpenter College of Embalming was organized in Des Moines in 1900, and shortly thereafter absorbed the Western College of Embalming. In 1930 it moved to St. Louis and merged with the American College of Embalming, founded in 1903 by another "pioneer," M. H. Alexander. In 1943 it merged with the Williams Institute of Mortuary Science to become the College of Mortuary Science, St. Louis, organized as a non-proprietary institution. Likewise the Los Angeles College of Anatomy, Embalming and Sanitation, founded in 1918, simplified its name to the California College of Embalming in 1929, and changed again in 1940 to the California College of Mortuary Science. Thus the mortuary schools in their changing structure have tended, on the whole, to follow the pattern set by other professional schools. The final stage seems to be incorporation into the organization of large universities and colleges. Examples of this trend among schools of mortuary science begin with the University of Minnesota, which as far back as 1914 offered a regular course in applied mortuary science. Wayne University of Detroit currently offers a three-year course, the first two years of which consist of liberal arts subjects, and the third of mortuary science courses. These requirements are in keeping with the college requirements for mortuary schools set by the State of Michigan. More recently Temple University of Philadelphia has incorporated into its college curriculum, a degree-granting program with special preparation in mortuary science.[6]

The genesis and development of schools of mortuary education represents one major dimension of the total pattern of the recruitment, indoctrination, technical training and control of personnel entering the field of embalming and funeral direction. It reflects the increasingly important influence exerted through associational committees, licensing boards, legislative acts, and the collective endeavors of other relevant and interested groups. (A list of accredited colleges of mortuary science is in the Appendix.)

(2) Agencies, Conferences and Councils: One of the most significant steps taken to raise examinational standards, and otherwise to improve the service of the State Boards of Examiners to the profession and general public, took place with the organization of the Joint Conference of Embalmers' Examining Boards and State Boards of Health in 1904, under the guiding genius of J. H. McCully of Idaville, Indiana.[7] The first meetings of this Conference were held in conjunction with the annual convention of the NFDA at St. Louis that year. The project had been talked about for some time before actual organization began; the first stirrings had come in 1900, at the Denver meetings of the NFDA with an informal conference of the members of the various boards for licensing embalmers. J. Newton Nind, Editor of *The Embalmers' Monthly* attended, and, about three years later, he and McCully joined forces to bring about the St. Louis meeting.

In a circular letter written to the field at large, the hope expressed by these two, seconded formally by H. M. Kilpatrick, Secretary of the NFDA, was that "such a conference might result in unifying the regulation of embalming in the several states, in the interchange of recognition of licenses issued by the different Boards, and expedite the adoption of the new transportation rules." Meanwhile, a Committee on Education of the NFDA, with McCully as chairman, had brought under scrutiny the problem of providing some uniform system of requirements both in the receiving of applicants for examination before licenses were granted, and in examining them. The work of this Committee was incorporated into the deliberations of the newly formed Joint Conference.

One of the first issues taken up by the latter was reciprocity with regard to licenses. Although it became increasingly apparent that the problems of the Examining Boards were more specific than the State Boards of Health would care to discuss, an effort was made to keep the two groups together. In 1906, at the Chicago meeting, the organization changed its name to The Association of State and Provincial Boards of Health and Embalmers' Examining Boards of North America. A prominent figure in Public Health, Dr. H. M. Bracken, of St. Paul, Secretary and Executive Officer for the Minnesota State Board of Health, was elected president, but the combination survived only for a year. In 1907, the Conference of State and Provincial Boards of Health of North America again returned to its unaffiliated status; and the Conference of Embalmers' Examining Boards of North America, with a slate of officers drawn from its own functionaries, was organized as a more limited interest group, dedicated to problems more specifically relating to embalming and funeral directing. Some of these were matters of concern to the entire field of funeral service: such as transportation of the dead; the quality, efficacy and reliability of embalming fluids; the relations of funeral directors with casket manufacturers; and self-improvement in the service of the State Boards.

Several developments, not necessarily representing direct actions of the Conference, need mentioning. In 1907 McCully was able to secure from the Attorney General of Indiana an opinion that the Burial Associations operating in that state were violating the insurance law. In the same year the Conference of State and Provincial Boards of Health endorsed a particular embalming fluid. In 1913, again due in most part to the persistence of McCully, acting in the capacity of a representative of the NFDA, the Conference, as one of its first important actions, adopted a set of rules pertaining to the transportation of the dead.

Meanwhile, the Conference of Examining Boards of North America reversed its name in 1914 to become the North American Conference of Embalmers' Examining Boards. For the next several years it devoted itself to pressing for adoption by individual legislatures and state boards of the transportation rules it had set in 1913. The difficulty of welding together such a Conference, representing about half of the State Boards of Health, and Embalmers' Examining Boards with membership in these boards often a matter of political appointment and in each state the result of a different legislative act, can well be imagined. Charles O. Dhonau, reminiscing over the early years of the Conference, underscores the differences that prevailed:

As I remember, particularly in the Conference meetings of and since 1914 at New Orleans, there were usually committees reporting on the possibilities of different kinds of uniformities. From the beginning, nearly every state delegate opined that his license law was superior in some provisions. Practically everyone thought his own law as a suitable pattern for all and was willing to try for uniformity provided his own law was the pattern. In 1914 much was talked about concerning license reciprocity between states and for a few years there was more actual reciprocity than in later years, when many Board members began to believe that there must be something iniquitous about a licensed individual changing his state of residence.[8]

After World War I and during the early twenties the Conference displayed a growing interest in the curricula of the schools. Under the inspiration of Dhonau it strove to convince State Board examiners that the responsibility for a student passing or failing an examination should in part be shared by the school which provided him with his training; and consequently it was incumbent upon the several Boards to learn more about the actual character and operation of embalming school programs.

Among education-minded funeral directors it has become traditional to look upon the date 1927 as marking the turning point for the Conference. In that year at its Cincinnati meeting a decision was reached to adopt a topical curriculum for a six months' course, then the longest being given. The length of term merits passing attention. As early as 1913 the Cincinnati School had offered a six months' course. By and large, however, other institutions in the field of mortuary training had not followed this advance, so that fourteen years later the average course still was of less than three months' duration, although a few schools had converted to a six months' basis. After the passage of the 1927 resolution, most of the schools which had been offering shorter courses voluntarily adjusted to it by lengthening their programs.

A second step toward raising standards was taken in 1927 when the Conference (still the "Conference of Embalmers' Examining Boards") decided to take positive action toward placing embalming college training on some basis of national accreditation. Its initial move was to adopt as standard one of the six month curricula in use in 1927. It also set four years of high school as an entrance requirement — which prerequisite had already been demanded by at least one existing college of embalming.[9] To complete the process of setting up an accreditation system, the Conference adopted a plan for the grading of colleges of embalming according to revised standards, as listed in part above. A three man Accreditation Committee was appointed to undertake this grading function. Although schools had already begun to revise their own programs, it was not until 1928 that the first grading system, consisting of the three letter grades, "A," "B," or "C," was worked out to the satisfaction of the Conference itself and of the eleven schools which were represented at its Kansas City meeting. Later the system was changed to "A," "AA," and "B."

In 1934 the "Grading Committee" became the National Conference Board Committee of Embalming Examiners, later to become the Examination and National Board Committee, operating under the authority of the Board of Directors of the Conference. Its functions were, and are, to develop examinations to be used by the State Boards; to distribute and, when directed, to grade these examinations for a stipulated charge; and to carry out continuous evaluation of its own efforts in the examination program with a view to constant improvement. Additionally, the Committee serves graduates of accredited schools of mortuary science by making available to them National Board Examinations. Certificates are granted to the successful applicant along with a travelling card, and a certification notice is sent to the state board of the applicant's choice. In 1938 the graded schools were encouraged to change their legal names from schools and colleges of "Embalming" to schools and colleges of "Mortuary Science." In 1940 the Conference became the Council of Funeral Service Examining Boards, Incorporated: and later substituted the term "Conference" for "Council." With this change the title took its present form.

Another mortuary education agency which came eventually to represent embalming schools and colleges was founded in 1942. Originally formed as the Mortuary Education Council, its corporate name was registered later as the National Council on Mortuary Education. The purposes of the Council were primarily educational and its operations non-profit. It sought to formulate the proper educational, scientific and professional principles and standards to be used in placing schools and colleges of mortuary science on an approved list. Acting as an agency independent of any one interest group—although trying to represent all impartially—it conceived its function to be to accredit and approve the programs of mortuary education and training being offered in the schools. It set up and carried out this function at the request of those schools which elected to join the Council.

Although the original intent of this Council was to include within its membership representatives from all the mortuary education interest groups, the Conference of Funeral Service Examining Boards elected not to participate, because its members for the most part felt that a duplication of the accreditation function would result. In some degree this feeling was also present among NFDA members; and although representatives of the latter did participate for several years, the Council suffered from diminishing returns, and by 1948 ceased to function, although its legal dissolution was not completed until 1953. While this agency was short-lived, it nevertheless brought under its influence most of the major schools and colleges of mortuary science, many of which revised upward their standards, facilities, and operations; and, apparently, benefited by the accreditation they received.

(3) Interest Group Committees: Turning for the moment to the various committees and groups which represented the different interest groups—other than those of

the colleges and the state examining boards—our attention is first drawn to the Committees on Education of the NFDA, which were first appointed in 1903 and whose initial report in 1904 coincided both in time and in point of view with the first meeting of the Conference of Embalmers Examining Boards.

Proposed and adopted at this time was the creation of a three man educational committee, whose members would be elected for periods of one to three years and whose function would be to prepare "a workable plan whereby this association may pass intelligent judgment upon the quality of professional attainment offered by any educational institution catering to the ranks of our profession."[10] In some detail the committee was also charged with the function of "working as far as possible in conjunction with the State Associations and State Embalmers' Licensing Boards." It was to "arrange and prescribe and present to this association for approval a detailed schedule of instruction which shall represent a standard that is in keeping with the dignity of our profession." Having determined upon such schedule it was further to "arrange with standard educational institutions for giving the necessary instruction to meet the requirements of such schedule."[11]

In the succeeding years this Committee and its various elected members worked in close cooperation with the newly formed Conference of Embalmers' Examining Boards. The meetings of this Conference were usually held just prior to those of the National Association and in the same city. Occasionally a member of the Conference would also be a member of the Educational Committee.

While the Educational Committee of the NFDA received many recommendations designed to better mortuary education, and recommended for adoption a considerable number of them, actual progress was not always as rapid as enthusiastic committee reports would seem to indicate; and it was not until the nineteen twenties, when the number of licensed embalmers in the field had soared above 35,000, that the Committee's repeated pleas for increased requirements and higher standards of educational and technical instruction began to receive serious notice. By 1924, an overture from the Conference of Embalmers' Examining Boards made to the NFDA through the Committee on Legislation, suggested the formation of a new joint committee consisting of three members from the Conference, three from the NFDA, and three from the National Selected Morticians. This joint committee would be set up to "coordinate activities looking toward the enactment of more uniform laws in the various states requiring higher standards of entrance into the profession."[12] In the same year the Committee on Education recommended the establishment of an American Institute of Funeral Directors.

1. The affairs of the Institute shall be in charge of a commission of five funeral directors who have state licenses . . . The purpose and duties of this Commission shall be: To endeavor to establish uniform preliminary requirements in all states willing to cooperate . . .

2. Said Commission shall be ready to furnish, under seal, original examination questions and answers for the use of those State Boards which may desire this service.

3. To provide increased opportunities for self-development for individual licensed funeral directors and embalmers by providing for the conducting of a course (or Institute) in funeral directing, embalming, cost accounting, and other business methods for funeral directors and embalmers . . .[13]

Only members in good standing of the NFDA were permitted to become students in the Institutes, which were to begin as soon as the Commissioners felt conditions so warranted. Two years later, plans to hold a two week Institute at the University of Chicago fell through, when an insufficient number of members enrolled. However, in the following year, 1927, eventful for important developments in the Conference of Embalmers' Examining Boards, the two days preliminary to the meeting of NFDA at Cincinnati were given over to a highly successful institute, presided over by "Dean" Harry G. Samson, son of Hudson Samson, one of the outstanding 19th century Pittsburg funeral directors, past president of the NFDA in 1885 and 1886, and resolute champion of increased educational standards and professionality among his colleagues. Lectures by well known experts in the field covered a variety of topics ranging from anatomical and physiological subject matter to discussions of modes of pricing funeral services. Attendance was excellent, and it was generally agreed that such institutes should become permanent adjuncts to annual NFDA meetings.

The year following saw this conviction fulfilled, and "Dean" Samson again presided over another two day session. At the second meeting fourteen speakers were present, each presenting a paper and carrying on discussions afterwards. These two meetings marked the high point of the NFDA Pre-Convention Institutes, and though they continued to be held regularly until 1932, and through the years 1937-1939, in length and educative quality the sessions diminished perceptibly, until at the end, they offered little more than an address or two, generally on trade matters.

Like many other similar ventures in occupational self-education, this one became a casualty to the depression of the thirties. It was reported by a representative of the burial goods industry, who was the main speaker at the 1932 Institute, that between 1929 and 1932 funeral directing had dropped one hundred million dollars in volume of business.[14] During these difficult times, in which shrinkage characterized all phases of professional and economic life, the minds of many funeral directors were taken up with the all-absorbing question of survival, to the exclusion of less urgent matters. The fact that a number went out of business is in itself eloquent of the crisis the group was facing.

With the return of moderately prosperous times, mortuary education for funeral directors already established in the field had assumed a somewhat different character. Two additions had been incorporated. One of these was a tendency to view business and marketing research problems as not only highly important, but as belonging in *any* program of education by "institutes," "forums," "in service-courses" or "lectures"; the other was the tendency to accept the growing field of "public relations" as likewise importantly a part of any program of mortuary education.

Among funeral directors, academic and technical subjects were gradually relegated to the formal schools of mortuary education, and when funeral directors or their representatives demanded additional training for admission to such schools their requests were not so likely to be for specific courses or course contents as they were for an increased number of years of formal schooling, that is, for more general education.

The conception of public relations as intrinsically a part of mortuary education—defined widely—received concrete expression in 1930 with the establishment, within the NFDA, of the Institute of Mortuary Research. The function of the Institute staff was to disseminate information favorable to organized funeral directing to the various media of communication: radio, newspapers, journals, spokesmen, and the like; and to "trouble shoot" points of hostility and attacks on the occupation.[15] It was also to serve as an information center for all persons, whether connected with funeral service or not, who sought answers to questions in any way related to the funeral field. It likewise published *The Director*, the trade organ of the NFDA. The Institute operated enterprisingly through 1939. After that year most of its functions were absorbed by the newly created office of Executive Secretary of the Association.

More specifically concerned with mortuary education, conceived in the narrower sense of the training and indoctrination of new personnel in the field, were the Joint Conference Committee and the Joint Education Committee, both closely related, though separated in time. These joint committees represented the various interest groups and agencies in the field of funeral service and licensing and examining boards. In 1924, the National Funeral Directors Association and the National Selected Morticians appointed three representatives to form with the Conference of Embalmers' Examining Boards a "Committee of Nine." This group, known in the NFDA as the "Joint Conference Committee," issued its first report in 1925. It stated in this its "readiness to function any time on matters pertaining to the Three Nationals," indicated its liaison activities, and pointed out its support of the American Institute of Funeral Directors. Substantively, "along the lines of educative advancement," the License Board of each state was urged to "step up its requirements of the applicant, and to make the examination, both oral and written of a still higher standard." However, the Committee felt that such harmony prevailed among the major organizations that it had no further usefulness, and despite its continued paper existence no meetings were held for the next several years, due to the difficulty of assembling the members from the different organizations at one time and at one place.

The 1929 Committee Report to the NFDA called for a cut in the representation to one from that group; but little more was heard of such committee in the next several years. In 1933 the Education Committee of the NFDA proposed in the National Meeting that a somewhat familiar sounding "committee of three be appointed to meet with the like committee from the Conference of Embalmers' Examining Boards and the National Association of Embalming Colleges, to be known as a Joint Educational Council . . . to consider any and all questions referred to it by its constituent bodies, and to make such recommendations as may be advisable."[16] This group, known in the NFDA as the "Joint Committee on Education"—with slight variations in its title—has found sufficient common interests and problems to hold together since its inception at Rochester in 1933, and has operated continuously since that time. It has kept its definition of mortuary education restricted to that of the recruitment, training and indoctrination of funeral service personnel, and although its decisions have been advisory in nature, this Committee remains as one of the major coordinating agencies in the field.

Meanwhile, by 1950, the Education Committee, specifically operating within the NFDA, had developed a program or set of ideals and goals toward which this organization may be thought officially to aspire. Too extensive to give in detail, the major points indicate a long-time developing concept of mortuary education, not too dissimilar from the educational models used generally in the professions: to gain and maintain a high educational background for all practitioners of funeral service; to secure high and uniform standards of requirements for entrance into schools of mortuary science; to help bring about a sound, realistic curriculum, geared to the needs of the occupation and everywhere standard in graded schools of mortuary science; to revise the apprentice system in the direction of internship-externship; and to press for the licensing of all funeral directors as well as embalmers, with training in a recognized college or university as a prerequisite.

A final set of interest groups in the realm of mortuary education, the associations of colleges of mortuary science, need mentioning. Two are currently operating, the National Association of Colleges of Mortuary Science, and the American Association of Mortuary Colleges.

The National Association of Embalming Schools and Colleges was organized in Atlanta, Georgia, at a meeting held on October 13, 1930. Ten colleges became charter members and Clifford Asken was elected first president. In 1935 the Association was incorporated in the State of Illinois and in 1942 the name was changed to the National Association of Colleges of Mortuary Science. Membership in the association increased progressively during its early years to a peak membership of seventeen schools and colleges during the period from 1948 to 1950. Beginning in 1950 membership declined as a result of the closing of some schools and the merger of others. Today (1955), the roster includes eleven schools.

From the beginning the National Association set as its goal the advancement of mortuary education. This purpose has been carried out through cooperation with accrediting agencies in recommendation of faculty qualifications, improvement of physical facilities and equipment, and progressive expansion in the educational program. The association is represented on the Joint Committee of Mortuary Education.

In 1947 the National Association sponsored a series of Teachers' Institutes and established Course Content Committees. The purpose of these Institutes and Committees is to standardize and improve course content and teaching methods in each subject of the curriculum. All accredited schools are represented on the committees which since 1947 have continued to work without interruption. Course content outlines have been certified to the Conference of Funeral Service Examining Boards for use in state and national board examinations.

A somewhat more recent group, the American Association of Mortuary Colleges, was organized in 1941 by a group of mortuary educators who belonged to the National Association of Colleges of Mortuary Science. In the fall of 1942 this new organization was formally established with Dr. L. W. Hosford as president.

The actions of this group in leaving the National Association created a three-way split. The third group consisted of the university schools which remained unaffiliated with both associations. The objectives which the American Association set for itself were: 1) To bring harmony between itself, the Nine Man Committee representing funeral directing and mortuary education, and the Conference of Funeral Service Examining Boards; 2) To promote educational standards and continuity in mortuary education; 3) To bring about harmony between association members; 4) To sponsor joint meetings between the various school and examining groups in an effort to improve examination and grading procedures and the correlation of course content material; 5) Generally, to promote better understanding in all areas of the profession.

Since its founding the American Association has worked for the development of standard textbooks, standard courses in mortuary education, and standard State Board examinations and correction procedures.

(4) Licensing Laws: One of the highest hurdles facing all agencies, councils and committees concerned with the betterment of mortuary education, has been the structure of state licensing laws. Although this matter has been referred to above, especially in the context of early associational developments, and will again be commented upon later in this chapter, its relevance at this point merits brief mention. The crux of the situation seems to be that in the haphazard growth of state licensing legislation, few if any of the states have identical or corresponding rules that pertain to the organ-

ization, curriculum, programing and operation of schools and colleges of mortuary science. Licensing as a state function in the realm of embalming and funeral directing has carried with it an inclination on the part of the several legislatures to spell out in some detail the substance, structure and function of mortuary education within their respective states. The difficulties of achieving such standardization is succinctly reviewed by Dr. Robert McFate, Professor of Pathology, and well known figure in the field of mortuary education:

. . . Some twenty or twenty-five years ago the scope of funeral service had grown so wide that our modern funeral director began to appear. With many demands made upon him, he realized the value of a more complete educational background. As a result, state legislatures passed new laws requiring a high school diploma for entrance into a college of embalming or mortuary science.

At this time, however, a major mistake was made. State laws were passed prescribing complete college curricula for the courses in embalming and funeral directing, so many hours of this subject, so many hours of that, and with no flexibility allowed. Furthermore, the requirements of one state would generally vary markedly from the requirements in a neighboring state. These requirements were not determined by a conference between the colleges and the members of the profession, but usually were based on the ideas of just one or two persons, often individuals not too well informed.

For the past twenty-five years then, the colleges of embalming and mortuary science have been faced with the problem of meeting the requirements set up by state laws with no opportunity to change their curricula to meet the advances in funeral service. In fact most state laws, as they refer to education in this field, are completely impracticable and impossible.[17]

Developments in Mortuary Law:[18] Although in England the framework of legal controls over sepulture was set in ecclesiastical law, which in turn was compounded out of earlier church or canon law generously mixed with components of civil, common and statute law, in America the tendency has been to ground these controls in common law, and to look for precedents no farther back than 1607, the year of the founding of Jamestown, the first English settlement. The common law of England, founded on a concept of property rights, had little to offer the Colonists in matters pertaining to the burial of the dead that was applicable to the New World situation. As a result, through the ensuing centuries Americans have evolved mortuary laws of their own. However, these are no less mixed and complex than those evolved by the English, this in spite of the fact that, with temporal courts in complete charge of matters pertaining to the dead, it might have been expected that an integrated, organized body of principle and precedent would have been developed. Such has not been the case; and to repeat for emphasis: in America traditional ecclesiastical usage has been mixed with common law, *ad hoc* decisions of the courts, statutes enacted by the several legislatures, and municipal ordinances, until the sum total has almost defied reason, much less codification.[19]

In the evolution of traditional usages, along with items of sumptuary legislation, now long in disuse, and scattered court decisions—there were only about twenty of any significance between 1821 and 1900 covering all aspects of sepulture[20]—there were few regulatory laws governing the actions of the embalmer and funeral director. Most of this type do not appear until the present century. Those of most significance were the first state licensing laws, mentioned earlier, beginning with Virginia in 1894, and in the next several decades encompassing a majority of the states. These, however, were statutes primarily dealing with the licensing and control of embalmers; and the impulse to license funeral directors or bring them under the control of state laws was a later development. Nevertheless, a few states had such laws before 1900: Pennsylvania, in 1895; Virginia, 1897; and New York, 1898. By 1910 the total had increased to 12, and by 1930, to 19. Today all states and the District of Columbia license embalmers, and funeral directors are licensed in 40. That these laws have been enacted for the purpose of protecting the public interest has been sustained as valid and constitutional without exception, whenever any attack has been made upon them.[21]

There has been some difference of opinion as to whether the funeral director and the embalmer should have separate licenses, or whether each should be compelled to have both licenses, or whether there should be a combination license. There have been decisions which have held that it is improper to compel a funeral director to have an embalmer's license and vice versa,[22] and there has been at least one decision which has upheld the provision that each should have both licenses, or that both should have the combination funeral director-embalmer license.[23] The majority of the court decisions have leaned towards the doctrine that the two callings differ so clearly that to compel one to take an examination for the license of the other is interfering with his constitutional rights.

From the very beginning, the laws regulating both embalmers and funeral directors were held to be right, proper and legal, and were regarded as a reasonable exercise of the police powers inherent in the state. Both legislatures and courts felt that the enactment of such laws was in the interest of public health and welfare. It must be recognized that even though embalming is not compulsory by law, it is regarded as a valid preservative and sanitary measure, and therefore as having implications for public health. This viewpoint, it should be remembered, is relatively recent both in its date of origin and in its increased acceptance.

There have been other indications of statutory recognition of the economic hazards flowing from the very nature of the functions of the funeral director. In setting priorities in estates the statutes of a majority of the states have placed the payment of funeral expenses after the costs of administration and taxes. This preference is based on an awareness that the funeral director must perform his services before the estate of the deceased is inventoried and declared.

A number of decisions have been rendered concerning the liability of the funeral director for the actions of the embalmer and of the drivers of funeral cars. A few cases supply some precedent governing the action of funeral directors themselves. The courts have decided, for instance, that a funeral director cannot hold a body as security for a debt;[24] nor can he delay a funeral against the wishes of the next of kin.[25] If he does, he is subject to legal penalty in the way of damages; likewise he is liable, if it is proved that his embalmer, while in his employ, improperly embalmed a body.[26]

Again, funeral directors have been held liable for injuries sustained to mourners driving to a funeral in a funeral procession. Legal opinion is not unanimous in this matter, the argument in these cases turning on the point as to whether or not the driver of the car in which the injured person was riding was acting under the supervision and direction of the funeral director. If he was not, then the funeral director has been held to be not liable.[27]

The practice of zoning a particular municipality into various districts such as residential, commercial, and industrial began about 1900 and in the past twenty-five years has become widespread. The purpose is to maintain property values and to limit the use of land in the public welfare. The establishment of zones is a legislative function; and before the courts will declare a zoning ordinance invalid, it must clearly appear that the ordinance is discriminatory or unreasonable in its operation, or has no substantial relation to the public health, safety or morals, or to the general welfare.[28] While a funeral home has generally been held not to constitute a nuisance as such, or as legally stated—"per se,"[29] nevertheless the general rule is to the effect that in the absence of zoning ordinance the operation of a funeral home in a strictly residential neighborhood does, by its very nature, constitute a nuisance. The reason behind these cases is the theory that the hearse, the ambulance, and the procession of mourners are reminders of the presence of death, and can bring depression and discomfort to the normal person unused to such conditions.[30]

Where a funeral home is being operated in an area permitted by the existing local zoning ordinances the courts will not interfere with the use of the home because it is not a nuisance "per se"; however, should the funeral home be so operated as to constitute a nuisance by the failure to observe such rules and regulations pertaining to the use of proper equipment for preservation of public health, a court may well grant injunctive relief to persons in the neighborhood who are suffering or who may suffer by the careless operation of the funeral home.

As taken up in a previous section, for the purpose of safeguarding the public health the various states have enacted laws and boards have prescribed regulations pertaining to the shipment of dead bodies, intrastate or interstate. These laws control generally the shipment of human bodies when death occurred from particular contagious diseases, prescribe the types of shipping cases and/or caskets, and set forth the various requirements regarding the care of dead human bodies where burial cannot readily be made.

Shortly after 1950, a number of pre-need, pre-financed funeral-cemetery schemes cropped up around the country. These promotional schemes were created and operated by persons outside the funeral directing profession. The basic danger in these plans was that they lacked adequate safeguards for the public. There were no assurances that the funeral merchandise or funeral or cemetery services contracted for would be available when needed. Through actions of the State and National Associations, statutes have been enacted by the several legislatures specifically designed to control these operations. Such statutes, framed in the interest of both the public and the funeral directing profession, provide that when a prearrangement contract shall be entered into, all or a considerable portion of the monies paid shall be placed in trust in a bank or trust company, and that the donor shall have the right at any time during his life to withdraw such funds.[31]

In the execution of his duties the funeral director is enjoined to respect the sentiments and feelings of the bereaved; yet such is the nature of his work that his obligations to his client can never be explicitly or totally defined by contract. There remains always a residue of things to be done and said appropriate to the circumstances of particular situations as they arise in the course of his care for the funeralization of the dead. While it is more or less universally accepted that his vocation is carried out within a context of individual enterprise, and for remuneration adequate to his support as a member of the community, it does not carry with it a sanction for dealing with the dead as merchandise, nor with the bereaved as merely customers seeking to maximize the value of their purchase. In the course of the last century, in dealing with the dead the funeral director has come to recognize that the legal and cultural sanctions for his vocation place him somewhat beyond general business practices in the light of the special care and judgment he must use in dealing with the bereaved. In other words, it has come to pass that the funeral director cannot seek to operate within the confines of our present legal and cultural definitions of judicious handling of the bereaved with a "let the buyer beware" attitude, nor can he cover all his obligations by the instrumentality of a simple contract.

Multiplication of Associations: During the 19th century the associational impulse found concrete expression in the founding of a number of Municipal and State Associations, and one National Association, the NFDA. During the 20th century this impulse to organize along occupational lines continued among funeral directors, as is evidenced by the fact of the further development of local and state associations, and by the appearance of several new national organizations. A brief outline of the members of this latter group follows.[32]

The National Selected Morticians, a limited membership organization, was formed on September 7, 1917, at the time when this country was heavily engaged in World War I. The founder was Beryl L. Boyer of Toledo, Ohio, who with eight other prominent funeral directors sought to organize an association the size of which would be limited and whose effectiveness would not be handicapped by local prejudice and by the inertia due to what they considered the inevitability of misunderstanding among groups including a large number of individuals. In the words of Wilber Krieger, longtime managing director of the organization:

These nine men were all Rotarians and they looked upon the non-competitive principle of Rotary International as something highly desirable. They felt that if they could achieve a Rotary Club of funeral directors—that is—with no competitors present, they could talk very freely about their problems and give each other the benefits of their ideas, methods, procedures, et cetera. It was with that thought in mind that the organization was formed.

George M. Olinger of Denver, Colorado, was the first president, serving in that capacity during the first three years of the organization's life.

As members were added from most of the principal cities of the United States, along with several firms from Canada, England, France and the Hawaiian Islands, the NSM grew in size. While the principle of restricting membership to one firm for each city or town was adhered to, with the later reservation that a second firm might be enrolled from a community provided such enrollment was sponsored by the member firm in that community, yet after two decades of organizational life, the small group of morticians who could freely talk over their problems together has developed into a substantial association, with all the organizational machinery of a well-instituted interest group, and with a complement of officers, committees, rules, regulations, usages and some sense of tradition.

As stated in the constitution and accepted by the membership, the purposes of the NSM were and are:

1. To ascertain and study the general principles governing the business and profession of the funeral director, and to promote their proper application.
2. To work toward higher standards, clearer ideals, a spirit of service, improved methods and organization and equipment, with an increasing satisfactory relation with patrons, manufacturers and the public generally, not only among its members but among all funeral directors.

Starting in 1923 the cost of membership was $100.00 and dues were $150.00 a year. An interesting by-law of the Association stipulated that representation in at least alternate national conventions and in at least alternate district group meetings was mandatory. By 1935 membership was held by about 325 firms.

Some indication of the developing and changing values of the NSM is given by the mere listing of the various special committees set up within it: "A Service Book Committee"; "A National Advertising Committee"; "A Conference Committee"; "A Bonded Extension Service Committee"; and "A Special Fact Finding Committee on the Model Mortuary."

By 1954, membership in the NSM had grown to about 500 firms, with a substantial number of probational members in addition, and annual dues had been increased to $300.00. Part of what seems the high cost of membership in NSM is accounted for by the services and advisement given directly to the members on matters of business management. In fact, it would probably be a fair statement that the NSM in the course of its existence has tended to develop a rather thorough going business conception of funeral directing operations. The relationship of mortician to client is basically seen as one of buyer and seller, scarcely different from that of merchant and customer, except that a few more intangibles are involved. Reduction of these intangibles to a minimum, through the use of cost-accounting procedures, is intrinsically a part of this point of view.

A rather recent development toward the realization of the goal to "study the general principles governing the business and profession of the funeral director" has been the establishment in 1945 of the National Foundation of Funeral Service, a tax-exempt institution, educational in nature, at Evanston, Illinois. Although the idea of a "Mortuary Institute" had been proposed as early as 1932, it was not until 1945 that the trust was officially recognized and qualified with the United States Treasury Department. Past NSM President George W. Olinger was the founder, and objectives for the Foundation were:

1. The establishment of a library wherein would be collected written and printed material relating to funeral service.

2. The creation of a model preparation room, and a model display room for funeral merchandise, wherein would be tested and shown the current arrangement, decoration, equipment, merchandise, etc., pertinent to each, for the edification of all who cared to come and see.

3. The establishment and maintenance of a School of Management, essentially a school of business administration geared to the specific needs of funeral service.

4. To make all these facilities available to members of the profession, students, writers, teachers, public officials, and responsible members of the general public interested in the elevation of the educational standards for the field.

5. To advance the education of the profession in higher professional and business standards as quoted from the Trust Agreement.

Thus far, the core of the Foundation's educational program has consisted of "Basic Courses" offered annually in two Summer Sessions of the School of Management. These courses are devoted exclusively to management policies, problems, and procedures in funeral service firms. The curriculum of these Basic Courses includes such subjects as Accounting, Advertising, Business English, Casket Materials and Construction, Credit and Collection, Funeral Insurance, Insurance, Legal Aspects of Funeral Service, Management, Merchandising, Personnel Management, Psychology in Funeral Service, Public Relations, and Public Speaking.

Additional short courses consisting of one week of intensive lectures, were added to the Foundation's educational program in 1952. Each of these deals with one specific subject, such as Public Relations, Sales Techniques, and the like. The Foundation has broadened the base of its program to become inclusive of other than NSM members.

Although the National Negro Funeral Directors Association was incorporated in the State of Illinois, June 30, 1938, its beginning dates back to 1925 when it was organized under the name of the Independent National Negro Funeral Directors Association. A few years later the name was changed to The Progressive Funeral Directors Association; and in 1938 the present name was adopted.

The NNFDA has expanded and constantly grown in membership, until it now includes twenty-four states and the Virgin Islands, divided into eight regions presided over by District Governors and a Board of Governors. The officials of the Association are composed of a President, who is limited to a term of two years, a Board of Directors, and a General Secretary.

The organization has set as its goal the full participation, representation and integration of its members in every phase of the burial profession, including local, state and national governmental departments regulating the profession. Currently five of its members serve on embalmers' boards in Maryland, the District of Columbia, California and Ohio.

The Association has championed higher education for its members, and has constantly supported legislation for raising the scholastic requirements for admission to embalming schools. Additionally, in an effort to encourage its members to give the public the highest type of service and maintain the dignity and integrity of the profession, it has adopted a code of ethics. The organization also has a National Women's Auxiliary, encourages mortuary fraternities, and holds clinics throughout the year for its members. The first president of the National Association was G. William Saffell of Kentucky.

The Jewish Funeral Directors of America, Inc., was chartered in October 1928 under the laws of the State of Illinois, and thus became the latest Funeral Association on the national scene. In 1928 through the accidental meeting of a small group of Jewish funeral directors at the National Funeral Directors convention in Kansas City, the Association came into being. This group was comprised of Herbert I. Berger of St. Louis, Bernard Dansansky of Washington, Charles Blauman, Harry Heiberg and Benjamin Weil of New York, Max Sugarman of Providence and Sam Piser of Chicago.

These men were struck with the idea that a national organization in the Jewish funeral field was necessary and important, and acting upon this idea during a transfer stopover in Chicago on the way back from the convention, they contacted Charles Kaye, Sam Piser's son-in-law, who was practicing law at the time, to implement that decision. The first officers were Herbert Berger, President; Bernard Dansansky and Max Sugarman, Vice Presidents; Sam Piser, Treasurer; and Charles Blauman, Secretary. The group immediately set about to recruit membership, and to work toward the realization of the purposes of the Association, i.e., to secure harmony in the profession among Jewish funeral directors; to cultivate a friendly professional spirit; to elevate the practice of the profession; to disseminate correct principles of business and ethical conduct; and to protect the interests of the membership.

For ten years the JFDA meetings followed the NFDA conventions. In 1938 it deemed itself numerically strong enough to support its own convention at a different time and place than the National. This practice has since been followed. The membership today consists of 150 Jewish firms. This represents 99.4% of all the Jewish funeral directors in America operating their own establishments, and extends from Montreal, Canada, to Los Angeles, California, and from St. Paul, Minnesota, to New Orleans, Louisiana.

Portions of this history dealing with developments from about 1880 on refer many times to the National Funeral Directors Association. This is necessary because this Association was a determining factor in many of the late 19th century and early 20th century developments. It remains to bring the picture up to date with a brief sketch of the Association in its most recent operations.

NFDA has grown from an association of 7,908 in 1935 to a membership of 12,552 in 1955. It is an affiliation of State Associations consisting of all state groups and the District of Columbia with the exception of New Jersey. The primary service of the National Association is to its affiliated groups. A bulletin service is provided, keeping State Association officers informed of important national developments. Legislative assistance is available. In recent years all state groups have been provided with a *reference guide to state licensing laws, information on burial allowances of the armed forces and the Veterans' Administration with a supplement on death claims under government insurance* and a *digest of the rules and regulations of the various states in the care and transportation of deceased human remains.* All of these are kept current by a loose-leaf method. The digest on transportation rules was prepared by NFDA in cooperation with the United States Air Force.

For years funeral directors and their Associations have interested themselves in public relations. In 1947 NFDA decided to ascertain the public's attitude toward funeral directors and funeral service and they retained Stewart Dougall and Associates of New York City to conduct a public opinion survey. A comprehensive report of the findings was given at the 1948 NFDA Convention in Detroit and later published in book form.

In addition to the program involving this survey, NFDA has made available to its affiliated associations and members a file of material on funeral service which is used as a basis for talks on the funeral profession before service, civic, church and other groups. The first film produced by an association to tell the story of funeral service is the Association's "Funeral Service—A Part of the American Way." For funeral directors who wish to give out material on funeral service, it has made

available a public relations brochure, "Spea.
and the Association of Better Business Bureau's .
Every Family Should Know About Funerals and .

In 1951 and again in 1952 NFDA retained Ernst a
a national firm of certified public accountants, to   -y
its membership to ascertain for management purposes certain
funeral home operating ratios and arranged for the findings
of both these surveys to be published.

NFDA has also sought to represent funeral directors to the
federal government. During the time of the National Recovery Administration, World War II and the Korean War, it
was especially effective as the field's leading representative.
The Association maintains constant liaison with all agencies of
government interested in funeral service operations as such.

The Association conducts a convention annually which has
an average attendance of close to 4,000. Following the pattern
laid down at the first meeting of the Association in 1882, an
exhibit of funeral merchandise is staged in conjunction with
the annual meeting. An average of 100 manufacturers and
suppliers of funeral merchandise and services display their
wares at each exhibit. The Association publishes the proceedings of each convention as well as an annual roster of members. It also has a monthly publication, *The Director*.

Of the several attempts made in the present century to
develop more sound and workable business relations between
funeral directors and casket manufacturers, and among funeral
directors themselves, the movement to introduce cost accounting into the funeral service field deserves paramount
attention. Although the need to know such an elemental
fact as the funeral director's business cost has been recognized by many funeral directors it was sharply underscored
at the Public Relations Conference called by the Casket Man-

ufacturers' Association in May 1923. Here it was discovered that without this datum it was impossible to organize an intelligent discussion of the business relations of the funeral directors and the manufacturers. Subsequently, in 1925, the NFDA and NSM jointly sponsored a uniform cost-accounting study. Although participation was less than expected, records were secured from a sufficient number of funeral directors from different sections of the country to indicate that most of them were operating without any certainty as to the soundness, from the business standpoint, of their practice.

The lessons of cost accounting were apparently so imperative to several of the officers and leaders of both the major associations that they were willing to put this subject above all other associational considerations. When their own enthusiasm failed to elicit the desired response they formed on October 8, 1927, the Funeral Service Bureau of America. Leaders in the new organization included Leroy C. Dunn, Des Moines; Charles R. Fiss, Oshkosh; George Olinger, Denver; Walter P. Quist, Minneapolis; Harry G. Samson, Pittsburg; Ferd P. Schoedinger, Columbus; Joseph N. Sletten, Chicago; and Colby E. Smith, Dallas. Although the new group was independent of both NSM and NFDA some of the groundwork had been laid in the latter organization's Cost Accounting Committee which had been in existence for several years previous to 1927.

Although the aims of the Funeral Service Bureau ranged widely it can be fairly stated that the basic purpose was to promote the study and use of cost accounting methods to foster the business interests of its members and to help dispel the aura of mystery that was felt to exist in the public mind regarding the business of funeral directing.

Seventy-six representatives of the better established funeral homes formed the nucleus of the organization. This number was broadened later to include nearly two hundred members. Ample funds were pledged to support the organization and insure the prosecution of its major aims. Not only were cost accounting procedures introduced to these members but actual observation over periods ranging up to a year were included by the agency which formulated them. Additionally, advertising problems were studied, and the organization also submitted to the Federal Trade Commission for its consideration the elements of a standard funeral service.

After a period of several years of rather intense activity these organizational projects tapered off, and little is heard of the activities of the Bureau during the early years of the depression. However the principle of cost accounting was given impetus through the work of the organization, and cost accounting remained to become an established practice in many, if not most, of the better run funeral homes.

A brief renaissance of the fortunes of the Bureau took place in 1933 when it joined with other groups representing the funeral service field and with federal officials to work out a Code for funeral directors in conjunction with the National Recovery Act which had been put into operation the previous year. At this time the Bureau, NFDA, NSM, and other associational representatives worked together, and although not always in complete accord, set up a Code Authority comprised of a committee representing twelve major geographical regions, with three at-large members. This group managed to work out a Code for the field, but the brief life of the NRA gave funeral directors only a short period in which a widely scattered field of practitioners could be brought under a specific code of operations. Two important results may be noted. First, in light of the deference shown by federal officials to the Funeral Service Bureau for its claims to have a vast body of information and data on the activities of funeral directors everywhere, it became clear that associations which claimed to be representative of the field, or a segment thereof, would henceforth have to build up bodies of reliable knowledge concerning the actual practices of their members. Secondly, in a figurative sense, notice was served on the field that funeral directors could no longer remain aloof of all that transpired outside the province of their immediate scope of operations—in other words, that occupational organization had become a necessity for all who wished to practice their vocation.

Shortly after the demise of the NRA the Funeral Service Bureau slipped out of public notice and by 1935 it had passed out of existence. Much of the data that were gathered and the experiences gained by its members were passed on to the major associations in the funeral service and allied fields. Some of these materials went to the NFDA, but the lion's share was passed on to the NSM and to the Casket Manufacturers' Association.

Economic Growth and Development:[33] From 1850 on, innovations in the manufacture of coffins, burial cases, and caskets, the spread of embalming as a sanitary and preservative measure, the rise of associations, and the changing popular taste in funerals, all combined to mark the great social and economic developments in funeral service in the 19th century. The task remains to point out some of the changing economics of modern funeral service—seen as a process of development in which the *organization* of economic relations has become something more than a promise, but less than a complete reality.

So closely are funeral directors and manufacturers of morticians' goods related in the total complex of funeral service that the economic features of one group can hardly be discussed without describing in the same breath the like features of the other. In this respect it has already been pointed out above that one of the first concerns of the associations of funeral directors was with the casket manufacturers, and until the passage of the Sherman Anti-Trust Act in 1890, vain efforts were made by the two groups to protect each others' business interests through compacts in restraint of trade. In 1899 there were 189 manufacturers of morticians' goods, emphasizing casket manufacture, of sufficient size to fall outside the United States Census designation "hand shop." The latter, and there were hundreds of them, consisted of small shops in which coffins and caskets were occasionally made by craftsmen, usually along with cabinet-making, furniture-making, rough carpentry, and the like.

By 1925 the total figure for both small and large scale manufacturers, again excluding "handshops," had risen to 326, and by 1947 to 568. The total volume of business of these establishments had increased likewise from a little better than 12 million dollars in 1889 to almost 190 million dollars in 1947. With this almost sixteen-fold increase of dollar volume there was for the most part little increase in the size of these industries, as the average number of employees per establishment grew only slightly during this period, from about 30 in 1889, to just under 40 in 1947, with less than one-fifth of all establishments having more than fifty workers each that year. Although there are currently a handful of casket manufacturing establishments which contain a work force of several hundred employees, and the National Casket Company with its 2,000 employed in thirty-three sales branches and factories constitutes the "giant" corporation in the field of the manufacture of morticians' goods, these concerns still account for only approximately 10 per cent of the market.[34] As the increase in value of the products manufactured has soared, so has the average wholesale cost of funerals. To the funeral director of 1889 the wholesale cost of his casket was about $10.00. By 1925 it had increased to almost $52.00, by 1947 to nearly $131.00. These bare facts serve only to indicate the rapid expansion of the morticians' goods industry and the increasing wholesale cost of funeral merchandise to the funeral director. Despite the depreciation of the dollar, the funeral director in the late 1940's still paid at least five times as much for his caskets as did the undertaker of the eighteen eighties.

Behind the scenes, the relationship of the manufacturers to the funeral directors through the early part of the current century continued to be unsettled and unorganized. In 1920 the wholesale mortuary and merchandising business involved five central elements: large manufacturers; small manufacturers; large-scale funeral directors; small-scale funeral directors; and, finally, travelling salesmen and jobbers. Jobbers represented many types of business: some manufactured certain products and jobbed others; some jobbed only one line; others jobbed several; some salesmen sold practically anything, and then shopped for it, and thus in a sense became a jobber as well. The circumstances of casket manufacture were such that small concerns could vary standards of quality, workmanship, materials, etc., to the extent that it was possible for them to cut wholesale prices and undersell the larger establishments whose products had long since been standardized in quality as well as price. Those funeral directors who operated, or tried to operate, on a large-scale basis, would often try "price pressure" tactics on casket salesmen, attempting to get special discounts for large orders. Salesmen of quality line products were often distressed by what they considered a misplaced emphasis on the price, as over against the quality of the merchandise. As a result, old-line casket accounts were lost when salesmen refused to cut prices, and smaller manufacturers found that by offering special and unscheduled discounts it was possible to capture new orders at the expense of the larger concerns. Volume buying funeral directors were not above entering the casket manufacturing field themselves, thus increasing the total number of establishments in an already crowded field.

In retaliation for competition in the form of funeral director-encouraged, or funeral director-operated small-scale casket manufacture, the larger and better established houses encouraged new talent to enter the field of funeral service and made introduction easy by setting up show rooms (display rooms to which the funeral director could take his client for purposes of casket selection, the price to be set by the funeral director), by the cheap rental of equipment, and through the use of quite liberal credit. During the twenties it was not uncommon for a casket house to have over a quarter of its assets tied up in accounts receivable from its funeral director customers.

Casket manufacturers were also in the habit of extending long term credit to competing funeral directors. For those who paid promptly this worked a hardship as it was their money which permitted the manufacturers to build working funds upon which to base such credit operations. On the other hand, manufacturers who were extending the normal trade discounts had a proper complaint against funeral directors who were paying in advance and financing competitive manufacturing concerns.

Still another intrusive factor, that of increasingly rapid style changes in caskets, made itself felt through the first quarter of the century. A funeral director who would buy a hundred caskets in 1910, would hesitate to stock a quarter that many ten years later, and five years later might consider ten caskets in any one style a precarious inventory. As the factor of taste in caskets gained strength, the manufacturers found the battleground of competition for style acceptance had widened its lines. The impulse to standardize a product for large scale distribution conflicted with consumer desires for a variety in styles. Often the funeral director would seek some kind of individual expression, demanding certain markings or refinements on all the caskets which he purchased. The upshot was opportunity for other, often quite small manufacturers, to enter into and remain in competition.

The overall effect of these activities and changing social and economic conditions was to increase the number of funeral directors, and indirectly, to make for an expansion in numbers of small casket manufacturing concerns. Competition had long since gone beyond the point where it functioned to distribute the best product for the least money, and the operation of the business cycle was reflected by a highly fluctuating number of such establishments in good times and bad. Nevertheless, the wholesale cost of funerals over the years continued to increase.

Funeral directors likewise continued to increase in number. Although the findings of the United States Census of Business and of the Department of Commerce tend to show a smaller total number of funeral directors than are known to be actually engaged in the profession, they may be used judiciously in connection with those reported in the Proceedings of the Annual Meetings of the NFDA. In round numbers, it was likely that the average number of funerals per year in 1888 for each funeral director was about 94 or 95. By 1900 it had fallen to 84; and by 1930 a low of about 48 deaths per funeral director was reached. Whatever the total cost of the depression of the 1930's, one of its effects was to squeeze out a number of funeral directors. Thus by 1940 some 23,000 established funeral directors averaged almost 62 funerals per year. The 1949 Census of the NFDA showed funeral homes just under the 24,000 mark, and deaths per established funeral director dropped to about 57 for that year. In 1955 this average will have increased to about 60.

One of the basic socio-biologic facts of the last 60 years has been the relatively constant number of deaths occurring annually in the United States in consequence of declining death rates, especially among infants. In the first 50 years of the century the total number of deaths per year has been increased by less than one hundred thousand, a little over seven per cent, although the population increased nearly 100 per cent in the same period. In light of the increase in funeral directors and embalmers, the sharp rise in wholesale costs of morticians' goods, and the very small increase in number of deaths per year, the result could only be increased competition among funeral directors, and increased costs of funeral service.

These bald facts need to be qualified somewhat because they tend to oversimplify a highly complex matter. The business of burying the dead is affected by other considerations, many of them not specifically economic, but social and cultural. One of the latter has been the tremendous increase in the purchase of insurance by the American public, with the consequence that all but the most destitute have ample funds with which to defray burial expenses (other sources of monies likely to be spent for funerals will be mentioned in the next chapter). Secondly, the general upgrading of consumer demands—for furniture, automobiles, housing, dress, and the like—has carried with it to some degree a demand for more expensive funerals. Thirdly, with the aging of the population and consequently a vastly increased number of deaths occurring at the higher age brackets, there are fewer deaths among infants, children, and young adults just getting established. Therefore, the amount spent per funeral has risen. Last, and perhaps most subtly pervasive, has been the drift in American culture toward putting the subject of death somewhat outside the reality of everyday life, where it was found in Colonial times, but at the same time rejecting the 19th century pattern of gloom that surrounded funerals in that period. The new "aesthetic" of death, which may have had its first expression in the desire to place the dead in a form of burial receptacle more pleasant than the crude coffin, has today reached its culmination in the popular demand for funeral homes, once rather plain, functional, and gloomy, but now beautiful and well appointed edifices with nothing or very little to suggest the funeral about them. Modern housing has been another factor making for the modern funeral home. It is the essence of modern funeral service to put the burial of the dead in a context of things pleasant and beautiful, and to consider the comfort of the bereaved. Whatever the motivations involved, the popular demand has been for such a mode of burial, and this in turn has meant more expensive merchandise and increased skills in the handling of individuals facing an emotional crisis.

In charting the growth and organization of the business enterprise end of funeral service certain divisions of the field need to be described. At the close of the last century funeral service establishments already showed several variations. In the rural and thinly populated areas many storekeepers sold funeral merchandise along with other goods—furniture especially—and, if necessary in rudimentary fashion helped to conduct funerals. His base of operations was a store, and coffins and cradles might well be displayed, side by side. Although in 1900 this type, later known as the "combination establishment," still predominated, by 1950, only one-fifth of all establishments were of this kind.

A different sort of part-time operator was the "curb-stone" undertaker of the large cities. Armed with very little capital investment, renting all his equipment and funeral paraphernalia, including hearse, or funeral coach, chapel, or "parlor," and possibly engaging a trade embalmer to prepare the body, this type would occasionally pick up a funeral—with several months often passing between cases. Between 1900 and 1935 "curb-stone" operators flourished in great numbers, especially in the big cities of the East, where they constituted—and still do to a lesser extent—some competition for the more conventional and established practitioners.

By 1900, rolling stock was the distinguishing mark of the well established undertaker. A parlor gave certain distinction to an individual or firm. It was generally a large room or chapel in connection with or proximity to the stable. With the transition from horse drawn to automotive equipment, the emphasis on rolling stock was partially removed, and a place of business or a telephone was enough to establish oneself. The need for a funeral home from which to operate has been a big deterrent to these "curb-stone" operators, however, except in territories where they can rent quarters for funerals.

Established practitioners, for the most part, were the independently operating funeral directors with their funeral "homes." Quite often they established partnerships, since the twenty-four hour a day schedule that came to feature the operation of the funeral home demanded competent personnel at hand at all times. The partnership in this respect seemed a form of organization well fitted to meet the special contingencies of the occupation.

The most recent development in the business organization of funeral service is the corporate form of mortuary establishment. Although few in number at the turn of the century, between World Wars I and II there was a large increase in the number of corporations. Since that time there has been little change.

By 1939 there were 2,247 corporations, or about 12 per cent of the total 18,196 mortuary establishments listed by the United States Bureau of the Census: *Census of Business.* Partnerships accounted for 3,524, or about 19 per cent, but the lion's share, 12,338 or nearly 68 per cent, were of individual proprietorships. Assuming the underenumeration of the Bureau of the Census to be consistent in the second *Census of Business*, for 1948, it appears that there was little significant change in either the number, the distribution of establishments in any one group, or of total receipts—with the exception that partnerships gained very slightly at the expense of the other two types of organization.

It is doubtful if the statistics of mortuary business operations for the two years, 1939 and 1948 can be construed to indicate a trend of any magnitude, or to show anything more than chance variations. On the contrary, in small measure, they do seem to support the contention that one of possibly several stabilizing influences is currently operative in modern funeral service business enterprise. This point will be touched upon again later.

Integration and Stabilization: We turn finally to an assessment of the factors and forces within the field of funeral directing for evidences of an integration of the actions and ideas of the various classes of men who make up the vocation. Some of the developments along this line have already been mentioned or alluded to, such as the tapering off of the number of funeral service establishments and the relative constancy of funeral service personnel in the past several decades. Although the historical lesson in regard to the number of persons engaged in embalming and funeral service teaches that the operations of the business cycle has *traditionally* accounted for the waxing and waning of this number, there are developments to be taken into account currently that have come about as a result of new factors, some because of the economics of modern funeral service, and some as a result of the deliberate actions of a majority of funeral directors and the agencies which represent them.

A completely unsettled occupation, in which the members have no assurance of what is coming next in their business operations or in their public relations, is hard to visualize. Such however may be the story of occupations which appear quickly and grow rapidly. To some extent this was the condition of undertaking in the last half of the 19th century; and the history of the occupation from then to the present day has been largely one of the attempt to put *order* and continuity into the actions of those within the field of funeral directing, and between them and other related areas of the general mortuary business—such as the casket manufacturers, baggagemen, public health officials and agencies, and the like.

The stabilization of the number of practitioners in any field where there is a limited demand for services is a *sine qua non* of any occupation. To entrust the problem of achieving such stabilization simply to the operations of competition and the fluctuation of the business cycle has apparently not sufficed for the funeral directors of the past seventy-five years. It should be noted that there are proportionately less business failures among funeral directors than among many other types of businesses, even those with expanding markets.

Licensing legislation, as noted before, has had the effect of setting up standards of competence and performance, as necessary to the public health and welfare of the community as to the funeral directing profession itself. Yet at the same time, licensing boards, consisting of mostly, and in some specific cases, all funeral directors, have become agencies for the control of the personnel in the field, and thus have exercised some small influence in the restriction of competition for the market. It should be recognized that both public *and* private interests are represented and realized by governmental restriction through State Boards.

Entrance to the vocation of funeral directing and embalming is controlled by state boards in all states; matters of reciprocity, renewal and assignability of license and other items pertaining to the circumstances of practicing these vocations likewise are almost universally covered in state licensing acts. The burden of this legislation goes beyond the stipulation of requirements for licensure; a somewhat ill-formed, but nevertheless recognizable image of the practitioner and the service he performs orients this legislation: the image of the funeral home, serving the community, "home operated" by a small number of skilled practitioners who dedicate all their vocational efforts to this task on a full-time basis. What the licensing legislation in a general way seeks to avoid or deter is the growth of funeral directing into big business mortuaries, vast chains of branch mortuaries, corporation operated, and staffed with paid functionaries. Although imperfectly realized, perhaps, by the lawmakers themselves and the funeral directors who have pressed for such legislation, there is, it seems, implicit a recognition of the need to keep the care of the dead from becoming perfunctory, impersonal, commercial, and from being brought into the workings of highly bureaucratized business organization.

Most states license a funeral director and embalmer, or issue separate licenses for each task, on the basis of knowledge and competence. Manifestly, such licenses cannot be assigned nor transferred, and while there is no valid reason why a funeral director or an embalmer cannot properly conduct his work from more than one location, because deaths are essentially the basis for emergency service, it must be clear that to render service at widely separated or distant points becomes a practical difficulty. In order to avoid all kinds of complications, many state boards have ruled that there must be a licensed funeral director for each establishment. While such rule does not prohibit an interchange of personnel, it does provide a minimum and fairly reasonable requirement. On the other hand, some western states issue a license for a licensee to engage in business only at a certain location. In some states, mostly in the far west, licensing laws tend to operate to discourage the small, part time operator.

A majority of the state licensure laws specify the physical equipment of the mortuary, with minimum requirements, such as a sanitary preparation room and the necessary instruments; a few require a display room; at least one hearse or funeral coach; and, often, a funeral chapel. The shoe-string operator of a half century or less ago thus finds himself prohibited by state law from handling funerals without a well-equipped funeral home. Likewise, display rooms in mortuaries have had the effect of limiting the number of manufacturers' display rooms—a reinforcing factor in the reducing of marginal and uneconomic funeral homes. It should be noted that such requirements for complete physical equipment apply to a minority of states and these mostly on the west coast. Any attempt to pass such legislation in the past in most of the eastern states could have legislated a large percentage of firms out of business. Because most firms are now of their own volition obtaining such equipment, this type of legislation may not be necessary.

Funeral directors, as well as most persons in occupations directly serving human beings, through their associations have developed or sought to develop a set of inner controls, or moral restraints, by creating codes, credos, and pledges to each other and to the public they serve. While these may often serve as goals or ideals of conduct, their appearance marks the recognition by those who have created them that their conduct must be subject to something other than simple, concrete rules of practice. In the funeral home the framed Code of Ethics complements the publicly displayed license to practice. Each deals with a form of control over vocational behavior, and while no absolute guarantee of orderly, ethical, competent, and professional behavior attaches to the display of these symbols, by their presence they nevertheless express a form of occupational and quasi-public consensus concerning the need for and value of *organization* in the field of funeral directing.

CITATIONS AND REFERENCES FOR CHAPTER XII

1. The authors are indebted to Mrs. Helene Carpenter Craig for putting unpublished materials dealing with early mortuary education at their disposal.

2. "Influence Back of Mortuary Education," by Charles O. Dhonau, unpublished document written specifically at the authors' request.

3. *Ibid.*

4. Advertised in the trade journals of the period.

5. Communication from John H. Eckels to Miss Elizabeth Foster, Office of NFDA, February 17, 1944.

6. Habenstein, "The American Funeral Director," *op. cit.*, pp. 134 ff.

7. For more details of the mechanics and operations of this Conference, consult the *Proceedings*, NFDA, 1904, ff.; also revealing is the correspondence of J. H. McCully, 1904-1917, copies of which are found in the archives of the NFDA in Milwaukee, Wisconsin, and in the records of the Conference of Funeral Service Examining Boards, Naperville, Illinois.

8. Dhonau, *op. cit.*

9. *Ibid.*

10. *Proceedings*, NFDA, 1904, *op. cit.*, pp. 60-61.

11. *Ibid.*

12. *Proceedings,* NFDA, 1924, *op. cit.,* p. 60.

13. *Ibid.,* p. 74.

14. *Proceedings,* NFDA, 1932, *op. cit.,* p. 147.

15. See the scattered reports of the Director of the Institute for Mortuary Research in the *Proceedings* of the NFDA, 1930-1939.

16. *Proceedings,* NFDA, 1933, p. 55.

17. *Proceedings,* NFDA, 1947, p. 33.

18. The authors are indebted to the Honorable James R. Clark, attorney, for his considerable help in preparing this section on development of mortuary law as it affects funeral directing.

19. Jackson, *The Law of Cadavers, op. cit.,* pp. lxxv-lxxvii.

20. Thomas F. H. Stueve, *Mortuary Law* (Cincinnati, Ohio: The Cincinnati College of Embalming). See "Table of Cases."

21. Prata Undertaking Co., vs. State Board of Embalming and Funeral Directing, 182 Atl. 808; Nugent Funeral Home Inc. vs. Beamish, 173 Atl. 177; People vs. Ringe, 197 N. Y. 143; Keller vs. State, 90 Atl. 603.

22. Wyeth vs. Board of Health, 200 Mass. 474; People vs. Ringe, Supra; State ex rel Kemplinger vs. Whyte, 188 N. W. 607.

23. State Board of Funeral Directors and Embalmers vs. Cooksey, 147 Fla. 337.

24. Gadbury vs. Bleitz, 133 Wash. 134.

25. Mass. 1932 Ch. 272, Sec. 42; N. Y. Penal Code, Sec. 2220; Okla Tit, 21, Sec. 1166; S. D. Sec. 13.1421; Wash. Sec. 2492.

26. Jackson, *The Law of Cadavers, op. cit.,* p. 462.

27. Grothmann vs. Herman, 241 SW 461; Greenberf Bond Co. vs. Yarbrough, 106 SE 642.

28. Pritz vs. Messer, 112 O.S. 628; Euclid vs. Ambler Realty Co., 272 U.S. 365.

29. Jordan vs. Wesmith, 269 Pac. 1096; Meldahl vs. Halberg 214 N.W. 902.

30. White vs. Luquire, 129 Southern 84; Leland vs. Turner, 230 Pac. 1061.

31. Ohio Revised Code Sec. 1317.12.

32. The authors acknowledge their debt to the representatives of the several associations for aid in gathering materials on this section: Wilber M. Krieger, National Selected Morticians; Howard C. Raether, National Funeral Directors Association; Ira Kaufman, Jewish Funeral Directors of America; and Robert H. Miller, National Negro Funeral Directors of America.

33. Statistical materials taken from the U. S. Bureau of the Census, *Census of Manufacturers: 1947;* U. S. Bureau of Census, *Census of Business, 1948;* Gebhart, *op. cit.,* Chapters IX-X; Habenstein, "The American Funeral Director," *op. cit.*

34. J. Richard Elliott, "The Funeral Business," *Barron's,* April 11, 1955, p. 6.

The Panorama of Modern Funeral Practice

Even to a most superficial observer, provided only that he has lived through the years concerned, it must be apparent that during the last half century significant changes have taken place in the American mode of life. To be noted among these changes are a general rise of the standard of living; a progressively increasing exodus from rural to metropolitan areas with a resultant urbanization of a much larger segment of the population; an increasing mobility of people within the country; growing centralization of government with the role of government constantly expanding into the lives of people; the decline of illiteracy and the rise in general education; the penetration of the machine age not only into the work by which people earn their livelihood but into the home and other areas of ordinary living; certain changes in family life; and, less tangible but no less real, certain changing patterns of thought concerning human relationships, among them the meaning of death. In the light of these and other changes, we may well stop at the mid-20th century to ask what, if any, changes have taken place in American burial beliefs and practices.

In the sections that follow, two complementary lenses will be used to focus on the modern panorama: first, the funeral patterns of modern America; and, second the work patterns common to the majority of American funeral directors today. In dealing with the former, the funeral patterns, wherever it is expedient to do so, comparison will be made with American funeral practices as described in Chapter 10; in dealing with the latter, the practices of funeral directors, contrast will be sought with former occupational usages.

THE FUNERAL PATTERN IN MODERN AMERICA

Responses to Death: In any society death stops the orderly processes of daily life and necessitates the remending of broken personal and social attachments. Societies differ, however, as to the way their members act in bereavement and the manner in which they dispose of their dead. Historically, that is, through a considerable period of time, the pattern of mortuary behavior in any society is subject to change, although basic death beliefs remain fundamentally unchanged. It bears repeating that the roots of American funeral behavior extend back in a direct line several thousand years to early Judaeo-Christian beliefs as to the nature of God, man, and the hereafter, and that, in turn, these beliefs and the practices were influenced to some extent by even older beliefs and practices. Despite the antiquity of these roots their importance as regards the treatment of the dead in the world that commonly calls itself Christian today cannot be overemphasized.

It would be difficult, too, to prove that in America the reverence for the dead, the conception that decent and respectful treatment, and proper disposal of the remains, have changed appreciably in the course of the seventy-five years elapsing between 1880, a period described in Chapter 10, and 1955. So far as basic death and funeral beliefs are concerned there is little that could be used for a "then and now" comparison.

Yet no one can doubt that American funeral beliefs have undergone some change, and, in the light of the anthropologists conception of culture, broadly conceived, as "man's way of meeting stressful situations, including the inevitable problems of procreation, hunger, shelter, and death,"[1] it might be profitable to examine the changing mortuary customs and usages as they reflect a portion of the culture of American society. Our quest then is for varying death customs and for the changing social conditions which accompany them, rather than a search for marked shifts in the very foundations of our funeral beliefs.

Two of the more significant social conditions, or social processes important in this connection, are the growth of an urban mass society, and the changing form and functions of the American family.

With industrial progress and business expansion has come the growth of cities, and the concentration of the American people in urban centers. Of the host of social consequences which have followed, one of the more important, especially from the standpoint of this study, has been the decline of communal or "folk" ways of living. Students of modern society have noted the manner in which groups of people held together by ties of blood, religion and ethnic background have become dispersed and scattered throughout cities and across the country. Although these groups still hold together with sufficient strength to keep many customs intact, and still demand and support their own institutions—including funeral service—the broader picture is one of a weakening of the influence of traditional community ties, and the appearance of *masses* of individuals, more aware of their individuality, self interests, and more responsive to the inducements of fashion, popular taste, and the currents of popular opinion.

A closely related development, the changing form and functions of the American family, has held the attention of many social scientists, officers of governmental agencies, religious leaders, and others. As the economic, protective, recreational, religious worship, and formal educational functions formerly fulfilled by the family have tended to be given over to outside institutional agencies, the family has become a unity of persons thrown together in more intimate association, with a higher degree of personal involvement and an intensification of emotional relationships. Because of smaller family size, problems and crises which produce stress on individuals tend to be distributed among proportionately fewer family members, much more so than was the case in the 19th century, when families were larger, and the sense of family ties extended to more distant relatives who still closely involved themselves in the affairs of any family.

In a family circle today, death produces precisely the kind of crisis with which few members are *completely* ready and able to cope. Aside from the shock of overwhelming loss, even among those who have expected the death, and the confusion which is magnified by the natural upsurge of grief, complicating questions develop to which the average person does not have certain and ready answers. How does one deal appropriately with an object both profane and sacred, the body? In what forms do the bereaved acceptably express mourning? What legal regulations bear on the subject of burial? These only sample a multitude of questions and problems that confront men and women at a time when their emotional condition lowers their capacity for deliberate thinking. And even without such disturbed conditions, there is a whole area of professional information and skill which in a society operating with a high division of labor and resultant specialization of competence, has been assigned to the funeral director.

Contrariwise in 1880, and particularly in less advanced rural areas, there were yet customary modes of response to death which, although perhaps not too well attuned to the tenor of the times, were generally well enough known to the bereaved to enable them, if they so desired, to see themselves through the trying situation produced by death. And there were clearly enough defined roles so that not only family members, but other relatives and often many persons in the community might be able to participate usefully in the care of the dead.

As noted above, in 1880 the role of the undertaker in rural areas was minimal. In the cities his work revolved around the deceased's home, the church of his choice and the cemetery. His assumption of the *direction* of funeral proceedings was as yet a new role, somewhat imperfectly if not less sincerely conceived, perhaps, and certainly not as important or as central to funeral matters as it is today.

In addition, then, to natural confusion and disorientation to death, Americans today, except for those who have experienced a recent death in their family or who have arranged the details of a funeral service, are somewhat at a loss for knowledge of what is appropriate behavior toward the dead. From one's religious and cultural background he may draw important cues as to what should be done, and there are legal rules and regulations that must be met. Yet with the general decline of birth and death rates, meaning smaller families and fewer deaths in them, one is less likely to have experienced a funeral in the family, and only a minority have actually taken charge in matters of death. For the most part, missing today are the friends and neighbors who laid out the dead as a simple matter of community duty; also missing in the culture of each family are the family traditions and the remembrances of all the actions necessary to the occasion of a death of one of its members.

Consequently, the burden of responsibility for immediate and subsequent action taken toward the deceased is shifted to the modern funeral director who is prepared for such action, and who makes his livelihood caring for the dead.

The Funeral Director's First Call: In 1880 when the undertaker received a call to come to a home and help prepare a body for burial, one of his major concerns was to arrive as quickly as possible in order to begin the embalming of the body. Currently the funeral director, or assistants, when called, consider not only the condition of the body but also the state of mind of the survivors.

The burden of the first call is therefore the removal of the body from the residence to the funeral home. Whereas, in 1880, embalming would most likely have taken place in the home of the deceased, ocassionally with someone observing the process, modern embalming almost always takes place inside the preparation room—specially designed and equipped for the purpose—by technically trained experts. Observation of the process is not only generally frowned upon by most funeral directors, but prohibited by law in many states, except for the members of the family.

In the course of his first call the funeral director secures certain necessary data. These include all essential items for the death certificate, which must be signed by the attending physician and filed by the funeral director with the Board of Health, which agency, in turn issues a burial permit. Publication of notices in newspapers, local and afar, the notification of relatives, and a few matters requiring immediate attention may also be taken care of at this time.

Approximately 40% of all deaths in the United States occurred in hospitals in 1954. The percentage is likely to increase. It follows that when the first call is at a hospital, many times the funeral director does not see a member of the family to get all the needed information. Some usually can be obtained from hospital authorities.

At some later time, whether the death occurred in the hospital or home, many more details must be decided by consultation between the person or persons responsible for the funeral arrangements and the funeral director. In order to avoid misunderstandings and possible subsequent embarrassment, every detail of the impending service must be discussed. In a recently published vocational guidance brochure the following points were listed as essential details of the average funeral service:

The place of service—church or mortuary; the time of service; the clergyman in charge—always contacting him before the time and place are finally determined; selecting cemetery space, or arranging for the opening of a grave in the family plot; music for the services—including organist, singer, and selection of titles; contacting lodge officials (if any); notifying pallbearers; selecting the clothing necessary; and choosing the casket and outside receptacle.

On the day of the services, which may be one, two, three or more days after the time of death, the funeral director must oversee every detail of the services. Some of these are obvious—the arranging of flowers, the seating of those attending the service, the transporting of the mourners to the church or cemetery, the assignment of the mourners to the proper vehicles, the marshalling of the funeral procession—but over and above all of these, the experienced and skillful Funeral Director is prepared to handle any eventuality. Some thirty to forty separate details in the funeral service have been listed as essentials to the conduct of a funeral.[2]

Rather than attempt to price these items separately, most funeral directors at mid-century generally combine them and lump them together with the cost of labor, supplies, business expense and other overhead, into one figure, predicated upon the wholesale cost of the casket. A few separate the merchandise and service charges.[3] As it was 75 years ago the selection of the casket is an important phase of funeral arrangements.

In the average funeral service the direct cost of the casket and other supplies approximates only 30% of the sale price of the funeral.[4] The balance of the costs are business expenses, such as heat, utilities, insurance, laundry, repairs and maintenance, telephone and telegraph, automobile, salaries, and others which make up the overhead. Federated Funeral Directors of America of Springfield, Illinois, a business counselling agency for a considerable number of funeral homes, has estimated that the funeral director's overhead for a standard adult service, not including the casket, in 1954 was $393.27.

Many services are rendered annually for a sum below the break even amount. Therefore, other funerals must be sold above this figure in order to keep the funeral establishment in a position to take care of those who must select funerals provided at a below cost price as well as for charity, indigent and welfare services.

Many people who purchase a funeral have a good idea of what they want to spend. Some, however, have difficulty determining what a reasonable funeral should cost because to judge what constitutes reasonable funeral expense is not a simple matter, as there are many grounds of reasonableness. Probate courts vary as to their standards; municipal, county, state and federal agencies have different ideas; and social reformers still others.

Age makes for a difference in opinion also. Youth is more likely to consider the amount of money spent on a funeral by adults as excessive. Young adults, likewise are prone to counsel those in later maturity to moderation in funeral spending. The experience among funeral directors over the last century is that racial, ethnic and social class factors all are not without some influence upon spending. An uninhibited giving way to grief, great floral display and open mourning are generally frowned upon in the middle and upper socio-economic classes. In the lower socio-economic classes and among certain ethnic groups, however, there is a feeling that a direct connection will be drawn between the money spent on the funeral and the respect judged to have been shown for the deceased.

In addition to these cultural factors which help to set prices and standards of quality in funeral services, there are several controls which more or less perfectly act to determine the business conduct of a funeral director. One of these is that the funeral director does not want to put himself in the position of having sold an expensive funeral service for which the family cannot or will not later pay. Most funeral directors write off only about two percent of their income to bad debt losses. A part of the reason for this modest figure may be their awareness that exhorbitant funerals are bad investments.

Another important control over the business practices of the funeral director is the pressure of the community in which he operates. For those funeral directors who have a community clientele and who see themselves in a position roughly analogous to that of the "family doctor," community opinion becomes a strong factor in determining the costs of their services. On the other hand for those urban mortuaries which have a large volume of business, such control is less effective, and the principles of business management are more likely to prevail. However, in the instance of both community and volume type funeral directors there is the further control of the state laws. Among other things these generally prohibit funeral directors from soliciting, taking advantage of a family, misrepresenting merchandise and services, and false advertising. The sale of the funeral service is not only an important phase of funeral arrangement but an action which needs to be understood generally in terms of the way the funeral director relates himself to his clients, to his community and to his professional and business world.

Caskets, years ago selected from catalogs issued to the undertaker by casket manufacturers, are now predominantly selected from the display rooms of the funeral director. The average display will comprise fifteen to thirty units, varying in price to fit the needs of the community being served. Choices are available as to colors of caskets and interiors, and materials used in their construction. All funeral directors sell vaults but usually this outside container is not included in the price of the standard funeral service.

In concluding the arrangements with the family or those responsible for the burial, and in all his contacts with the bereaved, the funeral director necessarily must use discretion as to what is appropriate to the particular circumstances; he must, moreover, have a good command of the social skills necessary in dealing successfully with persons who are distraught, highly suggestible, and easily susceptible to irritation. Again, he must be able to convey sympathy as a natural sentiment, evoked by the suffering of others, and not affected for commercial reasons.

It has been said previously that funeral directors serve the living while caring for the dead. Many times, days or weeks after a service has been conducted, the funeral director will be counseling with survivors.

Death benefits and burial allowances of the Social Security Administration, Veterans Administration, Armed Forces and other agencies of government can be secured only by completing proper forms within a prescribed period of time. The funeral director does this or helps get it done as well as assist the beneficiaries in the completing of papers to get insurance and lodge benefits and compensation awards.

The Funeral: In villages, small towns and open country, death and burial are still events which touch many, if not, most inhabitants of the community. In addition to the relatives, neighbors and friends of the deceased in one way or another are likely to participate in the proceedings, thus helping in many ways to relieve the bereaved of some of the responsibilities which urban dwellers tend to delegate to the funeral director.

Though less frequent than formerly, home services in rural areas are not exceptional. In many cases a majority of the town folk will still attend a funeral. Even so, in rural areas today, the funeral director is an indispensable person. The dead are mainly in his charge; they are embalmed in his preparation room; dressed, casketed and otherwise made ready for the funeral by him; and his general management of the funeral marks a wide departure from an earlier role as a seller of coffins or caskets, who was "in attendance" at the funeral service, and who provided transportation for the remains.

In contrast to the practice in rural areas, in urban America today a death touches a limited number of persons, and except for cases involving community or other leaders or, unfortunately sometimes, those who are notorious—its occurrence is made public only through the obituary columns of the daily papers. In a city of a million inhabitants, of the some ten thousand persons who yearly die only a handful are considered newsworthy in death. With the gradual dissolution of racial and ethnic groupings in the cities, those living in fairly close proximity to the deceased may not be affected by a death since they may not share the same customs, traditions, or other personal or social relations.

Home funerals in the cities are today a rarity. Even if the physical construction of apartment buildings—the smallness of the quarters, the inconvenience of the common lobby and stairways and corridors, the difficulty of bringing the casket in and out, the lack of privacy—did not make the home funeral inconvenient, other urban conditions would tend to place the funeral in the funeral home or church or both. For one thing, since the funeral director now prepares the dead in a part of his establishment equipped especially for the task, it has become expedient for him and convenient to his clientele to construct the kind of funeral home in which the funeral services as well as the preparation of the body can take place. At the turn of the century, the parlor, and the "homelike rooms" of the funeral home represent the preliminary step in the eventual change of site and function for funerals. If by 1925, less than ten percent of urban funeral homes advertised a funeral "chapel" in which the religious service of the funeral could be performed, at mid-century, such addition had become almost a standard part of nearly all urban and many, if not most, town and village funeral homes.

The typical funeral, originating in the urban funeral home, covers a period of about three days, beginning with the removal of the remains and ending with the journey to the grave. The preparation of the deceased for viewing is undertaken by a licensed embalmer who will have been trained in a School of Mortuary Science. To preservation and sanitation, the major purposes of embalming in the late 19th century has been added the function of *restoration*. Using skills akin to those of the sculptor, artist, and plastic surgeon, the embalmer, working, if possible from a photograph of the deceased, restores the tones to the face in such manner that resembles the appearance of the person in health and life, and is in aesthetic keeping with the beauty of the casket and its floral backdrop.

Once the remains of the deceased are placed in state in the funeral home, they may be viewed by friends and relatives, in much the same fashion as viewing took place a half, or even full century ago. In "paying their last respects" to the dead many of the friends of the deceased establish their only social contact with the immediately bereaved, since more persons in most sections of the country view the body than attend the funeral services and burial. The viewing is controlled in some parts of the country by the funeral director to the extent that certain visiting hours are established. The custom of the all night wakes and sitting up with the deceased has all but disappeared; certainly it is out of keeping with the routine of modern funeral home operations.

Most times on the third day following death the actual funeral service ceremony likely takes place. Custom today sanctions for most the use of either funeral home, church, or both. For those in regular practice of the Catholic faith, the church ceremony is required, except in case of infants; Jews may or may not bury their dead from the Synagogue; and most Protestants likewise enjoy free choice in the matter.

The funeral service ceremony marks a high dramatic point in the modern funeral. The chapel is physically so arranged that attention is focused on the casket, which, open or closed is placed on a catafalque in the center of the floral arrangement. The mourners gather along certain lines of protocol, and are seated in the body of the chapel while the family and immediate relatives often are withdrawn in a wing, which affords privacy in almost direct contrast to the older custom of putting the family on display. In the church, on the other hand, family members will most likely occupy the front seats, nearest to the casket. While Catholic funerals follow a rigidly prescribed pattern, the officiating Jewish rabbi has some leeway in the services which he provides. Least constrained by formula is the Protestant minister. Nevertheless, the general pattern for the Protestant funeral service comprises four segments; the ritual, consisting of the reading of the Scripture and prayers; the funeral sermon; music; and the committal service.

Prayers for the most part are intercessory, to bring comfort, consolation and strength to the bereaved. While some clergymen may still regard funeral sermons as offering opportunities to evangelize and to make converts—as was almost always the case in the last century—there has been more recently an increasing recognition of the utility of the sermon in expediting the mourning process. Cues for this approach are supplied by mid-century psychologists and psychiatrists who have turned their attention to the problems of bereavement. Hymns, although sometimes dispensed with along with all music, are seen as a mode of reinforcing the sense of sharing which the clergyman attempts to instill in the course of the funeral service. Protestant funeral ceremonies usually last between a half and three-quarters of an hour.[5]

The committal service at the grave is preceded by the funeral procession. In place of the long drawn-out array of vehicles (carriages before 1910, and afterwards motor cars whose number often was interpreted as indicating the respect in which the deceased was held and his popularity), the average funeral procession of today contains fewer persons, most of whom ride in privately owned automobiles. No longer is the furnishing of transportation one of the most profitable items in the list of services provided by the undertaker or funeral director as it was in the 19th and early 20th centuries. The most imposing aspects of the modern funeral procession are in the trim funeral hearses, and the seven passenger limousines. The journey to the grave takes the procession through the heavily trafficked city streets to the cemetery for the committal service and interment.

At the cemetery the traditional committal service is held, much the same as a century ago. Changes reflect, by and large, an increasing concern with the feelings and physical well-being of the bereaved. The harsh realities of the grave tend to be softened by the artifices of the funeral director. Most times graves are lined with artificial grass to cover the upturned earth, canopies are raised in inclement weather, and the casket in most cases is not lowered into the grave until the bereaved have departed. Committal services are usually short, but by the same token are no less trying. In the words of Irion, "The committal service provides, as nothing else . . . does so graphically, a symbolic demonstration that the kind of relationship which has existed between the mourner and the deceased is now at an end."[6]

The end of the committal service marks the end of the funeral, although not necessarily the relation of the funeral director to the bereaved. Filling the grave is the task of cemetery workmen, to be completed after the participants in the ceremony have left.

Following some services, a funeral luncheon or dinner awaits the returning mourners. Following others, what has been a group, held together by the bonds of ritual and ceremony, becomes only a crowd, a dispersing aggregate of individuals and small groups, some still caught up with the mood of sorrow, some in mourning, and others already easing out from under the strain of sustaining the harmony and discipline necessary to the conduct of the funeral.

OPERATING THE MODERN FUNERAL HOME

The Modern Funeral Establishment: In physical appearance the well-equipped funeral home of the mid-20th century bears only a passing resemblance to the funeral establishment of the 1880's. Whereas modern establishments are for the most part constructed around the chapel or service room, the earlier types, which in a majority of cases were not built as funeral homes but were private residences or stores convered into undertaking establishments, centered their emphasis around the "parlor," or "parlors." "Hominess" has never become the major item of consideration in the building of new funeral establishments, although the comfort of the bereaved is assured in many ways. Air-conditioning, soft upholstery, easy access from the street, the elimination of long stairs, separate rooms for the bereaved families, heavy carpeting, soft lighting, drinking fountains and many other items reflect this concern. In point of fact, after accessibility, beauty has undoubtedly become the foremost consideration in setting the motif of the funeral homes of the 1950's as they are either newly built or in process of rebuilding or redecoration.

Funeral homes are not located by chance or haphazardly, and in many locations they are limited by zoning laws. While nationality and other groups have long since had their own funeral directors, skilled and understanding in their respective special services and customs, fewer funeral directors today count on a single ethnic or religious group for their clientele. Two notable exceptions to the foregoing generalization are to be found: Negro funeral homes are still predominantly dependent upon what amounts to an all-Negro clientele, and to a lesser degree Jewish funeral homes specialize in funerals for Jewish clientele.

Factors other than the traditional accessibility to and service of racial, ethnic and religious groups are considered important in determining locations for funeral homes today. Important are such questions as how many establishments already exist in the same trade area, how much of an investment will be required to match the competitors' establishments, and what pertinent and significant population movements are taking place in the area. The funeral director who

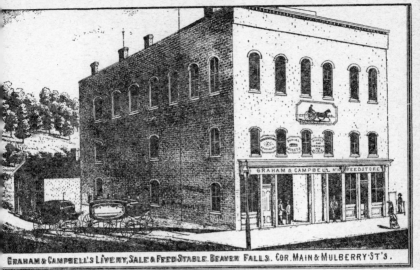

GRAHAM & CAMPBELL'S LIVERY, SALE & FEED STABLE, BEAVER FALLS. COR. MAIN & MULBERRY ST'S.

a) 19th Century Combination Establishment

b) Up to Date Funeral Home of 1926

PLATE 70

Mid-20th Century Suburban Style Funeral Home

PLATE 71

is considering taking over an established business might well ask, "How much of a clientele has been built up by the firm, and how much of this can I reasonably expect to keep?"

For a director without a clientele of his own and setting up a new establishment, the most promising location in a general sort of way would seem to be a growing suburban area where a large section of land could be used for the parking lot, garage, landscaped area, and other facilities in addition to the home itself. It has been noted before and bears repeating that it is characteristic of the business of funeral directing to persist under the same family name or operation, and to stay located in the same area or site for several generations. While there are advantages to such permanence of site, the development of the metropolitan areas nearly always brings with it an intensification of the problem of parking and to a lesser extent managing the traffic of funeral processions; and as cemeteries fill up within the cities themselves and new ones are located in the suburbs, the length of the drive required in a funeral procession becomes longer and more time consuming. The two related factors, increasing city size and density, have made permanency of site for funeral establishments somewhat less desirable than it was in the past. In 1955, funeral homes may move to new locations to follow their own moving clientele, or to escape from communities that are physically deteriorating or becoming filled with people who are not of their clientele type.

Because of the nature of the work performed, all funeral homes have a basic physical and operational similarity. Since people die at all hours, and as funeral directors are expected to answer calls immediately, mortuaries must keep operating on a twenty-four hour schedule. If ambulance service is maintained, calls must be answered promptly. So that service will be readily and quickly available, quite often living quarters, either for the funeral director or assistants, perhaps both, will be located above the establishment.

Inside the funeral home, and in addition to the service room or chapel which is central, the following rooms are most always necessary: 1) A preparation room for embalming; 2) a casket selection room; 3) an office; and 4) a family room. In addition to these, well furnished funeral homes will incorporate rest rooms, slumber rooms, clergyman's room, music room, room for employees, living quarters, anteroom, garage, and store room. The paraphernalia involved in operating such a funeral home is extensive. Even many of the more modest establishments will have the following items: hearse, ambulance, limousine, and service car; furniture, carpeting, drapes, venetian blinds, drinking fountain or water cooler, folding chairs, paintings, statuary, tables, lectern, candelabra, candles, bible, missal and hymnal; sundries such as smelling salts, spirits of ammonia, first-aid equipment; artificial grass and casket lowering device; maintenance supplies; stretchers and wheel carts; preparation room facilities and supplies, along with materials and instruments for restorative art; caskets, burial garments, a vault, or vault samples. This list is by no means exhaustive. Some funeral directors rent wheel chairs, folding chairs, beds and cots to the public.

The exterior appearance of a funeral home is as important as the interior. Well landscaped grounds, rock gardens, flower beds, evergreen plantings, are all resorted to in order to create favorable public sentiment. The buildings are constructed on many architectural styles, from Early Colonial and other traditional styles to severely functional "modern." Whatever the size or style of the buildings, all areas of a funeral home must be kept in good order for public view. The "show case" aspect of the funeral home adds to the self-image that the funeral director derives from the

A Modern Mahogany Casket

PLATE 72

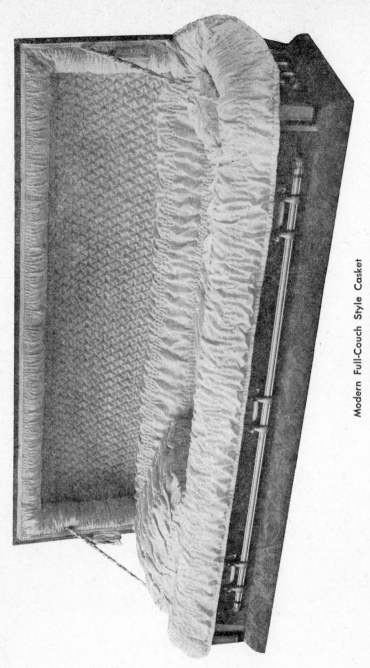

Modern Full-Couch Style Casket

PLATE 73

Modern Seamless Solid Copper Deposit Casket

PLATE 74

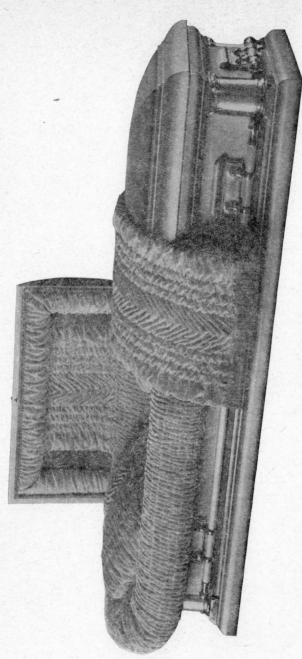

Modern Half-Couch Style Casket

PLATE 75

operation of his establishment, since he tends to think of himself as a person who carries out his vocation in surroundings that are scrupulously neat, sanitary, dignified, and even beautiful. Yet this makes for important problems in maintenance. Long before rolling stock wears out it becomes obsolete, and long before funeral homes actually begin to look shabby many funeral directors feel the urge to redecorate. Both the outside and inside of the establishment need constant maintenance and repair. Windows must be washed, lawns mowed, shrubs clipped, rolling stock washed and polished, walks swept, floors waxed, furniture and stock of caskets and other merchandise dusted, and equipment inspected and kept in good working order. This last precaution is especially true for the ambulance.

While funeral establishments do not exhibit the extreme variations in the number of workers that are to be found in commercial or industrial concerns, there is some significant difference between the small and the large funeral establishment. In the Careers Research Monograph No. 72 of The Institute For Research, of Chicago, the classification of job categories in funeral service includes Managerial or Supervisory, Professional, Clerical, Utility, and Miscellaneous. A total of thirty-one different positions are included under this classification scheme. By contrasting the type of establishment in which most of these thirty-one positions would be found with the small funeral home operated by one funeral director-embalmer with one or perhaps two assistants or helpers, we are able to establish the extremes of all ranges of funeral home operations—large to small. The nature of the relationships among the working personnel in funeral establishments depends in major degree upon their size and business perspective. In the larger mortuaries in which there is considerable division of labor with attendant specialization, it is convenient to classify occupational personnel into three groups: 1) Policy making—this group includes owners, proprietors, partners and active officers of the corporation if there be one. 2) Management—this classification includes funeral home managers, funeral directors, assistants, hostesses, credit managers, personnel managers and office staff. 3) Labor —this group would consist of embalmers, attendants, chauffeurs, garage mechanics, maintenance workers, handy men and elevator operators.

This classification is by no means universally valid for all the larger establishments and would be misleading if applied to smaller homes. The marginal or "gray areas" of the classification are made up of embalmers and attendants groups. To some extent the orientation of these groups depends upon the way in which the higher levels of management of particular mortuaries look upon their own personnel. In those establishments where the embalmers assist in arranging for and conducting funerals the classification of them on the side of "labor" is unrealistic. Yet during the present century embalmers as such have come to be regarded by many funeral directors and the courts more as technicians, performing a technical specialty that can scarcely be called professional, so that their training and functions cannot be placed at the same service level as that of the funeral director.

While many embalmers and funeral director-embalmers do not agree with this idea, the acceptance of embalmers in trade unions is an indication of the drift of this occupation toward the classification of highly skilled labor as over against that of professional practitioners. Another category of embalmers, "trade embalmers"—found only in the larger cities—are equivalent to self employed, and are independent trade workers who embalm for various funeral directors while not in the continuous employ of any. This group must not be put in the same classification with those embalmers

a) Modern Ambulance

b) Modern Flower Car

c) Mid-20th Century Funeral Hearse

PLATE 76

National Foundation of Funeral Service, Evanston, Illinois

PLATE 77

who work at one funeral establishment, nor are they likely to participate in labor-union organization.

In smaller funeral homes embalming is often done by the funeral director, who also will be a licensed embalmer. His relations to his working personnel are likely to be colored by the tradition of having his probable successor with him. His assistant is apt to be groomed from the beginning as his eventual successor. He may be a son, a relative or connection by marriage, or even a young man to whom he has taken a liking or fancy, because of his expressed interest in the funeral directing field. Such a person begins as an apprentice "helping out," and later goes to a school of mortuary science, passes his state board examination, receives his license, returns to the same home, and in the course of a long period of dedicated work and training in the necessary skills of funeral direction takes over the director's role upon the latter's retirement.

In larger mortuaries union organization is more likely to be accepted by management as the inevitable association of employees along lines of mutual interest. In funeral homes with a volume of less than one hundred funerals annually, union organization is less understandable and appears less reasonable to the funeral director, who may resist it. There are no industry wide collective bargaining patterns in the field of funeral service.

In addition to the two general points of view taken by funeral directors toward their employees there has been developing over the past half century a division in perspective as to the manner which a funeral establishment should function in regard to community and to clientele. Among the volume operators in chain-type funeral homes, and in a few multi-functional, or multi-purpose establishments, in addition to the care of the dead, cemetery space is provided along with facilities for weddings, baptisms and other ritual services. Here the service is not provided simply for a local community, that is, for people who live in the same general neighborhood and who have social contacts with one another, but rather for a trade area which may encompass whole metropolitan districts or even larger geographical regions.

Thus it is difficult for the larger, "volume" mortuaries to anchor themselves into a community by any other than a market relationship. Their clients come from near and afar; and the classification of the mortician in one of these mass-servicing mortuaries as a professional, equivalent of the "family doctor," is neither sound nor realistic. This is in marked contrast with the local funeral home where the community roots are comprised of a wide and deep network of personal services, many of which were performed a generation or more ago for the parents and even the grandparents of the present clientele. Such funeral homes and the practitioners within them constitute the "occupational essence," the characteristic way of doing business, of organized American funeral service at mid-20th century.

Alternative Forms of Operation: Over the last seventy-five years several alternative modes of burial, funeral service, or of providing funeral services, have appeared. Cremation as a different mode of disposal of the dead, along with the appearance of crematories to expedite the process, has been touched upon in an earlier chapter. It was pointed out that although the cremation movement found its initial impetus in a collective desire for funeral reform, the reform aspect vanished before World War I in the commercial spirit that accompanied the growth of crematories as business ventures. The growth of cremation has been slow, and its rate of growth has diminished slightly at mid-century. In 1955 cremation will account for somewhat less than five percent of all deaths; of this number slightly less than half will have taken place in the Pacific Coast states. Yet the custom, as an alternative to earth burial, has seemingly been firmly established in America, and is likely to persist.

Those funeral directors who operate crematories assert that they are providing another type of service, but for the majority of funeral directors, cremation is held to be a matter of personal choice, and their inclination is neither to encourage nor actively to resist the practice.

Governmental enterprise in the burial of the dead has been and is expressed in three ways: by the repatriation of the war dead, by the establishment of national cemeteries, and by the operation of municipal, county, state and federal crematories. The first two are detailed in their history and operations in Appendix I; the last, in light of smallness of scope, may be mentioned briefly in passing.

There are ten Government-operated crematories in the United States, less than five percent of the total of all crematories. Six (four of which are located in California, at Eldridge, Imola, Los Angeles and Talmadge, and two in Oregon at Pendleton and Salem), are state operated. Stockton County, California, and Allegheny County, Pennsylvania, have their own crematories, as does the city of Cleveland, Ohio. Finally, there is a crematory in the District of Columbia, which is managed by an agency of the federal government.

Two forms of competition face the funeral director outside his normal business operations. One is from cooperative funeral homes, operating as one phase of the broad cooperative movement. Such homes are likely to be found in the North Central States. Statistics are few, but in the United States Department of Labor's report on "Cooperative Burial Associations, 1939" it was stated that as of that time there were thirty-six cooperative associations made up of 31,247 members, reporting the handling of 1,180 funerals with an aggregate business for the year of $189,563. Nineteen of

these 36 were in Minnesota, nine in Iowa, five in South Da-
kota, two in Wisconsin, and one in Nebraska. Thirty-one
of the associations provided complete funerals, and five associations sold only funeral merchandise.[7] In 1946 the
number had risen to 52, but in 1948 the NFDA conducted
a survey of its constituent associations and found 32 still in
operation. While no data are readily available concerning
the more recent past of these cooperative funeral associations, in trade circles the feeling seems to be that the total
number has not increased since 1948.

The other form of competition directly to face the conventional funeral director comes from labor unions. As these
have grown apace with business and industrial expansion,
they have sought to extend the range of the services which
they offer members and their families. In the area of funeral
service this effort has been worked out in two plans. The first
type of union participation that offers direct competition in
the area of funeral service involves the actual ownership
and operation of a funeral home. Such establishments are
now operating, and have been for several years, in Gillespie
and West Frankfort, Illinois. Under the second type the
union develops a burial plan around funeral services contracted from a funeral director. In return for the contract to
bury members and their families such funeral director will
agree to a contract price, usually set at a figure presumed to
be below the average for the area. Union plans of this sort,
or a variant thereof, have been set up, or an attempt has
been made to set them up, in Detroit; Allentown, Pennsylvania; and Des Moines, Iowa. Union burial plans are currently operating (1955) in St. Louis, Minneapolis, and New
York.

Professionality — Benchmarks and Roadblocks: In 1880
the single most visible portent of professionality among
undertakers was the desire by outstanding members of

the occupation to come together and organize for reasons similar to those which had led other performers of personal services to form professional organizations. In public estimation and in the self-regard of its own practitioners undertaking was both highly necessary and yet highly demeaning, because it was considered disagreeable work. The historical association of the early English undertaker as a "dismal trader" clung to the 19th century American undertaker, and as we know, was reinforced by the gloomy mourning customs of the period. To move out of the shadows thus cast over the occupation, undertakers and funeral directors during the past three quarters of a century, have found it expedient to form associations in the purposes of mutual protection, of exercising a measure of control over the economic fortunes of their occupation, of colleagueship, and of building in the minds of the public a higher social estimation of the nature of their services.

The balance sheet of professionality may here be reviewed briefly. What specifically are the accomplishments and developments in the realm of funeral service which combine to make funeral directing a profession? Although precise standards of professionality are not universally agreed upon, to students of the professions and to the general public alike, there is a core of elements which seem to be most necessary to an acceptable definition.

A profession consists of a group of practitioners 1) who are possessed of a body of highly technical or specialized skills or knowledges; 2) who are set apart so that they may devote their full time efforts to this practice; 3) who are able to bring to the service of others, especially in the critical junctures of human affairs, a detached judgment which is beyond the resources of the average person and which draws upon their expert professional backgrounds; 4) who cooperate rather than compete with others, sharing professional information, enjoying the same privileges, and assuming the same risks; and 5) who associate formally to govern their own membership, setting standards of admittance, or practice, and procedures for controlling those who would violate their professional code.

In 1880 undertakers had mastered the rudiments of skills in dealing with the dead, although preservative arts were yet in their infancy and restorative arts—to complete the metaphor—were not yet born. In dealing with the bereaved, the undertaker had the example of the typical tradesman before him. He could act like a seller of goods, and in his role of giving some kind of service to the bereaved, the officiating clergy, public officials and the like, he could base his conduct on the pattern of the personal service handy man.

The skills of the modern funeral director transcend those of his 19th century counterpart. Two early claims to professionality, one based upon his services as a sanitarian—allying him with public health, and the other on his services in restoration of the features of the dead—allying him with the graphic arts, reached their peak of importance before mid-century, and do not today constitute the basis of the funeral director's claim to professionality. Sanitation is still important, but the early claims of the funeral director to be the central figure in protecting the nation's living from their dead, in an age of miracle drugs and tremendously improved medical and public health services, do not carry with them the prestige they did when the nation was swept with plagues and epidemics; and while restorative art has by no means lost its importance in funeral service, its practice, along with the embalming and preparation for funeral, has been increasingly delegated to the technically competent, hired embalmer.

The claim that the funeral director makes today to being a professional person is based not so much upon his possession of the technical skills that pertain to the handling of the dead, as upon the psychological skills in human relations necessary to the proper handling of the emotions and disposi- tions of the bereaved. To repeat, this is a personal service function which for obvious reasons cannot be carried out in the framework of a simple business, or market relationship. Above all, the claims to professionality of funeral directors must rest upon the necessity of their establishing a rela- tionship of *trust* with their clients. As does the physician, lawyer, priest and psychiatrist the funeral director, in the course of his work, must keep confidential the information he elicits from his clients.

It is somewhat difficult to estimate precisely how far this important criterion of trust has become centrally located in the definition the modern funeral director has built of his "occupational self." That he has brought into his vocabulary many of the terms used in professional discourse is evident. The prime example perhaps is the conscious attempt to sub- stitute "funeral director" for "undertaker"—an occupational title adequately descriptive of his work in the 19th century. In their individual efforts and through associational means fu- neral directors have attempted to gain public and official ac- ceptance of this newer term. Although success has not been universal, it is apparent that "undertaker" is falling slowly and inevitably into disuse. Telephone and city directories have reflected this change in terminology for some time; oc- cupational handbooks of various sorts have followed suit; and several agencies of the federal government have adopted the term "funeral director" in preference to "undertaker" or "mortician."

Insofar as general acceptance into the realm of profes- sionals is concerned the picture is somewhat more cloudy, but the direction of acceptance has definitely favored pro- fessional, or, at least semi-professional status. The *Alpha-*

betical Index of Occupations and Industries of the U. S. Government 1950 Census lists funeral directors under the "O" symbol, which is reserved for professional, technical and kindred workers. *The Occupational Outlook Handbook* of the United States Department of Labor in its 1951 edition includes funeral directors under "Professional, Semi-Professional and Administrative Occupations." The Better Business Bureau considers funeral directors as professionals, along with physicians and lawyers. The occupational status of the funeral director has been the subject of a number of court decisions. Many of these have arisen out of the licensing laws of the various states. The opinions rendered prior to 1920 were in general that there was a distinct line of demarcation between funeral directing and embalming, and that funeral directing was definitely a business or commercial venture as opposed to a profession. This position has been followed with some justification by the United States Department of Commerce, which brings the operations of funeral homes under the classification of "Service Establishments" whose primary activity is the sale of service, as distinguished from establishments dealing in merchandise. Not included under this classification are the business activities of "doctors, lawyers, dentists, and others performing a professional or scientific service." However in the Circuit Court of Wayne County, Michigan in 1944 the Commissioner ruled in the case of Michael A. Guest vs. Board of Education of the City of Detroit that "as a matter of law that one engaged in embalming and funeral directing is engaged in a profession" and, commenting on the historical development of the occupation, noted that:

While fifty years ago funeral directing might have been classed as a business, a tremendous step has been taken from the "horse and buggy" days of those years to the more scientific social viewpoint as reflected in the present day methods of embalming and funeral directing.

A motion for rehearing was denied early in the following year by the judge of the same circuit, and in default of further action the case stands as the most recent as regards the professionality of the funeral director and embalmer.

Even more recently, in June, 1955, in the Circuit Court of Hamilton County, Illinois, Judge Charles T. Randolph, in the case of Elmer Gholson vs. State of Illinois, held that the Illinois statute requiring, among other things, that the funeral director be an embalmer, was unconstitutional. It was the further sense of the decision that embalmers are to be classified as persons in hire of the funeral directors—in other words, apparently, skilled technicians.

For the past seventy-odd years funeral directors have had before them a code of ethics, which, though varying to some extent in content, provided the guideposts of professional practice for the occupation. It would be difficult to estimate the extent to which the present code has become an "inner control" over the behavior of some 50,000 to 55,000 practitioners of funeral directing and embalming. Some, a minority undoubtedly, reject the concept of professional morality completely and seek to operate either on the basis of expediency, or, with the ethics of the market place, as mere tradesmen. In dealing with this minority, funeral directors through their state associations may help maintain the high quality of their profession by recommending for prosecution those who violate the state statutes regarding funeral service; and while the controls of "professional ethics" remain, in the judgment of the authors, less effective than those of older and more firmly established professions, they are definitely more than simply a set of statements of honorable intentions made for public consumption.

Colleagueship, the sense of sharing or of making a concerted effort through cooperation rather than by competition, is a recent development among funeral directors, and is by no means as strong as it is among certain learned professions where the element of a competitive business aspect is not present. While funeral directors use the terms "ethics," and speak sincerely of "ethical behavior," the term "colleague" is only now coming into their working vocabulary. At the same time it should be pointed out that the raw competition and the suspicion of a fellow funeral director's acts and motives, attitudes widely prevalent seventy-five years ago, have been ameliorated mainly through the efforts of state and national associations to promote better man-to-group and man-to-man understandings.

Sufficient has been said about the development of associational activities to merit little more than a concluding observation. Funeral directors may still revert to expediency to meet their day-to-day problems, and the realities of operating a business in a competitive field do not dissolve in a change of vocabulary or in protests of professionality to the world at large. The principles of professional practice reside, if anywhere, in the *organizations* which not only represent funeral directors, but which having been given a measure of trusteeship over the field at large, find it necessary to reformulate and redefine these principles to the practitioners and to the public alike.

The lesson of professionalization of funeral service is the lesson of all personal service occupations that have sought to achieve professional status: personal service practices must be set in a context of social acceptance; social acceptance must be built by organizational actions; and organizational actions are themselves futile if they are not grounded in the proper responses of the practitioners.

CITATIONS AND REFERENCES FOR CHAPTER XIII

1. William Caudill, "Cultural Perspectives on Stress," in *Symposium on Stress* (Army Medical Service Graduate School, Walter Reed Army Medical Center, Washington, D.C., 1953).

2. F. Lloyd Hansen, "Funeral Service as a Profession," booklet (Milwaukee: National Funeral Directors Association of the United States, Inc., 1952), p. 5.

3. For an extended discussion of the business operations of modern funeral homes see James MacNaughton's "How Are You Doing?", *Proceedings*, NFDA, 1951, pp. 53-66.

4. *Ibid.*

5. Paul E. Irion, *The Funeral and the Mourners* (New York: Abingdon Press, 1954). See especially Chapter V.

6. *Ibid.*, p. 111.

7. James Meyers, Jr., *Cooperative Funeral Associations*, pamphlet (New York: Cooperative League of the U.S.A., 1946), pp. 16-17.

Appendixes

APPENDIX I

THE GRAVES REGISTRATION SERVICES AND THE RETURN OF THE WAR DEAD PROGRAM OF THE ARMED FORCES

The custom of gathering, identifying and giving special burial honors to the military dead of a nation is very ancient and general. Thus the Spartans were told to return either with their shields or on them, and the Athenian historian, Thucydides, has in some detail described the funeral ceremonies held at Athens in 436 B.C., when the first of those slain in the Peloponnesian war were brought home and given a funeral of state. The practice among the Greeks was then already old.[1]

Although some earlier provisions had been made for the care of American war dead, the Mexican War of 1846-1847 witnessed a major advance in American policy. In 1850 Congress appropriated funds for a cemetery in Mexico City to serve those of our armed forces who died along the route of the campaign to capture the city. The final result of establishing this cemetery pointed to the need for improved care of the dead, particularly for a registration service. When the bodies of the 750 Americans were exhumed from their casual graves along the way not a single remains could be identified.[2]

The Civil War: While the Civil war did not test the willingness and ability of a nation to care for or bring back from foreign soil great numbers of military dead, it was responsible for the development of many burial practices which in expanded form have become standard for the American armed forces. Decent burial of the war dead was felt to be an important morale factor both for the troops themselves and for the civilian population. In September, 1861, two months after the battle of Bull Run, the War Department ordered the Quartermaster General to supply all hospitals with forms for accurately registering the dead. In addition, he was to provide materials for registered headboards to be placed over soldiers' graves. The departmental or corps commanders were made responsible for the proper execution of burial blanks and forms.[3] Ten months later, in July, 1862, Congress authorized the President to purchase cemetery grounds for military burials. Government acquisition was supplemented by gifts. During the war patriotic persons or organizations put more than three hundred burial plots at the disposal of the armed forces. One of the most important decisions reached during 1862 was to transform the burial sites of major battles into national cemeteries. While this decision with implementing legislation marked a great advance, it nevertheless left much to be desired. Its greatest defect lay in the fact that its efficient operation was confined largely to what is now known as the "Zone of the Interior." In the absence of Quartermaster service troops, many services needed for the proper care of the dead were non-existent, particularly in combat zones. And yet, in spite of a failure to supply a specialized organization to do a defined task, considerable advance was made during the Civil War in the practice of battlefield burials and graves registration. Steere ascribes this improvement to the fact that the soldiers themselves would not tolerate the haphazard burial measures of previous wars, and, growing appalled at the carelessness around them, took it into their own hands to provide for their slain comrades the ideal of individual burial in a registered grave. Many instances are on record of private searches on old battlefields, and of the amateur use of identification techniques that later became standard procedure.[4]

The first known Graves Registration Unit was improvised in 1864 to handle the dead who fell during Jubal Early's attack on Washington. It made a perfect identification score.[5] That year, by the act of July 4th, 1864, the responsibilities and authority of the Quartermaster's Department for caring for the dead were enlarged, and for the first time the machinery was big enough for the task, if used as provided. In spite of improved procedures, however, in the final battles of the war insufficient burial details were assigned—probably because commanders did not wish to reduce their striking power at critical junctures—and graves registration services showed no marked improvement.[6]

When the war ended the task of clearing up war burials proved enormous. While this was no foreign fight, many battlefields had lain for several years in areas controlled by the Confederates. The first great achievement was the reinterring of Federal soldiers who died at Andersonville prison. Only 450 out of some 12,900 dead could not be identified. This was a much higher percentage of identification than that yielded by the battlefields. Of the total interred by 1870, positive identification was made for 172,000 or some 58 per cent, while 143,000 or some 42 per cent remained unknown.

Steere points up three significant aspects of this Civil war episode: 1. With about one-seventh of the 1950 population of the United States, the North suffered deaths roughly comparable in number to the fatalities in World War II; 2. The Civil War in some way, as indicated below, moved toward establishing the principle of returning remains to native soil; and 3. It set the policy that care and final disposition of American war dead would devolve upon the Quartermaster General.[7] Don Craig, special assistant in the office f the Quartermaster General, points out a limitation on 2 above: "While some Civil War dead were returned to their homes, there was no recognized policy to justify such procedure. Each was an individual case conducted with permission of the military and civil authorities. The precedent of return of the dead established by the Civil War was, as stated, reinterment in the concentration of a national cemetery. These dead were not returned to their homes. Their relatives were not consulted as to place of reinterment. The location of national cemeteries following the Civil War was determined by the distribution of the dead in temporary burials."[8]

The Civil War provided the Americans with an object lesson and a precedent useful in 1898, when the brief Spanish-American War—the Mexican War was the previous instance—again sent American soldiers to fight on foreign soil. In full realization that a considerable lapse of time between burial and accurate grave registration was largely responsible for an inability to identify almost half of the Civil War dead, President McKinley instructed the Secretary of War to proceed as quickly as possible to locate and properly mark all American military graves in the Cuban Theatre of operations.

To handle the job Mr. D. H. Rhodes, a landscape gardener with the National Cemeteries, was authorized to organize the Quartermaster Burial Corps. This unit, staffed with civilian undertakers and assistants, undertook to exhume and return the remains of American war dead to the United States.[9]

Having completed the task for the Cuban Theatre, Rhodes and his group undertook a similar assignment in the Philippines, where another agency was already operating in the field. By order of the Departmental Commander, Chaplain Charles C. Pierce had established the Army Morgue and Bureau of Identification at Manila. The two groups shared the duties of caring for the dead and returning the remains to the United States. Rhodes remained in active employment through the late 1920's, residing in a portion of the Lee Mansion at Arlington Cemetery.

Of the 1,222 casketed remains returned from Cuba to the United States by June 30, 1899, only 13.63 per cent—as compared to some 42 per cent for the Civil War—remained unidentified. An even better record was established in the Philippine Theatre for the Spanish-American War itself and for the Philippine Insurrection and the North China Expedition, which events followed the war. During 1901 only nine of the 1384 remains shipped from Manila to the United States were not identified. Although judged by the number of men involved and by total military deaths the Spanish-American War, compared to the Civil War, the two World Wars and the Korean War, was of lesser magnitude it pointed an emerging problem. With less than 6,000 remains returned home from the war itself and from the Philippine Insurrection and the China Expedition it became apparent that even though available burial space in the existing national military cemetery system was not immediately overtaxed, shortages in grave space might be expected by reason of the fact that an additional 400,000 veterans had become eligible for burial.[10]

In the years intervening before World War I two changes in the military organization of the United States were highly important to the problem of burial and registration. The first, which gave this country a modern command system, was the establishment of the General Army Staff in 1902. The second was the reconstruction in 1912 of the Quartermaster Department as a corps, with special duties—among others, graves registration—assigned to special services companies. Prior to this time the graves registration task had been carried out by civilian teams, or by detachments from the line. By unifying functions and placing them in the hands of a responsible military agency, it was made possible for theatre commanders to abolish the time lag between temporary burials and grave registration.

World War I enlarged both the problems of grave registration and the means available for their solution. Better organization, better means of identification, and the better planning of temporary cemeteries all worked toward better identification scores. At the same time the greater destructiveness of modern weapons tended to lower the percentage. Improved modern transportation eliminated in many cases the necessity of burying the dead where they had fallen.

Part of the anticipated immediate expansion of American military cemeteries at home did not take place. When the next-of-kin of dead fallen in the European Theatre were consulted a poll indicated that while 46,520 elected to have their dead brought back, 31,591 chose to have them remain in Europe. The European cemeteries were designed to serve as both memorials and burial places. The majority of European Cemeteries were established on battle sites. In 1934 the custody of them was transferred from the War Department to the American Battle Monument Commission. Only 2.2 per cent of the dead of World War I remained unidentified.[11]

World War I provided much burial experience that was used to advantage in World War II. In the course of the latter conflict the 15,000,000 men called to the colors by America suffered almost 360,-000 fatalities. Of these some 280,000 were recovered and given burial in temporary cemeteries established in the several zones of operation. A poll taken of the next-of-kin as to the final resting places for these dead produced a reaction very similar to that experienced after World War I. Three-fifths desired their war dead to be brought home; two-fifths to remain abroad.[12]

Of the total of 171,000 casketed remains returned to the United States, 134,000 or 80 per cent were buried in private plots and 37,000, or 20 per cent, in national cemeteries. All of these were known dead; the 10,000 unknown dead were left buried in foreign soil. Again, as in World War I the return of the dead had not been inaugurated until after the cessation of hostilities.[13] The experience of the Graves Registration Service which shows that the great majority of people prefer to have their soldier dead buried in family plots rather than in National Cemeteries either at home or abroad is evidence of the fact that the occasional statement that "we do not care how or where our kin are buried," even though not always contradicted is definitely a minority view point. The willingness of some families to allow their military dead to remain buried abroad is not certain indication that they particularly preferred this plan. In some cases this burial in foreign soil avoided what might have been personally embarrassing situations for the living, such as those produced by the remarriage of the wife, or religious and family differences among the survivors.

The Korean War witnessed a new policy development in military burials. In the Fall of 1950 thought was being given to a plan of removing casualties from temporary cemeteries in Korea and of returning them home while the fighting was going on. By the end of 1950 personnel and equipment were in Korea ready to do the job. With the advance of the enemy, wherever possible temporary American cemeteries were evacuated, and the remains were shipped to a central mortuary in Japan. While large temporary military cemeteries were established in Korea it was determined that these were not to be permanent, and that all American dead ultimately would be returned to the United States or its possessions. A considerable establishment for identifying the bodies and processing them was developed at Camp Kokura on the northern tip of Kyushu, the southernmost of the four major Japanese islands. There, a highly heterogeneous group of experts, equipped with the modern scientific apparatus carried on operations. Among the military personnel available were a "surprisingly large number of licensed embalmers in grades from private to major, who were screened from our service personnel throughout our Far East Command and the Continental United States." A large number of civilian embalmers and technical specialists were recruited in the United States.[14]

When this operation was established it was possible to inaugurate another "first" in the history of the Graves Registration Service. All casualties were directly evacuated from combat areas to the Kokura laboratory center, thus permitting for the first time the use of arterial embalming. Weekly retreat services in which the dead were brought from the laboratory center to the mausoleum area, and there given temporary burial with full military and religious rites were also made possible. Punched EAM cards were used to make preliminary screening of identification characteristics of unidentified remains against unresolved casualties, thus narrowing the area for research by the trained investigator. (14) The unidentified remains will ultimately all rest in the National Memorial Cemetery of the Pacific at Honolulu.[15]

By 1955 there were 97 national cemeteries in the United States, Alaska, Hawaii, and Porto Rico, 85 of them under supervision of the Department of the Army and 12 under the Department of the Interior.[16]

The Role of the Funeral Director: During the Civil War the funeral director frequently set up business as a civilian in military centers such as Washington or even made trips to battlefields to prepare and attend to the shipping of bodies on an individual assignment from the bereaved. In the Spanish-American War and in World War I bodies that were returned home for burial in nonmilitary cemeteries were met at points of destination and given final burial under the direction of local funeral directors.

The program for the return of the war dead of World War II provided survivors with four options:

1. They might elect to leave the remains of their loved ones undisturbed wherever they might be buried.

2. They might elect to have the remains buried in an overseas cemetery other than in a permanent, established United States overseas military cemetery.

3. They might choose to have the burial made in a permanent United States overseas military cemetery.

4. They might choose to have the remains returned to the United States for burial in such places as designated by them.[17]

Since it was determined that all bodies were to be returned to the United States after the Korean War the options granted after World War II were reduced to the selection of burial in either a national or private cemetery.

Funeral directors played an important role in both the World War II and the Korean War repatriation programs. When once the remains were delivered to the place in the United States designated by the next-of-kin the War Department's responsibility ended and that of the next-of-kin began. In the great majority of cases the next-of-kin turned the further proceedings over to a local funeral director. Again, in the great majority of instances, the services rendered by the funeral director went far beyond the minimum essential activities of arranging for and directing the final interment.

Survivors frequently were confused about their rights and privileges concerning the details of this program and quite naturally and reasonably sought advice and assistance from the funeral director, whose expertness came partly from his general familiarity with matters of this type, and partly from a study of the rehabilitation program and from previous experience in dealing with it.

The sealed casket frequently offered another problem. The next-of-kin, knowing little of the exceedingly great care exercised by the Graves Registration Service of the Quartermaster Corps, and the resultant high percentage of positive identification, were not always satisfied that identification could have been accurate, and sought to have the casket opened so that survivors might attempt needlessly and painfully to satisfy themselves that it did contain the remains of their son, husband, brother, etc. Funeral directors acting on many occasions as go-betweens, were able to counsel correctly and effectively in this matter, in assuring relatives that once positive identification by the Graves Registration Service was declared, such declaration could admit no doubt. Occasionally it was necessary for the funeral director to point out that while the identification originally was clearly established and continued so, the remains might have been buried in the earth for months or even years and would therefore no longer be recognizable. In this they were supported by the military escort—a trained group of selected personnel from each branch of the armed services—that accompanied the bodies of the returned to their final resting place. Despite their counsel, many families insisted on the caskets being opened, and there were even some court actions to enforce this legal right.

Many times the funeral director helped the escort to secure lodging, provided transportation about town for him, and rendered such other services to him as enabled him to carry out his assignment successfully.

These supplementary functions were of course in addition to the primary task of the funeral director in providing funeral home facilities and services, whether for a complete funeral or for a simple graveside ceremony.

CITATIONS AND REFERENCES FOR APPENDIX I

1. Edward Steere, *The Graves Registration Service in World War II* (Office of the Quartermaster General, Washington, D. C., 1951), p. 1 *seq.*

2. *Ibid.*, p. 3.

3. *Ibid.*, p. 4.

4. *Ibid.*, p. 5.

5. *Ibid.*, p. 7.

6. *Ibid.*, pp. 4, 7.

7. *Ibid.*, pp. 9, 10.

8. Don Craig to Howard C. Raether, June 1, 1955.

9. Department of the Army, *National Cemeteries, Military Cemeteries and Return of U. S. War Dead* (Office of the Quartermaster General, Washington, D. C., 1955), p. 2.

10. *Ibid.*, pp. 4, 5.

11. *Ibid.*, pp. 7, 13.

12. *Ibid.*, p. 15.

13. *Loc. cit.*

14. Department of the Army, *The Return of American Dead of the Korean Conflict* (Office of the Quartermaster General, Washington, D. C., 1955), pp. 13, 15.

15. *Ibid.*, pp. 3, 7, 8, 10.

16. Department of Defense, *Fact Sheet on National Cemeteries* (Office of Public Information, Washington, D. C., 1952), p. 1.

17. Report of Conference with Major Melvin A. Beyers, reported in January, 1946, *The Director* (National Funeral Directors Association, Milwaukee, Wis.), p. 9.

APPENDIX II

PAST PRESIDENTS OF THE
NATIONAL FUNERAL DIRECTORS ASSOCIATION OF THE
UNITED STATES, INC. **

1882-1884 *Charles L. Benjamin Saginaw, Mich.	1887-1891 *Robert R. Bringhurst Philadelphia, Pa.
1884-1885 *Oscar N. Crane Canandaigua, N. Y.	1891-1893 *Joseph W. Laube Richmond, Va.
1885-1887 *Hudson Samson Pittsburgh, Pa.	1893-1894 *S. Merrit Hook New York, N. Y.

1894-1896 *W. P. Hohenschuh
Iowa City, Ia.

1896-1898 *John H. Sharer
Alliance, Ohio

1898-1899 *Francke W.
Dickinson
Springfield, Mass.

1899-1900 *Josiah S. Pearce
Ardmore, Pa.

1900-1901 *Percy B. Dixon
Mobile, Ala.

1901-1902 *Fred Hulberg
New York, N. Y.

1902-1903 *J. H. McCully
Palo Alto, Calif.

1903-1904 *J. M. Connelley
Charleston, S. Car.

1904-1905 *L. M. Penwell
Topeka, Kansas

1905-1906 *L. T. Christian
Richmond, Va.

1906-1907 *D. B. Quinlan
Chicago, Illinois

1907-1908 *A. Eickelberg
New York, N. Y.

1908-1909 *W. D. Farley
Battle Creek, Mich.

1909-1910 *George L. Thomas
Milwaukee, Wis.

1910-1911 *Charles A. Miller
Cincinnati, Ohio

1911-1912 *J. W. Cookerly
Walla Walla, Wash.

1912-1913 *George Chandler
Paul
Philadelphia, Pa.

1913-1914 *James J. McLarney
New York, N. Y.

1914-1915 *George W. Lunt
San Francisco, Cal.

1915-1916 *Charles H.
Watkins, Jr.
Wheeling, W. Va.

1916-1917 *M. H. Alexander
St. Louis, Mo.

1917-1918 *Chas. C. Reel
Pittsburgh, Pa.

1918-1919 *John Maas
Louisville, Ky.

1919-1920 *John F. Martin
Elizabeth, N. J.

1920-1921 *Frank L. Ketcham
Chicago, Illinois

1921-1922 C. Albert Roth
Little Rock, Ark.

1922-1923 *Charles J. Dillon
Hartford, Conn.

1923-1925 *Fred P. Schoedinger
Columbus, Ohio

1925-1926 Martin W. Hysong
Washington, D.C.

1926-1927 *Colby E. Smith
Dallas, Tex.

1927-1928 *Henry Bosse
Louisville, Ky.

1928-1930 Harry J. Gilligan
Cincinnati, Ohio

1930-1931 *Thomas S. Wright
Temple, Tex.

1931-1932 *John T. Skelton
Sacramento, Calif.

1932-1933 John W. Mattle
Rochester, N. Y.

1933-1934 Bert S. Gadd
Indianapolis, Ind.

1934-1936 *Joseph L. Galen
Philadelphia, Pa.

1936-1937 John S. Rhodes
St. Petersburg, Fla.

1937-1938 *Samuel J. Waters
New York, N. Y.

1938-1939	Chas. W. Porterfield Holton, Kan.	1948-1949	Ronald C. Jones Scranton, Pa.
1939-1940	John W. Eberle Pasadena, Calif.	1949-1950	Edward A. Martin Grand Junction, Colo.
1940-1941	George A. Brewer, Jr. Dallas, Tex.	1950-1951	Jack Marshall Tilden, Neb.
1941-1943	Jacob Van't Hof Grand Rapids, Mich.	1951-1952	H. Fremont Alderson New London, Conn.
1943-1944	J. Leo Redgate Bridgeport, Conn.	1952-1953	W. Bruce Donaldson, Jr. Tifton, Ga.
1944-1945	R. P. Lee Minneapolis, Minn.	1953-1954	Fred W. Johnston St. Paul, Minn.
1945-1946	John E. Drummey Seattle, Wash.	1954-1955	A. B. Eckersell Rigby, Idaho
1946-1947	James C. Orr El Paso, Tex.		
1947-1948	*John W. Gennerich New York, N. Y.		

** *As submitted by the National Funeral Directors Association*

* *Deceased*

Past Presidents of the
National Negro Funeral Directors Association, Inc. **

1938-1939	B. J. McFalls Detroit, Mich.	1949-1951	J. W. Delaney Covington, Ky.
1939-1941	C. P. Hayes Richmond, Va.	1951-1953	C. L. Dennis New Orleans, La.
1941-1943	*W. J. Morsell Chicago, Ill.	1953-1955	Chas. Crook Chicago, Ill.
1943-1945	T.C.D. Hayes Memphis, Tenn.		
1945-1947	Duplain Rhodes New Orleans, La.		
1947-1949	W. E. Shortridge Birmingham, Ala.		

** *As submitted by the National Negro Funeral Directors Association, Inc.*

* *Deceased*

PAST PRESIDENTS OF THE
JEWISH FUNERAL DIRECTORS OF AMERICA, INC. **

1928-1930	*Herbert Berger St. Louis, Mo.	1949	Ben F. Solomon Brookline, Mass.
1931-1933	Bernard Danzansky Washington, D. C.	1950	Morton Etkin Buffalo, N. Y.
1934-1936	Judah Rosenberg Philadelphia, Pa.	1951	Leonard S. Labowitch Cleveland, Ohio
1937-1939	Ralph Schugar Pittsburgh, Pa.	1952	Issac Nieberg New York, N. Y.
1940-1941	Max Sugarman Providence, R. I.	1953	Harry Groman Los Angeles, Calif.
1942-1944	Isidor Alpert New York, N. Y.	1954	Milton Yaffe Chicago, Ill.
1945-1946	*Manuel Stanetsky Dorchester, Mass.	1955	Ira Kaufman Detroit, Mich.
1946-1947	Albert Kasdan Brooklyn, N. Y.	** *As submitted by the Jewish Funeral Directors of America, Inc.*	
1948	Charles Kaye Chicago, Ill.	* *Deceased*	

PAST PRESIDENTS OF THE
NATIONAL SELECTED MORTICIANS **

1917-1919	*George W. Olinger Denver, Colo.	1930-1931	R. L. Watrous Philadelphia, Pa.
1920-1921	*Harry Samson Pittsburgh, Pa.	1931-1932	B. C. Wallace Stockton, Calif.
1922-1923	*LeRoy Dunn Des Moines, Ia.	1932-1933	Russell D. Law Colorado Springs, Colo.
1923-1924	John Drummey Seattle, Wash.		
1924-1925	Fred W. Patterson Atlanta, Ga.	1933-1934	Floyd W. Estes Lansing, Mich.
1925-1926	Jack Matthews Lincoln, Neb.	1934-1936	Silas E. Ross Reno, Nev.
1926-1928	Arthur G. Mann Knoxville, Tenn.	1936-1937	*Clarence N. Bigelow Des Moines, Iowa
1928-1930	Porter Loring San Antonio, Tex.		

1937-1938	Earle K. Angstadt Reading, Pa.	1947-1948	R. M. Humphreys Urbana, Ohio
1938-1939	W. Emmet Milward Lexington, Ky.	1948-1949	Lyman S. Baird St. Paul, Minn.
1939-1940	Wade H. Kepner Wheeling, W. Va.	1949-1950	Lloyd G. Hay Portland, Maine
1940-1941	A. C. Connelley Charleston, S. Car.	1950-1951	George R. Schoedinger, Sr. Columbus, Ohio
1941-1942	T. Clyde Drennan Oakland, Calif.	1951-1952	James M. Brown Norfolk, Va.
1942-1943	George M. Davis, Jr. New Rochelle, N.Y.	1952-1953	Frank T. Walters Tacoma, Wash.
1943-1944	Edgar H. Turkle Alliance, Ohio	1953-1954	Knox E. Wright Houston, Tex.
1944-1945	George F. McCarthy Pueblo, Colo.	1954-1955	Donald C. Burton Erie, Pa.
1945-1946	George M. Algoe Flint, Mich.		
1946-1947	*George H. Waterman Boston, Mass.		

** *As submitted by the National Selected Morticians*

* *Deceased* •

APPENDIX III
CONFERENCE ACCREDITED COLLEGES

AMERICAN ACADEMY OF
FUNERAL SERVICE, INC.
1974 Broadway
New York 23, New York
Dr. Otto S. Margolis, Dean

ATLANTA COLLEGE OF
MORTUARY SCIENCE
3-5-7 Chestnut Street, N.W.
Atlanta, Georgia
J. Q. Caruthers, President

CALIFORNIA COLLEGE OF
MORTUARY SCIENCE
1920 Marengo Street
Los Angeles 33, California
Melvin Hilgenfeld, President

CINCINNATI COLLEGE OF
EMBALMING
3203 Reading Road
Cincinnati· 29, Ohio
Charles O. Dhonau, Dean

COMMONWEALTH COLLEGE
OF SCIENCES
102 Drew Street
Houston 6, Texas
Tex Garton, Dean

DALLAS INSTITUTE
GUPTON-JONES COLLEGE OF
MORTUARY SCIENCE
3906 Worth Street
Dallas 1, Texas
L. G. Frederick, President

Eckels College of
Mortuary Science
231 North Sixteenth Street
Philadelphia 2, Pennsylvania
John Eckels, President

John A. Gupton School of
Mortuary Science
2507 West End Avenue
Nashville 5, Tennessee
John A. Gupton, President

Indiana College of
Mortuary Science
1201 N. Capitol Ave.
Indianapolis 2, Indiana
Dr. William H. Crawford, Dean

Kentucky School of
Embalming
2nd Street at St. Catherine
Louisville 3, Kentucky
E. Leland Hughes, Dean

McAllister School of
Embalming
116 E. 27th Street
New York 17, New York
John McAllister, Dean

New England Institute of
Anatomy, Sanitary Science,
Embalming and Funeral
Directing
236 Huntington Avenue
Boston 15, Massachusetts
Joseph R. Parker, President

Pittsburgh Institute of
Mortuary Science
3337 Forbes Street
Pittsburgh 13, Pennsylvania
Dr. Emory S. James, Dean

San Francisco College of
Mortuary Science
1450 Post Street
San Francisco 9, California
Dr. L. W. Hosford, President

Simmons School of
Embalming
& Mortuary Science
2201 S. Salina Street
Syracuse 5, New York
Prof. Baxter G. Simmons,
President

Temple University,
Community College and
Technical Institute,
Eckels Curriculum in
Mortuary Science
Cheltenham Ave. and Sedgwick
Street
Philadelphia 19, Pennsylvania
William A. Schrag, Dean

University of Minnesota
Course in Applied
Mortuary Science
Minneapolis 14, Minnesota
Robert C. Slater, Asst. Director

Wayne University
Department of
Mortuary Science
2817 E. Grand Boulevard
Detroit 11, Michigan
Dr. Walter D. Pool,
Co-ordinator

Wisconsin Institute of
Mortuary Science
1205 N. Van Buren Street
Milwaukee 2, Wisconsin
Val Beyers, President

Worsham College of
Mortuary Science
1901 W. Jackson Boulevard
Chicago, Illinois
Dr. Milo E. Vacin, Dean

APPENDIX IV

FUNERAL SERVICE JOURNALS

American Funeral Director
Albert R. Kates, Editor
607 Fifth Avenue
New York 17, New York

Canadian Funeral Director
James O'Hagan, Editor
60 Fraont Street, West
Toronto, Ontario, Canada

Casket and Sunnyside
C. S. Baur, Publisher
487 Broadway
New York 13, New York

Northeast Funeral Director
John E. Powers, Editor
118 Summer Street
Boston 10, Massachusetts

Embalmers' Monthly
Fred Hadley, Editor
210 East Ohio Street
Chicago 11, Illinois

Mid-Continent Mortician
Grant Williams, Editor
905 Lumber Exchange Building
Minneapolis 2, Minnesota

Mortuary Management
William Berg, Editor
810 South Robertson
Los Angeles 35, California

Southern Funeral Director
John W. Yopp, Publisher
1070 Spring Street, N. W.
Atlanta, Georgia

Morticians of the Southwest
Dallas, Texas
P. O. Box 2683
Hugh Farrell, Publisher

APPENDIX V

COMPREHENSIVE TABLE OF BOOK CONTENT

Part One: Early Mortuary Behavior

1—PAGAN ROOTS OF MODERN FUNERAL PRACTICE   3

FUNERAL CUSTOMS OF THE ANCIENT EGYPTIANS: Death Beliefs—The Threat of Plague as a Burial Motive—Embalming—Coffins—Undertaking Specialists and the Ritual of Embalming—Influence of Egyptian Death Customs. FUNERAL CUSTOMS OF THE ANCIENT GREEKS: Death Beliefs—Burial Practices—Coffins and Tombs. FUNERAL CUSTOMS OF THE ANCIENT ROMANS: Roman View of Death and the Importance of Burial —Roman Burial Customs—Early Funeral Directing—Influence of Roman Burial Practices.

Index